Individuation and Liberty in a Globalized World

What is the best way to understand the narratives of self-identity at the beginning of the 21st century? This interdisciplinary collection brings together perspectives from analytical psychology, sociology, psychiatry, psychosocial studies, and psychoanalysis to consider questions about individuation and freedom in our unhinged world.

The contributors discuss the meaning of, and need for, individuation in individualized and liquid societies. The book begins with a comparison of three approaches: C.G. Jung's individuation, Ulrich Beck's individualization, and Zygmunt Bauman's liquidity. This sets the tone for further consideration of topics, including guilt, social media, global nomads, and surveillance. Theoretical reflections are enhanced by clinical material, and the book emphasizes the connections between sociology and psychoanalysis, offering significant insights into the importance of psychosocial approaches.

This timely work will be of great interest to academics and scholars of psychosocial studies, Jungian studies, sociology, and politics.

Stefano Carpani, M.A., M.Phil. is an Italian sociologist (post-graduate of the University of Cambridge) and psychoanalyst who trained at the C.G. Jung Institute, Zürich, accredited analyst CGJI-Z/IAAP, and a Ph.D. candidate in the Department of Psychosocial and Psychoanalytical Studies at University of Essex. He works in private practice in Berlin in English, Italian, and Spanish. He is the initiator of the YouTube interview series *Breakfast at Küsnacht*, which aims to capture the voices of senior Jungians. Since 2017, he has collected more than 70 interviews. He is among the initiators of *Psychosocial Wednesdays*, a digital salon modeled on Freud's Wednesday meetings in Vienna and Jung's meetings at the Psychological Club, which features speakers from various psychoanalytic traditions, schools, and associated fields. He is the author of numerous papers and edited volumes, including *Breakfast at Küsnacht: Conversations on C. G. Jung and Beyond* (Chiron, 2020—IAJS book award finalist, for "Best edited Book"); *The Plural Turn in Jungian and Post-Jungian Studies: The Work of Andrew Samuels* (Routledge, 2021); *Anthology of Contemporary Classics in Analytical psychology: The New Ancestors* (Routledge, 2022); *Lockdown Therapy: Jungian Perspectives on how the Pandemic Changed Psychoanalysis* (Routledge, in print, July 2022).

Individuation and Liberty in a Globalized World

Psychosocial Perspectives on Freedom after Freedom

Edited by Stefano Carpani
Preface by Andrew Samuels

Routledge
Taylor & Francis Group

LONDON AND NEW YORK

Cover image: Courtesy of Bianca Carpani Ruano

First published 2022
by Routledge
4 Park Square, Milton Park, Abingdon, Oxon OX14 4RN

and by Routledge
605 Third Avenue, New York, NY 10158

Routledge is an imprint of the Taylor & Francis Group, an informa business

British Library Cataloguing-in-Publication Data
A catalogue record for this book is available from the British Library

Library of Congress Cataloging-in-Publication Data
Names: Carpani, Stefano, editor.
Title: Individuation and liberty in a globalized world : psychosocial perspectives on freedom after freedom / edited by Stefano Carpani ; preface by Andrew Samuels.
Description: New York, NY : Routledge, 2022. | Includes bibliographical references and index.
Identifiers: LCCN 2021059342 (print) | LCCN 2021059343 (ebook) | ISBN 9780367768966 (hardback) | ISBN 9780367768959 (paperback) | ISBN 9781003168829 (ebook)
Subjects: LCSH: Identity (Psychology) | Self. | Individuation (Philosophy) | Liberty. | Globalization—Psychological aspects.
Classification: LCC BF697 .I537 2022 (print) | LCC BF697 (ebook) | DDC 155.2—dc23/eng/20220309
LC record available at https://lccn.loc.gov/2021059342
LC ebook record available at https://lccn.loc.gov/2021059343

ISBN: 978-0-367-76896-6 (hbk)
ISBN: 978-0-367-76895-9 (pbk)
ISBN: 978-1-003-16882-9 (ebk)

DOI: 10.4324/9781003168829

Typeset in Times New Roman
by Apex CoVantage, LLC

To István Kupper-Meynen,
friend, double, opposite, enemy,
this book is dedicated.

The time is out of joint; O cursed spite!
That ever I was born to set it right!

William Shakespeare (Hamlet)

It is not possible to solve a complex. It is only possible to solve
a conflict.

Günter Langwieler

Contents

Contributors

Dr. Galit Atlas is on the faculty at the NYU Postdoctoral Program in Psychotherapy and Psychoanalysis and faculty at the Four Year Adult and National Training Programs at NIP. She is the author of *The Enigma of Desire: Sex, Longing and Belonging in Psychoanalysis* (Routledge, 2015), *Dramatic Dialogue: Contemporary Clinical Practice* (co-authored with Lewis Aron, Routledge, 2017), and *Emotional Inheritance: A Therapist, Her Patients and the Legacy of Trauma* (Little Brown, 2022). She is the editor and a contributor to *When Minds Meet: The Work of Lewis Aron* (Routledge, 2020). Atlas serves on the editorial board of Psychoanalytic Perspectives and is the author of articles and book chapters that focus primarily on gender and sexuality. Her *New York Times* article "A Tale of Two Twins" was the winner of a 2016 Gradiva award. Atlas is a psychoanalyst and clinical supervisor in private practice in New York City.

Assoc. Prof. Ayse Devrim Basterzi, M.D., is a Turkish psychiatrist and psychotherapist. She is co-editor of several books, including *Women's Life and Women's Mental Health* (2012), *Book of Peace: The Mood of War from Individual to Society and Peace* (2015), and *Prevention, Intervention and Treatment Guideline for Mental Disorders in Mass Trauma and Disasters* (2021), all of which are published by PAT Publications. She was a past executive board member of Psychiatric Association of Turkey (PAT) for two terms (2009–2014), past member of the Board of PAT (2009–2016), and past president of the Curriculum and Program Development Section of the Board for two terms. Ayse Devrim Basterzi and her colleagues received an Association for Women in Psychology Distinguished Publication Award in 2019 with their article "Genocidal Sexual Assault on Women and the Role of Culture in the Rehabilitation Process: Experiences from Working with Yazidi Women in Turkey" (published in *Torture* 28(3), 124–132). She was removed and banned from public service with the Turkish Decree Law No. 689 on April 29, 2017, and dismissed from her academic post because she signed a petition called The Peace Petition. She works in private practice in Istanbul.

John Beebe, M.D., is a North American Jungian analyst in practice in San Francisco, USA. He received degrees from Harvard College and the University of Chicago School of Medicine. A past president of the C. G. Jung Institute of San Francisco, where he is currently on the teaching faculty, John is also a distinguished life fellow of the American Psychiatric Association. Books he has authored include *Integrity and Depth* and *Energies and Patterns in Psychological Type: The Reservoir of Consciousness*.

Stefano Candellieri, M.D., is an Italian psychiatrist and psychotherapist based in Turin. Between 1993 and 2001, he worked at the Fatebenefratelli psychiatric hospital in Turin, where he held the post of assistant head of department, specializing in psychotic disorders and forensic psychiatry. Since 2001, he has been engaged exclusively in private work as psychiatrist and psychotherapist. He is, together with the psychologist Davide Favero, founder and director of the Centro Medico Psicologico Torinese.

His current area of research is the intersection of psychoanalysis (with particular reference to the theoretical model of Antonino Ferro) and semiotics. On this last topic, he and Davide Favero wrote *Hyde Park – Officina di psicoanalisi potenziale*, published by Moretti & Vitali in 2019.

Roula-Maria Dib, Ph.D., is an assistant professor of English at the American University in Dubai and editor-in-chief of *Indelible*, the university's literary journal. A creative writer and scholar in the fields of literature and Jungian psychology, her poems, essays, and articles have appeared in several journals. She has authored *Jungian Metaphor in Modernist Literature* (Routledge, 2020). Her new poetry collection, *Simply Being*, will be published by Chiron Press in 2021. The themes that pervade her poetry usually revolve around different aspects of human nature, ekphrasis, surrealism, and mythology.

Davide Favero, psychologist and psychotherapist, is a CIPA and IAAP Jungian analyst and psychodramatist. A former psychologist at Fatebenefratelli psychiatric hospital and professor at the University of Turin, Faculty of Psychology, he is the founder and director of the Centro Medico Psicologico Torinese in Turin, along with psychiatrist Stefano Candellieri. He publishes articles in national and international journals and participates in congresses as a speaker, most notably at the International IAAP Congresses (Copenhagen 2013, Buenos Aires 2015, Kyoto 2016, Avignon 2018), the JAP International Conferences (Berlin 2014, New York 2017), the Tustin Conference (Boston 2014), the joint conferences of IAAP and IAJS, (New Haven 2015, Frankfurt 2018) and the IPA Congress (Boston 2015). His main interest is the intersection of analytical psychology and related subjects, particularly referring to the Zeitgeist, the semiotics, and the language.

Prof. Dr. Chiara Giaccardi is an Italian sociologist and full professor of sociology and teaches media sociology and anthropology at the Catholic University of Milan. She is Editor-in-Chief of *Comunicazioni Sociali – Journal of Media, Performing Arts and Cultural Studies*. Among her books are *Abitanti della rete* (2010), *La comunicazione interculturale nell'era digitale* (2012), *Generativi di tutto il mondo unitevi* (with M. Magatti, 2014), *Quale società dopo la crisi economica?* (2019, with Z. Bauman and Mauro Magatti), and *Nella fine è l'inizio* (with M. Magatti, 2020).

Roberto Grande M.D., is an Italian child and adolescent psychiatrist who graduated and specialized in Turin, Italy. From 1983 to 1997, he acquired training – personal and didactic – on Jungian group psychodrama (Coirag). He earned a diploma in analytical psychology for adults, children, and adolescents in 2015 at the CG Jung Institute, Zurich, where he is an instructor and leads lectures and seminars. He worked as a clinician in Geneva (Switzerland) and currently works in private praxis in Turin (Italy) as psychiatrist and psychoanalyst for adults, children, and adolescents, dealing with psychiatric drugs if needed. The passion for human life brought him to write a book of stories about his clinical work, entitled: *The Chocolate Child – Stories of Children and Adolescents Narrated by Their Psychotherapist*, (ed. Ponte alle Grazie – Mauri Spagnol Group, 2009). He has been a IAAP member since 2015.

Niccolò Fiorentino Polipo is a clinical psychologist and a Ph.D. student at the Psychological Sciences Research Institute of the Université catholique de Louvain in Belgium. He holds a bachelor's degree in philosophy (University Vita-Salute San Raffaele), a second cycle degree in clinical psychology (University of Bologna), and an M.Sc. in forensic psychology (University of Kent). He is training as a Jungian analyst with the Belgian School of Jungian Psychoanalysis. One of his main research interestsis the relation between Jungian psychology and normative ethics. He is the author of "Vulnerability and incorruptibility: An aretaic model of the transcendent function" in *Jungian Perspectives on indeterminate states: Betwixt and between borders* (Brodersen, & Amezaga, 2020).

Elizabeth Leuenberger-Kajs, M.A., is a US-born Swiss depth psychologist and Jungian psychoanalyst-in-training based in Zürich, Switzerland. Following many years in social work counseling advocating for families and children in the area of international adoption, she received her M.A. in depth psychology/ Jungian and archetypal studies from Pacifica Graduate Institute. A diploma candidate at the CG Jung Institute in Küsnacht, Switzerland, Elizabeth is currently a psychotherapist at the CG Jung Ambulatorium in Zürich and has been a Personal Development Analyst with IMD Business School for Management and Leadership in Lausanne. She has also served as a trainer and is an international advisory board member representing Jungian/analytical psychology and expressive arts since 2016 with BeautifulMind, a Nairobi-based mental health and psycho-social support enterprise. Elizabeth has authored a number of papers, including "Typological Refugees: Pearls of Conflict in Culture and Marriage" (*Personality Type in Depth*, 2018).

Monica Luci, Ph.D., is an Italian clinical psychologist and Jungian and relational psychoanalyst (IAAP and IARPP), working in private practice in Rome. She collaborates with NGOs and national and international institutions in the field of research, clinical evaluation, and psychotherapy for vulnerable people, especially survivors of torture and violence linked to wars and migration and unaccompanied minors. She speaks at national and international conferences and conducts training in academic and professional contexts. She is the author, translator, and editor of publications on the themes of trauma, displacement, collective violence, transcultural psychology, sexuality, and gender, including the monograph *Torture, Psychoanalysis & Human Rights* (Routledge, 2017). She was awarded the 2018 Fordham Prize by the *Journal of Analytical Psychology*.

Prof. Dr. Mauro Magatti is an Italian sociologist and economist, full professor of sociology in the Faculty of Sociology of the Catholic University of the Sacred Heart of Milan, and editor at *Corriere della Sera*. Since 2008, he has been director of the ARC – Center for the Anthropology of Religion and Generative Studies. His main scientific interests are focused on the relationship between economy and society, the role of civic society, and globalization in its cultural and social implications. More recently, his focus has moved to social generativity as a strategy to overcome the consumeristic society and its narcissistic individualism. Among his most recent books are *Generativi di tutto il mondo unitevi* (2014, with Chiara Giaccardi), *Cambio di Paradigna* (2017), *Social Generativity: A Relational Paradigm for Social Change* (2018), and *Nella fine è l'inizio* (2020, with Chiara Giaccardi).

Prof. M.D. Gamze Özçürümez Bilgili is a Turkish psychiatrist and a psychoanalytic psychotherapist. She graduated from Hacettepe University School of Medicine in 1996 and did her psychiatry residency at Baskent University Faculty of Medicine, where she is Full Professor at the Department of Psychiatry. She is a visiting professor and guest lecturer at International Psychoanalytic University-Berlin and a past executive board member of the Psychiatric Association of Turkey (PAT) (2011–2013). She is a member of the Migration-Trauma in Transition (MTT) and Social Trauma in Changing Societies (STICS) Networks, which are supported by the German Academic Exchange Service (DAAD). She and her colleagues received the Gradiva Award for Best Edited Book in 2020 with their work *Forced Migration and Social Trauma: Interdisciplinary Perspectives from Psychoanalysis,*

Psychology, Sociology and Politics. The title of her chapter is "Syrian 'Guests' and the Receiving Communities: Traumatisation of Being an Insider/Outsider" (pp. 85–94).

Marcus Quintaes is a Brazilian Jungian psychoanalyst and coordinator of seminars on James Hillman's archetypal psychology and post-Jungian thought. He is the Founder of Lapa (Laboratory of Archetypal Psychology) and of Thiasos. He is the author of *Letras Imaginativas: brief essays in archetypal psychology* (Editora Paulus). He lives and works in Rio de Janeiro.

Prof. Andrew Samuels, has, for almost 40 years, evolved a clinical blend of post-Jungian, relational psychoanalytic, and humanistic approaches to therapy work. He is recognized internationally as one of the leading commentators from a psychotherapeutic perspective on political and social problems. His work on the father, sexuality, spirituality, and countertransference has also been widely appreciated. He is a training analyst of the Society of Analytical Psychology and was chair of the UK Council for Psychotherapy 2009–2012. He is a co-founder of Psychotherapists and Counsellors for Social Responsibility. He was Professor of Analytical Psychology at Essex (until 2019) and holds visiting chairs at New York, London Roehampton, and Macau Universities. Samuels's books have been translated into 19 languages and include *Jung and the Post-Jungians* (1985); *A Critical Dictionary of Jungian Analysis* (1986); *The Father* (1986); *The Plural Psyche* (1989); *Psychopathology* (1989); *The Political Psyche* (1993); *Politics on the Couch* (2001); *Relational Psychotherapy, Psychoanalysis and Counselling: Appraisals and Reappraisals* (2014); *Passions, Persons, Psychotherapy, Politics* (2014); and *A New Therapy for Politics* (2015). A selection of video lectures may be found on www.andrew samuels.com.

Huan Wang, Ph.D., graduated from PPS University of Essex. She was a psychotherapist for five years in the clinic department of a hospital in Wuhan, a city in China. At present, her research interests mainly focus on the effects of political interventions on relationships within family and how to address the individual position in a collectivist setting. Her Ph.D. dissertation is on femininity and masculinity in romantic relationships in contemporary China. The study is mainly from Jungian and Post-Jungian perspectives and focuses on how young Chinese couples have been affected by traditional values, Westernization, and the One-Child policy.

Elias Winterton, Ph.D., is an analytical psychologist and psychotherapist dedicated to expanding Jungian and post-Jungian ideas beyond the clinical setting. This interdisciplinary approach aims to apply depth psychology to emerging fields of knowledge and experience.

Preface

It used to be possible to think in terms of an inner freedom that survives whatever offences and insults the social and political world throws up against it. This Romantic and, in a sense, psychoanalytic idealism has not withstood twentieth-century totalitarianism and its successors whose specific goal was to colonise the mind. As Ayse Devrim Basterzi and Gamze Özçürümez Bilgili put it in their chapter in the book ('The Impossibility of Freedom: From Psychoanalytical Conceptions to Political Objections'): 'Exterior power that regulates acceptable behaviour became an interior power resulting in the pressure to conform to the norms of others.'

Yet I sense that the over-arching thrust and importance of Stefano Carpani's extraordinary and ingenious edited collection is to return to the idea of something on a psychological level that can survive whatever the social order may hurl at it. Hence his shrewd nuancing of the tensions between 'individualization' and 'individuation' and many other related aspects of his writings.

Carpani's project is extremely ambitious because he seeks to add a Jungian dimension to psychoanalytically informed psychosocial studies. That said, this is not a Jungian book, though at times one can but wonder at what intellectual life would be like if there had been a Jungian Frankfurt School, so to speak.

It is important that many of the writers are clinicians. Therapists are not usually interested in freedom *per se* (as a sociological category), and sociologists are not usually interested in freedom from a psychological point of view. Hence, the collection contains something to unsettle and destabilise both divides of the psychosocial *Weltanschauung*. Make no mistake, the divide between them still exists, just as attempts to bring together the clinical and academic ways of proceeding have made but limited progress.

So – freedom, what about it? Freedom will never be more than good-enough because there will always be failures of freedom, often but not always caused by one's opponents or by oppressive tendencies within societies. Plus, the limits each person puts on their own freedom, for whatever reasons, are never to be overlooked. In the collection, this ineluctable failure of freedom is probed by writings from sociology, psychiatry, psychosocial studies, relational psychoanalysis, analytical psychology, and psychoanalysis. Such a plurality of perspectives is remarkable and a tribute to Carpani's incredible capacity to get people to work together.

From the personal perspective of my own writing, what the book problematises is the role and function of 'the individual' in relation to social and political processes, specifically processes of change and transformation. Is it not time to consider the fate of the individual in the liquid societies we are told we live in? Something other than a cork tossed by waves? Something active and autonomous? (See Samuels, 2014.)

For what many elements in the book suggest is that the way in which sociologists such as Beck, Giddens *et al.* have written about the individual is primarily as a symptom, a second-order phenomenon, extremely far from being a driver. It has occurred to me that the 'sociological individual' of the past forty years could be summarised as being interested mainly in her or his life and issues and not in the life of the times and its issues.

Although the claims of Camusian existentialism might have been hyperbolic, there is something there that has got lost if we just see the individual as a dedicated follower of fashion, as a consumerist – or, at the other pole, a homeless and drifting person in a Western society living on the streets.

I specifically wrote about Western society because the concept and image of freedom are not only historically relative but vary enormously from society to society. Freedom is therefore a culturally created idea. Nevertheless, what we have seen since the end of the Second World War is the export of Western varieties of freedom to many geographical locales outside the original Hellenically inspired areas.

To return to the individual, Carpani's chapter on the fall of the Berlin Wall utilises an account of the role played by the East German Communist politician Gunter Schabowski. Without in any way subscribing to the 'great person of history' school of historiography, Carpani proposes that Schabowski's role in the fall of the Wall deserves more than a cursory mention. The chapter is fascinating and original. But it is also important in terms of the history of ideas, as he explores the lines of the tensions between the social and psychological dimensions of experience.

And this adds to the value of the book as a whole: To show how interdisciplinarity and transdisciplinarity are, in our time, pretty much the only forms of disciplinarity that work. It follows that we need to allow ourselves freedom to travel the route mapped out by the book.

Andrew Samuels

Reference

Samuels, Andrew (2014) 'Appraising the Role of the Individual in Political and Social Change Processes: Jung, Camus, and the Question of Personal Responsibility – Possibilities and Impossibilities of "Making a Difference"'. *Psychotherapy and Politics International* 12(2), 99–110.

Introduction

Absolute Freedom is 'Freedom After Freedom'

Stefano Carpani

If you are looking to understand what freedom is (or looking for a description of what freedom is), this book is not for you. But don't despair, because perhaps – thanks to serendipity and enantiodromia – this book has reached you for another reason and is, in fact, for you! While not examining what freedom is *per se*, this book does examine the concept of freedom after freedom.[1]

How this book came about

Expanding on my idea[2] that in current 21st-century individualized and liquid societies, there is a renewed need for individuation, this book comprises a series of essays and clinical vignettes (including unconscious material) and interpretations by senior scholars and clinicians (in sociology, psychiatry, psychosocial studies, relational psychoanalysis, analytical psychology, and psychoanalytical psychoanalysis), providing an in-depth look at the concepts of individualization, liquidity, and individuation, as well as freedom. Therefore, this book is entirely composed of solid academic, scholarly, and clinical writings.

After publishing my aforementioned paper, I continued my own research on freedom and what I called *the consequences of freedom*, and I realized that there is a gap when examining freedom from the psychoanalytical and sociological perspectives. This gap has to do with the bridging (or lack thereof) of the two fields. I came to observe that therapists are not usually interested in freedom *per se* (as a sociological category), and sociologists are not interested in freedom from a psychological (or logical metaphysical) point of view.

Therefore, I invited colleagues to bridge these two categories in a psychosocial effort to work on the theme of *freedom after freedom* from different perspectives. Hence, all the chapters included in this book find a theoretical standpoint of reference in my paper titled 'The Consequences of Freedom: Moving beyond the Intermediate States of Broken Individualization and Liquidity'.

In this paper, I attempted a psychosocial comparative study of Swiss psychoanalyst C.G. Jung's individuation process, German sociologist Ulrich Beck's individualization theory, and Polish sociologist Zygmunt Bauman's concept

DOI: 10.4324/9781003168829-1

of liquidity, leading to the proposal that in current 'second-late modernity' or 'second-late individualized society',[3] there is a renewed need for individuation. In doing so, I looked into the sociological concept of anomie and explored its role as a possible 'indeterminate state'.

In attempting to demonstrate the validity of this approach, I answered the following research question: What is the best tool to understand the nature of development of narratives of self-identity at the beginning of the 21st century? To do so, I claimed that there is an imminent necessity to build a bridge from sociology toward psychoanalysis, or from Beck's individualization and Bauman's liquidity to Jung's individuation (and not vice versa) and in so doing leave behind traditional sociology in order to open the door to the unconscious with a psychosocial approach. To illustrate my findings, I used a clinical vignette, inspired by a patient who – during our first session – reported a 'sense of emptiness', of 'feeling stuck' and that 'sentimental relationships don't last'. While this patient is sociologically individualized and (apparently) well adapted in a liquid society, it remains to be seen if she is individuated.

Therefore, I employed the work of feminist and relational psychoanalyst Susie Orbach (2014, p. 17), who underlined that 'being is constituted out of the enactment and living of both conscious behaviour and behaviour of which we are unaware' and that agents mutually influence each other, while structure and agency are also mutually influential. Orbach (2014, p. 16) also claimed that 'the individual is born into a set of social and psychological circumstances. The human infant is a set of possibilities – not id based, not instinctually driven – but in order to become recognized as a human, will need to attach' and later to separate. Following this, I proposed that traditional sociology is not equipped to consider the unconscious, because it relies exclusively on classical drive theory and has an ontological bias toward the rational and cognitive aspects of human behaviour. To this could also be added its loyalty to Durkheim's[4] view of psychology and the Frankfurt school's inability to go beyond Freud's dogma and examine the irrational side of the psyche. Finally, making Jung a *persona non grata* in 20th-century sociology, the Frankfurters saw – following Walter Benjamin (cited in Samuels, 1993) – Jung's psychology as 'the devil's work' and an 'auxiliary service to National Socialism'. In contrast, I proposed adopting Jung's psychosocial and relational viewpoint.

I also propose that Beck, Bauman, and traditional sociology lack the tools to examine the unconscious and emotions, since they look at these factors theoretically (sociologically) instead of clinically (symbolically). We must ask why, at a time where people have gained freedoms that were unthinkable in earlier times, suicide rates have increased by 25% across the United States over nearly two decades (US Centers for Disease Control and Prevention, 2018). This fact alone is sufficient reason to look anew at the concepts of individualization, liquidity, and individuation and to realize that to truly *become* liberated[5] in an individualized and liquid society, people need to individuate. Thus, Jung's individuation process constitutes a valid theory for understanding the world as it is (thus opposing the idea that the world is out of joint). I propose that Jung's individuation is a theory of metamorphosis of the individual and therefore of the world. Moreover, metamorphosis is always linked to self-responsibility, in opposition to anomie.

What, then, is the link between precarious freedom, self-responsibility, and leading a life made up of a succession of new beginnings, disorientation, and the absence of itinerary and direction? Beck and Beck-Gernsheim (2002) claim that when living an experimental life, everything is a matter of self-responsibility, and Bauman (2000) underlined that the burden of responsibility that fluid modernism places on the individual consists of the need to replace traditional patterns with self-elected ones. Self-responsibility and its burdens, I propose, are where individualization and liquidity crack, because people have difficulty taking responsibility and instead engage in brooding, 'a sterile activity . . . not work but a weakness, even a vice' (Jung, CW18/II, para.1810), before succumbing to depression and suicidal ideation, per anomie.

In this regard, both sociologist Mauro Magatti (2018) in his recent column 'There Is No Freedom without Responsibility' (*Corriere della Sera*) and Erich Fromm (1941) in *Escape from Freedom* underlined that 'Modern man still is anxious and tempted to surrender his freedom to dictators of all kinds'. Fromm (1941) also noted that 'If humanity cannot live with the dangers and responsibilities inherent in freedom, it will probably turn into authoritarianism'. However, in the words of Magatti and media sociologist and anthropologist Chiara Giaccardi (2014), if, in Western society, we have already liberated ourselves, 'what other liberation must we therefore seek?' Why are people not yet free if they have liberated themselves – again following Fromm (1941) – from the political, economic, and spiritual shackles that have bound them? Why are people not yet happy, as Václav Havel wrote already in 1976 in the play titled *Horský Hotel*? Why are anxiety, depression, and suicide rates increasing? This is, I propose, when the dichotomy between the wish for autonomy and anomie become apparent. Therefore, when there is a *broken individualization* that equals 'the betrayed promise of freedom and happiness for all',[6] there can be no individuation.

Based on this, Jung's individuation could provide an answer, perhaps even an antidote, to the current broken individualization/liquidity and consequent anomie. This is because, following Watkins (2003), it is the capacity for dialogue, not reason, that distinguishes humankind from other living creatures. Furthermore, such dialogue takes place with oneself, with one's neighbour, and with God (Niebuhr, 1955, cited in Watkins, 2003), and this 'capacity for dialogue is a necessary precondition for human liberation' (2003, p. 87), particularly 'from rigid, stereotypic, and unidimensional narrowness'. In this view, development (which she calls liberation) is based 'on a paradigm of interdependence, where the liberation of one is intimately tied to the liberation of the other' (2003, p. 88). In this sense, 'the other' may constitute 'economic, political, sociocultural, spiritual, and psychological' entities. Additionally, Samuels (1989, p. 1) – who introduced the concept of the plural psyche to 'hold unity and diversity in balance' and underlined that 'our inner worlds and our private lives reel from the impact of policy decisions and the existing political culture' – suggested that within both the microcosm of an individual and the macrocosm of the global village, 'we are flooded by psychological themes'. If this is the case, however, why does mainstream sociology fail to investigate these themes? Why does Beck argue that individualization might 'unleash the conflicts and devils that lie slumbering among the details' but does not say more? Why did Bauman underline that instead of facing their conflicts and devils, people prefer to look at new beginnings because they are unable to cope with painful endings? To all this – and as an antidote to broken individualization and liquidity – I suggest examining Jung's concept of meditation.

In his essay 'Self-Knowledge', Jung (CW14, para. 497) claimed that 'what I call coming to terms with the unconscious the alchemists called "meditation"' and added, citing Ruland, that meditation is 'an Internal talk of one person with another who is invisible, as in the invocation of the Deity, or communion with one's self, or with one's good angel"'. In an individualized and liquid society, there is fresh need for renewed internal talk, and one way of engaging in such is through Jungian psychoanalysis. Jung (CW14, para. 498) claimed that modern meditation methods are 'only for increasing concentration and consolidating consciousness, but have no significance as regards effecting a synthesis of the personality. On the contrary, their purpose is to shield consciousness from the unconscious and to suppress it'. That being the case, such methods are of no therapeutic value. Instead, Jung (CW14, para. 498) proposes analysis as meditation, although 'there are relatively few people who have experienced the effects of an analysis of the unconscious on themselves, and almost nobody hits on the idea of using the objective hints given by dreams as a theme for meditation'.

More than 70 years since the publication of this essay, little has changed. While in Jung's day, meditation had a bad reputation in the West, today, the *à la mode* forms of meditation and contemplation – yoga at lunchtime, daily morning meditation, weekend or holistic 'holiday' retreats, and so on – that have been adopted in the West do not facilitate internal talk. Instead, they facilitate a momentary calmness before returning (recharged) to the jungle of an affluent society. Thus, these techniques are akin to smartphone battery chargers: indispensable for recharging in our society but never fully disconnecting.

Therefore, I agree with Jung's view that:

> No one has time for self-knowledge or believes that it could serve any sensible purpose. Also, one knows in advance that it is not worth the trouble to know oneself, for any fool can know what he is. We believe exclusively in doing and do not ask about the doer, who is judged only by achievements that have collective value. . . . Western man confronts himself as a stranger and that self-knowledge is one of the most difficult and exacting of the arts.
>
> (CW14, para. 498)

To further investigate the concept of inner talk (as a means to contrast the emptiness and meaninglessness of the affluent life) and the need people have in Western societies to find a momentary calm-ness before returning (recharged) to the jungle of an affluent society, I here examine the German psychotherapist Wolfgang Giegerich.

In *The End of Meaning and the Birth of Man*, Giegerich (2010) suggests making a person fully aware through confrontation with her/his unconscious ideas. However, he wonders whether lack of meaning is sufficient cause to make one neurotic, or whether the quest for meaning is merely 'the expression of a neurotic pretentiousness, a claim to metaphysical grandiosity. It is the delusion that life is only life if there is, like in a dog race, that never-to-be reached one thing, the sausage "to race after"'. Giegerich (2010, p. 233) claims that Jung refused to see this, despite being aware of 'the danger of pointless seeking', which I compare to Beckett's (2010) 'waiting' for Godot: both actions are a sign of *légèresse*, indicating an impossible depth, substance, or purpose in life.

As Simone de Beauvoir noted, 'une femme libre est exactement le contraire d'une femme légère'. Going beyond sex and gender, depth (substance) may be the antidote to *légèresse*, and a free individual is the opposite to a *légère* individual. Therefore, the concepts of emptiness, meaning, searching, and waiting are interwoven: all show traits of ambivalence, wanting, and rejecting, and meaninglessness is linked to a never-ending searching and waiting, until 'something' (perhaps the numinous) happens to the individual or a symbol appears. But what if this numinous event, this symbol, never arises, or we are so distracted by the daily noise of our affluent lives that we fail to recognize it when it does come? This is what I call broken individualization and liquidity.

In this regard, Giegerich (2010, p. 233) recalls Jung's example of a woman who

> does not live the life that makes sense . . . because she is nothing. But if she could say, "I am the daughter of the Moon. Every night I must help the Moon, my Mother, over the horizon" – ha, that is something else! Then she lives, then her life makes sense.
>
> (CW18, para. 630)

Giegerich claims that this is, in fact, not a cure, as Jung claimed, and that the 'Pueblo-Indian model' cannot be applied to the modern woman because it would involve 'an endless, futile search' (2010, p. 233); thus, 'Jung's suggestion feeds her neurotic craving, her "addiction"' (2010). Instead, Giegerich (2010) proposes as a 'real cure' that she goes, I believe, toward what Thomas Bernhard (1994) calls *the opposite direction*; that is, that she be made fully aware that her unconscious idea that 'she ought to be the daughter of the moon . . . is why she is desperately travelling'. Thus, she is confronted 'with the exaltedness, inflatedness of the unconscious demands and expectations'. This is the very opposite attitude to that described by Bauman (and Calvino). Therefore, Giegerich (2010) claims: 'why should she not be able, like everybody else, to find satisfaction, contentedness, in ordinary life?' In this way, Giegerich's realism helps to understand the limitations of contemporary mainstream sociology, which does not examine unconscious motives. By realising that she is not 'a Queen in search for . . . the recognition due but denied to her', it could permit her to accept, following Orbach, her ordinary unhappiness (Orbach, 2020) – in contrast to the hystericized and narcissistic desire for accomplishment – and even allow new developments to arise.

At the end of my paper – with the help of a clinical vignette, I sought to propose that *substance* and *purpose* are required to replace *emptiness* and *meaninglessness*. Otherwise, as suggested by Bauman (2005), people will continually move from one life/identity to another in a perpetual cycle of dissatisfaction (and search), of killing time and of being 'tired like the residents of Calvino's Eutropia of everything they have enjoyed thus far'.

Therefore, to return to the question asked in the introduction, whether Bauman's liquidity is a 21st-century existentialism in the line of Kierkegaard, Nietzsche, Camus, Sartre, and Laing, I propose that liquidity is the consequence of early existential theory (minus purpose and substance); the more we turn to existentialism, the more we turn to anomie (anxiety, depression, and suicide). This is because if, following Bauman, in the 21st century, becoming never reaches completion, this is a symptom of our own lack of substance and purpose, and the only certainty is impermanence. Meditation in the sense used by Jung, however, would allow individuals to look inward, to find substance and purpose in life, and by this means to compensate for emptiness and meaninglessness. As Jung suggested, to become 'one's own creator' is key (*The Red Book*, 2009, p. 188).

Finally, I propose that the anxiety and depression related to anomie, which are rife in our society, should not be viewed as pathological but rather as attitudes toward life, as an opportunity for development and liberation, and as a key aspect of intermediate (pre-individuated) states. In sociological terms, anxiety and depression are linked to anomie, the state wherein individuals lose sight of the fact that they can actively shape their lives. Thus, when creativity and the contents of the unconscious are repressed, anxiety and depression result, and this enables anomie. In this context, Jung's individuation is fundamental because the goal of psychotherapy, according to Jung (CW16, para. 99), is 'to bring about a psychic state in which my patient begins to experiment with his own nature – a state of fluidity, change and growth where nothing is eternally fixed and hopelessly petrified'. This, Jung claims, is always related to the opportunity to express oneself creatively, through dreams, painting, active imagination, or through the body. Moreover, Jung notes that the creative fantasy is an 'intrusion from the unconscious, a sort of lucky hunch, different in kind from the slow reasoning of the conscious mind' (CW16, para. 16).

Thus, one can equate individualization and liquidity with the conscious mind, while fluidity can be equated with the unconscious mind. In this sense, authentic creativity (creative fantasy) is what is lacking in a liquid society, because, following George Berkeley (cited in Giegerich, 2010), 'few men think, yet all will have opinions'. Therefore, creativity and creative fantasy help fluidity (and pluralism), and if fluidity, rather than liquidity, is fostered, there will be a chance to contrast anxiety, depression, suicidality, and, therefore, anomie. Anomie occurs when emotions are stuck, while, when one is able to 'translate the emotions into images – that is to say, to find the images which were concealed in the emotions' (Jung, MDR), one becomes inwardly calmed and reassured.

If we follow these lines, we could also say, with Hillman (2013, p. 94), that 'Individuation is a path of salvation' from the

> modern condition of cut-offness from the world, cut-offness from others, from the community, from nature and all the rest, the dead world of Descartes, where we are more and more individual and more and more alone, more and more isolated – anomie.

I therefore propose that – if individualization and liquidity lead to solipsism and anomie – individuation is a way out through meditation.

But if we have already freed ourselves, from what are we seeking freedom?

Italian sociologists Chiara Giaccardi and Mauro Magatti, in their book titled *Generativi di tutto il mondo unitevi* (2014), asked themselves "but if we have already freed ourselves, from what are we seeking freedom"? This book attempts to answer this question (from the perspectives of sociology, psychiatry, psychosocial studies, relational psychoanalysis, analytical psychology, and psychoanalytical psychoanalysis) and examines freedom not so much to answer the question what freedom is but – if anything – to understand what freedom is after freedom – that is, the freedom acquired in the West since the Second World War, the '68, the fall of the communist/capitalist dualism, and the fall of the Berlin wall, when people have acquired physical but probably not absolute (psychological) freedom.

German Jungian psychoanalyst Wolfgang Giegerich (2020, p. 58) claims that psychotherapy 'should fundamentally be comprehended as improvisation', which, for him, 'is the opposite of the application of a technique or of expert knowledge'. Therefore, when stressing that 'it is of course not enough if the *patient* starts to swim. The *therapist* has to do the same thing', he underlines that therapy is about co-participation and mutuality. Is freedom, too, about improvisation and co-participation? I intentionally leave this question unanswered, hoping that readers of this book will find their own answer.

Therefore, as suggested by Giegerich, 'we must here keep in mind the difference between the psychological (or logical metaphysical) level and a pragmatic level' (2020, p. 92) of freedom.

Nelson Mandela (one of the giants of 20th-century freedom) helps us in this regard. In his autobiography *Long Walk to Freedom* (1994), he reminds us that 'to be free is not merely to cast off one's chains, but to live in a way that respects and enhances the freedom of others' – which to me sounds like *co-participation*. The chains of which Mandela speaks and from which we have freed ourselves are Giegerich's pragmatic level; the rest, I propose, is psychological freedom, and that we must earn ourselves.

The theme of this book is as follows: it is not sufficient to acquire pragmatic (physical) freedom; it is our duty to become absolutely free, which means becoming free at the psychological or logical metaphysical level. I will later describe what I propose absolute freedom to be.

Boris Groys, in his book *Antiphilosophy* (2012, p. XXII+XXIII), reminds us of what Husserl termed *phenomenological reduction*. This consists,

> in the subject's taking a mental distance from his own life interests – even the interests in his own survival – and in this way opening up a perspective in considering the world that is no longer confined by the needs of his empirical ego. By way of this broad phenomenological prospective one obtains the ability to do Justice to all commands, by starting to experiment freely both in obeying them and refusing them. At the same time, the subject of the phenomenological reduction finds himself no longer required to transform the commands he receives into his conduct of life, or, conversely, to oppose them, since the phenomenological ego thinks as if it were not living. In this way one acquires for one's phenomenological ego a real 'as if' – an imaginary perspective of limitless life, in which all decisions of life lose their urgency, so that the opposition between carrying out and rejecting a command dissolves into the infinite play of life possibilities.

This, I propose, is psychoanalysis's supreme duty.

It can be said that once Husserl's *phenomenological reduction* has been reached, and only then, will it be possible to reach another step that corresponds to 'releasing oneself, namely one's releasing to or rather into oneself' (Giegerich, 2020, p. 82). Giegerich underlines that this means 'releasing ourselves from our imprisonment in our subjectivity', and he adds that 'Jung wanted that we learn to face ourselves objectively, see ourselves from outside, as an objective vis-à-vis'. This means, according to the German therapist, becoming 'an other for myself, that is to say, I have to take myself as an objective fact' (Giegerich, 2020, p. 82).

However, Giegerich also emphasizes that this is no easy task (as it is not easy to reach *phenomenological reduction*), because – he claims – 'we are enclosed within in our own subjectivity' and because 'we see ourselves only subjectively, in terms of our self-image, our ego-ideal and our demands upon ourselves' (Giegerich, 2020, p. 82). Therefore, Giegerich adds, 'many people feel guilty or ashamed because they are not the way they ought to be', and this is when 'they think that *they* should be able to decide how they are', forgetting that 'their subjective thoughts and wishes' are 'molded after general moral principles or the values of one's social environment, which shows that our subjectivity is by no means isolated, solely subjective, but from the outset socially constructed' (Giegerich, 2020, p. 82).

Only following this is it possible to understand a comment made by Giegerich in clinical supervision on the dream of a patient of mine; he suggested that the patient *must drop all hopes and expectations*. This means, I propose, allowing *longings to arise* from one's own soul. When examining this, it is possible to understand that hopes and expectation are ego driven, while longings are related to the Self and arise from the soul. Thus, they come from God. Longings are *vox Dei*, the voice of God, 'which often cuts sharply across our subjective intentions and may sometimes force an extremely disagreeable decision' (CW10: 842).

Only then will people stop feeling in/a constant void and suspended in a never-ending vacuum (similar to Italo Calvino's *Eutropia*). Only then will the sublation happen and will people move from what Giegerich called the *pragmatic level of freedom* to psychological (or logical metaphysical) freedom, which I term *absolute freedom* (which also equates to becoming individuated and individualized in late modern society). Only then will people lose the neurotic need to move from city to city (as described by Calvino in *Invisible Cities*).

Italian Jungian psychotherapist Luigi Zoja wrote in his book *La morte del prossimo* (2009) that the French revolution helped to subvert the vertical order of power and that the rigid, top-down patriarchal order that prevailed in 20th-century families and society was 'without uncertainty: and, in this sense, reassuring'[7] (2009, p. 84). Zoja then reminds us that people have social duties but also 'the right to personal inspiration' and that 'the tension between freedom of desires and solidarity cannot find solutions, it can only reach balance' (2009, p. 84). Zoja also reminds us that 'unlike solidarity, which can respond to some objective measurement and which supports personal limits shoulder to shoulder. . . . Individual frenzies insinuate themselves into unconscious motivations' and ultimately end up poisoning the very organisms that feed on them (2009, p. 85).

In line with Giegerich's suggestion to *drop all hopes and expectations*, Zoja proposes that we should replace desire, or animal appetites, with learning 'how to behave with others' and eschewing herd mentality (2009, p. 85/86). He also notes the 'tragic antinomy' between solidarity and equality on the one hand and 'the modern <<right>> to desire' on the other (2009, p. 85/86), with the 21st century favouring individual needs over the freedom that comes with fraternity and equality (2009, p. 84). This, he says, is what positions us 'all on the side of evil: all responsible for the environmental and cultural degeneration of the planet' (2009, p. 103), and he claims that 'self-criticism and personal assumption of responsibility are indispensable for a transformation to be lasting. This is not only a necessary condition in psychoanalytic therapy: it is even more so in attempts to transform society' (2009, p. 100/101). Thus, 'what is necessary is to de-individualise' (2009, p. 100).

I concur with Zoja and propose that the concept of freedom after freedom is related to self-criticism and personal assumption as well as the phenomenological reduction in a society such as the post-1989 one. Therefore, freedom after freedom (absolute freedom) is about *Letitia*, which, as Spinoza puts it, is when 'the Mind moves on to greater perfection' (2021, 'Ethica', III, prop.11). One could also say it is when the soul moves on to greater perfection, ending ego-supremacy. It is the soul's move to an expansion of knowledge and gathering of insights.

Absolute freedom

What I call absolute freedom is a possible merging (which I called 'the I+I' in my Ph.D. thesis, 2022) of individualization and individuation. It is the process of become individuated in an individualized society.

Absolute freedom is our innate *striving for wholeness*, in a late-modern (Beck, 2002), Liquid (Bauman, 2000), Self-reflexive (Giddens, 1998) society. Absolute freedom is the capacity to fulfil one's own destiny (von Franz, 1964; Hillman, 1997) in an individualized and late modern 21st-century society. It is a sense of one's own inner realization (authentic, not material) and therefore, not in a will-to-power effort but in an intimate process (that per Jung's individuation process might occur unnoticed or during analysis) to fulfil one's own destiny.

Absolute freedom is a non-linear, uroboric process that starts much before one's birth. It is a trans-generational path, inherited from our parents, grandparents, and ancestors, that we leave in the hands of our children and grandchildren. When one is absolutely free, one becomes God. One becomes one-Self: whole. This correlates with Jung's idea that the Self is (the archetype of) the God-image. The absolute.

I employ the term absolute freedom not to mean that an individual should become like God, or God himself, but to reach a knowledge of oneself (and an acceptance of what one is) that will allow us to live our lives with awareness of some of the most devouring complexes that limit our path to freedom.

However, just as absolute certainty is impossible, absolute freedom is also impossible. This is because people can reach a state of absolute freedom during their lifetimes, but they can also lose it (due to inner or outer circumstances) and gain it and lose it again (in an uroboric circle). Thomas Bernhard (1995) is eloquent in this regard when he claims that our whole life is nothing but a continuous effort to find ourselves again and again. Or Ribi (2020), who claims that life must be a continuous transformation; otherwise, stagnation will bring death.

Therefore, absolute freedom, which is a generative process, means becoming individuated ('A process by which man lives out his innate human nature'[8] [von Franz, 1978]) in an individualized society. It is the opportunity to become oneself (*farsi sé*) in an individualized society; thus, a society where 'man and woman are released from the gender roles prescribed by industrial society for life in the nuclear family' while simultaneously

> forced, under pain of material disadvantage, to build up a life of their own by way of the labor market, training and mobility, and if need be to pursue this life at the cost of their commitments to family, relations and friends.
>
> (Beck & Beck, 1995 [1990], p. 6)

Absolute freedom occurs when people are able to live a life free from authorities. By this, I mean that it is a state of psychological freedom from the negative influence (or rather, say, devouring influence) of authorities and of social (cultural) freedom beyond the class and gender roles prescribed by industrial (modern) society.

Absolute freedom is psychological and social (psychosocial) freedom from authorities; it is psychological and social dis-enchainment (unleashing) from authorities. Therefore, it is a state of psychological and social freedom from the constellating complexes (or, at least, an opportunity to look at their devouring aspects) in relation to authorities. Authorities, in this regard, are not to be seen as *authoritarian regimes* only. Authorities, in this case, are anything that constellates our complexes (and that limits our psycho-social freedom): family, father, mother, partner, teacher, siblings, boss, school, institutions, communities, the government, and so on. An authority is therefore anything that oppresses our individuation (particularly if we consider individuation a conscious/unconscious process, as C.G. Jung observed). The concept of absolute freedom, then, is directly related to the Jungian concept of complexes (the via regia to the unconscious) and Beck's individualization.

Notes

1 This book was assembled before February 24th 2022. Therefore before the invasion of Ukraine by Russian troops.
2 See: 'The Consequences of Freedom: Moving beyond the Intermediate States of Broken Individualization and Liquidity' in Elizabeth Brodersen and Pilar Amezaga's book titled *Jungian Perspectives on Indeterminate States: 'Betwixt and Between' Borders*, Routledge, 2020b
3 According to British sociologist Anthony Giddens (1998, p. 94), modernity 'is associated with a certain set of attitudes toward the world, the idea of the world as open to transformation by human invention'. Modernity evolves into what Beck (2002) calls 'reflexive modernization' or 'second modernity', what Giddens (1991) calls 'high' or 'late' modernity, and what sociologist Zygmunt Bauman (2000) calls 'liquid' modernity. In this work, amongst the wide range of possible definitions, I prefer to refer to the present epoch as a 'second-late modernity' or 'second-late individualized society', as I consider the current era to have followed the previous without a break. The start of this epoch can be traced back to the launch of the first iPhone in 2007, because the incorporation of this technology in our daily lives changed it radically in terms of how and when we relate to others and the world. When looking at Giddens' (1990) claim that late modernity reduces the separation of space and time, second-late modernity does so even more. Also, Umbach and Huppauf's (2005, p. 8) concepts of flux, change, and unpredictability become accelerated. This period, in the radicalization of Marcuse's definition of modernity as 'advanced industrial society' (Marcuse, 1986, p. XV), can also be named 'advanced electronic society' or 'accelerated electronic society'.
4 Following Lukes's (1982) introduction to Durkheim's *The Rules of Sociological Method*, we understand that Durkheim sought to demarcate sociology from psychology, claiming sociology to be a 'special psychology, having its own subject-matter and a distinctive method' (Durkheim, 1982, p. 253), while psychology is 'the science of the individual mind', whose object or domain is as follows (Durkheim, ibid, p. 40): 1. states of individual consciousness; 2. explanation in terms of 'organico-psychic' factors, pre-social features of the individual organism, given at birth and independent of social influences; 3. explanation in terms of particular or 'individual' as opposed to general or 'social'

conditions (focusing, say, on individuals' intentions or their particular circumstances); 4. explanation in terms of individual mental states or dispositions. However, if we look carefully into a psychosocial parallel between Durkheim and Jung, we might recognize that these four points can be linked respectively to Jung's concepts of (1) the personal unconscious, (2) archetypes and the collective unconscious, (3) the persona, and (4) Jung's theory of neurosis and psychodynamics (the Syzygy).

5 *Liberation* is a term/concept I borrow from Mary Watkins (Lorenz and Watkins, 2003; Watkins and Shulman, 2008).

6 As Giaccardi underlined in 'Individuation and generative social action', a paper given at the international conference titled *Social Generativity. What It Is and What It Is Good For.*

7 My translation from Italian for all quotes from Zoja.

8 M.L. von Franz, *Man and his Symbols*, p. 164.

References

Bauman, Z. (2000). *Liquid modernity*. Cambridge: Polity Press.

Bauman, Z. (2005). *Liquid life*. Cambridge: Polity Press.

Beck, U., and Beck-Gernsheim, E. (1995). *The normal chaos of love*. Cambridge: Polity Press.

Beck, U., and Beck-Gernsheim, E. (2002). *Individualization: Institutionalized individualism and its social and political consequences*. London: Sage.

Beckett, S. (2010). *Waiting for Godot*. London: Faber and Faber.

Bernhard, T. (1994). *La cantina. Una via di scampo*. Milano: Adelphi.

Bernhard, T. (1995). *Perturbamento*. Milano: Adelphi.

Carpani, S. (2020a). *Breakfast at Küsnacht: Conversations on C. G. Jung and beyond*. Nashville, NC: Chiron Publications.

Carpani, S. (2020b). 'The consequences of freedom: Moving beyond the intermediate states of broken individualization and liquidity'. In Elizabeth Brodersen and Pilar Amezaga (eds.), *Jungian perspectives on indeterminate states: 'Betwixt and between' borders*. New York, NY/London: Routledge.

Carpani, S. (2022). *Absolute Freedom: The 'I+I' (Individuation + Individualization) as a Metanarrative of Self-Development in a Second-Late-Modern Society*. Unpublished Ph.D. thesis. Colchester, UK: University of Essex.

Durkheim, E. (1982). *The rules of sociological method*. New York, NY: The Free Press.

Fromm, E. (1941). *Escape from freedom*. New York, NY: Holt Paperbacks.

Giaccardi, C. (2018, unpublished). 'Individuation and generative social action'. Paper given at the international conference titled *Social Generativity. What It Is and What It Is Good For.*

Giaccardi, C., and Magatti, M. (2014). *Generativi di tutto il mondo unitevi*. Milano: Feltrinelli.

Giddens, A. (1990). *The consequences of modernity*. Cambridge: Polity Press.

Giddens, A. (1991). *Modernity and self-identity. Self and society in the late modern age*. Cambridge: Polity.

Giddens, A., and Pierson, C. (1998). *Conversations with Anthony Giddens: Making sense of modernity*. Cambridge: Polity Press.

Giegerich, W. (2010). *The soul always thinks*. New Orleans, LA: Spring Journal.

Giegerich, W. (2020). *What are the factors that heal?* London/Ontario: Dusk Owl Books

Groys, B. (2012). *Antiphilosophy*. London/New York: Verso.

Havel, V. (1976). *Horský hotel*. Venezia: Marsilio.

Hillman, J. (1997). *Il Codice dell'Anima*. Milano: Adelphi.

Hillman, J., and Shamdasani, S. (2013). *Lament of the dead: Psychology after the red book.*

New York, NY: Norton & Company.

Jung, C. G. (1993a). 'A psychological view of conscience'. In *Collected works*, vol. 10: *Civilization in transition* (2nd edn.). London: Routledge and Kegan Paul.

Jung, C. G. (1993b). 'Self-knowledge'. In *Collected works*, vol. 14, *Mysterium coniunctionis* (2nd edn.). London: Routledge and Kegan Paul.

Jung, C. G. (1993c). 'Principles of practical psychotherapy'. In *Collected works*, vol. 16, *The practice of psychotherapy* (2nd edn.). London: Routledge and Kegan Paul.

Jung, C. G. (1993d). 'The aims of psychotherapy'. In *Collected works*, vol. 16, *The practice of psychotherapy* (2nd edn.). London: Routledge and Kegan Paul.

Jung, C. G. (1993e). 'Depth psychology and self knowledge'. In *Collected works*, vol. 18, *The symbolic life* (2nd edn.). London: Routledge and Kegan Paul.

Jung, C. G. (1993f). 'The symbolic life'. In *Collected works*, vol. 18, *The symbolic life* (2nd edn.). London: Routledge and Kegan Paul.

Jung, C. G. (1963). *Memories, dreams, reflections*. A. Jaffe (ed.). London: Collins; Routledge and Kegan Paul.

Jung, C. G. (2009). *The red book*. New York, NY: Norton & Company.

Lorenz, H., and Watkins, M. (2003). 'Depth psychology and colonialism: Individuation, seeing-through, and liberation'. *Quadrant*, 33, 11–32.

Lukes, S. (1982). 'Introduction'. In E. Durkheim (ed.), *The rules of sociological method*. New York, NY: The Free Press.

Magatti, M. (2018). 'Non può esserci libertà senza responsabilità'. In *Corriere della Sera*. Retrieved on 11 November 2018 from www.corriere.it/opinioni/18_settembre _10/non-puo-esserci-liberta-007b4212-b450-11e8-8b0b-dff47915528b.shtml.

Mandela, N. (1994). *Long walk to freedom*. New York: Little, Brown & Company

Marcuse, H. (1986). *One-dimensional man*. London: Ark.

Orbach, S. (2014). 'Democratizing psychoanalysis'. In D. Loewenthal and A. Samuels (eds.), *Relational psychotherapy, psychoanalysis and counselling: Appraisals and reappraisals*. New York, NY/London: Routledge.

Orbach, S. (2020). 'How are women today? Feminism, love and revolution'. In S. Carpani (ed.), *Breakfast at Küsnacht: Conversation on C. G. Jung and beyond*. Asheville, NC: Chiron Publications.

Ribi, A. (2020). 'Jung, von Franz and Alchemy'. In S. Carpani (ed.), *Breakfast at Küsnacht: Conversation on C. G. Jung and Beyond*. Asheville, NC: Chiron Publications.

Samuels, A. (1989). *The plural psyche*. London: Routledge.

Samuels, A. (1993). *The political psyche*. London: Routledge.

Spinoza, B. (2021). *Ethica*. Kindle Edition.

Umbach, M., and Huppauf, B. (2005). *Vernacular modernism: Heimat, globalisation, and the built environment*. Stanford: Stanford University Press.

US Centers for Disease Control and Prevention. (2018). 'Suicide rates rising across the U.S.' *CDC Newsroom*. Retrieved on 10 January 2022 from https://www.cdc.gov/media/releases/2018/p0607-suicide-prevention.html

von Franz, M.-L. (1964). 'The process of individuation'. In C. G. Jung (ed.), *Man and his symbols*. Garden City, NY: Doubleday.

von Franz, M.-L. (1978). 'The process of individuation'. In C. G. Jung (ed.), *Man and his symbols*. London: Picador.

Watkins, M. (2003). 'Dialogue, development, and liberation'. In I. Josephs (ed.), *Dialogicality in development*. Westport, CT: Greenwood.

Watkins, M., and Shulman, H. (2008). *Towards psychologies of liberation*. New York, NY: Palgrave Macmillan.

Zoja, L. (2009). *La morte del prossimo*. Torino: Einaudi.

Chapter 1

Dreaming Your Future. Dreaming Your Freedom

Galit Atlas

Sophie, a 34-year-old, successful Israeli businesswoman, started her analysis pre-occupied with her future, filled with dread that she would never be able to become a mother and that "the clock is ticking, time passes too fast, and I just can't make it." Sophie begins the analysis in a state of agitation, very concrete, desperately asking again and again, "What should I do? Is anything going to change soon?" Our main focus is on her desperation and hunger. Sophie expresses her longing for a baby, while I experience her as a demanding girl who requests that I feed her as an omnipotent mother who knows everything about the past, present, and future. "What do you think, does he love me?" "What should I do? Tell me . . ." she asks again and again. I am supposed to know her future and help her to make it happen, but in my mind I hear myself echoing her: "Oh, what a hopeless treatment. . . . Will anything ever change?" At that point, we are both frustrated. She has a limited ability to know her mind, use symbolic language, or play. Rather, it's as if Sophie is so hungry and empty that she has to immediately "swallow" everything I give her.

Sophie is the youngest of five children and the only girl. Her mother was excited to finally have a daughter, and Sophie admires and idealizes her mother. The mother is the one who shows restraint, who contains everyone, listens, and knows everything. "She's God," Sophie says. Sophie's mother comes from an Orthodox Jewish home. Although her mother was religious, Sophie and her four older brothers renounced religion. "At home," she says, "no one dared rebel against mother, but everyone rebelled against God." Only the household rules remained. Mother's rules, not God's. It is not God then who knows the future, but mother, and in the transference, it is her analyst.

We work in a preliminary way with Sophie's dreams (see Atlas, 2015, 2013a, 2013b). Food was the main theme in most of these, and the use of dreams as a shared third enables a shift to more playful and symbolic thinking (Aron, 2006; Benjamin, 2004; Ogden, 1994). "We are cooking," Sophie used to call the analysis of her dreams, referring to the profound form of thinking that we shared.

One day, during the fourth year of her treatment, Sophie begins a session saying that she feels empty, that sometimes after our sessions she feels like she is vomiting water. She explains that it feels like it does after having vomited everything;

DOI: 10.4324/9781003168829-2

when there is nothing there, she is empty, and it is painful and exhausting. She
tells me the following dream:

> I am in a wedding hall, where I meet an Israeli friend of mine who is a psy-
> chologist, who has come there to give a talk. I sit down at the table and see
> leftovers from lunch that look delicious, many dishes, and everything looks
> appetizing and fresh. But since I was so late, there is almost nothing left on
> the tables. I go over to the organizers' table, a women's table, and ask if there
> is more to eat. For a moment it seems to me that the girl whom I am asking
> is ignoring me, but a few seconds later she says, "There is no food left, but
> it's being taken care of [in Hebrew, *Betipul*, also meaning "it's in treatment]."
> I say, "OK, thanks," and return to the table. But I'm impatient. I think to
> myself, why do I have to wait for them? It's easier to just go out and get some
> fast food so that I won't be hungry. I ask myself if I should trust them. It feels
> like I have no control. It is much simpler to buy something with my money
> than to wait.

We begin by exploring the inherent question concerning whether she can trust
whatever is happening in the kitchen. Since food is a main theme in this treatment,
the kitchen became a metaphor for the unconscious and for the analytic process.
In the kitchen, something is being cooked, but Sophie cannot always know what it
is. "It's better to have control and go outside, to the real world and buy something
with my money, the money I know I have," she says. She makes her own money
and can pay for anything she needs, but she can't trust what she can't see, touch,
or know. The process of waiting for the food to be cooked is too frustrating; she
feels helpless, she is hungry, and she feels dependent and asks herself if she can
trust the process.

There is another implicit question: Maybe *I* ate everything and left nothing for
her? Maybe I took all the men, I have everything, just like her mother. And maybe
in therapy, food belongs only to me. I cook it and I serve it – maybe I even with-
hold it, and she needs to go back to her place and be patient, be a patient. Can she
trust me? Can she trust herself? Can she trust the analytic process? Here, she is
explicitly raising these questions while presenting the option that there is something that belongs only to her. "Maybe it is not empty, maybe there is something
there, in the unseen kitchen," she says. "I suddenly exist, and maybe I don't have
to run and fill myself up. Maybe I am full. Maybe someone will soon fall in love
with me . . ."

The following week, Sophie shares another dream. She goes to visit in the
kitchen. "It's the kitchen from last week's dream," she says,

> and I see a man from afar. I don't understand what's special about him and
> why I notice him. He's a simple man. He touches my hand and consoles me
> for all of the things I have lost while riding the motorcycle with my brother
> [an image from an earlier dream]. I was so happy as he hugged me in front of

other people and wasn't embarrassed, and I say to him, "I love you," and he answers, "I know. I love you, too." And they lived happily ever after,

she jokes. Somewhat uncannily, a day after presenting this dream in therapy, Sophie would meet the man who eventually becomes her husband. "He is a simple man," she says. "And I probably wouldn't even notice him if I didn't see him in my dream the night before. You know," she adds, "I'm sure I cooked my own food in that kitchen."

While not prophetic, I believe Sophie's dream was prospective, and the dream process itself – I believe like any other process – was looking toward and cooking the future, unconsciously preparing and procedurally rehearsing for it. The conflict between self-reliance and dependency appears in all of Sophie's dreams, as she has been mentally and symbolically exercising her sense of agency. She was cooking and gaining a sense of mastery of the kitchen and of riding her own powerful motorcycle so that she now has the autonomy to begin to envision a relationship with a man. Hence the dream is forward-looking; she can cook in that kitchen without feeling that in doing so she abandons her mother or analyst.

Elaborating on Bion's alimentary model of the container/contained, Ferro (2009) uses the metaphor of cooking when he defines how "emotions can be 'cooked' through their narrative transformation, with unsaturated interpretations, as the patient's response is always being 'sampled' in order to determine which ingredients are required to enrich or lighten the dish" (p. 217). In Ferro's mythic narrative, the analyst is the chef who cooks, processes raw beta elements, and transforms them into digestible form for the patient, always sampling the dish and adjusting, modulating, and regulating what is served up in the kitchen in response to the patient's unconscious feedback. When Aron and I (Atlas & Aron, 2017) use this metaphor, rather than envisioning the analyst as the cook and the patient being served up a dish, we view the analyst as inviting the patient into the kitchen itself where the analyst and patient cook and process the ingredients together, jointly tasting and modifying the dishes collaboratively. The process that Sophie herself called "cooking together" was a way of co-creating a profound form of thinking and feeling that belongs neither to patient nor analyst alone (Atlas, 2013a). Our attention was thus not limited to the outcome of the prepared dish but highlights the shared activity and process. Bion's digestive model of containment was transformed in his later writings into a sexual model of co-creativity (Brown, 2011), where mutuality and intersubjectivity are highlighted. Sophie's and my approach shares that later emphasis on reciprocity.

Sophie was preoccupied with becoming a mother. She could not get there so long as she relied on splitting the images of baby and mother, so long as she believed that a mother must be an omnipotent god, not a dependent baby. This splitting was repeatedly enacted between Sophie and her analyst. Either she expected me to be the all-powerful mother/God who provided for her, or she exerted omnipotent control over her own mind, but in a way that left her feeling both empty and unable to produce. In the process of "cooking together," oscillating and mutually enacting the functions of mother and infant, we co-created a third that transcended mother-baby oppositions and reversals. That process, as Sophie defines it, helped her to believe she is fertile and capable of dreaming, imagining, and producing – thus ready to become a mother. Her dreams, as they were enacted with me, were a way to rehearse for her future.

When I first asked Sophie's permission to present her story, she was proud and jokingly said, "Do you think people will realize how amazingly my mind works? Will they see how I learned to dream my existence and make my dreams come true?" Thinking of Ferro's (2009) ideas, following Bion's (1991) lines in *A Memoir of the Future*, I believe the analytic process can help our patients dream their future. Sophie believed she invited her future loving husband and the future father of her three children to her life in her dreams. Bion (1991) reminds us that our future, enigmatically, is always already ours, and that we don't remember it only for the pragmatic reason that it didn't happen yet. Linking Bion's approach with Jung's prospective function, Aron and I put forward the proposition that in studying the mind, we need to consider the unconscious will and urge to create, envision our future, give birth to ourselves, exercise our destiny drives, and even die our own individual deaths. As Freud (1920) memorably observed "the organism wishes to die only in its own fashion" (p. 312).

These are all conscious and unconscious processes that are based on the assumption that the mind is aimed toward mental evolution and toward the developmental capacity to bear the emotional anxiety of the confrontation with life. Whereas Freud's pleasure principle is rooted in the idea that the mind strives to avoid pain and frustration, Bion argues to the contrary that the mind develops towards transformation, to tolerate and bear pain so as to grasp Truth. In Bion's understanding, emotional growth manifests in developing the tolerance for our deepest anxieties, including psychological birth and annihilation, fear of our future death, and disintegration. If Freud emphasized the causality of the past and Jung the future orientation, Bion cautioned that both the past and future can distract from the immediacy of the present, and his effort to restrict memory and desire is in the service of immediate experience.[1]

This chapter, which was originally developed as an earlier paper with Lewis Aron (Atlas & Aron, 2017), focuses on the individual's effort to anticipate their psychic future and thus to transform fate into destiny. While some of the earlier theorists had conceptualized this function in terms of a one-person psychology, Aron and I weaved this theme into the tapestry of the relational matrix, where individuals can only fashion their destiny in intersubjective contact with others.

The Prospective Function

Whereas traditional psychoanalysis emphasized the psychological causation driven by our past and present wishes, in our theory, we highlight how our unconscious hopes and dreams, our goals and ends, pull us toward our destiny. Our mind anticipates and rehearses for that future, and we argue that all productions of the mind, all compromise formations, include some unconscious anticipation of the future and efforts to transform our fate into destiny. Human beings, we propose, can potentially transform their fate and thus create their destiny. From objects of fate, we become agentic subjects, creators of our destiny, of our futures. Indeed, we suggest that this goal represents an additional layer of meaning to Benjamin's (1998) call, "where objects were, subjects must be" (p. 29). We argue that contemporary psychoanalysis, with its hermeneutic, constructivist, humanistic, and relational leanings, is now in a position to reevaluate the use of what Carl Jung (1916), a century ago, called the prospective function. Prospective does not mean prophetic, or literally predictive, but rather refers to a visionary function; we unconsciously "look forward" to future possibilities. The mind exercises or rehearses; it anticipates, prepares, shapes, and constructs.

Freud depicted the mind as stratified in layers and the analyst as archeologist, digging from the surface to the depths. However, this does not mean that memory is buried underground like an artifact preserved in its original form, waiting to be dug up. Rather, Freud viewed memory as a fluid entity that was constantly changing and being reworked over time. He referred to this dynamic as *Nachträglichkeit*, translated in English as "afterwardness," or "deferred action," and in French as *après coup*. For Freud, the past and present mutually influence one another. Later events lead to the reworking of earlier events, affecting subsequent development. Such a complex view of time fits contemporary models of development as nonlinear complex systems (Harris, 2005). Faimberg (2013), in broadening the concept of *Nachträglichkeit*, introduced the "as-yet situation," a clinical form of temporality that includes a phase of anticipation and a phase of retrospective meaning. In illustrating her thesis, she describes Winnnicott as being "careful to propose an interpretation that points time's arrow toward an open future" (p. 871). Throughout his work, Freud emphasized the determinism of the past, and yet he also recognized that all fantasy anticipates the future. Freudian theory, despite this nonlinear, complex view of time, remained deterministic – unlike Jung's use of psychological teleology. Freud's attachment to natural science and determinism left no room for human agency in his metapsychology.

A view of psychoanalysis as transforming passivity into activity, objects into subjects, fate into destiny, inconsistent with Jung's use of teleology, referring to the psyche's purposiveness, orients interpretations away from causal formulations, which look back to the events of early life and to the contingencies of personal history. Jung disagreed with Freud about the nature of symbols and understood them as anticipations of new possibilities, new transformations; instead of a way backward to the past and scenes of childhood, they are a way forward to the psychological future. What Jung called the prospective function of the unconscious is what Deleuze, following Bergson, called the memory of the future (Semetsky, 2013). Deleuze's future-oriented epistemology is leaning towards meanings "that are yet to come" (Deleuze & Guattari, 1987, p. 5), while Freud's analytic approach was considered reductive by Jung, and then by Deleuze, because of its exclusive orientation toward the past as marked by oedipal conflict (Semetsky, 2013).

Whereas Freud traced the dynamics of the psyche back to early childhood experiences, and especially to those of a sexual nature, Jung (1912) understood symbols not fundamentally as serving distortion or disguise but rather as playing an active role in pushing the psyche forward in a development toward greater wholeness. The shift from a natural model mechanical formulation to an existential and prospective approach posits active agents who are not simply objects of historical forces beyond their control but active subjects who shape and design their futures and whose psychic lives must always be understood as unconsciously determined attempts to take hold of their future. From this perspective, Jung's visionary teleology, unhinged from careful analysis, can lead too far from material reality to mysticism, just as Freud's natural science approach eschews too much of psychological and spiritual life. In this chapter, I look to incorporate insights from both vertices, combining Pragmatic and Enigmatic registers.

The distinction between fate and destiny is a central theme in the existential philosophy (developed in the 1950s) of Joseph Soloveitchik. For Soloveitchik (2000), fate refers to a level of human existence in which the human being is a passive object acted upon by external forces beyond the individual's control, whereas destiny refers to a realm in which the person is an active subject imbuing life with meaning and significance. "Man's task in the world is to transform fate into destiny; a passive existence into an active existence" (p. 6).

Destiny, in contrast to fate, makes room for human agency, but fulfilling the destiny drive leads to inevitable conflict; destiny calls for the determined agentic taking hold of one's future. Building on Winnicott's theory, for Bollas (1989), to exercise one's destiny drive is to creatively make use of objects in the environment to establish one's true self. By contrast, to be passively fated by forces outside of one's control is associated with the development of a false self. "It may be an essential part of analytic work to help a patient transform fatedness into destiny and to gain futures" (p. 44).[2]

Self-psychological formulations have much in common with the line of thought Aron and I (Atlas & Aron, 2017) have been developing,[3] wherein we link Jung's prospective function, Bion's memories of the future, and Bollas's destiny drive, all of which we understand as efforts to shift from a natural science to an existential model in which human beings have the potential to transform fate into destiny – in other words, to become subjects where they had been only objects (Benjamin, 1998), to be existentially free agents where they had been determined by circumstance.

In the history of dream analysis, there have been several efforts to understand the function of dreaming in "generative" terms. Maeder, a friend of Jung's, proposed as early as 1911 that in addition to fulfilling childhood wishes, dreaming might also serve the purpose of preparing the dreamer for upcoming tasks. Did dreams represent only attempts to discharge disguised childhood wishes, or "did they also sometimes have as their purpose attempts to anticipate and solve problems that lay in the near future?" (Kerr, 1993, p. 461). By 1914, the idea of a prospective interpretation of dreams and symptoms was in the air. Adler was proposing a teleological function of neurotic symptoms, and both Stekel and Adler claimed priority in suggesting the prospective function of dreams. Kerr (1993) suggests that the prospective theory of dreams was the biggest threat facing Freud in these years of defection. By 1916, Jung posited that dreams serve both compensatory and prospective functions. Fosshage (2000) suggests that dream mentation can contribute to the development of psychological organization through the creation or consolidation of a new solution or synthesis. In Fosshage's view, dreaming does not just foreshadow developments but is actively engaged in bringing about those internal changes.

As we have seen, a prospective function may be attributed not only to dreams but also to symptoms, to play, or to fantasy. In her comprehensive survey of fantasy in psychoanalysis, Ethel Person (1995) writes,

> fantasy can act as a rehearsal for future action and can provide a template for life choices that may be either literal translations (enactments) or symbolic expressions of the fantasy's narrative content. Fantasy is a theatre in which we preview the possible scenarios of our life to come.
>
> (p. 6)

She terms "generative fantasies" those that do not just repeat the past but rather focus on the future (p. 95). Like make-believe and play, "generative fantasy represents a creative effort to find our way in the real world" (p. 121).

Enactment as a Rehearsal

In our previous work (Atlas & Aron, 2017), we suggested that just as dreams, fantasies, and play have been understood as generative, as having prospective functions, so too do enactments. *Enactment* has become a widely employed term across schools of contemporary psychoanalysis. Relational psychoanalysis, in particular, has emphasized the affirmative and beneficial contribution of enactments rather than stressing only their counterproductive or problematic aspects, and our exploration of the prospective function of enactment is a development that continues along these lines. Enactments may well be a central means by which *patients and analysts enter into each other's inner world and discover themselves as participants within each other's psychic life*, mutually constructing the relational matrix that constitutes the medium of psychoanalysis (Aron, 1996; Mitchell, 1988).

Enactment speaks to the unique way in which the analyst is affectively pulled into and discovers him- or herself as a participant in the patient's relational world in ways that the analyst had not predicted and might not recognize until later (Aron & Lechich, 2012). Bass (2003) observes that "Enactments" constitute especially challenging moments for the analyst and may be decisive turning points in the analysis. These, he argues, are times of high risk and high gain for both patient and analyst. He demonstrates an important function of enactment: allowing the analytic dyad to contain opposing realities and to enable incongruous self-states to coexist. In doing so, he builds on the work of Bromberg, Davies, Mitchell, Stern, and others in connecting relational theorizing about the multiplicity of selves to the clinical literature on enactment.

Enactment is not simply an overt event but an unconscious, continuously evolving, dynamically meaningful process (Katz, 2013). In all treatments, a new version of the patient's early conflicts, traumas, and formative object relationships is inevitably created, without awareness or intent, in the here-and-now of the analytic dyad. Within the enacted dimension of psychoanalytic process, repressed or dissociated aspects of the patient's past are not just remembered, they are *relived*. Katz (2013) and the Boston Change Process Study Group (2013) situate enactment within the larger flow of therapeutic process, not as a return of past dissociated memories but rather as the threshold for the introduction of emergent ways of being, of an opening toward new relational possibilities.

Aron and I addressed an aspect of enactment that is somewhat different from the usual focus in the relational literature. The more common emphasis, following the pioneering contributions of Levenson (1983), is on the process of resolving enactments, "getting out of enactments," questioning them, understanding them, and interpreting them. Of course, we agreed that this unpacking is often necessary and beneficial. However, we suggested that the flow of enactive engagement, the enactive dimension of analysis, may at times be more Enigmatic than Pragmatic, generative and transformative in and of itself, not only by working one's way out of it. Our argument for the prospective function of enactment is tied to and builds on our assumption that enactments dramatize and bring to life not only the individual's conflicts but the entire intersubjective field, allowing for growth and transformation.

Stern (2013) suggests that it is precisely because enactments "inhibit the free unfolding of the future, their resolution is one of the most important influences liberating the future to unfold more freely than the past did" (p. 232, n. 8). Regardless of the different emphases, Aron and I joined both Stern and the Boston Change Process Study Group in their focus on looking toward the future while also working through the past. Our own emphasis, and the focus of this chapter, represents a further development of this approach, in that we do not view enactment only as the blockage or interference with the future, which leaves the focus only on resolving or eliminating the enactment; rather, we imagine enactment as a rehearsal, a practicing for the unknown future, an early effort to "work toward the future" rather than only a "working through of the past" (see Aron, 1991, p. 81). It emphasizes what the enactment is for – its constructive side – rather than how it gets in the way or interferes with the process. The prospective function highlights that enactments are an improvised form of mutual play or dramatization (Ringstrom, 2001) that anticipate, practice, and rehearse forms of relationship and behavior looking toward the future. Enactments, from this perspective, develop and elaborate characters as a means of exploring, dramatizing, and bringing to life future potentialities, what Steven Cooper (2000) has called, after Loewald (1962), our "psychic futures." Enactments, and not only their interpretation or resolution, are thus a creative medium for giving psychological birth to or actual-izing the self. Our unconscious participation in enactment is not only pushed or driven, determined by our past history or present circumstances, but is shaped by our psychic futures. Enactments are one of the royal roads to the fulfillment of our destinies.

The End

Sarah has been complaining about her marriage since she began her analysis seven years ago. She came to treatment suffering from bodily pain – pain in her knees that interfered with walking, and pain in her elbows. She believed that her physical condition was in some way related to the pain she felt in her 12 years of marriage, pain caused by feeling that she was not heard by and could not get through to her husband, even though he was a "good guy." At night, she tried to avoid him and moved to sleep with her three-year-old son, while her husband stayed alone in their bedroom. Sarah felt much safer when sleeping with her son. She felt close to and loved by him. She said she was afraid of the end, but the end of what? The end of her marriage? The end of her analysis? The end of her life?

As a child, Sarah was a popular girl with many friends, and later in adoles-cence, she had several boyfriends but felt that no one really knew her, and if they did, they would not like her because there was something bad hidden inside of her. Sarah was always told that she was a beautiful child, and in fact was regarded by others as a beautiful woman, but she never thought of herself as either popular or attractive. Rather, she believed her beauty hid internal ugliness, perhaps in the same way that she believed her parents' advanced education disguised their ignorance. Sarah's father was a judge in a state court. Both parents were highly educated and economically and socially successful, but they were morally rigid, emphasizing strict standards of right and wrong, and were unable to tolerate the expression of affect. Sarah knew that it was "right" to keep her marriage. She knew her parents wouldn't accept any other behavior. She knew it was "wrong" to express so much dissatisfaction and agony.

Sarah decided to start therapy when her joint pain became insufferable. She tells me that she is afraid she is about to become paralyzed, that she is worried about her future. As the years went on, she became increasingly clear about her feelings of dissatisfaction and was better able to articulate her concerns. Sarah would at times become convinced that her husband, Josh, like her mother, was dissociative, incapable of expressing or even identifying feelings, was depriv-ing, punishing, and could never join in her feeling states. But neither of us was convinced that this was what he was really like. In fact, it was confusing since we both knew Josh was also protective, stable, solid, often encouraging her to do what she most desired, and we genuinely believed that they had a good enough marriage. Josh was committed to her as his wife and the mother of his child and thought that in her ongoing complaints she was somewhat hysterical and overly dramatic, exaggerating the problems between them. I joined in her confusion. To what extent were her perceptions related to childhood experiences, we wondered, noting the parallel of her past and present convictions? She had also always felt that her parents were solidly there and committed to the family, and yet she did not really believe they loved her.

Very often, I felt in a position similar to the one she experienced with her husband; Sarah would come to the sessions on time, worked hard, paid promptly, and yet something was missing. I felt that there was something we were still unable to touch, as if there were no ability to think about what was actually happening inside and outside the analysis. Thinking and affect started and ended with her intolerable pain. As I started to recognize my own inability to think, I became more aware of the ways her insights and introspection were used masochistically in the service of guilt and stasis. Sarah began treatment blaming herself and quickly moved to explore the many reasons she felt at fault for her marital discontent. There was a thin line between Sarah's insight and her self-recrimination in the service of not being able to move, physically because of her joint pain, and emotionally, as she was trapped in the masochistic position. She was paralyzed.

Focused on her pain, I was trying to grasp any vision she or I could have of her future. The future seemed empty. There was no imaginary scenario of what she would like to have inside or outside of her analysis, inside or outside of her marriage, no fantasy of creating something new with her husband or with me, not even a forbidden fantasy of being with another man, who could perhaps love her the way she needed. At times, I felt that her mind attacked all linking (Bion, 1959), between objects, ideas, affects, images, different aspects of her personality and of our interaction. These attacks on linking kept her fragmented, disjointed, and unable to dream or think and therefore unable to move, incapable of transformation, of learning from experience (Bion, 1959).

In the room with Sarah, my own reverie included life filled with light, children, music, food . . . and sexual thoughts, which Sarah asserted she certainly didn't need. I wondered if my reveries of abundance were only a way to keep myself alive with her, to soothe the pain; in what way were they connected to her process, in what way was I dreaming her life, my life, and our future? I think about reverie as belonging not only to the analyst but also as part of a shared process, existing within the intersubjective field. In that sense, I understand my reverie as a co-creation and assume a flow of unconscious communication between us and linking us together. I realized that I dreamt a future, and as I started to silently connect my reverie with a potential for a full life, Sarah notified me that she was ending her analysis. Sarah didn't want to discuss or process that decision, and I was left with the feeling that maybe I dreamt something she had to attack and cut off, so that no transformation would occur. I did not yet know that our ongoing enactment – including this sudden end without discussion – was a step forward for both of us and not only a repetition of destructive attacks and paralysis. Thinking along more conventional lines, I inferred that quitting the treatment was a defensive displacement, that she was cutting me off as she wanted to cut off her husband because she still couldn't face the catastrophe of ending her marriage; instead, she ended her analysis. To some degree, I could think of the analysis as repeating the deadness and hopelessness of her marriage and of me as a participant in those dynamics. One question that I asked myself was whether Sarah's unwillingness to discuss these considerations with me might have been related to some reciprocal conflict or avoidance on my part. Could it be that there was some relief for me in her leaving because her marital struggle was too close to my own? All of these reflections and considerations emerged in an attempt to search for the repetition of old object relations, and in that respect, they needed to be uncovered and processed. Alternatively, I suggest that at times what seem like mutually engaged old scenarios, the trailing edge, may instead turn out, from a different vertex, to be new developments in the process of transformation, a leading edge of development. There is always more ambiguity and multiplicity of meanings than we can ever know or consciously articulate. Sometimes, and perhaps often, only the future can teach us about the meanings of the past.

Another Beginning

Six months later, Sarah calls me. She asks to resume her analysis. "I left," she says, and as I am about to acknowledge her wish to return to treatment, she adds, "I don't mean the analysis. I left him. Right after I ended the analysis, I left Josh." Years later, we came to understand her interruption of the analysis as an enactment. She left the analysis not only as a defense or resistance but rather as a way of rehearsing for her future, a preparation for the end, for leaving her marriage and starting a new life, with new love, hopes, and dreams. Enactment, as Aron and I have noted, is a process rather than a discrete episode. One might question whether Sarah's interruption was itself an enactment or whether it is more accurately viewed as the end of what had been a sadomasochistic enactment between the two of us that preceded it.

The clinical understanding that I am proposing is that the disruption of the analysis was not only defensive but rather was adaptive and constructive in at least some respects. In interrupting the analysis, Sarah took an initial step in a move from passivity and paralysis to activity and decisiveness. There was a gradual transformation from someone who could not dream, who had to express herself concretely by attacking her joints, her links, attacks that kept her from knowing and having an emotional experience for which she did not feel prepared. She slowly developed the ability to use her mind, make connections, and imagine her future. She used her analyst's mind to transform her night terrors into a dream with connections, with joints that could move, so that she could think and symbolize (see Ogden, 2005). The enactment was also a way to transform an experience of masochistic submission into agency and self-authorization, from being disjointed to feeling connected, and thus she slowly transformed her life experience from fate to destiny.

I consider the possibility that the enactment was not only a rehearsal for Sarah's future, but in fact was also a co-created rehearsal for my own future, as my marriage ended a few months later. In that sense, Sarah and I co-created a scene where we enacted our similar and different hopes, possibilities, and potential future. In contrast to the term *acting out*, which emerged within the context of a one-person psychology, the concept of enactment, as it has been developed and elaborated on since the 1980s, is embedded within a two-person or bidirectional model (for the historical development, see Aron, 1996). I believe that enactments are co-constructed even at times when it might superficially look as if one person is "acting out." The analyst is always a participant in the unconscious shaping of the patient's future, but the assumption that we can always come to know the analyst's contribution is of course an illusion. The analyst's unconscious is no less complex than the patient's, and so our focus is on those things that we cannot fully know or that we cannot know at all. In this case, while eschewing any sense of certainty or mastery of the analyst's unconscious, we can play with the idea that it was the analyst's reverie that was an expression of dreaming her patient's life as well as her own. Perhaps it was this reverie that contributed to the enactment of a jointly constructed treatment interruption, possibly even including as one component the analyst's unconscious wish to get rid of the patient who "has no future."

In sum, what seem like impasses, disruptions, stalemates, gridlock, even interruptions, may at another time, from a different perspective, look more like progress and transformation. Whereas much of the contemporary literature has considered the analysis of enactments therapeutic – the explication of these repetitive patterns, "getting out" of enactments, resolving impasses and stalemates by understanding and explaining them – Aron and I (Atlas & Aron, 2017) suggest another approach: conceptualizing in another register. There is much we may never be able to understand about what happened between two people and in an enactment, but *the enactment itself*, and not only its resolution, may be a dimension of a transformative process. Enactments, like anything else between patient and analyst, can be restrictive, limiting, and destructive or may be expansive, growth promoting, and creative. The analyst therefore must straddle a paradox, always skeptical, questioning, seeking hidden meanings, searching for unconscious dynamics at play, the trailing edge, a hermeneutics of suspicion – while also, paradoxically, trusting unconscious process and surrendering to the continuous flow of the enactive dimension of analysis, relying on a hermeneutics of faith (Ricoeur, 1970).

In many ways, it is tempting to work with what we assume we know – the past that already happened, the patient's history – while it is more challenging to think of enactment as anticipating an uncertain future, a future that may be filled with promise and hope but that also inevitably entails pain and loss. Thus the prospective function contains the light and the dark, hope and dread (Mitchell, 1993). Recognizing and containing our ignorance of both of our futures is an important aspect of the mutual vulnerability that is an ethos of psychoanalytic praxis (Atlas & Aron, 2017).

In conclusion, I suggest that it is essential for clinicians to take an affirmative approach to our patient's presentations, which are to be understood in at least one register as their best effort to develop their psychic futures. One aspect of such an approach, as mentioned, is to think prospectively as well as retrospectively. Both are necessary, as to think only prospectively would neglect causation and repetition, might promote the denial of aggression and conflict, and would encourage a naïve optimism and utopianism. We must consider both what enactment avoids, defends against, and repeats – its trailing edge, the repeated dimension of the relationship – as well as what it is for, what it accomplishes, and how it prepares us for our future – its leading edge or the needed relationship. At times, we may prematurely interpret our way out of enactments that would have been better off further lived through. Just as clinicians need to see how we participate in being used as both old and new objects, so too, and as a very important part of such a view, do enactments both repeat and work through the past and also anticipate, rehearse, and work toward the future, toward the transformation from fatedness to destiny.

Notes

1 Grotstein suggests that Bion not only heard Jung lecture but was deeply influenced by him (Culbert-Koehn, 1997).
2 For recent studies of agency within psychoanalysis, especially those emphasizing the development of agency through the negotiation of recognition and mutuality, see Gentile (2010), Hoffman (2006), and Pollock and Slavin (1998).
3 Kohut's suggests that the analyst attend to the "leading edge" as well as the "trailing edge" of the patient's transference (Miller, 1985, p. 19). The leading edge addresses the evolving and developing aspects of the patient's transference, whereas the trailing edge is concerned with genetic causal configurations. The trailing edge addresses what is old and repeated, whereas the leading edge speaks to what is new. Analyzing both trailing and forward edge transferences, according to Tolpin (2002), frees the patient from repeating nuclear pathology while supporting the aim of regaining developmental momentum.

References

Aron, L. (1991). Working through the past – Working toward the future. *Contemporary Psychoanalysis, 27*, 81–109.

Aron, L. (1996). *A meeting of minds: Mutuality in psychoanalysis*. Hillsdale, NJ: The Analytic Press.

Aron, L. (2006). Analytic impasse and the third: Clinical implications of intersubjectivity theory. *International Journal of Psychoanalysis, 87*, 350–368.

Aron, L., & Lechich, M. (2012). Relational psychoanalysis. In O. Gabbard, B. E. Litowitz, & P. Williams (Eds.), *Textbook of psychoanalysis* (2nd ed., pp. 211–224). Washington, DC: American Psychiatric Publishing.

Atlas, G. (2013a). Eat, pray, dream: Contemporary use of dreams in psychoanalysis. *Contemporary Psychoanalysis, 49*, 239–246.

Atlas, G. (2013b). Eating, cooking and the space between: Response to panelists' commentaries. *Contemporary Psychoanalysis, 49*, 276–286.

Atlas, G. (2015). *The enigma of desire: Sex, longing and belonging in psychoanalysis*. London: Routledge.

Atlas, G., & Aron, L. (2017). *Dramatic dialogue: Contemporary clinical practice* (1st ed.). London: Routledge.

Bass, A. (2003). "E" enactments in psychoanalysis: Another medium, another message. *Psychoanalytic Dialogues, 13*, 657–675. doi:10.1080/10481881309348762

Benjamin, J. (1998). *Like subjects, love objects: Essays on recognition and sexual difference.* New Haven, CT: Yale University Press.

Benjamin, J. (2004). Beyond doer and done-to: An intersubjective view of thirdness. *Psychoanalytic Quarterly, 73*, 5–46.

Bion, W. R. (1959). Attacks on linking. *International Journal of Psychoanalysis, 40*, 308–315.

Bion, W. R. (1991). *A memoir of the future*: Books 1–3. London: Karnac.

Bollas, C. (1989). *Forces of destiny: Psychoanalysis and human idiom.* London: Free Association Books.

Boston Change Process Study Group. (2013). Enactment and the emergence of new relational organization. *Journal of the American Psychoanalytic Association, 61*, 727–749.

Brown, L. J. (2011). *Intersubjective processes and the unconscious: An integration of Freudian, Kleinian and Bionian perspectives.* London: Routledge.

Cooper, S. H. (2000). *Objects of hope: Exploring possibility and limit in psychoanalysis.* Hillsdale, NJ: The Analytic Press.

Culbert-Koehn, J. (1997). Between Bion and Jung: A talk with James Grotstein. *The San Francisco Jung Institute Library Journal, 15*, 15–32.

Deleuze, G., & Guattari, F. (1987). *A thousand plateaus: Capitalism and schizophrenia* (B. Massumi, Trans.). Minneapolis, MN: University of Minnesota Press.

Faimberg, H. (2013). The "as-yet situation" in Winnicott's "Fragment of an analysis": Your father "never did you the honor of" . . . yet. *Psychoanalytic Quarterly, 82*, 849–875.

Ferro, A. (2009). Transformations in dreaming and characters in the psychoanalytic field. *International Journal of Psychoanalysis, 90*, 209–230.

Fosshage, J. L. (2000). The organizing functions of dreaming – A contemporary psychoanalytic model: Commentary on paper by Hazel Ipp. *Psychoanalytic Dialogues, 10*, 103–117.

Freud, S. (1920). Beyond the pleasure principle. In J. Strachey (Ed. & Trans.), *The standard edition of the complete psychological works of Sigmund Freud* (Vol. 18, pp. 1–64). London: Hogarth Press.

Gentile, J. (2010). Weeds on the ruins: Agency, compromise formation, and the quest for intersubjective truth. *Psychoanalytic Dialogues, 20*, 88–109.

Harris, A. (2005). *Gender as soft assembly* (1st ed.). London: Routledge.

Hoffman, I. Z. (2006). The myths of free association and the potentials of the analytic relationship. *International Journal of Psychoanalysis, 87*, 43–61.

Jung, C. G. (1912). *Wandlungen und Symbole der Libido: Beiträge zur Entwicklungsgeschichte des Denkens.* Leipzig: F. Deuticke.

Jung, C. G. (1916). *Psychology of the unconscious: A study of the transformations and symbolisms of the Libido. A contribution to the history of the evolution of thought* (Beatrice M. Hinkle, Trans.). New York: Moffat, Yard and Vo.

Katz, G. (2013). *The play within the play: The enacted dimension of psychoanalytic process.* New York, NY: Routledge.

Kerr, J. (1993). *A most dangerous method: The story of Jung, Freud, and Sabina Spielrein.* New York: Knopf.

Levenson, E. A. (1983). *The ambiguity of change: An inquiry into the nature of psychoanalytic reality.* New York: Basic Books.

Loewald, H. W. (1962). The superego and the ego-ideal. *International Journal of Psychoanalysis, 43*, 264–268.

Miller, J. P. (1985). How Kohut actually worked. *Progress in Self Psychology, 1*, 13–30.

Mitchell, S. A. (1988). *Relational concepts in psychoanalysis.* Cambridge, MA: Harvard University Press.

Mitchell, S. A. (1993). *Hope and dread in psychoanalysis.* New York: Basic Books.

Ogden, T. H. (1994). *Subjects of analysis.* Northvale, NJ: Jason Aronson.

Ogden, T. H. (2005). *This art of psychoanalysis: Dreaming undreamt dreams and interrupted cries.* London: Routledge.

Person, E. S. (1995). *By force of fantasy: How we make our lives.* New York: Basic Books.

Pollock, L., & Slavin, J. H. (1998). The struggle for recognition: Disruption and reintegration in the experience of agency. *Psychoanalytic Dialogues, 8*, 857–873.

Ricoeur, P. (1970). *Freud and philosophy* (D. Savage, Trans.). New Haven, CT: Yale University Press.

Ringstrom, P. A. (2001). Cultivating the improvisational in psychoanalytic treatment. *Psychoanalytic Dialogues, 11*, 727–754.

Semetsky, I. (2013). *Jung and educational theory.* Hoboken, NJ: Wiley-Blackwell.

Soloveitchik, J. B. (2000). *Fate and destiny: From Holocaust to the State of Israel* (L. Kaplan, Trans.). Hoboken, NJ: KTAV Publishing.

Stern, D. B. (2013). Relational freedom and therapeutic action. *Journal of the American Psychoanalytic Association, 61*, 227–256.

Tolpin, M. (2002). Doing psychoanalysis of normal development. *Progress in Self Psychology, 18*, 167–190.

Chapter 2

In Defense of the Freedoms of the Self

John Beebe

During Shakespeare's *Julius Caesar*, just after the self-declared 'Dictator for life' has fallen dead from the stabs of Republican patriots, Cassius, the senator who masterminded the assassination, gives a command of his own: 'Some to the common pulpits and cry out "Liberty, freedom, and enfranchisement" ' (Shakespeare, 1998, p. 346). This message was delivered by Cassius without cynicism, but since what really happened after Caesar's assassination is that the Roman Republic completely disappeared, it is likely that the playwright intended a dramatic irony by inserting between the thrilling "liberty" and the empowering "enfranchisement" so dangerous a word as "freedom." He knew, and I think counted upon us to realize, that the words on either side of it had never been political realities in the centuries since Cassius might have spoken them.

In our own time, so many political ironies have resulted when an autocratically disposed political party has wrapped around its repressive policies a promise to guarantee "freedom" that it seems naive to argue that the concept of freedom can be trusted to nourish more than its own abuse. Yet that is what I am going to attempt. I will refuse to heed George Orwell's warning in his novel *1984* – which I first read about in the July 4, 1949 issue of *Life* magazine, when I had just turned 10 – that in a future modern country speaking my own English language, it could be the received opinion that "Freedom is Slavery" and that this recognition would be used to justify a domestic agenda guided by the knowledge that "Ignorance is Strength" and a foreign policy which understood that "War is Peace" (Orwell, 1961, p. 4). The dystopian novelist's ironic dismissal of the possibility of a future worldview guided by a more naive idea of freedom did not convince me that this was my own democracy's fate, and it does not convince me now, even acknowledging that Orwell's socialist political vision was instantly subverted by the editors of *Life*, who, working under right-wing Editor-in-Chief Henry Luce, introduced his novel to middle America with the sentence "An Englishman writes a frightening satire about the cruel fate of man in a regimented left-wing police state which controls his mind and soul" (Life Magazine, 1949, p. 78).

Ten years earlier, emerging American attitudes had been very different. In that year before Franklin Roosevelt ran for his third term as president, it was just dawning on America that it might be called to realize the promises he was starting

DOI: 10.4324/9781003168829-3

to make for it as the leader of the free world. Nazi German forces had invaded Czechoslovakia in March, and in April, Roosevelt had written to Chancellor Adolf Hitler asking him "to agree not to attack any other sovereign nation in Europe." Orwell, who had been born in India in 1903, grew up as a writer witnessing the effects of the colonialism that Rudyard Kipling had celebrated, in an ironic reversal of the ideals England pretended to. In his literary work, Orwell's command of irony would take on the quality of prophecy. He was able to see the reality of the shadow that pervades Western democracies today, even when it does not prevail, which includes a notion of freedom that is designed to rationalize taking advantage of people who wield less power. What has gotten lost in the ironic realism that became fashionable among millennials (Jedediah Purdy [1999] has called theirs a 'terminal irony') is the concept of freedom that Roosevelt was able to successfully construct for political discourse at a time when even Britain's ability to sustain its democracy on its own island was under attack. Roosevelt's conception, happily, is beginning to get a rehearing in America today when democracy is under similar threat from a different understanding of freedom between the country's own shores.

What particularly impresses me about Roosevelt's success in harnessing the idea of freedom to renew the energy needed to stand up to tyranny is the psychological way in which he was able to argue for the idea. How he spoke to the Congress just after being elected, in his Annual Message to Congress on January 6, 1941 (which today would be called his "State of the Union"), was entirely psychological in a way that I find uncannily congruent with the political attitude that has always guided my own work as a Jungian analyst. This is not an accident. As an American Jungian, training in San Francisco where the United Nations got its start, the values of Franklin Roosevelt were evident in two of my most influential analyst trainers, Jo Wheelwright and Joseph Henderson. The two Joes took Roosevelt's liberal vision for granted, and they welcomed me because I shared it.

From my earliest days, at 17, as a volunteer at the state mental hospital for disturbed children in Waltham, Massachusetts, not far from Walden Pond, my life as a healer has been organized by the idea of psychology as a way of bringing service to others. Sixty-five years later, Roosevelt's vision still guides me in my work as a Jungian analyst and consultant to people in many parts of the world.

Thanks to the investigative efforts of Jung historian Jay Sherry, I have come to recognize that Franklin Roosevelt may have had similar inspiration from this kind of Jungian attitude from America's first Jungian analyst, Beatrice Hinkle, who was born in San Francisco and after graduating from the Cooper Medical College served in 1900 as San Francisco's "city physician," the first woman in America to hold such a position. Following the death of her husband in 1905, she came to New York and, after working at New Thought sanatorium in Kingston, New York, became part of one of the first psychotherapy clinics in America. It was organized at Cornell Medical College by the neurologist Charles H. Dana, who was familiar with both Freud's work and Jung's. Remarrying, Hinkle went to Europe to study psychoanalysis and travelled on the same train with Freud and Jung to attend the

1911 Weimar psychoanalytic congress. Back in America, she became a member
of the Liberal Club in New York that brought professionally distinguished women
together, and through her membership in Chi Omega, a society for professional
women, met Eleanor Roosevelt. As Sherry recounts, "There is a family story that
Franklin Roosevelt met with Hinkle at Roughlands [her country home in Con-
necticut] for help in regaining his self-confidence after contracting polio in 1921"
(Sherry, 2013, p. 497). Jan Jarboe Russell (2021) confirms that

> When asked if he wanted to talk about it, Franklin usually said no. He would
> not allow negative talk about his illness. However, on one occasion in 1921,
> he had a bad day and met with Beatrice Hinkle, the Jungian psychologist,
> to discuss how he could deal with the onset of dark depression. . . . It was
> Eleanor who asked Hinkle to help Franklin lift up his spirits as he dealt with
> his paralysis.
>
> (p. 95)

As Russell also reveals, Hinkle and Eleanor had both been influenced by the
politically and sexually liberated men and women they met in Greenwich Village,
who, by setting themselves free from patriarchal constrictions, were experiencing, in the early 1920s, a personal freedom that was entirely cognate with Jung's
emphasis on individuation as a way to overcome the limitations of collective
thinking.

Near the end of one of Jung's most difficult but rewarding essays, "Transformation Symbolism in the Mass," in which he explores the psychological meaning of
sacrifice to clarify why that concept is so central to the Christian understanding
of God's coming to the earth in human form only to be crucified, the following
passage offers insight into the value we have inherited by Divinity's making such
a choice:

> the Christian spirit of the West has become the defender of the irrational,
> since, in spite of having fathered rationalism and intellectualism, it has not
> succumbed to them so far as to give up its belief in the rights of man, and
> especially the freedom of the individual. But this freedom guarantees a recog-
> nition of the irrational principle, despite the lurking danger of chaotic individ-
> ualism. By appealing to the eternal rights of man, faith binds itself inalienably
> to a higher order, not only on account of the historical fact that Christ has
> proved to be an ordering factor for many hundreds of years, but also because
> the self effectively compensates chaotic conditions no matter by what name
> it is known: for the self is the Anthropos above and beyond this world, and in
> him is contained the freedom and dignity of the individual man.
>
> (Jung, 1954/1958, p. 292, para 444)

It is important to realize that Jung was also speaking as an analyst when he per-
mitted himself this anthropological interpretation of a religious mystery. He had

already met that mystery in the phenomenon of the analytic transference, while still regarding himself a psychoanalyst. His correspondence between January and March 1913 with his analysand, Dr. R. Loÿ, who was a psychiatrist working in Switzerland some distance away at a sanatorium in Montreux on "Crucial Points in Psychoanalysis," is Jung's farewell to all he had learned while being a Freudian and, not incidentally, working through a self-confessed "'religious' crush" on Freud himself (McGuire, 1974, p. 95). It reaches its conclusion in a letter from Jung dated March 1913, in which he makes the following statement:

> Recapitulating, I would like to say this of the positive transference:
> The patient's libido fastens on the person of the analyst in the form of expectation, hope, interest, trust, friendship, and love. The transference first produces a projection of infantile fantasies, often with a predominantly erotic tinge. At this stage it is, as a rule, of a decidedly sexual character, even though the sexual component remains relatively unconscious. But this emotional process serves as a bridge for the higher aspect of empathy, whereby the patient becomes conscious of the inadequacy of his own attitude through recognition of the analyst's attitude, which is accepted as being adapted to life's demands and as normal. Through remembrance of the childhood relationship with the help of analysis the patient is shown the way which leads out of the subsidiary, purely sexual or power values acquired in puberty and reinforced by social prejudice. This road leads to a purely human relationship and to an intimacy based not on the existence of sexual or power factors but on the value of personality. This is the road to freedom which the analyst should show his patient.
>
> (Jung & Loÿ, 1914/1961, p. 286, para. 663)

By the time Jung wrote these words, he had already given his 1912 lectures at Fordham University in New York City and was still in New York in March, 1913, where he got to see the Armory Show of Modern Art and was taken by Beatrice Hinkle to Patchin Place, a cul-de-sac off 10th Avenue between Greenwich Avenue and Sixth Avenue, the elegant heart of Greenwich Village, for a dinner party hosted by the members of the Heterodoxy Club, which had been founded the year before by a group of radical feminists who had become Hinkle's friends. Women connected to Hinkle even tried to have Jung meet the pioneering black civil rights activist W. E. B. Dubois, an opportunity Jung did not take up (Sherry, 2015, p. 66) but which might have opened his eyes to the "New Negro Movement" that was successfully giving the lie to the Kiplingesque stereotypes Jung was not alone among white psychoanalysts in allowing himself to succumb to.

Because it is both so freeing and so vulnerable to premature framing that would turn it into a new elitism of individuation for the already culturally privileged, it is important to explore exactly what it is in the Jungian analyst's stance that can provide "the road to freedom" for the analytic patient.

Freedom, as Jung used it in describing to Dr. Loÿ in 1913 the aim of what today would be called "relational psychoanalysis," is a political term that in its essential meaning refers to "the ability to act without undue hindrance or restraint" (Merriam-Webster, 1986, p. 906, def.1c [2]). Freedom can only be a socially viable reality when someone with the power to hinder and restrain has granted someone else "the right of participating as a member or a citizen often conferred as an honorary distinction upon one who is not a member or a citizen" (Ibid., def. 2a). This was a power Jung was willing to grant within the analytic transference as a doctor to the patients who had come to him to dispense his medical psychology in a therapeutic way, and he knew what he was doing in speaking for the psychoanalytic patient's right to receive that honor.

Today, however, it is necessary to political discourse to amplify adequately what Jung was implying: what the analyst has to provide so that his essential argument can be heard in as democratic a way as it was intended and not just an elitist claim by a white middle-class Protestant who, though regarding himself a Swiss democrat, had secured his own position by marrying well after getting an excellent education and could afford to dispense such honors to those who would also pay his fees. So, given that Eleanor Roosevelt had afforded Beatrice Hinkle the chance to re-empower someone as privileged, politically, as her own husband with a talk inspired by Jungian method, it may not be amiss to note that in Jung's own time what that method consisted of was glossed in political terms by a speech that Franklin Roosevelt delivered when he became America's president. And this at a time when not he, but his country, was, with regard to the problems of Europe, paralyzed by its fear of coming out of its isolation and needed to summon the courage to stand up for freedom wherever challenged.

Presidential speeches are often ghosted by wordsmiths, and Roosevelt had a team that included the playwright Robert E. Sherwood, who had written *Abe Lincoln in Illinois*, which had won the Pulitzer Prize in 1939. Sherwood could voice Lincoln for the stage because he himself had sat at the Hotel Algonquin Table with Dorothy Parker and Robert Benchley across the street from their offices at *The New Yorker* magazine where they were paid to set the style for American eloquence. No doubt Sherwood helped Roosevelt frame the remarks he wanted to make to Congress, but both eyewitnesses and the still-existing handwritten evidence make it clear that it was Franklin Roosevelt who penned the section on the four freedoms that was the payoff of his greatest speech. It reads to me like a spontaneous utterance from the Self. In its robust four-foldedness, it has the rhetorical structure of a four-sided pyramid of the kind a bright older child might have constructed by folding a piece of essay paper, so that each face of its argument would meet at the same point. That point was the inexpressible essence of freedom, arrived at by the trick of naming out of all the possible political meanings of that term, most of them inviting controversy, just four with which to make the case for defending freedom. This was the intuitive simplicity with which Franklin Roosevelt constructed what he knew America had to face as its responsibility to defend freedom throughout a world threatened by war. Because of the part that only he could have written, the speech as a whole today is known as his Four Freedoms speech. Here, from Roosevelt's original reading copy, which gives the punctuation and separated spelling of compound nouns he chose to guide him, is the peroration that gave the speech this name:

> In the future days which we seek to make secure, we look forward to a world founded upon four essential human freedoms.
>
> The first is freedom of speech and expression – everywhere in the world.
>
> The second is freedom of every person to worship God in his own way – everywhere in the world.
>
> The third is freedom from want – which, translated into world terms, means economic understandings which will secure to every nation a healthy peace time life for its inhabitants – everywhere in the world.
>
> The fourth is freedom from fear – which translated into world terms, means a world-wide reduction of armaments to such a point and in such a thorough fashion that no nation will be in a position to commit an act of physical aggression against any neighbor – anywhere in the world.
>
> (Text from Engel, 2016, pp. x–xi; see also Kaye, 2020, pp. 211–212, for the published version)

It is important to point out, as Jeffrey Engel (p. 1) does in his introduction to the book of essays he has produced to unpack the meanings embedded in the differentiations Roosevelt was able to discriminate, that "Freedom has no universally accepted definition." In one sense, what it means depends on the context in which the word is summoned. Here, in this context of an essay I am writing from the perspective of a psychotherapist schooled in a psychoanalytic tradition that evolved because Jung had to free himself from something arbitrary and tyrannical that he experienced in the way Freud held his original ideas, I am going to claim the Four Freedoms speech for Jungian psychology. Although written by President Roosevelt to rouse Congress in the face of the threat posed to all democracies by the Axis powers of Germany, Italy, and Japan, Roosevelt articulated his defense of freedom in a way that would shape my own evolution as a depth psychotherapist. The freedom of the self, in both its meanings, little-s self and big-S self, can be fostered so as to be able to survive extreme challenges. For that reason, the four freedoms that Roosevelt identified and insisted that America needed to defend serve just as well to inform a psychotherapist interested in treating the self as well as the ego of the patient as to what must be brought attitudinally to the dialogue. People who seek analytic treatment often do not trust that they can say what is on their minds yet doubt that any other form of self-expression would even be allowed. Analysands, especially new analysands, presume that their core beliefs will be challenged if ever they take the risk of revealing them. They feel a want of psychological nourishment and are frightened about what will become of them in a world that has not been made safe for psychological democracy.

We have to admit that, for many, freedom is a word that has been invoked to support a right to tyrannize and as a way to enact envy. This is the burden of the remarkable book *Myths of Freedom* by Stephen Gardner, which argues from the standpoint of a French anthropology informed by René Girard that freedom as a philosophy of life is often at odds with, because envious of, other people's liberty. Anyone pausing to contemplate the "Tulsa Race Massacre" that occurred in the United States on May 30, 1921, finally covered in full by the *New York Times* on the centennial of that atrocity (Purshina-Kottas et al., 2021) will find ample evidence of what Gardner is talking about. In the Greenwood neighborhood of Tulsa, Oklahoma, a black-owned business community was attacked, bombed, and virtually leveled, with hundreds of its 10,000 African American residents brutally killed by a mob of angry whites. They had heard that a white girl operating the elevator in one of the upwardly mobile businesses of this thriving Negro section of the city had screamed because a young black man had in some way come on to her – a complaint that was never verified or even voiced by the putative victim of the original aggression. It is hard not to see envy in this attack on a racially defined minority community that had succeeded, just after World War I, in enacting the American dream, validating Gardner's Girardian claim that viewed narrowly from the standpoint of how it is an imitative and rival form of desire, "'freedom' is an illusion fueled by the regime of modern democracy but by no means the same as liberty" because the "natural tendency of freedom is to sever the bonds of ordinary human reality" (Gardner, 1998, pp. 1–2). In Tulsa's case a hundred years ago, that was the reality of racism, which reified itself in freely destroying the economic freedom black people had felt entitled to take advantage of in a time of postwar boom, an envious attack that was never punished because the crimes involved were never charged or prosecuted by city, state, or federal authorities. Joe Biden, who visited Tulsa on the centenary, was the first American president even to refer to it.

Roosevelt's 1941 speech, a scant twenty years after the attack, though grounded in values that transcend such immediate domestic conflicts, is no less decisive in the positive way it defines freedom in terms that no one had done as completely before. One of his ways of accomplishing this rhetorical feat was by refusing freedom as a unitary concept that could too easily be co-opted by those who wished to tyrannize and instead deconstructing it into four essential freedoms that must (and can) be kept in balance (the pyramidal structure again coming to the point of the concept in a heavenward direction) if the notion of freedom were not to become an invitation to license. The intuitive wisdom of his speech is that it knows we cannot do without any of its essential faces if freedom is to have any chance of becoming something that liberates us from tyranny. Roosevelt's everyday reality was informed by a political gift that was centered in his remarkable extraverted feeling, which made him both an aristocrat and a democrat at once. But he had to reach deep inside himself to get to the profound level of integrity in depth that this speech commands. We know (from Harold Holzer, 2018, p. 107) that he worked closely with his speechwriters, constantly redoing, and simplifying, their formulations, until at last his own, more introverted, thinking became animated enough to say what only his self could have allowed him to say.

That is how I have learned to read Jung's *Psychological Types* published the same year as the Tulsa Race Massacre, as a self-psychology in which the fourfold structure of the functions of everyday consciousness, when they converge, can create a transcendent function that frees the self to generate a new consciousness suited to the situation at hand (Jung, 1921/1971, p. 252). Something like this seems to me to have enabled Roosevelt, still perhaps benefitting from his one-day Jungian analysis, to define freedom more completely and less violently than it had ever been presented before by an American president. His speech, though as idealistic as anything Wilson had uttered, had a peculiar feeling for the pragmatic effect of balancing opposites that not only Jung, but Jung's special mentor William James, would have recognized and James' godfather Ralph Waldo Emerson would have hailed. Roosevelt's transcendent image of freedom as a form of self-reliance being shared had to it an Emersonian perfection. His speech proved for America's greatest generation a galvanizing set of ideals.

Aside from its simplicity in bringing the essentials of freedom together to point the way to what its speaker's democracy needed to rouse itself to protect at a time when all democracies were under attack, what is remarkable in the way the speech is constructed is that it parses the balance it is striving for by the skillful use of prepositions. This is its way of recognizing the opposites of ego and shadow that must be held in check if freedom is to serve liberty for all rather than the victory of the greed and envy of some. Roosevelt achieved this by the way he deployed the words "of" and "from" to play off the difference between what one should be free to have and must refrain from having to experience.

As a working analyst, trying to set people free from what has kept them from accessing the goods of life, and at the same time protecting their initiative to articulate the higher self that they feel should guide them, I have needed to be clear in myself as to the freedom I have to speak and to value from my own perspective. Not to be abstract about this, I need my patients, eventually, to secure me from being afraid of them and to take care of me in basic ways that do not leave me wanting more from them than they can reasonably give. It is a wondrous thing when we both reach what Winnicott has called "the stage of concern," (Merkur, 2010, pp. 155, 178–183) when neither of us wants to manipulate the other into wanting or fearing us. The fact that we know this is not always possible is a realism learned in the first years of any analysis of any length, and that we see that it can be achieved is the wonder of very long-term work. Just this is what Roosevelt was imagining for his nation.

Despite the fact that we are nowhere near the disarmament he dreamed would occur at the end of the war and that we can feel in this speech he knew was coming does not mean that this long-term goal is beyond eventual attainment. What I have seen, working with character armaments of anger, fear, envy, and desire in analysis and watching 'freedom of' and 'freedom from' do their magic, has made me feel that taking narcissistic defenses down is and will continue to be helpful in all human affairs. If I have realized any part of the agenda Roosevelt set out for Americans before I was old enough to think about it, it is because I have recognized that the idea of freedom he most wanted to assert was a freedom we all have: to choose to take care of each other.

Roosevelt was being, when he spoke, not someone aiming to keep himself in power (he knew what he was asking would create stiff resistance from those who felt America should simply mind its own business) (Kaye, 2014, p. 5). He was being, instead, a father showing the direction of duty at a time when it was quite unclear what Americans needed to do for others, and for him, as imperfect in his generosity as any of us. This meant assisting everyone everywhere and anywhere in the world who desired, and was willing to accept, the balance of freedoms involved. We would be wise to explore this option in the way we conduct and offer therapy to one another.

References

Engel, J. A. (ed). (2016). *The Four Freedoms: Franklin D. Roosevelt and the Evolution of an American Idea*. New York: Oxford University Press (Kindle)

Gardner, S. L. (1998). *Myths of Freedom: Equality, Modern Thought, and Philosophical Radicalism*. Westport, CT & London: Greenwood Press.

Holzer, H. (2018). Freedom from speech: Lincoln, Roosevelt & the myth of impromptu oratory. In *Enduring Ideals: Rockwell, Roosevelt & the Four Freedoms*, S. H. Plunkett & J. J. Kimble (eds). New York & London: Abbeville Press, pp. 107–117.

Jung, C. G. (1921/1971). Psychological types. *CW* 6.

Jung, C. G. (1954/1958). Transformation symbolism in the mass. *CW* 11.

Jung, C. G. & Loÿ, R. (1914/1961). Some crucial points in psychoanalysis. *CW* 4, pp. 252–289.

Kaye, H. J. (2014). *The Fight for the Four Freedoms: What Made FDR and the Greatest Generation Truly Great*. New York: Simon & Schuster (Kindle)

Kaye, H. J. (ed) (2020). *FDR on Democracy: The Greatest Speeches and Writings of President Franklin Delano Roosevelt*. New York: Skyhorse Publishing (Kindle)

Life Magazine (1949). Orwell's Strange World of 1984. July 4 issue. 78–86. (Online https://daviddunnico.files.wordpress.com/2011/03/life-in-orwells-1984.pdf consulted 6.1.21)

McGuire, W. (1974). *The Freud/Jung Letters: The Correspondence between Sigmund Freud and C.G. Jung*. Princeton: Princeton University Press.

Merkur, D. (2010). *Explorations of the Psychoanalytic Mystics*. Leiden: Brill. Kindle, pp. 155, 178–183.

Merriam-Webster, inc. (1986). *Webster's Third New International Dictionary*. P. V. Gove (ed). Chicago: Encyclopedia Britannica.

Orwell, G. (1961). *1984*. New York: Signet Classics (paper).

Purdy, J. (1999). *For Common Things: Irony, Trust, and Commitment in America Today*. New York: Knopf.

Purshina-Kottas, Y., Singhvi, A., Burch, A. D. S., Gates, G., Griggs, T., Gröndahl, M., Huang, L., Lutz, E., Wallace, T., White, J. & Williams, J. (2021). What was lost in the Tulsa Race Massacre. *The New York Times*, Vol. CLXX, No. 59,0974 (Sunday, May 30) National, pp. 19–23.

Russell, J. J. (2021). *Eleanor in the Village: Eleanor Roosevelt's Search for Freedom and Identity in New York's Greenwich Village*. New York: Scribner.

Shakespeare, W. (1998). *The Arden Shakespeare Complete Works*. R. Proudfoot, A. Thompson, and D. Kastan (eds). Walton-on-Thames, Surrey: Thomas Nelson and Sons.

Sherry, J. (2013). Beatrice Hinkle and the early history of Jungian psychology in New York. *Behavioral Sciences,* Vol. 3, pp. 492–500.

Sherry, J. (2015). "Carl Jung, Beatrice Hinkle, and Charlotte Teller, *The New York Times Reporter*." In *Jung in the Academy and Beyond: The Fordham Lectures 100 Years Later.* New Orleans: Spring Journal Books, pp. 65–73.

Chapter 3

The Paradox of Metaphor

Stefano Candellieri and Davide Favero

The two fundamental axes of language[1] are known as the paradigmatic axis, or that of system, and the syntagmatic axis, of process.

Briefly, the former comprises all the possible forms of a linguistic or more generically communicative element: we have the paradigm of a certain verb just as, according to Roland Barthes's illustration, the paradigm of a particular garment (that of "shoe" includes, for example, ballet shoes, boots, loafers, desert boots, sandals, slippers, trainers and so on).

This dimension is governed by a criterion of *substitution*: within a given paradigm or system, the elements are similar among themselves but exclude each other reciprocally (a pair of shoes by definition excludes the possibility of wearing another pair).

The second, syntagmatic, axis represents concretisation or actualisation along a *continuum*, which, to keep to our two examples, may be a sentence or a combination of clothing with a wide range of paradigmatic potentialities: a verb will appear in a sentence conjugated according to person, tense and mood, accompanying other grammatical elements in linear succession; a garment may consist of a specific pair of loafers worn on a particular occasion, coordinated with other items of clothing. Within this syntagmatic dimension, that of process, the relationship between the elements is one of *contiguity*.

Every act of communication – and items of clothing also are certainly this – is therefore a sort of "big bang" which "precipitates", as in a chemical reaction, all the possible forms of an element, the paradigm or system, into a precise and irreversible manifestation, which maintains a relationship of contiguity with other elements in the series, that is, the syntagm or process. Every time a potentiality is actualised as a concrete occurrence, be it linguistic term or any other semiotic phenomenon, an "enunciation" has taken place; it can thus easily be understood, when speaking of enunciation and therefore also of rhetorical figures, how a strict correlation of the opposition process/system is the fundamental rhetorical opposition between metonymy and metaphor. As Ugo Volli (2000/2004, p. 39) succinctly puts it:

> The first figure in fact substitutes one linguistic element with another which is contiguous on the axis of process ("the bows" for "the ships"), the second an

DOI: 10.4324/9781003168829-4

element with another "similar" one according to the system ("shining eyes" with "stars").

In Saussurian terms, the relationship between paradigm and syntagm corresponds linguistically to that between *langue* and *parole* and is akin to the relationship between signified and signifier.

It is a theoretical approach with no lack of analogies, echoes and correspondences also in psychoanalysis, but we shall limit ourselves to calling attention to the different conceptualisation relating to "symbol" and "sign" found in Freud and Jung. In extreme synthesis, for the father of psychoanalysis, the "symbol" would appear to be essentially characterised by an impoverished paradigmatic dimension, being understood in point of fact as mere "sign" which points unequivocally to something else, "aliquid pro aliquo". Conversely, Jung understands the "symbol" in a constantly allusive and unsaturated dimension, fully paradigmatic and metaphorical, making a complete understanding impossible in any attempt at processual enunciation, similar to what takes place in the case of poetic language, which, by its very nature, resists paraphrase or naïve decoding (despite the efforts of school textbooks to do just that).

Having thus defined, albeit briefly, the two axes of language, we may now proceed with our reflection and examine whether and how these two dimensions are modified reciprocally, in perhaps novel ways, moving from the more intuitive example of spoken or written language in traditional terms (a book, for example) to the modern linguistic universe of the Web and digital communication; we mean by this, of course, the overall system of social media, within which we can find, on the multitude of platforms available and to a practically unlimited degree, traditional texts such as books, newspapers, individual articles, films, videos and music, as well as posts and memes shared by millions of users.

We shall consider first of all the question of immediacy in the use of social media from which to draw theoretical and clinical conclusions later on.

Anyone and everyone now uses social media, whether for work or for play. The almost limitless possibilities offered by the Web to surf from post to post, link to link, from one platform to another, are there to be enjoyed by all. A post which tags us on Facebook, for example, might share a music video from YouTube which we can watch on the same app or by switching over to the original platform, where we will find, on the basis of our viewing habits analysed by purposely created algorithms, suggestions for even more videos which we can choose to watch or not; or a tweet on Twitter might send us to a LinkedIn page from where we are directed to a newspaper's homepage; the same goes, of course, for all social media, including Instagram, TikTok, WhatsApp and many others not listed here. We are talking of the concept of "hypertext", defined for the first time in 1965 by Ted Nelson (1992, p. 0/2) as follows:

By hypertext I mean non-sequential writing – text that branches and allows choice to the reader, best read at an interactive screen. As popularly conceived, this is a series of text chunks connected by links which offer the reader different pathways.

In this definition we find, as an integral distinctive part of hypertext, the notion of "non-sequentiality", as opposed to the sequentiality of traditional writing, and in a part of reading, which sees the book as its typical object. It is, to be more precise, a double level of sequentiality, that of the traditional text set against that of the hypertext and most importantly a sequentiality – or "linearity" to use Saussure's term, that is, the syntagmatic axis described briefly previously – which is intrinsic to language; for example, "a written verbalised text, at the level of signifier, puts into spatial sequence graphemes, words, phrases and simple and complex sentences" (Cosenza, 2010, p. 102); second, a "typographical" sequentiality, in relation to the book-form, the *codex* of the Romans, which has remained essentially unchanged since it replaced the scroll (*volumen*) some time between the 2nd and 3rd century AD. The typographical sequentiality Nelson is talking about concerns in particular the organisation of the book's paratextual elements: paragraphs, sections, chapters, page numbering and so on, a second-level, subterranean structuring of written language, which, until the advent of Web 2.0, provided the basis for our ideas of language and communication. Any illustrated, and therefore non-verbalised, accompaniment to the text also follows a sequential order respecting the customary numbering of figures and images.

Hypertext throws this dual linearity into disarray, especially if it is collocated within the notion of "hypermedia", again as proposed by Nelson and understood as a hypertext including not only words, but also images, sound and animations. Hypermedia was at the heart of Nelson's vision, which was

to make available via IT all texts, past, present and future, organised and interconnected in hypertextual form: it was Project Xanadu.

(Cosenza, p. 99)

which would not only be a veritable universal library, no longer linked to a physical place, but a multimedia library to boot.[2]

Going back to the two axes of language, we might ask what the implications, especially psychological, are therefore of the essentially hypertextual nature of the Web in general and of social media in particular. First and foremost, it is evident that we are dealing with a repositioning of emphasis: the syntagmatic axis, or of process, cannot be eliminated without the risk of falling into the dissolution of language, thus giving rise to a paradoxical aphasia.

In this regard, Jung likened the disorganisative psychotic process to being inflated by the "symbol", that is, being completely absorbed in a paradigmatic dimension. In clinical work, this shows up as severe forms of disorganised schizophrenia but also as disorders found in the organic forms of aphasia, where it is the syntagmatic or metonymic axis which is more affected by neurological damage, according to Roman Jakobson (1956/2012). In this latter case, syntactic rules in the aphasic individual are lost and the sentence becomes destructured, resulting in a heap of disorderly words; the first words to disappear in these forms of aphasia characterised by what is known as *contiguity disorder*, the function words expressing purely grammatical or structural relationships such as conjunctions, pronouns and prepositions, thus leaving an overall condition of *agrammatism*.

While not excluding a possible "aphasic" drift among compulsive users of the Web, we must assume that the syntagmatic axis is not destructured to such a degree but is, more simply, considerably redimensioned in favour of the paradigmatic dimension, of system.

One experience common to all users of social media is when any posted content becomes immediately – within the space of a few hours or days – obsolescent; another is represented by the difficulty encountered in the attempt to retrieve any trace of content posted previously. Social media create and determine a perennial present; past and future become devoid of any interest and are weakened.

The Web's impact on the paradigmatic expansion of the present, at the expense of the syntagmatic retrieval of the past and equally syntagmatic projection into the future, is stigmatised by some authors such as Adriano Prosperi, who in his recent work (Prosperi, 2021) speaks out against the imprisonment of society in an asphyxial *hic et nunc* deprived of the fecundative depth which the past provides.

The theme of the implosion of the present – increasingly fast, fleeting and inconsistent right up to its transformation into a one-dimensional point, losing the three-dimensionality it derives from its intersection with the other two temporal dimensions – is one that is also dear to Paulo Barone. Quoting the well-known Joycean image which depicted the present as "a crumpled throwaway", he decries its emptying of any substance.

Going back to the "fashion system" which opened our discussion and on which the well-known reflection by Roland Barthes is centred, the difference between process and system, syntagm and paradigm, or even between metonymic and metaphoric is, put briefly, that which exists between the concrete realisation of a person's attire (dressed in a certain moment in a certain way) and her/his wardrobe or, at a more general level, the whole "fashion system" potentially available to her/him. If the Web can be metaphorically represented as the aspiration to a universal library, we might likewise represent it metaphorically as a "universal wardrobe", a virtual space full of "idea-garments" ready for use.

What consequences might this extreme overabundance of idea-garments, that is to say, of signifiers more than of signifieds, have? At an initial and more elementary level, we may think that the consequence is paralysing. Paradoxically, the average user of the Web is inhibited in the quest for deeper understanding, which is facilitated by modern information technology to a greater degree than ever before, with the risk that the undertaking turns into a "hit-and-run" affair, surfing the superficial waves of an essentially disquieting world. This first consequence is psychological and individual in nature.

A second consequence, ascribable this time more to the complex system created by the architects of the Web (from platform proprietors to software producers), arises from the need to organise the immense quantity of material available. The never-ending catalogues of films, TV series and documentaries on platforms such as Prime Video, Netflix or Sky would be virtually impossible to access if they were not in some way indexed, and the most intuitive way to index them is by organising them into the "categories" now familiar to all (New Releases, Italian Movies, Comedy Movies, Drama Movies, etc.). This places us fully within the paradigmatic dimension, dominated, as pointed out at the beginning, by relationships among the various elements constituting it which are classified as *in absentia*, because if we choose one element, the other elements in a relationship of association with it are automatically excluded.[3]

The problem is that the choice of how to organise categories, in particular with reference to the Web, is an operation whose outcome is far from being a foregone conclusion or neutral. Inevitably the organisation into categories ends up creating actual pathways of "reading" and use which are given precedence but remain hidden, as is indicated by the autological "index-" in indexisation (Latin for "pointer, indicator" [cf. index finger]): certain pathways are indicated tacitly and therefore privileged, and the persuasive, perlocutionary and ultimately manipulative function of the Web assumes a central position within a multimedia universe, which aims in the final analysis to "cause to be", "cause to do" or "cause to think": a world which is, from a narrative point of view – and with reference to the structuralism of Algirdas Greimas – essentially *performative*.

To render visible this tacit process of privileged use and indexisation of content, we turn to the particularly evocative image drawn by Leon Battista Alberti, who in *De Pictura* postulates as a rule of composition the role of the so-called *commentator*, a figure whose presence in a painting has a deictic function, that is, as an auxiliary with regard to the spectator, to guide the latter, by means of gesture or direction of gaze, in discerning what needs to be noted within the pictorial work according to the intentions of the artist.

To recapitulate, we have on the one hand a frightened user/consumer, ready to "clutch hold", as Bion observed speaking more generally of the human psyche, of anything which might have the semblance of a structure:

> when we are at a loss we invent something to fill the gap of our ignorance – this vast area of ignorance, of non-knowledge, in which we have to move. The more frightening the gap, the more terrifying it is to realize how utterly ignorant we are of even the most elementary and simplest requirements for survival, the more we are pressed from outside and inside to fill the gap. . . . You only have to ask yourself what to do individually in a situation where you feel completely lost; you are thankful to clutch hold of any system, anything whatever that is available on which to build a kind of structure.
>
> (Bion, 2005, p. 2)

On the other hand, we have a complex universe of "enunciating subjects", who not only produce the textual and multimedia utterances they share on the Web but, as real-life *commentatores*, also provide the tacit "instructions for use" of what they are putting at the users' disposal, to meet the need to "clutch hold of any system" that Bion talks of in his Tavistock seminar.

The final result of this "secret marriage" between digital producers and consumers can be metaphorised reflecting on the universe of online pornography, around which an interesting and multifaceted analysis flourishes within the fields of semiotics and cultural studies. Originally, the porn movie as "consumed" in cinemas already displayed fully a marked depletion in the syntagmatic component, being based on a pared-down narrative *fabula*, whose sole function was to provide a frame for the explicit sex scenes. The narrative plots used to this end were extremely weak and repetitive. Such narrative weakness has become further accentuated in online pornography. All the specialised platforms are, in fact, organised in categories (the paradigmatic dimension) in similar fashion to the websites already mentioned offering more orthodox entertainment, with each category representing an archive of brief film sequences characterised by a tenuous narrative thread, often only suggested by the various sets used (office, massage parlour, gym, villa, etc.). The consumer's use here is more than ever "hit and run" and generally oriented towards sexual gratification.

In the universe of pornography, therefore, we see represented in essence the main characteristics of the use of social media by the average user. We are speaking, of course, of a *naïve reader* (attuned to semantic content), namely one who:

> actualizes the linear surface of the text according to the indications provided by the text itself with the sole aim of extracting the literal meaning.
>
> (Volli, 2000/2004, p. 130)

Essentially it is a question of the reader passively, or actively only in minimal part, adhering to the pathways of interpretation written into the universe of the text presented to her/him; this type of reader, according to Umberto Eco, differs from the *critical* (or *semiotic*) *reader* who, also contravening the role of *model reader*[4] requested of her/him, uses the text autonomously and creatively (for example, the semiologist studying pornography).

In other words, in the pornographic universe and, *mutatis mutandis*, in the more extensive one of social media, a passive user enters the scene in search of sexual satisfaction (a variation of the "clutching hold of" something in Bion's observation) interacting in predatory fashion with a system (the Web and its producers) whose goals are to persuade and manipulate, something ultimately in itself equally predatory; the semiotic-linguistic structure of this interaction appears heavily biased towards an extensive paradigmatic supply at the expense of the (syntagmatic) *processual* construction of pathways of knowledge. It is a universe which can be represented, to add a further, novel metaphor, as a vast market which allows only minimal, predictable, repetitive pathways to move around it but which, on the other hand, offers a vast profusion of merchandise.

With the premise that in Aristotle's Poetics the term μῦθος (mythos) designates the plot, understood as "the arrangement of a series of acts or facts", and if this "myth" meets the need, vital for the mind both at the individual and collective level, to organise its content in narratives in order to be able to represent, share and examine it more deeply, the world of hypertext and hypermedia risks inhabiting a "demythologised" dimension,[5] one which as a result is deeply concretistic and literal: a world, from a Jungian perspective, of dead symbols, as a result of the weakened syntagmatic axis which should otherwise exist in a vital relationship with the paradigmatic one, dead symbols which propagate in viral fashion, like the memes conceptualised by Richard Dawkins in the 1970s. The risk is that what we are witnessing is not limited simply to the conspicuous decline in book reading and resultant marked impoverishment of the average person's vocabulary; rather, it represents a profound qualitative change in the semio-narrative abilities of the individual and collective mind, one which is more and more "denarrativised" and "pornographic", impulsive and primitive and, ultimately, bidimensional.

The increasingly frequent cases of impulsivity and violence in social media, up to the extreme phenomenon of the shitstorm, are eloquent examples of the psychological impoverishment we are talking about. The enormous potentialities offered by modern digital technologies stand in startling contrast to the psychologically regressive shift we have attempted to describe and which is inevitably associated with significant issues of dependency and weakening of individual identity in favour of the more or less conscious adoption of "partial identities" afforded by digital profiles which, by their very nature, bear little or no resemblance to the reality of people's biographical or historical data.

The first effects of these changes are beginning to become apparent in the consulting room, particularly among younger patients. It is too early to talk of new pathologies, we hasten to add, but rather of an intensifying of psycho-social traits which have already been present for some time in modern industrialised societies, and of which the *hikikomori* phenomenon is a classic example.

This consists of the progressive withdrawal from social life and the outside world. The term itself derives from the two Japanese verbs *hiku* (to pull, to [with] draw) and *komoru* (to seclude oneself).

It was initially described at the beginning of the 1980s in relation to Japan, where its predominance may be accounted for by the country's traditional cultural features and which we may discern in the samurai ethic (the seven principles of *bushido* which, as a whole, shun the possibility of failure), in the idea of sacrifice as an absolute value (as demonstrated by the actions of kamikazes), in excessive machismo, in the worship of the work ethic, and in pride and chauvinism perceived as national sentiments, leaving to shame and humiliation the dubious pleasure of acting as counterpoint.

Subsequently *hikikomori* was recognised at a global level, divorced from a specific national origin. New hypotheses were formulated as to its aetio(patho) genesis, which, when they exclude a psychiatric comorbidity, focus mostly on mechanisms of competition or relating to performance dynamics which characterise globalised society.

Young *hikikomori*, the great majority of whom are male, can live for years in their room, spending their time engaged in various activities mediated by the Web. Our opinion, corroborated by substantial clinical feedback, is that the presence of social media, MMORPGs and other apps which can be enjoyed via the Web has a marked impact, if not on the genesis of the phenomenon, then certainly on how it is structured and on its permanence over time. We recall in this respect McLuhan's well-known refrain "the medium is the message": for the Canadian semiologist, any technology constitutes a *medium* in the sense that it represents an extension and a strengthening of human faculties and, as such, retroactively conditions both the social environment in which the individual lives and her/his lifestyle; for this reason, it is necessary to consider the impact of the media in terms of their sociological and psychological implications.

At this point, it would appear insightful to recognise the specifics of the influence of the paradigmatic bias present in Web apps, an influence which might foster permanence in an aprocessual present and, as mentioned previously, with no possibility of connecting with the past nor ability to project into the future.

For an understanding of the phenomenon at the psychodynamic level, we need to have recourse to the individuation process and to the *Bildungsroman*, which we shall talk about in the following: while it is true that novels of a failed coming of age existed well before the birth of the Web – Goncharov's Oblomov comes to mind – with regard to *hikikomori* individuals, it is hard not to think of the individuation process as other than regressive, as if they had returned to the ouroboric intrauterine condition, one of non-birth, devoid of processuality. Psychological birth, in fact, implies differentiation from the maternal element, by definition understood as a homeostatic environment. Then again, we know from biology that stem cells are totipotent and reach maturity only by differentiating and not remaining within the "possible". This is essentially the Aristotelian difference between "potentiality" and "actuality".

The "anomic"[6] subject, described over seventy years ago by Robert MacIver as someone who "lives on the thin line of sensation between no future and no past" (MacIver, 1950, p. 85), is fully aligned with this individual, "de-mythologised" and prisoner of the present, perpetually at the confines of the *hikikomori* dimension.

The case of Pietro (see Candellieri, Favero, 2019, pp. 169–173) is representative of this typology.

Pietro is a young man whose emotive intensity has led him in life to build robust relational barriers of an autistic nature, akin to those investigated by Frances Tustin (1990).

Pietro begins analysis after earlier disappointing experiences of psychotherapy following several periods of treatment in rapid succession in a psychiatric intensive-care unit (Servizio Psichiatrico di Diagnosi e Cura) as a result of pantoclastic destructive acts. At the start of therapy, Pietro is taking high doses of psychotropic medication, which help him to keep his impulsivity in check, but he remains imprisoned behind the autistic barriers he has built up for himself over the years: on the cusp of turning thirty, he lives with his mother, has no job, does not study and spends most of his time shut up in his room at home; in short, he displays many of the characteristics of the *hikikomori* clinical picture described previously. He maintains social contacts via the Internet exclusively by means of message boards and chatrooms, in some cases assuming a female identity in order to receive greater attention. He visits pornographic sites online, compulsively engaging in masturbation. During sessions, Pietro appears "normal": he has a fairly good level of education and displays a keen intelligence; his use of language is correct and collaborative, even if emotively constricted; he takes care of his appearance and dress, even if in a nondescript way, but gives the distinct impression of exhibiting a carefully constructed exterior which hides a turbulent inner world. He is an anomic young man, with no future and no past, either on the individual level or socially: he does not want to remember his own past, he has no projects and is completely unaware of history (which, once therapy has commenced, he begins to study, turning again to his old school books); he cannot find his way around town, being ignorant of street names, except for a few in the vicinity of his home. He seldom dreams and is unwilling to talk about any dreams he does have: for Pietro they mean nothing, and talking about them is consequently a waste of time. Instead, in psychotherapy, he is seeking "practical" tools to learn how to dialogue with others without being afraid, a sort of coaching which might help him to be master of himself, to which he can dedicate most of his energies, and also the social mask he feels he lacks which he needs to enter into relationships with the rest of the world. The dreams that he does manage to talk about, however, are rather bareboned: situations of danger, great or small, which see him engaged, inevitably, in hiding away, and where the danger is often represented by bullies or overbearing people.

One of the first and most important therapeutic factors in a story such as Pietro's is that of proceeding regularly with the sessions, to reconstitute at the most basic level, session after session, the syntagmatic Ariadne's thread which throughout the individual's existence has struggled to take shape or has become destructured. We might define this level as "macro-syntagmatic" (or "of the individuation process" or "of the diachronic axis" or "of the personal coming-of-age novel") to distinguish it from the "micro-syntagmatic" (or "of the *hic et nunc*") represented by the articulated narrative within each individual session.[7]

In the attempt to render even more comprehensible and evocative what we mean by the macro-syntagmatic and micro-syntagmatic dimension, it is the "individuation process" conceptualised by Jung which comes to our aid, together with its well-known literary counterpart, the *Bildungsroman*/coming-of-age novel mentioned previously.

We shall not deal further with the individuation process in the strict sense, taking as given that it will be known to the reader. Rather, we are interested in showing what happens in the *Bildungsroman*, where the protagonist is engaged in a process of progression towards maturation, a process which generally starts in childhood or early adulthood and is marked by a gradual detachment from the security of the early years and continues through various adventures, moments of initiation and complex existential vicissitudes, which all come together again at the end of the novel, leaving the protagonist completely transformed. To discern the "unitariness" of the transformation, we naturally have to wait until the end of the novel, in the same way that we have to wait until the end of analysis to be able to discern the overall transformations which have taken place in the patient: in this case, we are talking, therefore, as we were saying, of the macro-syntagmatic dimension.

We know, however, that the progression towards a new adaptation to the world such as that which occurs in the coming-of-age novel does not happen suddenly but that the metonymic chain (the process of maturation) is made up of as many links as the number of single experiences which dot the everyday lives of individuals, be they literary characters or patients during a session of analysis: it is here, though, that it is possible to discern micro-syntagmatic processuality. There is no need to add that the processualities described are possible in that they are a coagulum, a precipitate, single and unique, of potentialities present in the paradigmatic dimension.

The micro-syntagmatic interweaving of accounts in each individual session and their metonymic assembling over different sessions allows, therefore, the slow reinstating within the setting of the psychological and narrative "*nomos*" that the anomic individual has lost, an individual literally "devoid of norms", "without *nomos*". In Pietro's case, as a direction of meaning slowly took form, the start of a richer and more varied oneiric production was made possible. A group of dreams of particular interest appeared in a single session;[8] some of these expressed disorientation and paralysis,[9] whereas a more elaborate dream presented new subject matter which is relevant to our argument:

> Pietro is wandering around a big but rather sad and anonymous shopping centre with some friends. Coming out of the mall, he sees in front of him a cinema which has the peculiarity of being wide open on one side, due to the absence of one of the walls: the people inside can be seen intent on watching a film. Drawing closer, Pietro notices that the cinema is also a stadium, inasmuch as a section of stand, the curva, can be made out, one frequented by the most fanatical tifosi. He realises that he too should have gone to the stadium for work.

This oneiric segment seems to represent well the passage from the anomic, confusive dimension (wandering aimlessly around the featureless shopping centre) to an emotionally warm representational world, in which the syntagmatic dimension (the cinema, the stadium, with the latter seen from the point of view of its most emotionally charged characteristic) again takes on a central role. Of course, we also know that the shopping centres of referential reality, which dreams draw upon as if from an immense encyclopaedia, contain invisible narrative sequences developed by their designers, but it is evident that the cinema and the stadium both have strong theatrical significance and therefore represent quite markedly the centrality of the syntagmatic narrative sequence that Pietro was slowly reappropriating for himself.

It is worth pausing for a moment, incidentally, to reflect on the importance of such a narrative sequence on a socio-cultural level and ask ourselves whether this is, in fact, the reason for the veritable boom in TV series that we have been witness to over the past few years, a boom accompanied by the phenomenon of binge-watching, a sort of bulimic tendency to watch multiple episodes of the same show back to back. The "series" is by definition the succession of particular discursive segments, individual episodes, and thus authentically constitutes the macro-syntagmatic axis, the object of our discussion. In light of this line of reasoning, the phenomenon of TV series being accompanied by binge-watching does not appear coincidental, binge-watching appearing as a sort of psychic enantiodromic compensation for the bias towards a confusive, anomic, paradigmatic universe whose "ensign" is to be seen in the now-ubiquitous "icons" found today throughout the vast digital universe, from Netflix to the online edition of a newspaper to pornographic websites. In short, if we are witnessing a widespread "demand" for syntagm and processual pathway, psychotherapy, serial by definition, can now more than ever present itself as a useful instrument to prevent such enantiodromic compensation from going too far in the direction of the syntagmatic impoverishment of soap operas, TV series within which the possibility – which remains fundamental – of a metaphorical and paradigmatic expansion withers away, trapped as it is within the rigid confines of the characters and the plots which involve them. Psychotherapy, then, presents as a pathway of harmonisation between *langue* and *parole*, paradigm and syntagm, system and process, metaphor and metonymy, signified and signifier, potentiality and actuality; or, in psychoanalytic terms, between expansion of the "analytic field", as prompted primarily by developments after Bion, and the traditional individuation process of the individual's psychological biography, as favoured by Jungians.

Expressed in other terms, we are talking about the reciprocal inter-relating of the two axes, syntagmatic and paradigmatic, present at the very heart of psychoanalysis as a "talking cure", an authentically linguistic therapeutic practice; as Bion succinctly put it:

The medium in which the psycho-analyst works is verbalized thoughts.

(Bion, 2018, pp. 37–38)

It is no coincidence if at the very origins of the psychoanalytic edifice we find, in the works of Freud, his particular formula to integrate the two axes: on the one hand, meticulous biographical inquiry, based on the authentically metonymic and rectilinear line of thought of the conscious Ego which investigates the depths of the Id according to the well-known formula: "Where Id was, there Ego shall be" (Freud, 1933, p. 80), and, on the other, the *regola aurea* of free association, reaching for the metaphorical expansion of thought thanks to the loosening, stimulated by the setting, of logical connections and the consequent access to a more genuinely oneiric dimension – in short, the consulting room as the place of choice of integration, in new and creative terms for the individual, of these two fundamental dimensions. It is interesting to observe how also at the root of Jungian thought is to be found a systematic reflection on language, investigated using psychological instruments. We are referring here to the word-association experiments carried out at the Burghölzli by Jung together with Franz Riklin. It is well known that Jung and Riklin revisited experimentally the work of Gustav Aschaffenburg, assistant to Emil Kraepelin in Heidelberg, who had studied the effects of fatigue on word association. According to Aschaffenburg, in particular, with increased fatigue, induced in the subjects studied during the experiments, it was noted that there was a decrease in semantically based word associations (for example, "pear" associated with "fruit") while phonetically-based ("clang-reaction") word associations ("pear" associated with "bear") increased, explainable as a consequence of motor excitation and therefore in exclusively organicistic terms.

Jung and Riklin drew a different conclusion:

> Therefore, the clang-reactions are not in any demonstrable connexion with motor excitation; rather we perceive the cause of their appearance in the decline of attention. . . . With weak attention the stimulus-image does not rise to its full height of clearness, or, in other words, it remains in a peripheral region of the field of consciousness and is merely apprehended by means of its external, clang-like manifestation. . . . Every apperceptive process of an acoustic stimulus begins at the stage of clang-like apprehension. At each of these stages associations can be expressed through speech centres which are ready for discharge at the moment. That this does not occur normally depends upon the inhibition exercised by the direction of the attention, i.e. by the raising of the threshold of the stimulus for all inferior and non-directed forms of association.
>
> (Jung, 1919, pp. 41–42)

In other words, as Paul Kugler summarises:

> Ego-consciousness tends to associate words metonymically, according to a consideration of linear contiguity, i.e., to predicative and spatio-temporal associations,

while

> [a] lowering of consciousness, whether produced by a distraction of attention, sleep, or a psychic disturbance, is marked by a dramatic shift in the

associative process from the metonymic to the metaphoric mode of association emphasizing a similarity in sound-image and analogy.

(Kugler, 1982/2002, pp. 67–68)

And again:

The psychic movement from conscious to unconscious is accompanied by a
linguistic shift from an ego emphasis on the signified (meaning) to an unconscious insistence on the signifier (sound-image).

(*ibidem*, pp. 67–68)

This is essentially, expressed in more strictly linguistic terms, what had already
been observed by Freud in distinguishing primary and secondary process.

At this juncture, we might further refine the provisional identikit we are putting
together of *homo digitalis*: an individual not only *anomic*, without past or future,
but also profoundly *sensory*, with mental mechanisms in which the metaphoric
association (image-sound) prevails, deprived, however, of poetic and polysemic
potentiality – which paradoxically should be intrinsic precisely to the metaphoric/
paradigmatic universe – as it is too far removed from pathways of knowledge
and signification of a metonymic/syntagmatic nature. This hypertextual and metaphoric universe would be unable, in other words, to express the enormous potentialities it contains, becoming a chaotic and confusive dimension. The inevitable
consequence of this psychological and linguistic bias, as we saw in the case of
Pietro, is the difficulty of entering into contact with one's own inner world and,
likewise, with external reality. To quote Bion, we might say that this human type
manifests extreme difficulty in *learning from experience*, as a result seeking ref-
uge in an altogether conformist modality of behaviour, guided by an alexithymic
pseudo-rationality very similar to the *pensée opératoire* conceptualised, at the
beginning of the 1960s, by Pierre Marty and Michel de M'Uzan as a modality
of thought characteristic of the psychosomatic personality: men and women,
especially younger people, who thus meld a hyper-stimulated imaginary from the
digital universe with an overall emotive constriction and a conformist, repetitive
and somewhat concretistic modality of behaviour. It is no co-incidence, then, that
often during a session, these patients feel the need to use their smartphones, to
read to their analyst exchanges of messages with people they are connected to or
to show a photo which illustrates what they are talking about: a place, a person or
perhaps a cartoon found on the Web. Verbal language in these cases seems insuf-
ficiently developed to express the confused interior sentiment.

Psychotherapists' open-mindedness in accepting these new, increasingly widespread behaviours is, in our opinion, inevitable; otherwise there is a risk that what
are, in any case, authentic attempts to communicate might be frustrated, even if
the communication is by means of the "*débrayage*" of fragments of meaning,
while waiting for a better signification, on the cold display of a smartphone. If the
semiotic slogan "put sense in a position to signify" is also valid for psychoanalysis

as a whole, it seems even right and proper that psychotherapists should embrace new technologies as a tool, born of the *Zeitgeist* of psychological expression.

The situation encountered during sessions with another patient, Carla, is a case in point, representative of the many which evince the presence of excessive bias as a result of the impact of the paradigmatic axis (deprived, however, as we were saying, of its poetic and polysemic potentiality) in the analytic dyad's internal narrative construction and the concomitant need on the part of the patient to use, as a communications prosthesis, an electronic device to be able to fully express her-/himself.

It would be opportune to ask ourselves as to the sense still now, in the era of the deconstruction of space/temporal *topoi*, in distinguishing dichotomously between inside and outside the setting, recalling Deridda's "*il n'y a pas de hors texte*"; in fact, Carla readily uses, to accompany her verbal language, a wide assortment of multimedia material which she brings to the analyst's attention both during analysis and outside the sessions by means of email and WhatsApp.

To simplify, let us consider only those situations in which the analyst comes into contact with material of a non-spoken nature produced by patients during sessions (leaving aside the material produced outside the sessions): screenshots of messages with the people they are connected to, selfies, photos, songs, videos, memes and everything that the Web effortlessly offers by means of a simple click.

The "physical" time needed to visualise multimedia products is, logically speaking, time subtracted from the analyst's *rêverie*, given that the processes of perception prevail over the activities of the imagination, and the analyst's work as decoder and generator of meaning of the raw material brought in by the patient is thus limited by an excess of signifiers present in the *hic et nunc*.

To use a culinary simile, it would be like seeing the analyst in chef's uniform, without doubt able to transform the uncooked foodstuffs into palatable (and perhaps tasty) comestibles, having to grapple with such an overabundance of produce, cartons and packets, ingredients to defrost or otherwise clean and prepare, that it all obstructs or seriously limits the available space, the use of the kitchen utensils and, ultimately, the very process of "cooking". If truth be told, even without multimedia, the analyst/chef will indeed always find her-/himself faced with the responsibility which comes from having to select[10] between the material present in the analytic field/kitchen what s/he considers pertinent or which generates insight, the herald of "meaning".

What we wish to underline, therefore, is that the analyst/chef risks in this case finding her-/himself faced with the paradox of no longer being able to cook, or cooking badly due to the overabundance of produce to deal with.

Like the chef in question, the analyst experiences a sense of paralysis from overabundance and must try rapidly to reorganise her/his "thought-thinking apparatus" in order to try to accomplish the task.

What strategies does the analyst have at her/his disposal?

One possibility would be to take even greater recourse than in the past to the evenly hovering attention of Freudian fame and so to try to select episodic fragments of material in an attempt to semanticise them and insert them into a metonymic/syntagmatic flow. We would be looking at the chef who tries to get on with the job by randomly picking or, in the best-case scenario, rapidly seeking inspiration from the first products to come to hand.

An alternative strategy for the chef would be to try to regulate the flow of provisions, choosing what to let into the kitchen (and with likely tailbacks building up outside the door). For the analyst, it would mean regulating *a priori*, without the relational *coniunctio*, which contents are meant to be dealt with.

Clearly both alternatives are unsatisfactory for obvious reasons.

What is to be done therefore?

To sketch out an answer in conclusion, it appears to us that what is needed is not so much a modification of analytical technique as a remodulation of it. If over the last few decades there has been a progressively greater accentuation of the relational dimension of the session's *hic et nunc*, up to the post-Bionian model of the *analytic field*, developed above all in Italy by Antonino Ferro and his collaborators, it is not so much a redimensioning of this type of listening and interpretative attitude which seems important to us today, undoubtedly fertile as this is, as it is accompanying it with a constant underlining of the (macro)syntagmatic axis in the interventions with the patient. It is important that the latter should not lose track of her/his psychological pathway in order to be able to re-emerge progressively from the "atemporal" confusion of the hyper-paradigmatic universe which we have attempted to describe here. Interventions which connect processually the various phases of the work accomplished thus seem important, for example, by periodically looking again at sequences of dreams which were dreamt on different occasions or by highlighting specific psychological themes which reoccur over various sessions (known in semiotics as thematic isotopies). Also, the frequent knitting together, where possible, of the analytic material with the existential pathway outside the analysis (the *referent* of every narrative during sessions), can contribute significantly to the work of strengthening the syntagmatic-processual function of the mind. The activity of interpretation, freer from the processual axis, with a constant poetic and playful amplification of the patient's account, "without memory or desire", as advocated by Bion, will best be developed at later stages of the therapeutic pathway, when "psycho-narrative" harmony has already been sufficiently re-established between paradigm and syntagm and between metaphor and metonymy and, to use different terms, between the anomic patient's hypertrophic, prefabricated imaginary and her/his historical pathway, which has often been largely lost when s/he sets out along the avenue of analysis.

Notes

1 And – taking into account Lacan's assertion whereby "the unconscious is structured like a language" – of the mind *tout court*.
2 Xanadu can be considered a sort of precursor to the Web 2.0, even if Nelson was opposed to such a comparison since, from his point of view, the Web is excessively

unidirectional and does not allow its end-users any genuine freedom of manoeuvre, at least within the digital space.

3 As Spinoza puts it, "*Omnis determinatio est negatio*". If we open our wardrobe to select a garment from those hanging on the skirt or trouser rail, we automatically exclude all the others in the same category but are still free to choose a shirt, again excluding all the other shirts available. In the same way, returning to Saussure, the selection of a word in the construction of a sentence excludes all the other words semantically associated with it. Incidentally, syntagmatic construction, which progresses in linear fashion by joining together various elements (words as much as items of clothing, or a sequence of musical pieces as accompaniment to a particular event), can only work *in praesentia*, because the selected elements will all be present in the final "text".

4 Eco, talking about the empirical author of any given text, states that the author "will thus envisage a Model Reader able to cooperate with the actualization of the text as he, the author, imagined, and to proceed interpretatively as he proceeded generatively" (Eco, 1979, pp. 53–55).

5 Care is needed, however, in understanding what we mean by mythical/mythological. If we refer to Roland Barthes's notion of "mythology", it is quite a different matter. In his famous work *Mythologies* (1957), and most noticeably in the concluding theoretical essay *Le mythe, aujourd'hui*, Roland Barthes reflects on the ideological force of what he calls "mythology", which holds sway in the language of advertising and, today more then ever, of politics. This is the semiotic phenomenon of connotation, by which a sign becomes the signifier of a second sign and a second "hidden" semiotic system which is ideological and manipulative in nature. The world of the Web is dominated by this phenomenon, and most of the signs which we encounter there "signify" something else (a value, a desirable object, an "instruction" for a certain type of behaviour, etc.). The "demythologised" individual we are describing is, paradoxically, particularly receptive to and manipulable by these mythologies of Barthes's.

6 Anomie – literally "without norms" – is a term which originated in the works of Émile Durkheim and became current among social scientists.

7 This is a pragmatic distinction, since the syntagmatic plane of language can be segmented, according to the linguistic analysis required, at many levels.

8 A more exhaustive treatment of this material is to be found in the referenced work (Candellieri, Favero, 2019).

9 *Ibid*. In particular, of the likeable manager of Torino F.C. giving a practically unintelligible reply to a TV reporter, and of a suspicious note left on the windscreen of Pietro's parked car.

10 For an in-depth examination of the delicate topic of the selection of material present in the analytic field, see the description of the concept of *découpage* presented in Candellieri, S., Favero, D. (2019).

Bibliography

Alberti, L. B. (c.1450) *De Pictura*. Polistampa, Firenze, 2012.

Aristotle (330 BC) *Poetica*. Einaudi, Torino, 2008.

Barone, P. (2012) *Utopia del presente*. Mimesis, Milano.

Bion, W.R. (1965) *Transformations*. Routledge, London, 2018.

Bion, W.R. (2005) *The Tavistock Seminars*. Karnac Books, London.

Candellieri, S., Favero, D. (2019) *Hyde Park. Officina di psicoanalisi potenziale*. Moretti e Vitali, Bergamo.

Cosenza, G. (2010) *Semiotica dei nuovi media*. Editori Laterza, Bari.

Eco, U. (1979) *Lector in fabula*. Bompiani, Milano, 2004.

Freud, S. (1933) *New Introductory Lectures on Psycho-Analysis*. In *The Standard Edition of the Complete Psychological Works of Sigmund Freud*, Volume XXII (1932–1936): New Introductory Lectures on Psycho-Analysis and Other Works, 1–182. Hogarth Press, London.

Goncarov, I. (1859) *Oblomov*. Feltrinelli, Milano, 2014.

Jakobson, R. (1956) *Due aspetti del linguaggio e due tipi di afasia* (1956), in *Saggi di linguistica generale* (1963), a cura di Heilmann L. Feltrinelli, Milano, 2012.

Jung, C.G. (1904) *Studies in Word-Association*. Moffat, Yard & Company, New York, 1919.

Kugler, P. (1982) *The Alchemy of Discourse. Image, Sound and Psyche*. Daimon Verlag, Einsiedeln, 2002.

MacIver, R.M. (1950) *The Ramparts We Guard*. MacMillan, New York.

McLuhan, M. (1964) *Understanding Media: The Extensions of Man*. McGraw Hill, New York.

Nelson, T.H. (1981) *Literary Machines: The Report on, and of, Project Xanadu, Concerning Word Processing, Electronic Publishing, Hypertext, Thinkertoys, Tomorrow's Intellectual Revolution, and Certain Other Topics Including Knowledge, Education and Freedom*. Mindful Press, Sausalito, CA, 1992.

Prosperi, A. (2021) *Un tempo senza storia*. Einaudi, Torino.

Tustin, F. (1990) *The Protective Shell in Children and Adults*. Karnac Books, London.

Volli, U. (2000) *Manuale di semiotica*. Editori Laterza, Bari, 2004.

Chapter 4

The Fall of the Berlin Wall

Complex Theory and the Numinous in the Development of History (a neo-Jungian Approach)

Stefano Carpani

Introduction

On the evening of November 9th 1989, something unexpected (and numinous), happened that changed history forever! This something, I propose, cannot be explained only rationally.

In this chapter,[1] I investigate Jung's complex theory and the concept of the numinous in the development of history, looking specifically at the fall of the Berlin Wall and the events of November 9th, 1989. This example of the Berlin Wall – which takes into consideration Jung's basic premise that the unconscious is continually compensating for what is dominant in consciousness (also on a collective level) – might help to verify, criticize, and enhance Jung's idea that

> incisive changes in history are generally attributed exclusively to external causes. It seems to me, however, that external circumstances often serve merely as occasions for a new attitude to life and the world, long prepared in the unconscious, to become manifest. Social, political, and religious conditions affect the collective unconscious in the sense that all those factors which are suppressed by the prevailing views or attitudes in the life of a society gradually accumulate in the collective unconscious and activate its contents.
>
> (CW8, 594)

Following Jung (CW6, 923), I propose that complexes, which are "emotionally-toned contents having a certain amount of autonomy," also determine history due to "the capacity of the complexes to resist conscious intentions, and to come and go as they please" (CW6, 923). Furthermore, "they are psychic entities which are outside the control of the conscious mind. They have been split off from consciousness and lead a separate existence in the dark realm of the unconscious, being at all times ready to hinder or reinforce the conscious functioning." (CW6, 923) Again following Jung, it is important to remember that

> when we look at human history, we see only that which happens on the surface and even this is distorted in the faded mirror of tradition. But what is

DOI: 10.4324/9781003168829-5

really happening eludes the inquiring eye of the historian, for the true historical event lies deeply buried.

(CW10, 315)

In this work, I employ a psychosocial approach to examine how psychic experience and social life are fundamentally entangled and propose that this approach is
the best at hand to examine both the theatre/stage and actors/play of history at the
border between the conscious and unconscious realms. I will recount the events
of November 9th 1989 and examine those events in lights of Jung's concept of the
numinous. I will also examine the concept of meaning with reference to Wolfgang
Giegerich's "End of Meaning" (2010).

November 9th 1989: A numinous day

In the months leading up to November 9th 1989, millions of people manifested
their wish for a change in the DDR by marching in the streets of Leipzig, Dresden,
Berlin, and other east German cities. Then, on the evening of the day in question,
something numinous occurred that changed history forever! This something cannot be explained rationally; it is a complex phenomenon that mingled the conscious and unconscious realms.

The facts: Mr. Günter Schabowski was the regime's unofficial spokesman (so
named by the SED's[2] General Secretary Egon Krenz), member of the Politbüro,
and an experienced journalist, whose role (since Krenz's coming to office) was
to hold several daily press conferences to announce changes (Sebestyen, 2009).
Additionally, "Schabowski had spent most of his career in Communist-style journalism, in which reporters were told what to write after events had already happened" (Sarotte, 2014, p. 115).

Shortly before the press conference on the evening of November 9th 1989,
"Krenz handed Schabowski a text containing new, temporary travel regulations"
(Sarotte, 2014, p. 115) and stipulating "that East German citizens could apply
for permission to travel abroad without having to meet the previous requirements for those trips, and also allowed for permanent emigration between all
border crossings-including those between East and West Berlin" (Sarotte, 2014,
pp. 107/108). Although this revolutionary information was supposed to be embar-
goed until the next morning, "Schabowski had not been on hand when Krenz read
the text earlier in the day to several Politbüro members . . ., nor had he been there
when it was discussed before the full committee. However, he felt comfortable
discussing it at the press conference" (Sarotte, 2014, p. 115).

According to the TV recording,[3] Schabowski met the press for almost one hour
and touched upon such subjects as how to modernize socialism. Schabowski (who
looked confident and in control for almost the entire press conference) – answer-
ing Italian journalist Riccardo Ehrman, who asked him if the new travel legisla-
tion could be a mistake – said: "one cannot implement all steps at the same time.
There is a sequence of steps necessary." He smiled as if satisfied with his handling

of the press and looked self-confident and in control. He then reiterated that granting travel opportunities to DDR citizens was an effort to stop illegal fleeing and to
"free people from psychological pressure."

In this regard, I sense that he – unconsciously – began to feel uncomfortable
and under pressure but did not recognize it (being one-sided, ego-centered, and
too much in his persona). Thus, he continued to speak, believing himself to be in
control of the situation. He added that many of the aforementioned steps had been
"taken without reflection." Again, I propose, his unconscious was warning him to
reflect before speaking. It was taming him. However, he did not understand this
and continued, allowing the *force of the change* itself to push into consciousness,
thus giving voice to the collective unconscious as well as to all those who had
marched in the previous days and months.

He then laid the groundwork for the subsequent error. As mentioned, he was too
unconscious and in his persona and – accidentally – pushed forward the collapse
of the Berlin wall. He first said that

> we are of course concerned that this possibility of a new travel legislation,
> which is still only a draft and not yet a law that is effective, but as much as
> I know there has today been a decision based on a proposal of the Politbüro
> that one adjust the law . . . to let it become effective so that people can leave
> the republic on a permanent basis, especially also because we don't want to
> see this movement affect the relations to a foreign state we are friendly with.
> This is also not an easy situation for that state.

He then contradicted himself, saying "therefore we decided today to enact leg-
islation that shall make it possible for every citizen to cross the border directly
through a checkpoint of the DDR."

Suddenly, after almost an hour of monologue, a journalist (Sonnevend, 2016,
pp. 64–66) – disregarding protocol – interrupted Schabowski and asked, "From
when on will this become effective?" This was immediately followed by another
journalist's[4] question: "Without passport?" and then yet a third one[5] asked:
"Immediately? From now on?" Schabowski was puzzled and replied only "*Bitte?*"
(excuse me?), as if he hadn't quite caught the questions or as if stalling for time.
This reaction, according to Jung's association experiment, is a sign of a complex
indicator (misunderstanding or mishearing) and therefore relevant.

The TV close-up of Schabowski's face demonstrates that he also frowned
(another complex indicator) and suddenly became lost. In my opinion, he became
overwhelmed by unconscious elements and did not know how to answer. Here is
when – I sense – he entered a sort of trance,[6] or what Jung would call a psychoid
state that took control over this experienced politician who *should have known*
how to answer because he had been trained to deal with such situations. From a
senior party executive, one would expect a political answer, such as: "more information will be disclosed soon." But instead, Schabowski looked again at the paper
he had been given. He scratched his forehead with his right hand and looked left

(two more important complex indicators), sharing the text with a colleague, as if crying for help, and said: "Well, Comrades, I have been told that there is a press release that has been circulated today so it should be with you already."[7]

He then donned his reading-glasses, as if preparing to read a non-existent text, as if hiding from the crowd, or, symbolically, as if to see better, more clearly. Perhaps he sought to help his eyes (symbols of intellectual perception and recipients of light [Chevalier and Gheerbrant, 1996, p. 362]) to become illuminated by the changing power of the numinous and the collective unconscious; to help his eyes, which are symbolically the "eyes of heart," (Chevalier and Gheerbrant, 1996, p. 362) to receive "spiritual enlightenment" (Chevalier and Gheerbrant, 1996, p. 362).

By this means, he unconsciously changed the world forever and said, as if reading aloud from the paper, "Private journeys to foreign countries can be applied for without special reasons such as family visits for which permissions will be granted ad-hoc. The relevant office of the Volkspolizei is ordered to grant visas for permanent leave immediately." Immediately, another journalist piped up: "From when does this become effective?" Schabowski replied – looking again to the note, as if hoping to find the right answer there (Sonnevend, 2016, p. 65) – "that goes into effect, according to my information, immediately, without delay." Hearing this answer, Mr. Beil[8] (who was sitting next to Schabowski) looked at him and said[9] – very quietly – "that has to be decided by the council of ministers."

Here was the moment when the numinous occurred, when the psychoid[10] was at its best and demolished the Berlin Wall forever. Here is when, in Schabowski's own words, "all steps (were implemented) at the same time" and "without reflection," "free(ing) people from psychological pressure."

Immediately, the conference room was inundated with a sense of "sublimity, awe, excitement, bliss, rapture, exaltation, entrancement, fascination, attraction, allure" and "impelling motive power" (Otto, 1958, p. 29) but also a sense of "fear, trembling, weirdness, eeriness, humility (an acute sense of unworthiness), urgency, stupor (blank wonder), bewilderment, horror, mental agitation, repulsion, and haunting, daunting, monstrous feelings that 'overbrim the heart'" (Otto, 1958, p. 29).

Schabowski ended the conference and prepared to return to the Politbüro, but he was confronted by more questions from journalists. He had meanwhile returned to his persona and could respond politically. Simultaneously, while saying goodbye to the journalists, he said: "I am interested to go back to the general committee," as though sensing that something big was about to happen.

The numinous according to C.G. Jung

What is the numinous, and what is its relevance in the development of history? Can the facts just underlined be seen as a numinous event or as a "stroke of fate that changes history," as German media outlet Deutsche Welle reported in 2014?[11]

Jung, following theologist Rudolf Otto, saw the numinous as

> a dynamic agency or effect not caused by an arbitrary act of will. On the
> contrary, it seizes and controls the human subject, who is always rather its
> victim than its creator. The numinosum – whatever its cause may be – is an
> experience of the subject independent of his will.
>
> (CW11 §6)

He also put such experience down to "a cause external to the individual. The
numinosum is either a quality belonging to a visible object or the influence of an
invisible presence that causes a peculiar alteration of consciousness."

According to Otto (1958, p. 29), the *numinosum* is a paradox, containing both
positive (sublimity, awe, excitement, bliss, rapture, exaltation, etc.) and negative (overwhelm, fear, trembling, weirdness, eeriness, etc.) qualities (Otto, 1958,
p. 29). Thus, the numinous, as Otto (Otto, 1958, p. 59) underlined, "eludes appre-
hension in terms of concepts," "being a mystery, it bewilders the rational mind"
(Otto, 1958, p. 31); "being divine, it links us to the ground of the soul," (Otto,
1958, p. 36); and "being 'unevolvable,' it is not to be derived from any other feeling" (Otto, 1958, p. 44).

Jung (CW18 §581) underlined that "things whose enormity nobody could have
imagined in the idyllic innocence of the first decade of our century[12] have happened and have turned the world upside down," and because of this "the Western
world feels uneasy, for it does not know how much it plays into the hands of the
uproarious underworld and what it has lost through the destruction of its numi-
nosities." Saying so, he claimed that numinous events must be seen as compensation for the loss of numinosity, and "their *raison d'être*, the order of their social
organizations" (CW18 §582).

He added that since the early 20th century,

> our spiritual leaders cannot be spared the blame for having been more inter-
> ested in protecting their institutions than in understanding the mystery that
> symbols present. . . . they turn a blind eye to the numinous psychic powers
> that forever control man's fate.
>
> (CW18 §582)

We can also add that "psychology can only indicate the relation of psyche to
matter without being able to make out the least thing about its nature" and that

> certain complexes arise on account of painful or distressing experiences in a
> person's life, experiences of an emotional nature which leave lasting psychic
> wounds behind them. . . . All these produce unconscious complexes of a per-
> sonal nature.
>
> (CW8 §594)

Therefore, Jung speaks of loss of the soul, "because certain portions of the psyche have indeed disappeared" and

> a great many autonomous complexes arise in this way. But there are others that come from quite a different source. While the first source is easily understood, since it concerns the outward life everyone can see, this other source is obscure and difficult to understand because it has to do with perceptions or impressions of the collective unconscious.
>
> (CW8 §594)

In this regard, Jung added,

> usually the individual tries to rationalize these inner perceptions in terms of external causes, but that does not get at the root of the matter. At bottom they are irrational contents of which the individual had never been conscious before, and which he therefore vainly seeks to discover somewhere outside him. The primitive expresses this very aptly when he says that some spirit is interfering with him.
>
> (CW8 §594)

Jung (CW8 §594) underlined that

> these experiences occur either when something so devastating happens to the individual that his whole previous attitude to life breaks down, or when for some reason the contents of the collective unconscious accumulate so much energy that they start influencing the conscious mind.

I propose that this is what happened to Schabowski on November 9th 1989.

Jung also underlined that "this happens when the life of a large social group or of a nation undergoes a profound change of a political, social, or religious nature. Such a change always involves an alteration of the psychological attitude" (CW8 §594). He added that

> incisive changes in history are generally attributed exclusively to external causes. It seems to me, however, that external circumstances often serve merely as occasions for a new attitude to life and the world, long prepared in the unconscious, to become manifest.

Therefore, he claimed – sharing a perspective dear to psychosocial scholars – that

> social, political, and religious conditions affect the collective unconscious in the sense that all those factors which are suppressed by the prevailing views or attitudes in the life of a society gradually accumulate in the collective unconscious and activate its contents.[13]

This is what happened in the months and years before the collapse of the Berlin Wall. But why did Budapest (1956) and Prague (1968) not experience similar changes? Nor South Africa, Ulster, Gaza, Kurdistan, Hong Kong, or Catalunya, to name just a few?

One could also say, like Kast,[14] that "in terms of experience, something similar to numinous happened in Prague at the time – it was only perceived differently. And no Schabowski was there." But what about Budapest? Nagy's role cannot be compared to that of Schabowski (not even to the roles Václav Havel and Nelson Mandela played in their respective countries), and the Soviet invasion can certainly be compared to many other *Golias* (past and present) whose aim has been to suppress change and reestablish the authoritarian order.

According to Jung (CW8 §47), this is because development – which is always paralleled by psychic development – "cannot be accomplished by intention and will alone," and therefore

> it needs the attraction of the symbol, whose value quantum exceeds that of the cause. But the formation of a symbol cannot take place until the mind has dwelt long enough on the elementary facts, that is to say until the inner or outer necessities of the life-process have brought about a transformation of energy.

Therefore, Jung claims that "certain individuals gifted with particularly strong intuition then become aware of the changes going on in society and translate these changes into communicable ideas." During the 20th century (focusing on Western society), we can recall many such figures: Rosa Parks, Malcolm X, Martin Luther King, Nelson Mandela, Lech Wałęsa, Václav Havel, and perhaps even Gorbachev, Saint Karol Wojtyla, Malala Yousafza, and Greta Thunberg. Jung added that

> new ideas spread rapidly because parallel changes have been taking place in the unconscious of other people. There is a general readiness to accept the new ideas, although on the other hand they often meet with violent resistance. New ideas are not just the enemies of the old; they also appear as a rule in an extremely unacceptable form.

According to Jung,

> whenever contents of the collective unconscious become activated, they have a disturbing effect on the conscious mind and confusion ensues. If the activation is due to the collapse of the individual's hopes and expectations, there is a danger that the collective unconscious may take the place of reality.
>
> (CW8 §595)

In my opinion, this is exactly what happened to Schabowski. That being the case, could Schabowski be considered an involuntary (because unconscious) un-locker of contents locked in the collective unconscious? In this regard, Jung claimed that "spirits are not under all circumstances dangerous and harmful. They can, when translated into ideas, also have beneficial effects" (CW8 §596). He added that an

> example of this transformation of a content of the collective unconscious into communicable language is the miracle of Pentecost. From the point of view of the onlookers, the apostles were in a state of ecstatic intoxication ('These men are full of new wine': Acts 2: 13). But it was just when they were in this state that they communicated the new teaching which gave expression to the unconscious expectations of the people and spread with astonishing rapidity through the whole Roman Empire.

Metaphorically, I compare the apostles' state of ecstatic intoxication with Schabowski's. I propose that he was intoxicated by the contents of the collective unconscious because "the experience of the self is always a defeat for the ego" (CW 14 §778) and because, quoting Walter Benjamin (1929, pp. 1018–1044), "every revolution has an intoxicating component."

The unconscious constantly recombines in a dialectical way from the ego to the self, aiming for the realization of the self. I see Schabowski's intoxication and state of trance (psychoid's transcendent) as the realization of the Self, possibly his individual self and the collective self. When examining Schabowski's experience, it can be said with Jung that

> the unconscious also contains all the material that has not yet reached the threshold of consciousness. These are the seeds of future conscious contents. Equally we have reason to suppose that the unconscious is never quiescent in the sense of being inactive but is ceaselessly engaged in grouping and regrouping its contents. This activity should be thought of as completely autonomous only in pathological cases; normally it is coordinated with the conscious mind in a compensatory relationship.
>
> (CW7 §204)

Conclusions

In the previous pages, I have proposed, following Jung, that history is shaped by complexes and the numinous, by both conscious and unconscious contents. In the fall of the Berlin Wall, we see the conscious effort of Krenz's Politbüro to change the DDR according to Gorbachev's perestroika and the boiling pressure of the demonstration and riots in East-Germany, followed by Schabowski's unconscious action.

I have examined the concept of the numinous in history, recognizing, like Jung, that the numinous can feed the "hunger of the soul" (CW10 §651) and "provide feelings of liberation and relief" (CW13 §342). Jung adds that "as much as it is ineffable, the numinous is also ineluctable: it cannot be ignored" (CW12 §247).

Therefore, the numinous "is wholly outside conscious volition, for it transports the subject into the state of rapture, which is a state of will-less surrender" (CW8 §383).

In this light, it is interesting to examine both conscious and unconscious contents in regard to the individual and society and claim that the Berlin Wall was brought down by both the conscious efforts of the many who marched on the streets of the DDR as well as the numinous. Thus, the interconnectedness of conscious and unconscious contents, of the individual and collective and society, are inseparable from any understanding.

On this, Jung (CW8 §417) also underlines that psychological theory cannot be formulated mathematically

> because we have no measuring rod with which to measure psychic quantities. We have to rely solely upon qualities, that is, upon perceptible phenomena. Consequently, psychology is incapacitated from making any valid statement about unconscious states, or to put it another way, there is no hope that the validity of any statement about unconscious states or processes will ever be verified scientifically.

He adds that "We must, however, constantly bear in mind that what we mean by 'archetype' is in itself irrepresentable, but has effects which make visualizations of it possible, namely the archetypal images and ideas." Physics shares a similar ground where atoms are "the smallest particles [which] are themselves irrepresentable but have effects from the nature of which we can build up a model. The archetypal image, the motif or mythologem, is a construction of this kind." He adds, "the identity or non-identity of two irrepresentable quantities is something that cannot be proved" mathematically and, on this basis, when "psychology assumes the existence of certain irrepresentable psychoid factors, it is doing the same thing in principle as physics does when the physicist constructs an atomic model." He concludes that

> just as the atom is not indivisible, so, as we shall see, the unconscious is not merely unconscious. And just as physics in its psychological aspect can do no more than establish the existence of an observer without being able to assert anything about the nature of that observer, so psychology can only indicate the relation of psyche to matter without being able to make out the least thing about its nature.

Therefore, we cannot regard a numinous event as a miracle. Miracles are *deo concedente*, while numinous events are not merely unconscious; as underlined previously, they are already contained in the individual or collective psyche. From this, we can claim that "the unconscious actually creates new contents" and "everything that the human mind has ever created sprang from contents which, in the last analysis, existed once as unconscious seeds" (CW8 §702).

Post scriptum: from "the end of history" to "the end of meaning"

I would now like to examine the link between the numinous and *meaning*. In so doing, I reengage with the question posed previously: why might a numinous event lie behind the fall of the Berlin Wall but not behind Budapest (1956) or Prague (1968)? If we follow Jung (CW8 §47), conditions for *development* were not adequate in the latter places: there was too much "intention and will alone" and possibly not (enough) "attraction of the symbol" because "the formation of a symbol cannot take place until the mind has dwelt long enough . . . until the inner or outer necessities of the life process" make possible "transformation of energy."

This brings me to ask: is there any meaning behind the numinous? Is there any meaning in history? It would be disrespectful to dismiss those events that do not bring about *concrete* development. One example is the Palestinian liberation movement, where the power of *Goliath* is too strong to let *David*[15] and the numinous occur and thus to allow for development. Another example is Irish reunification, where the power of the *Crown* will not allow for liberation[16] (Watkins, 2003, p. 3) and the numinous, thus reunification, to happen. The same applies to Kurdistan, Hong Kong, and Catalunya, where liberation is – apparently – about separation and independence.

In this light, I claim that there is no rational meaning behind historic events (not even when they seem crystal clear), and it is this that makes them so difficult to understand. The only possible way is to think, as sociologists do (with rationality – logic – mind), that the current world has gone out of joint (Beck, 2017).

Giegerich (2010, p. 232) helps to clarify the question on meaning. He claims that since the Bible has become an historical rather than a holy book and has therefore become desacralized and demystified, we can no longer speak of meaning. In my opinion, we live in a post-Biblical society where Biblical symbolism has – apparently – lost its metaphorical meaning for the conscious mind but not for the soul.

Giegerich (2010, p. 232) also claims that "one can, to be sure, agree with Jung when he states that, 'Meaninglessness inhibits the fullest of life and therefore is equivalent to illness'" (Jung, 1963, p. 340); however, "The feeling that there should be a higher meaning of life and that it is missing is the illness But this . . . is not how the sentence is meant" because "as the example of most people living in the modern world shows, one can live quite well without meaning." Giegerich (2010, p. 234) claims that "there has not been one case where the meaninglessness of life was the cause of illness" and that the quest for meaning "is the expression of a neurotic pretentiousness, a claim to metaphysical grandiosity." Giegerich (2010, p. 234) claims that Jung refused to see this, although he was aware of "the danger of pointless seeking" (Giegerich, 2010, p. 233). I compare this infinite seeking to Becket's "waiting" for Godot and see both actions as a sign of *légèresse*, or impossible depth (superficiality). Depth could be the antidote to this *légèresse*, and an (absolutely) free individual is the opposite of a légère one. I also propose that absolute freedom occurs when all projections withdraw and cease (to have us).

The concepts of *meaning, searching and seeking*, and *waiting* are interwoven. They all show bulimic traits of ambivalence, wanting, and rejecting. Therefore, meaninglessness is linked to a never-ending *search* and *waiting* and ultimately to increased *légèresse*, until "something" (perhaps the numinous) happens to the individual or until a symbol appears. However, this might also not happen at all.

In this regard, Giegerich (2010, p. 233) recalls Jung's example of a woman that

> does not live the life that makes sense . . . because she is nothing. But if she could say, 'I am the daughter of the Moon. Every night I must help the Moon, my Mother, over the horizon' – ha, that is something else! Then she lives, then her life makes sense, and makes sense in all continuity, and for the whole humanity.
>
> (CW18 §630)

Giegerich adds that, while, according to Jung, "she would be cured" (2010, p. 233), this is no cure at all, just "a repetition of that illness that he himself[17] diagnosed." He claims that the "pueblo-Indian model" cannot be prescribed to the modern woman because "it is an idea that could only be sought in an endless, futile search" and that "Jung's suggestion feeds her neurotic craving, her 'addiction'" (2010, p. 234).

I propose that the problem faced by Western society since the end of WWII (and especially since the fall of the Berlin Wall) with the move into a "post" (class, gender, commitment, biblical) society is that a vast majority of individuals neurotically (and narcissistically) think that they are the sons or daughters of the moon. Westerners have also fallen prey to *grandma syndrome*, whereby grandmas see their grandchildren as so perfect that they can accomplish anything. The problem is that grandchildren take grandma's opinion to heart and acratically. Another problem is the missed transition from what Kierkegaard (2016) calls the esthetic and ethical phase of life. To think one is the daughter of the moon is to live an esthetic, not an ethical, life (even less a spiritual one) and is thus to be trapped – as Kast suggests[18] – in a narcissistic search for meaning. In this case, I propose that seeking can only be a compensation (for deprivation).

Therefore, Giegerich (2010, p. 234) proposes as a "real cure" to "make her fully aware that unconsciously she obviously thinks she ought to be the daughter of the moon or some such thing and that this is why she is desperately travelling, constantly seeking" and "to confront her with the exaltedness, inflatedness of the unconscious demands and expectations" and adds, "why should she not be able, like everybody else, to find satisfaction, *contentedness*, in ordinary life? . . . devoting her life to some useful task" (Giegerich, 2010, p. 234). In this regard, Hillman (1997) suggested learning to give something back to society, while Magatti and Giaccardi (2014) suggested becoming generative. This would – in Giegerich's lexicon – imply a *sublation*, therefore presenting the opportunity for development and the realization that she is not "a Queen in search for . . . the recognition due but denied to her."

Now, this is not about sex or a gender-specific problem. It is a problem for the whole Western world, which is not out of joint but has become narcissistic and grandiose and therefore is undoubtedly exalted, inflated, and unconscious. Perhaps there is no better example nowadays than the 45th US president, a man in "cloud-cuckoo-land, still living with grandiose ideas" (Giegerich, 2010, p. 234). Other examples are Brexit and the rise of neo-populism.

Following Giegerich and asking whether history has meaning,[19] it is possible to say "that there is nothing to be sought, nothing that would be somewhere else, be in the future or in the transcendence" (2010, p. 234). It could also be said that "this is it" and that "this real life of hers . . . contains everything it needs within itself. This life of hers here and now. . . *is* the source and circumference of all happiness, productivity and fulfilment possible for her." We can conclude that "nothing needs to be sought at all. On the contrary, her seeking is her running away from her fulfilment" (Giegerich, 2010, p. 234).

Therefore, I sense – when looking into the concept of the numinous and how this affects history (especially when looking at the fall of the Berlin Wall) – that meaning needs not to be sought at all and, above all, contradicting Fukuyama, who theorized that

> what we may be witnessing is not just the end of the Cold War, or the passing of a particular period of post-war history, but the end of history as such: that is, the end point of mankind's ideological evolution and the universalization of Western liberal democracy as the final form of human government.
>
> (1992)

there has been no end of history, as there has been no shift from a modern to a post-modern era. On the one hand, ideologies are substituted by new ones (perhaps even by the universalization of Western liberal democracy as a form of government that will eventually be substituted by a new one, and so on *ad infinitum*) and that, on the other hand, the so-called Western liberal model has demonstrated itself to be anything but liberal (thus engendering the rise of fundamentalism and populism, fanaticism, and antagonism). President George H.W. Bush's *New Order*[20] speech on September 11th 1989 is confirmation of this.

Therefore, the idea of a global "liberal democracy" based on the Western model has proven both naïve and *wotanistic* (the empire myth based on domination of the other [which is always the weaker]),[21] and a *new myth* is now required. The world seems stuck and in pain, or *out of joint*, as sociology suggests. To think that the world will become a global liberal democracy is to live in another cuckooland, and, rather than predicting a profit-driven future model, we should instead denounce the narcissism, will to power and domination, anxiety and aggressivity, corruption and hypocrisy, hedonism, anger, inflation, and grandiosity of our society and in this way perhaps help to put forward a development (with or without the advent of the numinous) to enable us to live in a less schizophrenic world than that pictured by Jung.

The world will continue evolving in an a-temporal and uroboric (cyclic) way, just as it always has. It will continue to swing uninterruptedly through the seasons of the year, between days of sun and rain, between war and peace, and wars fought in the name of peace. Thus, when examining history, and paraphrasing Giegerich (2010, p. 234), *this is it, the world contains everything it needs within itself,* and our continuous seeking is merely our running away from our own fulfillment.

I wish, following Otto Gross (2012), that we could move from a society based on *will to power* to one based on *will to reciprocity*, where mutuality (Orbach, 2014), equality and equivalence (Erickson, 1968), and social generativity (Giaccardi and Magatti, 2014) are key features. But we are far from this, and every attempt toward this model will no doubt be compensated by its opposite.

Notes

1   This chapter was originally written in partial fulfillment of the training requirements at the Carl Gustav Jung Institute Zürich, for which it received the Kim Arndt Award in 2019.
2   SED: Socialist Unity Party of Germany
3   www.youtube.com/watch?v=eLErVjwmrQY&t=720s or https://youtu.be/kZiAxgYY75Y
4   Mr. Ehrmann (Agentur Ansa, Italy).
5   Mr. Brinkmann (Bild-Zeitung, Germany).
6   Jung refers to this state as an intoxication. Please see subsequently.
7   It is important to underline that according to historical and journalistic reconstruction, there was no text yet in the hands of the journalist and that the press release he referred to would have been circulated only the following day.
8   Colleague of Shabowski and member of the DDR' *Zentralkomitees.*
9   Ibid.
10 Jung (CW8 §417) explains the psychoid as follows: "The archetype as such is a psychoid factor that belongs, as it were, to the invisible, ultraviolet end of the psychic spectrum. It does not appear, in itself, to be capable of reaching consciousness. I venture this hypothesis because everything archetypal which is perceived by consciousness seems to represent a set of variations on a ground theme" and "the real nature of the archetype is not capable of being made conscious, that it is transcendent, on which account I call it psychoid. Moreover every archetype, when represented to the mind, is already conscious and therefore differs to an indeterminable extent from that which caused the representation."
11 www.youtube.com/watch?v=DTBnOoBEJP0&t=77s
12 Jung refers to the 20th century.
13 Stephen Frosh (2013) underlined that "Psychosocial studies is a new terrain for interrogating the 'social subject', at odds with both psychology and sociology and drowning on a range of deliberately 'trans' spaces, such as postcolonial theory, queer theory, psychoanalysis, feminism and relational ethics." Frosh (2014) noted that one of the first definitions of psychosocial studies appeared on the Palgrave website authored by Redman, Holloway, and Frosh: "psychosocial studies seek to investigate the ways in which psychic and social processes demand to be understood as always implicated in each other, as mutually constitutive, coproduced, or abstracted levels of a single

dialectical process. As such it can be understood as an interdisciplinary field in search of transdisciplinary objects of knowledge. Psychosocial Studies is also distinguished by its emphasis on affect, the irrational and unconscious process, often, but not necessary, understood psychoanalytically." It is my opinion, therefore, that Jung must be considered one of the forerunners of psychosocial studies since his emphasis is on the previous.

14 Private conversation (2019).
15 How awkward it is to swap characters and write David here! But this, in my opinion, also proves the law of enantiodromia to be correct. Therefore, it gives hope for change and liberation.
16 Mary Watkins (2003, 3) prefers the term "liberation" to "development," because "with regard to economic and cultural progress, 'development' of one group seems often to require an oppression of the other." She adds that "a dominant culture's idea of development is too often imposed on a culture, depriving it of undertaking its own path of development."
17 Jung.
18 Private conversation (2019).
19 What a question in a post-Nietzschean, Marxian, and Freudian society where God is dead and religion is considered opium for the people and an illusion!
20 President George H.W. Bush in his speech to the Nation dated 11th September 1990 (https://youtu.be/MADYzQstpsU) – in front of a congress crowded with only men and top-rank military – promoted a New Order, "freed from the threat of terror, stronger in the pursuits of justice and more secure in the quest for peace. An era in which the nations of the world, east and west, north and south, can prosper and live in harmony." He continued: "Hundreds of generations have searched for this elusive path to peace, while a thousand wars rage across the human endeavour and today that new world is struggling to be born. A world quite different than the one we've known. A world where the rule of law supplants the rule of the jungle. A world in which the nations recognize the shared responsibility for freedom and justice. A world where the strong respect the rights of the weak." Events since this speech include (but are not limited to) the first invasion of Iraq, Sarajevo, the war in the former Yugoslavia, 9/11, the war in Afghanistan, the second invasion of Iraq, the bombing of Belgrade, Al Qaeda, Syria, and ISIS. The keywords that come to my mind when watching this speech are: will to power, hypocrisy, and greed. I also wonder whether Fukuyama's "end of history" was inspired by this speech. A new era did start, although not one of peace. Not one where the rule of law supplanted the rule of the jungle, and especially not one in which nations recognized their shared responsibility for freedom and justice, where the strong respect the rights of the weak. To believe so would be naïve. As psychoanalysts, what is our role (taking into consideration Jung's quote that "to cure one individual is to cure the world")? Is it possible to accomplish this? How can we accomplish "will to reciprocity" (Gross) and "plurality" (Samuels)?
21 On this, see Vice-President Dick Cheney's foreign policy post 9/11, which could be seen as a continuation of President Bush's *New Order*.

Bibliography

Beck, Ulrich. *The Metamorphosis of the World*. Cambridge: Polity Press, 2017.
Benjamin, Walter. "[Notes to] Der Sürrealismus." *GS II* 3 (1929): 1018–1044.
Chevalier, Jean, and Alain Gheerbrant. *The Penguin Dictionary of Symbols*. London: Penguin, 1996.

Craib, Ian. *Psychoanalysis and Social Theory*. Amherst: The University of Massachusetts Press, 1989.

Erickson, Erik Homburger. *Identity, Youth and Crisis*. New York, NY: W.W. Norton Company, 1968.

Frosh, Stephen. "Psychoanalysis and Psychosocial Studies." *Psychoanalysis Culture & Society* 13(4) (2008): 346–365.

Frosh, Stephen. "Transdisciplinary Tension and Psychosocial Studies." *Enquire* 6(1) (2013): 1–15.

Frosh, Steven, ed. *Psychosocial Imaginaries: Perspectives on Temporality, Subjectivities and Activism*. London: Palgrave Macmillan, 2014.

Fukuyama, Francis. *The End of History and the Last Man*. London: Penguin Books, 1992.

Fukuyama, Francis. *Identity: The Demand for Dignity and the Politics of Resentment*. London: Profile Books, 2018.

Giaccardi, C., and M. Magatti. *Generativi di tutto il mondo unitevi*. Milano: Feltrinelli, 2014.

Giegerich, Wolfgang. *The Soul Always Thinks*. New Orleans: Spring Journal, 2010.

Gross, Otto. *Selected Works 1901–1920*. Hamilton – New York: Mindpiece, 2012.

Heller, Agnes. *The Time Is Out of Joint*. Oxford: Rowman & Littlefield Publishers, 2002.

Hillman, J. *The Soul's Code: In Search of Character and Calling*. New York: Ballantine Books, 1997.

Jung, C.G. Except as below, references are to the Collected Works (CW) and by volume and paragraph number.

Jung, C.G. "Psychological Types." *CW* 6. Princeton: Princeton University Press, 1954.

Jung, C.G. "The Structure and Dynamics of the Psyche." *CW* 8. Princeton: Princeton University Press, 1960.

Jung, C.G. *Memories, Dreams, Reflections*. New York: Random House, 1963.

Jung, C.G. "Civilization in Transition." *CW* 10. Princeton: Princeton University Press, 1964.

Jung, C.G. "Psychology and Religion: West and East." *CW* 11. Princeton: Princeton University Press, 1969.

Jung, C.G. "The Symbolic Life." *CW* 18. Princeton: Princeton University Press, 1976.

Jung, C.G. "Mysterium Coniunctionis." *CW* 14. Princeton: Princeton University Press, 1977.

Kierkegaard, Soren. *Aut-Aut (Either/Or)*. Milano Mondadori, 2016.

Magatti, Mauro, and Chiara Giaccardi. *Generativi di Tutto il Mondo Unitevi*. Milano: Feltrinelli, 2014.

Orbach, Susie. "Democratizing Psychoanalysis." In *Relational Psychotherapy, Psychoanalysis and Counselling: Appraisals and Reappraisals*, ed. Dan Loewenthal and Andrew Samuels. New York and London: Routledge, 2014.

Progoff, Ira. *Jung's Psychology and Its Social Meaning*. London: Routledge, 2013 [1955].

Otto, Rudolf. *The Idea of the Holy*. New York: Oxford University Press, 1958.

Samuels, Andrew. *Politics on the Couch*. London: Profile Books, 2001.

Samuels, Andrew. *Politics on the Couch: Citizenship and the Internal Life*. London: Karnac Books, 2001.

Sarotte, Mary Elise. *The Collapse: The Accidental Opening of the Berlin Wall*. New York City: Basic Books, 2014.

Sebestyen, Victor. *Revolution 1989: The Fall of the Soviet Empire*. New York City: Pantheon Books, 2009.

Sonnevend, Julia. *Stories Without Borders: The Berlin Wall and the Making of a Global Iconic Event*. Oxford: Oxford University Press, 2016.

Watkins, Mary. "Dialogue, Development, and Liberation." In *Dialogicality in Development*, ed. I. Josephs. Westport, CT: Greenwood, 2003.

Chapter 5

The Impossibility of Freedom

From Psychoanalytical Conceptions to Political Objections

Ayse Devrim Basterzi and Gamze
Özçürümez Bilgili

Shape Matters!

> Our freedom does not lie outside us, but within us. One can be bound outside, and one yet still feel free since one has burst inner bonds. One can certainly gain outer freedom through powerful actions, but one creates inner freedom through symbols.
>
> (Jung 2009, 311)

We are in the heart of a plague where a tiny deadly virus tyrannizes the whole world. As science struggles to develop efficient vaccines and medications, leaving our houses freely, walking on the streets without face masks, and even *carefree* breathing are all strictly prohibited. The power of this virus is perhaps best reflected in its name, *corona*, because its shape resembles the royal crown. Royal crowns have long been a symbol of authority, power, and sovereignty. What other than the struggle for freedom against crowns is the whole written history of humanity? Shape matters!

The Reforms of Urukagina is a conical Sumerian tablet housed in the Louvre Museum, Paris (Frayne 2007). Urukagina was ruler of the city-state Lagash in Mesopotamia. The oldest known word for freedom comes from "ama-ar-gi" found on this conical tablet. Urukagina's code has been widely hailed as the first recorded specimen of government reform, seeking to achieve a higher level of freedom and equality. Urukagina did not describe himself as a "king"; he used the title of "governor" (ensi). He also released large segments of the population from such compulsory service as slaves for the king. Samuel Noah Kramer – one of the foremost authorities on the ancient Sumerian language and literature – describes the first use of the word "freedom" in written history in his seminal book *Sumerians* (1963, 79):

> Beginning about 2700 B.C., we find actual deeds of sales, including sales of fields, houses, and slaves. From about 2350 B.C., during the reign of

DOI: 10.4324/9781003168829-6

Urukagina of Lagash, we have one of the most precious and revealing documents in the history of man and his perennial and unrelenting struggle for freedom from tyranny and oppression. . . . Reading between its lines, we also get a glimpse of a bitter struggle for power between the temple and the palace – the "church" and the "state" – with the citizens of Lagash taking the side of the temple. Finally, it is in this document that we find the word "freedom" used for the first time in man's recorded history; the word is amargi, which, as has recently been pointed out by Adam Falkenstein, means literally *"return to the mother"*.

Amargi defines the condition of emancipated servants who returned to their own free families (Fischer 2005a). Early monarchs in history used indebtedness for taxes as a means of binding people in service to the king. To release one back to one's family was often literally to be returned to one's mother (Postgate 2017).

We encountered another conical shape associated with freedom in Ancient Rome: *pileus*. The pileus was a conical cap given to slaves after their manumission. Libertas is a Roman goddess and personification of liberty. She is usually portrayed with two accoutrements: the rod (the Vindicta) and the soft pileus (Tate 2005). The Vindicta ceremonial rod was used in the manumission of slaves. In the ceremony, the master would bring his slave to the lictor, who would proceed to lay the rod on the head of the slave and formally declare him free. When a slave obtained his freedom, he had his head shaved and wore instead of his hair an undyed pileus. Hence, a person with libertas in Rome means that she/he had been granted some degree of autonomy, unlike a slave. The pileus became a political symbol following the assassination of Julius Caesar in 44 BC; Brutus and his co-conspirators instrumentalized the symbolism of the pileus to signify the end of Caesar's dictatorship and a return to the (Roman) republican system.

In summary, both amargi and liberty originate from manumission. A person who had *Freiheit* in northern Europe or *Ama-ar-gi* in southern Mesopotamia was the one who could unite either by kinship or affection with a tribe of free people, unlike a slave. But freedom has another etymological origin. The English word *free* is related to the Norse *jri*, the German *frei*, the Dutch *vrij*, the Flemish *vrig*, the Celtic *rheidd*, and the Welsh *rhydd*. These words share an unexpected common root. They descend from the Indo-European word *priya* or *friya* or *riya*, which means dear or beloved. Hence, in English, *freedom* and *free* have the same etymology as *friend*, as in German *frei* and *freund*. Accordingly, "free" meant someone who was joined to a tribe of free people by ties of kinship and rights of belonging (Fischer 2005b). Then, we come across *amargi* once more, "returning to the mother". This brief journey to etymology shows that *liberty* means separation, whereas *freedom* implies uniting. Liberty embodies the privileges of independence, freedom, on the other hand, the rights of belonging.

History and language illustrate how deeply we are embedded in society and culture. Psychoanalysis, alongside these, focuses on personal history for excavating the hidden symbols of subjectivity. James Baldwin, American novelist, poet, and activist, wrote in his essay "Stranger in the Village" (1953): "People are trapped in history and history is trapped in them". The essay is about his experiences in Leukerbad, Switzerland, after he suffered a breakdown. Baldwin, declares that, while he is a stranger in the village of Leukerbad as the only black inhabitant, he also feels like a stranger in the village of the United States as an African American. More than 60 years have passed since, and one wonders if there is any substantial shift from the effects of centuries of oppression, discrimination, and racism. Some even claim that we are on the verge of a new world crisis, pointing back to the one which led Freud to write *Civilization and Its Discontents* (1930, 145):

> The fateful question for the human species seems to me to be whether and to what extent their cultural development will succeed in mastering the disturbance of their communal life by the human instinct of aggression and self-destruction. . . . And now it is to be expected that the other of the two 'Heavenly Powers', eternal Eros, will make an effort to assert himself in the struggle with his equally immortal adversary. But who can foresee with what success and with what result?

The final sentence was added in 1931, when the menace of Hitler was already beginning to be apparent.

Richard (2011) outlines the present-day forms of discontent in culture and claims that the modern crowd of individuals, who believe themselves to be autonomous, is far closer to the "masses" discussed by Freud than to the educated participative citizen, who is today being singled out for supposedly having definitively transcended the embodiments of totalitarianism, populism, and even the subtle destruction of democracy by democracy itself. To top it all off, in countries with authoritarian regimes, quarantine-like regulations that are dictated by the COVID-19 pandemic created an opportunity for restricting freedom of speech and freedom of peaceful assembly. As the authors of this chapter – two women scholars from the border between East and West – restriction of freedom is all too familiar to us. In the following, an overview of psychoanalytical conceptions on freedom is provided along with certain political objections.

Returning to Father

> Normally, there is nothing of which we are more certain than the feeling of our own self, of our own ego. This ego appears to us something autonomous and unitary, marked off distinctly from everything else. That such an appearance is deceptive.
>
> (Freud 1930, 65)

The naked truth is Freud saw no possibility that a free or autonomous ego might exist unless a therapeutic success is achieved through the *talking cure*. He sees the ego as a kind of vacant intersection for conflicting urges of varying frequency and intensity (Groves & Greif 1987). He characterizes consciousness as "a hierarchy of superordinated and subordinated agents, a labyrinth of impulses striving independently of one another towards action, corresponding with the multiplicity of drives and of relations with the outer world, many of which are antagonistic and incompatible" (Freud 1917a, 141). In a passage which portrays "mind" as little more than a mechanistic pleasure-seeker, Freud argues that

> all thinking is no more than a circuitous path from the memory of a satisfaction (a memory which has been adopted as a purposive idea) to an identical cathexis of the same memory which it is hoped to obtain once more through an intermediate stage of motor experiences.
>
> (1900, 602)

Here, there is little room for a free or autonomous consciousness, for the most that consciousness would seem capable of is mediating between drives and their objects.

In line with this conceptualization, there is his famous horse and rider analogy. This metaphorical allusion to the roles played by various parts of the mental apparatus appears more than once in Freud's writings, and each time the ego is equated with the rider, who, "if he is not to be parted from his horse, is obliged to guide it where it wants to go; so in the same way the ego is in the habit of transforming the id's will into action as if it were its own" (Freud 1923, 25). The judgment is damning and the implication clear: the ego is held hostage by powers originating elsewhere, such that, as the saying goes, the id pulls the strings and consciousness dances (Groves & Greif 1987). Moreover, the ego is "not only a helper to the Id; it is also a submissive slave who courts his master's love" (Freud 1923, 56). Shakow and Rapaport go so far as to say that Freud's "theory implies that these internal forces and their external objects are innately coordinated and that experience only modifies and amplifies this coordination during the developmental process" (1964, 114).

Determinism is the thesis that all events, including all mental events, are caused by prior events in the natural order of things. Freud asserts that determinism is definitive for the psychic life:

> There are also all the unfulfilled but possible futures to which we still like to cling in phantasy, all the strivings which adverse external circumstances have crushed, and all our suppressed acts of volition which nourish in us the illusion of Free Will.
>
> (1919, 236)

Spinoza, arguing along lines similar to Freud's, held that human beings believe themselves to be free only because they are unconscious of the causes whereby their actions are determined (1955). Such model posits that *consciousness* is only like the eye of the ego, merely "a sense organ which perceives data which arise elsewhere" (Freud 1900, 149). This "eye" receives information from both within and outside the organism, and its main purpose "is restricted once and for all to directing along the most expedient paths the wishful impulses that arise from the unconscious" (1900, 603). Then, for Freud, the ego is merely the locus for a meeting of conflicting urges such that one urge overpowers the other(s).

In sum, Freud's position is that "the ego is not master in its own house" (Freud 1917a, 143). To further fuel the fires of antifreedom, we can add to the fact that the ego is "caught between the two powerful forces of fate" (the id and superego) (Rank 1978, 4). In this view, the ego emerges as a response to the combined pressure of the id and the reality with which it must come to terms. In the *New Introductory Lectures on Psycho-Analysis*, it reads as follows:

> Thus the ego, driven by the id, confined by the super-ego, repulsed by reality, struggles to master its economic task of bringing about harmony among the forces and influences working in and upon it; and we can understand how it is that so often we cannot suppress a cry; "Life is not easy!" If the ego is obliged to admit its weakness, it breaks out in anxiety – realistic anxiety regarding the external world, moral anxiety regarding the super-ego, and neurotic anxiety regarding the strength of the passions in the id.
>
> (1933, 78)

Once again in his *New Introductory Lectures on Psychoanalysis*, Freud remarks that "the ego must on the whole carry out the id's intentions" (1933, 77), that it is at most a steering mechanism for urges which arise elsewhere. As an *ingenious modification of the id*, it is, as Anna Freud remarks, "made to measure, i.e., nicely adapted to hold the balance between the two forces" (1982, 143–144).

If we reduce Freudian psychology to only his words quoted previously, it could be claimed that there is no way to see the ego as an autonomous mental construct with agency. Ego is neither able to control passion nor the external world in the name of reason or freedom. The description of neuroses further outlines the siege ego is under:

> The ego feels uneasy; it comes up against limits to its power in its own house, the mind. Thoughts emerge suddenly without one's knowing where they come from, nor can one do anything to drive them away. These alien guests even seem to be more powerful than those which are at the ego's command. They resist all the well-proved measures of enforcement used by the will, remain unmoved by logical refutation, and are unaffected by the contradictory assertions of reality. Or else impulses appear which seem like those of a stranger, so that the ego disowns them; yet it has to fear them and take precautions against them. The ego says to itself: "This is an illness, a foreign invasion." It increases its vigilance, but cannot understand why it feels so strangely paralyzed.
>
> (Freud 1917a, 141–142)

Not surprisingly, the account presented thus far has led certain prominent observers such as Jung to accuse Freud of an overly simplistic positivism; he has been criticized for his determinism (Wilson 1981). Add to this criticism the fact that Freud's mechanistic annulment of the ego flies in the face of his whole therapeutic project. It is difficult to reconcile his apparent preference for determinism with his own action-oriented prescription for therapeutic success, the goal of which is:

> [T]o restore the ego, to free it from its restrictions, and to give it back the command over the id which it has lost owing to its early repressions. It is for this one purpose that we carry out analysis, our whole technique is directed toward this aim. We have to seek out the repressions . . . and urge the ego to correct them.
>
> (Freud 1926, 205)

Putting it simply, there is an ambiguity in Freud which sees individuals as free and developing subjects with a certain agency in their self-creation on the one hand and as passive and inert objects embedded in a swirling "labyrinth of impulses" (Freud 1917a, 141) on the other.

One could claim that Freud was not of one mind in his discussions of the individual in relation to freedom. Though he is a determinist in many respects, he does not throw up his hands and abandon the ego to the *powerful forces of fate*. The Freudian ego does have room to move and can develop greater degrees of flexibility and freedom. For all of Freud's stoical qualifications on both rationalism and the power of autonomous consciousness, something of the rationalist remains in him as a man of enlightenment. He offers a cultivation of "the patient's ego-*freedom*" (emphasis Freud's) as his therapeutic goal (1923, 50). This "rationalist" dimension of psychoanalysis is evident in Freud's description of the ideal relationship between the ego and its *adversaries* – the superego and the id. Overcoming these adversaries is "to strengthen the ego, to make it more independent of the super-ego, to widen its field of perception and enlarge its organization so that it can appropriate fresh portions of the id" (Freud 1933, 80). In a word, the goal of therapy is to increase the relative strength of the ego, to subject unconscious energies to the light of reason so that they might be brought under the ego's conscious control.

Obviously, dredging information up from the id is an insufficient condition for bringing the variety of urges into confrontation so that conflicts might be resolved. Rather, this information must be interpreted such that it can be integrated into the patient's life in a meaningful way, and the act of interpretation presupposes an executive capacity on the part of ego which accounts for the individual's ability to choose, to "find his own solutions" (Freud 1917b, 433), all of which explains Freud's therapeutic mission of giving the patient "ego *freedom* to decide one way or the other" (Freud 1923, 50). This is the core formula for Freud's psychoanalytic version of enlightenment.

Ansermet and Magistretti (2007) discuss Freud's core formula as follows:

> Thus we contend that the work of psychoanalysis is to decode internal reality by including the processes particular to somatic states, that is, by referring in a fundamental way to the drive dimension, so as to allow for direct access to external reality and make possible an action free of the fantasy constructions that so greatly interfered with it.
>
> (178)

Here, they stress that fantasy is in itself a synchronic constraint that disturbs the mental handling of external reality, placing it in a context that is determined and determinative (190). Hence, the work of analysis is aimed at making the person conscious of the phantasmatic nature of the scenario that he has constructed. Through a newly won freedom from the constraints of fantasy, the course of a psychoanalysis should enable the person to approach reality from a different perspective, to pass from the restrictions of an unconscious internal reality to the possibilities offered by whatever may happen. Ansermet and Magistretti, by pointing to *the work of psychoanalysis*, like a number of philosophers who have argued in different ways, among them Locke, Hobbes, Kant, Mill, and even Spinoza, imply that causal determinism is not only compatible with freedom but also a necessary condition for it. We become more free as we become more conscious of the causes for our actions. Thus, neither freedom nor agency is a condition which we absolutely have or lack but a matter of degree (Cavell 2003).

Freedom as a Concept

> The replacement of the power of the individual by the power of the community constitutes the decisive step of civilization.
>
> (Freud 1930, 95)

As outlined previously, Freud saw the individual as driven by bodily instincts and showed, precisely by way of his discovering the unconscious, that we are determined by irrational forces beyond our control, forces that are in no way governed by our own choices. Consistent with his aim, Freud saw freedom as an illusion and redefined it as the recognition of necessity. According to Binswanger (1963, 35–47), Freud is not wrong but incomplete: People also exist in the mode of *being-as-free*. The individual is determined by many factors such as constitution, personal history, culture, and so on, but what psychoanalysis considers psychopathological limitation is self-chosen unfreedom – that is, surrender to a constricted world of one's own structuring. The person structures the meaning context of his world and then gives up the freedom to understand or experience the world in any other way.

Eyal Rozmarin, in his seminal paper "To Be Is to Betray: On the Place of Collective History and Freedom in Psychoanalysis" (2011), explores the question how contemporary psychoanalysis might facilitate thinking on freedom:

> freedom is very much a concern of psychoanalysis, a discipline that both in theory and practice is dedicated to the plight of the individual who strives to be free of his misery. The subject of psychoanalysis, from the turn of the 19th century to the present, is founded in a struggle between choice and inevitability, will and repression, expression and prohibition. It is a subject constituted as a project of exploring the possibilities and limitations inherent in this dialectic, which is the fundamental dialectic of a self-consciousness aspiring for intelligibility and agency in a world that in its materiality, sociality, and historicity never fully makes sense and never fully yields. This is true of the originary hysteric who found herself as if possessed by unintelligible somatic demons, a possession Freud (1905) conceptualized as an embodiment of conflict between norm and desire.
>
> (320–321)

Rozmarin asserts that the conflict between norm and desire described by Freud is still true for the analytic subject of western late-capitalism who, when not similarly possessed by somatic and affective experiences that he has no means of apprehending, complains of a more diffuse yet no less incomprehensible sense of self-estrangement in a life full of confusion and antagonism.

Basescu (1974), in this regard, reflects on the subjective experience of freedom as not unitary but able to be described in a number of different but related dimensions. He defines one such dimension as the contrast between freedom "from" and freedom "to". *Freedom from* is related to the restrictions, constraints, and obligations imposed rather than chosen that exist as an obstacle to the experience of freedom. Similarly, responsibilities and emotional attachments, chosen but then regretted, result in the same thing. Relief from these felt burdens is then experienced as freedom. In contrast, *freedom to* focuses on one's availability to commit oneself. Active participation in the events of living, involvement in meaningful relationships, forming one's values are all accompanied by the experience of freedom. In fact, without this kind of participatory commitment, the simple freedom from constraint leads to the experience of emptiness. In one sense, freedom is greatest where most potentialities exist, where the widest range of choices prevails. However, if one has not committed oneself to choose or decide among the available potentialities, the experience is that of not using one's powers, of emptiness. This resonates with what Rozmarin (2011) refers to as "an incomprehensible sense of self-estrangement in a life full of confusion and antagonism". Such a state is one of potential power but actual powerlessness. On the other hand, as soon as commitment occurs to one set of potentialities, or possible modes of being, others are precluded and freedom is limited. In this regard, Sartre (1947) in *The Republic of Silence*, describes the concentration camp experience as one of maximum freedom. This is an extreme statement, but it is meant to convey that where *outer* freedom was nonexistent, where life and death were arbitrarily determined by forces outside oneself, where one could not function in terms of usual concerns, emotional ties, and commitments, one was most free to be accountable to oneself.

Sartre's statement brings to mind another dimension acknowledged by Basescu (1974), this time in terms of the contrast between *inner* and *outer* freedom. Basescu describes this dimension through Robert Bolt's drama, *A Man for All Seasons*, which effectively portrays his assertion. At the beginning of the drama, Sir Thomas More, as the king's best friend and prime minister, literally has the *keys of the kingdom*. It is not until the king demands of him a decision that goes against his convictions that More experiences the difference between *inner* and *outer* freedom. His continuing refusal to accede to the king's demand leads to increasing loss of *outer* freedom, imprisonment, and execution. However, accompanying this is an increasing sense of *inner* freedom to be true to himself, even in jail awaiting death. However, Hannah Arendt (1951, 148) reminds us that freedom is first established in our relationship with others, not ourselves:

> Human would know nothing of inner freedom if he had not first experienced a condition of being free as a worldly tangible reality. We first become aware of freedom or its opposite in our intercourse with others, not in the intercourse with ourselves. Before it became an attribute of thought or a quality of the will, freedom was understood to be the free man's status, which enabled him to move, to get away from home, to go out into the world and meet other people in deed and word.

Basescu's illustration for inner and outer dimension of freedom and Arendt's remark recall the views of Adorno (*Negative Dialectics* 1966 and *History and Freedom* 2006) and Foucault (*Society Must Be Defended* 2003 and *The Politics of Truth* 2007) on how subjectivity and notions of freedom change with historical shifts in power and government and what constitutes truth. In place of the power of absolute monarchy and the king's arbitrary rule, the enlightenment placed self-sufficient reason. The enlightenment is therefore a project of questioning the traditionally and religiously given, towards establishing means for defining free and independent truths. In the notion of reason, the Enlightenment finds the promise and realization of freedom for the king's discontented subjects. Then, reason is a king whose subjects are free. The bourgeois subject, increasingly free of the old ruler's power but now himself a sovereign with an interest in social order and a need to define a new mode of government, shapes the idea of government in his own image, the image of a subject free of arbitrary, exterior domination. He creates a new kind of truth and new means of power: his mode of government is self-government, and his truth is the truth of power invested in subjectivity itself.

By the end of the 19th century, the bourgeois subject leaps in feats of progress, sowing the seeds of reason and gaining control over nature, but he finds himself torn, uncertain, and unhappy. Because now he is imprisoned in his own norms and threatened by his own desires and those of others. He is deeply discontented in this civilization of his own making, a civilization that, as Levinas (2003) showed, is preoccupied with the wish to control the world and, necessarily unsuccessful, with generating means for binding the inevitable anxiety and sense of failure. It is at this historical junction that psychoanalysis emerges. In psychoanalysis join three constitutive questions of its epoch (Rozmarin 2011, 324): the focus on subjectivity as the legitimate origin and the core of experience, the recognition of the internalization and presence of social power in the subject, and the consequent preoccupation with the potential and limitations of reason, which is also a preoccupation with the question of freedom under the paradoxical condition of self-government.

Foucault (2003) describes in great detail how this historical turn is accompanied by a change in the way power is exercised and experienced. Rather than being subjected to the sovereign's techniques of bodily discipline and punishment, new state technologies created a self-governing subject who internalized "an obligation to be normal". Exterior power that regulates acceptable behavior became an interior power resulting in the pressure to conform to the norms of others. Adorno (1966), on the other hand, examines psychoanalysis' engagement with the question of social power as a subjective condition through the notion of the superego. The superego is the subjective trace of the old king, whose power has since been delegated to a matrix of social institutions, including – as Foucault argues, that which psychoanalysis has made its primary object – the family. What is freedom when the subject of psychoanalysis is under the spell of a superego that maintains an internalized pressure to comply with the demands of society for "normalcy" (these demands being most effectively communicated through the social institution of the family)?

Hanna Segal (1981, 51–53) emphasizes the liberating effects of psychoanalysis while taking superego into consideration as the inner authority

> Psychoanalysis belongs to the great scientific tradition of freeing thought from dogma, whether religious or arising out of an established scientific tradition itself. . . . In the same way in which the fear of an external authority can make us afraid to speak, the fear of an internal authority can make us afraid to think.

Segal continues addressing the possible oppressive influences of parenting by referring to Freud's definition of the superego and uses well-known mythological figures to corroborate her point of view: the superego, according to Freud, is the internalized parental figure carrying the parental prohibitions, which becomes a structure in our unconscious mind, but while the external authority can forbid only actions, including speech, this internal authority can forbid thought. The prohibition may be directed not only to certain thoughts – say, hostile thoughts directed against the parents and siblings – it may also be against searching for knowledge and thought itself. Some myths lend themselves to this interpretation – for instance, the myth of the Garden of Eden. Eating from the tree of knowledge is the first sin and leads to a fall from grace. The myth of the Tower of Babel – the pursuit of knowledge of God is punished by an attack on language – that is, verbal thought – an attack that leads to confusion of thought. The myth of Prometheus, punished for seeking fire – light. One root of the inhibition of thought and therefore of searching for knowledge is the demand felt to spread from the superego that it be deified. When Oedipus finds the answer to the riddle of the Sphinx, the Sphinx has to kill herself. A god cannot survive being known too well. Such a god is also a terrible god.

For Adorno (1966), the superego is the unconscious presence of social power. As an unconscious presence, the superego acts like a *spell*. Adorno uses the term *spell* often to describe the relations between the subject and the social, attempting to evoke a sense of subjective experience as constituted under the enigmatic effect of power that relies on dimming individual will and consciousness to maintain its effectiveness. He uses this term also because it evokes the opposite sense – spells can be lifted, conspiracies can be unmasked, truths can be discovered (Rozmarin 2011, 339). Both in *Negative Dialectics* and in *History and Freedom*, Adorno recognizes that psychoanalysis, at least initially, offered the promise of radical reason and full engagement with the idea of freedom:

> The Freudian school in its heroic period, agreeing with . . . Kant of the enlightenment, used to call for a ruthless criticism of the superego as something truly heteronomous and alien to the ego. The super-ego was recognized, then, as blindly, unconsciously internalized social coercion.
>
> (1966, 272)

Adorno claims that psychoanalysis failed to pursue this possibility and instead became a repressive discourse of social control. He also asserts that the idea of a 'pure subjectivity' is a perverted notion, a defense that denies the reality of the subject's inseparability from the world. The call for the elimination of the superego can be made only in relation to an ideal of subjectivity that is completely independent of its environment, a notion that for Adorno represents the bourgeois' delusions of grandeur and his denial of dependence. Any concept of freedom must concede that there is no subjective life outside the collective, that subjectivity and society are interdependent and co-created. This is illuminated by Adorno's further reflections on the superego as "the presence in the subject of all that is other than the subject, of the interests and needs of others, of sociality in general" (Rozmarin 2011, 327). This expanded notion of the superego points to the possibility of new forms of freedom. But, as Adorno suggests, this can be done only alongside a critique of society so far as society is organized around a notion that a conflict between the subject and sociality is universal and necessary.

Kristeva (2004) argues after the fall of the Berlin Wall, there are two different types of democratic societies with a sense of freedom. One of them is inspired by Kant, and the other leans on Heidegger. For Kant, freedom is not "an absence of constraint"; it is the possibility of self-beginning, "Selbstanfang". He subordinates the freedom of Reason, be it pure or practical, to a cause, divine or moral. Thus, he opens the way for praise of the enterprising individual for the initiative of the "self". In Arendt's words, this type of freedom calculates the consequences. Therefore, "to be free" would be to profit from adaptations to this logic of causes and effects and to the economic market. The second kind of freedom Kristeva (2004) defines is very different from the kind of *calculating logic* that leads to unbridled consumerism: it is the language-being, leaning on Heidegger's *Dasein*. The freedom of the language-being buds from the encounter between the self and the other. It is driven by a real concern for the uniqueness and fragility of each and every human life. It also requires special attention to gender and ethnic differences: men and women are considered in their unique intimacy rather than as simple groups of consumers. Kristeva concludes with reference to Heidegger's view on freedom (30–31);

> from that perspective what matters is the particular, the art of living, taste, leisure, the so-called "idle" pleasures, grace, pure chance, playfulness, wastefulness, our "darker side" even, or, to put it in a nutshell, freedom as the essence of "Being-in-the-World" prior to any "Cause".

Following Adorno's idea on "pure-subjectivity" and in line with Kristeva's contradicting "Self-Being" and "Language-Being" conceptualizations, Rozmarin elucidates the kind of freedom that he believes can be sought through psychoanalysis:

> The potential for freedom lies in the difference between a subject who is conscious of his embeddedness in society and his consequent dependence and responsibility and a subject intent on defying his embeddedness, destined to existence in self-estrangement in a foreign world that is hostile to his pleas.
> (328)

He passionately asserts that psychoanalysis must not condemn individuals to an illusion of separateness and unquestionable social normativity where the only question that the individual in trouble can ask is "What's wrong with me?" For there to be freedom we must also ask and allow the subject to ask "What's wrong with the world?" (329). This reminds Kohut's criticism of traditional psychoanalysis:

> Specifically, traditional analysis believes that man's essential nature is comprehensively defined when he is seen as "Guilty Man", as man in hopeless conflict between the drives that spring from the biological bedrock of homo natura and the civilizing influences emanating from the social environment as embodied in the superego. . . . Is it not the most significant dynamic-genetic feature of the Oedipus story that Oedipus was a rejected child? . . . The fact

is that Oedipus was not wanted by his parents and that he was put out into the cold by them. He was abandoned in the wilderness to die.

(1982, 402–404)

Kohut's assertion overlaps with Adorno's that a critique of the superego would have to be a critique of the society that produces the superego. For Kohut, the loss of protection by the parents and its transmutation into homicidal impulses toward the child by the father is the main theme of *Oedipus Rex*. Freud, on the other hand, focused on different aspects of this tragedy; the Oedipus complex, guilt, super-ego, and the repression theory (Goldberg 1989). The expression that contains both Kohut's and Adorno's outcries comes from the Soviet theatre and film director Grigori Kozintsev, best known for his book *Shakespeare: Time and Conscience* (1966), and for his films of *Hamlet* (1964) and *King Lear* (1970):

It is impossible to combine human worth with existence in a society based on a contempt for man. To reconcile oneself, to swim with the current, is igno-miny. It is better "not to be." . . . The society portrayed in Hamlet is frighten-ing neither by its resemblance to the savage existence of beasts of prey nor by the particular cruelty of bloodthirsty fiends, but by its callous emptiness. The noble and the spiritual have vanished from life. It is not bestial crimes that around horror; it is normal human relations which have lost their humanity.

(1966, 163)

Freedom in the Time of Corona: From Oedipus to *Pharmakos*

"They don't realize we're bringing them the plague." S. Freud

(Lacan 1996, 336)

There is an intriguing neglect in the psychoanalytic literature regarding a *plague*, which feeds the Freudian *determinism* immensely that *fate* is inevitable – even for a king – and there is no room for Free Will. Such a neglect is compelling because the sovereign in question is no other than one of the most influential characters in Freud's oeuvre, Sophocles' *Oedipus Rex*. Rather like the contagion that he causes in Thebes, Oedipus spreads infectiously throughout Freud's oeuvre (Cooke 2009).

Freud's first reference to the Sophoclean tragedy occurs in a posthumously pub-lished letter addressed to Wilhelm Fliess on 15th October, 1897:

I have found, in my own case too, [the phenomenon of] being in love with my mother and jealous of my father, and I now consider it a universal event in early childhood. . . . If this is so, we can understand the gripping power of Oedipus Rex, in spite of all the objections that reason raises against the pre-supposition of fate. . . . [T]he Greek legend seizes upon a compulsion which everyone recognizes because he senses its existence within himself. Everyone in the audience was once a budding Oedipus in fantasy and each recoil in horror from the dream fulfillment here transplanted into reality, with the full quantity of repression which separates his infantile state from his present one.

(Freud 1985, 270–273)

At the time, Freud was subjecting himself to self-analysis and reporting his findings in their regular correspondence to Fliess. Rejecting the prevalent interpretation of the play as a contrast between destiny and human will, Freud expanded this germ of a thought in *The Interpretation of Dreams* (1900). There he once again asserts that the long-lasting popularity of the play lies in witnessing the fulfillment of "those primaeval wishes of our childhood", the acts of parricide and incest unwittingly committed by the ill-fated Oedipus. To this first public exposition of *Oedipus Rex*, Freud later affixed a remarkable footnote in 1919 which, with an undisguised dream-pun, makes a claim for his work in *Totem and Taboo*:

Later studies have shown that the "Oedipus complex", which was touched upon for the first time in the above paragraphs in *The Interpretation of Dreams*, throws a light of undreamt-of importance on the history of the human race and the evolution of religion and morality.

(365)

The play opens with a priest beseeching the king of Thebes on behalf of the people to act to avert the "raging plague" which is relentlessly destroying the citizens. Oedipus has already dispatched Creon, his brother-in-law, to consult Apollo's oracle at Delphi and is awaiting the answer. Upon his return, Creon announces Apollo's instructions (Cooke 2009, 79): "Drive the corruption from the land,/don't harbour it any longer, past all cure,/don't nurse it in your soil – root it out!" According to Apollo's proclamation, the plague will recede only when Laius' murderer is found and the crime is atoned for. Through interrogating the blind seer Teiresias and learning new revelations from other sources, Oedipus at last discovers his true ancestry. Jocasta hangs herself, and Oedipus stabs out his eyes. He surrenders his sovereignty and leaves Thebes to begin a wanderer's life, as depicted in Sophocles' *Oedipus at Colonus*. His rapturous death at Attic Colonus alone liberates him from his homelessness.

In *Legacies of Plague in Literature, Theory and Film*, Cooke (2009) brings to light the neglected side of Sophocles' *Oedipus Rex*: it is that the physical body becomes the locus where the state's metaphorical disease is inscribed and suffered (79). It seems to us here the "state's metaphorical disease" is the "normal human relations which have lost their humanity" (Kozintsev 1966, 163). Otherwise, how shall we think of parents, who happen to be the head of the state – the king and the queen – abandoning their own child to wilderness to die, so that the father defeats his own death? Only a society with utmost hypocrisy could turn a blind eye to such a vicious crime. *Something is rotten in the state of Thebes*. It looks like this terrible act is first *denied* and then *projected* onto Oedipus, making the victim himself the infectious example, tabooed taboo-breaker, carrier and cure of plague.

The relationship of plague with discourses of blame and acts of scapegoating has a long history. But it is in Sophocles' *Oedipus Rex* that the Greek word for scapegoat, *pharmakos*, finds one of its finest illustrations: Oedipus is the *pharmakos* in relation to the plague-ridden Thebes. The ancient Greek plague rituals suggest that where there is plague, there is a *pharmakos* to be found. The *pharmakos* supposedly carried plague out of the city, transferring the disease from the general populace to be concentrated in one body: their exclusion or death was supposed to be curative. That is to say, the *pharmakos* is both carrier of plague and cure; at the same time and in the same ritual, he or she is the poison to be removed and its antidote. Similar to *pharmakos* being the poison and the antidote, the ritual merges the symbolic and the literal in itself: the healthy body of the *pharmakos* is symbolically and metaphorically polluted with disease; they "embody" plague, but their death, also symbolic of the death of plague, is literal. This shifting from the literal to metaphoric and back again shows that plague marks a time when the distinctions between healthy/infected, symbolic/literal, community/individual are threatened. Such polarities usually establish and maintain order: they are the straitjackets for civilization. Hence, Freud argues in *Civilization and Its Discontents* (1930) that civilization is too costly; it is at the expense of freedom:

> Individual liberty is not an asset of civilization. It was greatest before there was any civilization. . . . With the development of civilization, it underwent restrictions, and justice requires that no one shall be spared these restrictions. . . . The urge for freedom is thus directed against particular forms and claims of civilization, or against civilization as a whole. It does not seem as though any influence can induce human beings to change their nature and become like termites; they will probably always defend their claim to individual freedom against the will of the mass.
>
> (95–96)

Time and again, plague is wielded as a political or rhetorical weapon in the service of social discrimination or stigmatization, fiercely restricting all kinds of individual freedom, even leading to total destruction. An echo of the *pharmakos* mechanism can be identified at work within Hitler's anti-Semitism: the Jews were depicted as the scourge of German Aryanism and their removal proposed as the cure. Used in this way, plague is frequently accompanied by the powerful "body metaphor", which renders a state, nation, or people the "body" that can be labeled "sick" or "healthy", thus making it, with plague alongside, a convenient vector for political and social rhetoric. The body metaphor is so ubiquitous, so familiar, that its status as metaphor, and therefore as a linguistic construct, is often obscured and the lines between real sickness and metaphorical sickness blur (Cooke 2009, 2). For example, appellations such as the "gay plague" swiftly make the transition from being a euphemism for AIDS and the people it affects to becoming a way of stigmatizing the gay community.

Today, with all the past and present, known and hidden events, it is evident that the *pharmakos* ritual is no ancient creation. It is still active as a strong and effective way of controlling people, robbing them of freedom. Concluding this chapter, we wish to exhibit just a few examples which provide a clear picture of how plague could be instrumentalized to further consolidate power through modern *pharmakoi*. We choose not to name the state that these examples are from because every state carries such a potential if the *right kind* of people are appointed and the masses support.

The following is the list of only few examples among hundreds regarding the period since COVID-19 was declared a pandemic (Annual Report of Amnesty International 2020).

In April 2020, the government used the COVID-19 crisis to further crack down on the opposition, banning several opposition-run municipal donation campaigns and launching investigations into pandemic fundraising efforts by the mayors of . . .

A disciplinary investigation initiated by the Council of Judges and Prosecutors against the three judges who on 18 February acquitted the . . . trial defendants, including civil society leader . . . The investigation followed the President's public criticism of the acquittal decision.

In July 2020, Parliament passed a law changing the structure of bar associations. Thousands of lawyers protested and 78 out of 80 bar associations signed a statement opposing the reform. The new law weakens the associations' authority and independence.

Criminal investigations and prosecutions under anti-terrorism laws and punitive pre-trial detention continued to be used, in the absence of evidence of criminal wrongdoing, to silence dissent.

Under the guise of combating "fake news", "incitement" or "spreading fear and panic", the authorities used criminal law to target those discussing the COVID-19 pandemic online. The Cyber Crimes Unit of the Interior Ministry alleged that 1,105 social media users had made "propaganda for a terrorist organization", including by "sharing provocative COVID-19 posts" between 11 March and 21 May; reportedly 510 were detained for questioning.

In October, the President targeted the . . . Medical Association and called its new chair "a terrorist" after the . . . Medical Association repeatedly criticized the government's response to COVID-19.

Journalists and other media workers remained in pre-trial detention or served custodial sentences. Some prosecuted under anti-terrorism laws were convicted and sentenced to years of imprisonment, their legitimate work presented as evidence of criminal offences.

In April 2020, a senior state official at the Religious Affairs Directorate blamed homosexuality and people in extra-marital relationships for the spread of HIV/AIDS. He urged followers to combat this "evil" in a Friday sermon focusing on the COVID-19 pandemic, a call supported by the President. Bar associations criticizing the statements faced criminal investigation under Article 216/3 of the Penal Code that criminalizes "insulting religious values".

In March 2020, for the second year running, the authorities banned the International Women's Day march in . . . Police used tear gas and plastic bullets to disperse peaceful protesters who had defied the ban.

In August 2020, suggestions by some politicians in the ruling . . . Party to withdraw from the . . . Convention sparked country-wide demonstrations. Women's rights organizations criticized the lack of implementation of the Convention, including an adequate response to rising domestic violence during COVID-19 restrictions. Finally in April 2021, by a Presidential decree . . . withdrew from the . . . Convention.

We would like to add this last example just to give a crude idea about the state of academic freedom: Mr. . . ., who has ties to the ruling . . . Party, was appointed as rector to the most prestigious University in . . . by presidential decree on 2 January 2021. According to faculty, Mr. . . . was the first rector chosen outside the university since the 1980 coup d'état. In a shared statement, faculty regarded the appointment as a violation of "academic freedom and scientific autonomy, as well as the democratic values" of the . . . University. After police harshly dispersed protests at the campus on January 4, the . . . prosecutor at 3 a.m. on January 5 issued arrest warrants and ordered the confiscation of cellphones, laptops, and data storage devices of at least 28 students, allegedly at the request of the city's governor. At around 5:30 a.m., police raided at least 17 houses, in a few cases the wrong houses, and broke down doors, and in one case walls, to arrest students who took part in protests a day before. Also, as part of an art exhibition organized for the protest, artwork on campus reportedly depicting the Kaaba alongside a LGBT flag and a figure of Shahmaran led to the arrest of four students, who were in the exhibition team. . . . Ministry of Interior . . . referred to the arrested students as "four LGBT perverts", causing Twitter to later restrict his tweet. After this event, . . . University LGBT Studies Club was closed by order from the appointed rector. President . . . said that "a routine appointment" was "being used to provoke the universities." He also called protestors "terrorists" and denounced LGBT youth . . . authorities have placed hundreds of student protesters under possible criminal investigation. As of July 2021, protests by students and faculty outside the rector's office still continue.

We conclude this chapter by commemorating Eric Garner and George Floyd, whose last words were: "I can't breathe!"

References

Adorno, T. 1966. *Negative Dialectics*. Ed. Ashton, E. New York: Continuum.

Adorno, T. 2006. *History and Freedom*. Ed. Livingstone, R. Cambridge: Polity Press.

Amnesty International Turkey 2020. www.amnesty.org/en/countries/europe-and-central-asia/turkey/report-turkey/

Ansermet, F. & Magistretti, P. 2007. *Biology of Freedom: Neural Plasticity, Experience and the Unconscious*. London: Karnac.

Arendt, Hannah. 1951. *The Origins of Totalitarianism*. New York: Harcourt Brace.

Baldwin, James. 1953. Stranger in the Village. *Harper's Magazine*.

Basescu, S. 1974. The Concept of Freedom. *Contemp Psychoanal*, 10:231–238.

Binswanger, L. 1963. *Being-in-the-World*. New York: Basic Books.

Cavell, M. 2003. Freedom and Forgiveness. *International Journal of Psycho-Analysis*, 84(3):515–531.

Cooke, Jennifer. 2009. *Legacies of Plague in Literature, Theory and Film*. New York: Palgrave Macmillan.

Fischer, D.H. 2005a. *Liberty and Freedom*. Oxford University Press, 2005.

Fischer, D.H. 2005b. Freedom's Not Just Another Word. *New York Times*. www.nytimes.com/2005/02/07/opinion/freedoms-not-just-another-word.html.

Foucault, M. 2003. *Society Must Be Defended: Lectures at the College de France 1975–76*. Ed. Macey, D. New York: Picador.

Foucault, M. 2007. What Is Critique (A lecture first published in the Bulletin de la Societe francaise de philosophie, 1990). In Hochroth, L. & Porter, C. (Eds.). *The Politics of Truth*. Los Angeles, CA: Semiotext(e).

Frayne, D.R. 2007. The Reforms of Urukagina. https://cdli.ucla.edu/search/search_results.php?CompositeNumber=Q001124.

Freud, Anna. 1982. *The Ego and the Mechanisms of Defense*. New York: International Universities Press.

Freud, Sigmund. 1900. *The Interpretation of Dreams*. Standard Edition, IV–V:603. London: Hogarth Press, 1953.

Freud, Sigmund. 1917a. *A Difficulty in the Path of Psychoanalysis*. Standard Edition, XVII:137–144. London: Hogarth Press, 1955.

Freud, Sigmund. 1917b. *Mourning and Melancholia*. Standard Edition, XIV. Trans. James Strachey. New York: W. W. Norton & Company, 1990.

Freud, Sigmund. 1919. *The 'Uncanny'*. Standard Edition, XVII:217–256. London: Hogarth Press, 1961.

Freud, Sigmund. 1923. *The Ego and the Id*. Standard Edition, XIX:1–59. London: Hogarth Press, 1961.

Freud, Sigmund. 1926. *Inhibitions, Symptoms and Anxiety*. Standard Edition, Volume XX. London: Hogarth Press, 1986.

Freud, Sigmund. 1930. *Civilization and Its Discontents*. Standard Edition, XXI:64–146. London: Hogarth Press, 1961.

Freud, Sigmund. 1933. *New Introductory Lectures on Psychoanalysis*. Standard Edition, XXIII:1–182. London: Hogarth Press, 1961.

Freud, Sigmund. 1985. *The Complete Letters of Sigmund Freud to Wilhelm Fliess: 1887–1904*. Trans. Jeffrey Moussaieff Masson. Cambridge, MA: The Belknap Press of Harvard University Press.

Goldberg, C. 1989. The Shame of Hamlet and Oedipus. *Psychoanalytic Review*, 76(4): 581–603.

Groves, W.B. & Greif, G.F. 1987. Freud and Freedom. *Psychoanal. Contemp. Thought*, 10(1):69–101.

Jung, C.G. 2009. *The Red Book: Liber Novus*. Philemon series. Shamdasani, S. (Ed.) (M. Kyburz & J. Peck, Trans.). New York: W. W. Norton & Co.

Kohut, H. 1982. Introspection, Empathy, and the Semi-Circle of Mental Health. *International Journal of Psycho-Analysis*, 63:395–407.

Kozintsev, Grigori. 1966. *Shakespeare: Time and Conscience*. Trans. Vining, Joyce. New York: Hill and Wang.

Kramer, S.N. 1963. *The Sumerians: Their History, Culture, and Character*. Chicago, IL: University of Chicago Press. p. 79. ISBN 0226452387.

Kristeva, J. 2004. Thinking About Liberty in the Dark Times. The Holberg Prize Seminar 2004.

Lacan, J. 1996. *Écrits: The First Complete Edition in English*. New York: W. W. Norton.

Levinas, E. 2003. *On Escape*. Ed. Bergo, B. Stanford, CA: Stanford University Press.

Postgate, N. 2017. *Early Mesopotamia Society and Economy at the Dawn of History*. London: Routledge.

Rank, O. 1978. Truth and Reality. New York: W. W. Norton.

Richard, F. 2011. The Present-Day Forms of Discontent in Culture. *Journal of Psychoanalytic Studies Current Perspectives*, 11:6–17.

Rozmarin, E. 2011. To Be Is to Betray: On the Place of Collective History and Freedom in Psychoanalysis. *Psychoanalytic Dialogues*, 21:320–345.

Sartre, J.P. 1947. *The Republic of Silence*. New York: Harcourt Brace.

Segal, H. 1981. Psychoanalysis and Freedom of Thought. In Sandler, J. (Ed.) (1989). *The Dimensions of Psychoanalysis*. London: Karnac Books.

Shakow, D. & Rapaport, D. 1964. *The Influence of Freud on American Psychology*. Psychological Issues, Monograph 13, 4/1. New York: International Universities Press.

Spinoza, de B. 1955. *Chief Works*. New York: Dover.

Tate, Karen. 2005. *Sacred Places of Goddess: 108 Destinations*. New York: CCC Publishing.

Wilson, C. 1981. *The Quest for Wilhelm Reich*. Garden City, NY: Anchor Press/Doubleday.

Chapter 6

Individuation, Textuality, and Sexuality in Ursula Le Guin's *Lavinia*

Roula-Maria Dib

Ursula Le Guin's *Lavinia* is a novel about freedom via the process of creative, imaginative writing as much as it is about Lavinia the heroine – as opposed to Lavinia the shadow who appeared in the background of Vergil's *Aeneid*. The novel is about the freedom and existence granted to heroes and heroines, and it reveals how liberty – and reality – lies in fantasy and fiction. It does not matter to the author whether Lavinia had actually ever existed historically, because the way we know her is through the medium of text – through the *Aeneid*, the epic that is all about heroes of war, in which she is merely a silent character: her existence is confined within the lines of the poem, and Vergil had invented her (or had he?). According to *Lavinia*, Vergil had sat down at a table, started to write, and she came to him of her own accord. This is one thing about which Le Guin has always been quite clear: that imaginative storytelling – when properly done – is a process of exploration and discovery, not that of goal-directed making. It is what Jung and the post-Jungians call active imagination, which, as I will argue, paves the way for different freedoms through textual sluices.

Overall Summary of the Novel

In 'The Carrier Bag Theory of Fiction', Le Guin suggests that the earliest form of art and culture is the story. Le Guin speculates on the possibility of having two original cultural tales: that of the more masculine, heroic *spear* (war stories/ patriarchy) and that of the carrier bag, where un-associated things are put together (like characters in a story), rendering the sack 'ultimately behind the literary form of the novel, a form distinguished by relationships between characters.'[1] Not only does *Lavinia*, the novel, originate in a feminine, eros-charged 'carrier bag' of the heroine, but so does her kingdom (Lavinium) and its culture. More interestingly, the novel shows how the advent of Lavinium is not prophesied by an oracle but by a poet.

In *Lavinia*, the author makes a 'love offering' to the female character who is almost forgotten in the *Aeneid*, but who also makes a return away from the meek and demure diffidence that the epic poem labeled her with. In the novel, narrated by the heroine herself, Lavinia first appears as a young teenage princess living in

DOI: 10.4324/9781003168829-7

Latium with her loving father, King Latinus, and her emotionally unstable mother, Queen Amata (both of whom she refers to by their first names). Lavinia is an independent girl endowed with the gift of prophesy, which she inherited from her father; thus, she is assigned with performing and leading the palace's daily religious tasks. In the beginning of the novel, Latium had been quite peaceful and war free, so the princess would roam around freely, traveling to the sacred forest (Albunea) with only one of her maids for receiving prophetic visions. Lavinia continuously refuses her suitors, including her arrogant cousin Turnus, whom her mother is deeply obsessed with. However, on one night spent in Albunea, Lavinia has in vision in which she meets Vergil, and she engages in a series of conversations with him about her life according to the *Aeneid*. The poet warns her about the impending war with the Trojans, and she accepts the fact that she will be married to a foreigner, the Trojan warrior Aeneas, until he dies three years later. After their first encounter, Lavinia and Vergil meet a few times before his 'death' (he had traveled to the distant past to tell her about her life), and more details are told and created as the worlds of both the poet and the heroine intertwine. During this time, Vergil is surprised at how much of an 'unkept promise' Lavinia turns out to be, referring to how unjustly the poem had portrayed her. After much of what the poem states happens with Lavinia, her brief but happy marriage with Aeneas results in a son, and both live under the corrupt rule of Aeneas's older son Ascanius, who threats to take Lavinia's son away from her after the death of his father. To escape Ascanius's control, Lavinia and her son then decide to seek freedom by going into self-imposed exile in the forest for a few years, after which her son becomes a wise, just, and graceful king.

From Epic to Novel: The Spear vs. the Carrier Bag

Lavinia lives her own poem as she creates it and becomes aware of it through her encounters with Vergil. Unlike her voiceless, barely palpable existence in *The Aeneid*, Lavinia is given a voice and presence in Le Guin's novel, in which she says:

> If you'd met me when I was a girl at home you might well have thought that my poet's faint portrait of me, sketched as if with a brass pin on a wax tablet, was quite sufficient: a girl, a king's daughter, a marriageable virgin, chaste, silent, obedient, ready to a man's will as a field in spring is ready for the plow.[2]

In the beginning, upon her first stepping out of the poem version and into the novel, Lavinia seems to be limited by the boundaries of her own destiny, drawn by Vergil in the *Aeneid*, which is mainly the story of Aeneas. In the novel, Lavinia's encounters with Vergil help her speak and create her own destiny through her vivid active imagination; Vergil confesses that the unconfined quality of her existence is not bound to the lines of the poem: 'But that's not where it ends for you, Lavinia.'[3] Perhaps this is a hint at the continuity of her life through the liberating format of the novel. In order to achieve this liberating function, Le Guin weaves the story in non-conventional form by including the element of active imagination, offering the heroine a unique dimension of 'possibilities-become-worlds.' Lavinia is given life in an alternative form of writing mirroring an alternative form of reality.

It is my contention, then, to show that the freedom given to the female protagonist within this new dimension is the product of vivid active imagination, textual individuation, and the realm of possibilities rendered by the combination of reality, surreality, and possibilities within the novel's quantum-like structure.

In the beginning of the novel, Lavinia states:

> And yet my part of them, the life he gave me in his poem, is so dull, except for the one moment when my hair catches fire – so colorless, except when my maiden cheeks blush like ivory stained with crimson dye – so conventional, I can't bear it any longer. If I must go on existing century after century, then once at least I must break out and speak. He didn't let me say a word. I have to take the word from him. He gave me a long life but a small one. I need room, I need air.[4]

Indeed, Lavinia is referring to the *Aeneid*, which is a patriarchic celebration of the victories of male heroes in war, told by a man and about men (the spear stories mentioned earlier). It is also the original home of Lavinia's existence:

> No doubt someone with my name, Lavinia, did exist, but she may have been so different from my own idea of myself, or my poet's idea of me, that it only confuses me to think about her. As far as I know, it was my poet who gave me any reality at all.[5]

Lavinia the novel is a rewriting and redemption of the silenced feminine in the epic, with a heroine who is aware of this redemptive act. The new form is an attempt at redeeming a history told through fiction but this time focusing on a different kind of truth hidden in a different kind of fiction. According to Marc Slavin:

> When it is re-visioned in terms of the poetic basis of mind, 'fiction' becomes the condition of possibility for case history. The imaginal becomes the a priori of the historical. It does not ensconce itself as noumena, but, in a *quasi-transcendental* or de-literalized sense, as differend, the border of unfolding phenomena.[6]

What happens with Lavinia, as well as Le Guin (through Vergil), is a re-visioning, also 'in terms of the poetic basis of mind' that offers possibilities for a resurfacing of a history suppressed through silence. And fiction as a new hosting environment for history – or rather, *herstory*. Lavinia's imaginal realm of story-making was indeed, as Slavin would call it 'the border of unfolding phenomena'. Perhaps it would help to look more closely at the history of story making within early societies in Ursula Le Guin's 'The Carrier Bag Theory'. Le Guin reflects on the way stories have molded the patriarchal perspective on the origins of culture. She mentions that hunting (traditionally a male role) has left many artifacts such as the spear, one of the earliest tools used by humans. With the spear culture comes a legacy of stories teeming with details of excitement and (male) heroism. But, Le Guin asks, are these the only types of stories that emerged from the earliest forms of culture? She invites her readers to think more deeply about humanity's first artifacts and visualize two types of stories rather than just the hunting-related ones – namely the ones stemming from the gathering tradition. She suggests that people probably invented other tools way before the spear: 'A leaf a gourd shell a net a bag a sling a sack a bottle a pot a box a container. A holder. A recipient.'[7] She proposes that parallel to the spear would probably be another invention: the carrier bag, which definitely does not elicit as many tales of drama, danger, and excitement as the spear; however, it is known for encasing and nurturing many unrelated things together: the diversity of objects inside a carrier bag is like the making of a novel, where characters are also homed together in one text:

> the natural, proper, fitting shape of the novel might be that of a sack, a bag. A book holds words. Words hold things. They bear meanings. A novel is a medicine bundle, holding things in a particular, powerful relation to one another and to us.[8]

The carrier-bag is the eros version of the logos-spear. Telling history through the *Aeneid*'s spear-story model is a telling of the battles and heroes – a reductionist approach Le Guin seeks to revise through the novel, which is like the carrier-bag. Lavinia's story, however, in its novel form, shows us that conflicts are not everything, and the overemphasis on details of the battles and heroes has muffled the voice and existence of the princess in the *Aeneid*. The silence of Lavinia in the *Aeneid* is the suppression of those tales of being that appear in the novel, which tells about wars but also about people, showing how 'One relationship among elements in the novel may well be that of conflict, but the reduction of narrative to conflict is absurd.'[9] Instead of being the warrior here, Lavinia as a heroine is the girl whom wars were fought for, 'the nobody that everybody was fighting a war about.'[10]

More Than a Novel: Active Imagination

According to Susan Rowland, 'active imagination is a way of improving and enhancing individuation,' which we can see the novel doing with Lavinia; myth-like in its archetypal manifestations, with its plot and characters, it is in an active dialogue and relationship with the *Aeneid*, the performance of a living conversation between Lavinia and Virgil. It is a self-realization of the heroine through the textual space she is offered by the writer. Ursula Le Guin creates this effect by practicing this form of active imagination while allowing the text to come to life, bringing the characters along with it and letting them perform their own active imagination through the conversations between Lavinia and Vergil. In doing so, the author endows the text with its own autonomy – her claim is that she was re-writing along Vergil, but the novel itself seemed to wake up to its own life: 'My desire was to follow Vergil, not to improve or reprove him. But Lavinia herself sometimes insisted that the poet was mistaken about some details – about the color of her hair, for instance.'[11]

Lavinia, freed in textuality, has emerged in the autonomy allowed her by active imagination that she performed as a character. Le Guin, by disclaiming the text and its details as her own property, simply starts freeing the heroine – an act of active imagination in itself, where the image (Lavinia) has its own autonomy. By not 'owning' the ideas in the novel, and by handing it over to Lavinia, Le Guin is not only presenting Lavinia as engaging in active imagination with the poet, but the author goes even further in showing how she herself has, like her protagonist, engaged in this practice, too, in perceiving the novel as a separate entity she engages with. This, again, echoes Susan Rowland:

> In effect, treat the image as the text of another, a missive from the unknown, unconscious psyche. Eventually the image with its overwhelming affect will truly show itself to be alive. Acting true to its autonomous archetypal nature, it will move, expand, breathe, develop, and may even speak.[12]

But how does Lavinia start the active imagination process? It starts with her gift, which annoyed her mother:

> My mother's anger was chafed by the idea that I had some gift like my father's of conversation with the spirits. It gave me a kind of uncanny importance, which she despised. I agreed with her in my heart: the importance was false. But the gift was real. And it was useful to me as my reason not to be always at home, dressed in white, the meek garlanded sacrifice, while the suitors paraded through and drank their wine, and Turnus flattered my mother and laughed with my father and looked at me as the butcher looks at the cow.[13]

Lavinia, filled with the emotional distress, dread, and sense of entrapment because of her mother's madness and obsession with marrying her daughter to her own relative, finally finds her own projection in Albunea, a sacred space in the forest where the gifted like herself may receive visions: her vision came in the image of Vergil as a dying poet, an incarnation of her own feelings. Albunea is where Lavinia prepares her mind to enter its imaginal space, during the time when her conscious mind is quieted and focused, allowing her ego to receive the guiding message from her unconscious. This is when Vergil becomes alive and real, enabling Lavinia to relate to him productively. Her active imagination comes into play, when it 'develops a relationship with an image that manifests part of the unknown and uncontrollable psyche; in other words, a symbol.'[14] From the beginning of the novel, Lavinia makes the link between Albunea and freedom:

> The walk there was an escape, too, a time of freedom.'[15] Her life in the castle, despite her father's doting and love, was a form of imprisonment for her: it was a place to stay until she is handed over to another suitor. However, Lavinia resorts to her special gift: 'All I wanted when I went there was to sleep there, in that silence, with freedom in Albunea those spirits around me, in the numen of Albunea. A night there clarified my heart and quieted my mind, so that I could come back home and do my duty.'[16]

During her retreat, the silent maiden of the *Aeneid* merges with the silence of Albunea, where she discovers the language of the archetypes within:

> I watched the light grow reddish across the misty pools, and listened to the troubled voice of the water. After a while I moved farther up the hill, where I could hear birds singing near and far in the silence of the trees. The presence of the trees was very strong. For the first time I wondered if I might hear the voice that my father heard speak from among them in the dark. The big oaks stood so many, so massive in their other life, in their deep, rooted silence: the awe of them came on me, the religion.[17]

Visions become meditations upon images with the appearance of Vergil. There are many layers of dreams being unfolded to unravel the 'textual' existence of Lavinia through the poet's imagination. At the same time, this existence is mirrored with that of the poet, who also appears to be a projection, a 'vision' whom Lavinia engages into conversations with. Vergil tells her that imagination is a whole world, one parallel to the one she was experiencing. But it is not a world of definite and determined details: 'Perhaps it never did – never will happen. You should not be concerned about it. I made it up. I imagined it. A dream within a dream . . . within the dream that has been my life.'[18] This is active imagination in the making, in the poet's brief explanation of his meditation upon an image, which, simultaneously, is what Lavinia also does: she is meditating on the image of the poet and engaging with it, bringing this unconscious element into consciousness, which is the projected image of Vergil, for 'the unconscious appears in projected and symbolized form, as there is no other way by which it might be perceived.'[19] Lavinia's active imagination opens the door to the world of possibilities that grants her some form of freedom: 'So my mind ran from possibility to possibility like a hare dodging hounds, while the three old women, the Fates, spun out the measured thread of what was to be.'[20] Lavinia does not want determined outcomes. She is intrigued by the idea that the poet is not a prophet, not an oracle, and she wants a different type of relationship with him, since he does not dictate her life to her or give her the final outcome of her destiny; instead, her life unravels through her conversations with him. He asks her: 'I am searching for my duty here. How much is it right for me to tell you? Do you want to know your future, Lavinia?'[21] To which Lavinia answers: 'I want to know what's right to do, but I don't want to know what's to come of it.'[22] This is the beginning of Lavinia's individuation, and she is ready to explore it with all its unfolding possibilities.

By going to Albunea on dark, starless nights, Lavinia delves into the depths of her unconscious, or, as Jung calls it 'the nocturnal side of the psyche,'[23] and sets up communication with it:

> And he sat up straighter, there on the dark ground, a shadow among shadows, and began to sing. . . . There was no tune to it. Its words were all the music of it, its words were its drumbeat, clack of the loom, tread of feet, oarstroke, heartbeat, waves breaking on the beach at Troy away across the world.[24]

This is what Robert A. Johnson would call a balancing act, where we find a 'constant flow of energy and information between the two levels as they meet in the dimension of dream, vision, ritual, and imagination.'[25] Lavinia's trips to the forest are a journey towards her visionary experiences, which are a conscious engagement with her unconscious through active imagination:

> I sat talking with a shadow, a dying man who had not yet been born and who knew my past and my future and my soul, who knew who it was that I should marry, the true hero. . . . And he said that perhaps he had imagined it, that it was a dream within a dream. And I had imagined it. It had not happened. It would not happen. False dreams, visions, follies.[26]

Le Guin's active imagination is very much alive through the character of Vergil, for she, too, not only narrates Lavinia's life story: she meets her, meditates upon her image, and gets to know her better as the story moves forward. The initial portrayal of Lavinia as a minor character of the *Aeneid* is limiting and inaccurate, manifested by the patriarchic gaze (like that of Turnus, her cousin-suitor) that favors battles: 'Turnus would certainly have recognised the poet's portrait of me as a shrinking silent maiden.'[27] Through the character of Vergil in the novel, however, the author gets to know Lavinia better and discovers features that were previously unknown – she allows the novel to portray the princess more accurately. This is expressed by Vergil:

> I know very little. And what I thought I knew of you – what little I thought of at all – was stupid, conventional, unimagined. I thought you were a blonde! . . . But you can't have two love stories in an epic. Where would the battles fit? In any case, how could one possibly end a story with a marriage?[28]

What shows here is the 'reality' of people and characters in active imagination. It is an autonomous reality, one that is independent from the poet's imagination, for, as Jung claims in his 1935 Tavistock lectures, '*Active imagination*, as the term denotes, means that the images have a life of their own and that the symbolic events develop according to their own logic.'[29] This is another facet of the freedom Lavinia is given through active imagination and the text: as a living textual entity, she is able to have a complete life of her own, surprising even her 'maker(s)' (the poet and the author). The active imagination of Lavinia, as well as Le Guin in writing the novel, is an act of freeing the heroine from the silent bonds of the epic poem: 'Though all my poet sang was true and is true, yet there are small mistakes in the truth of it, and I have tried to mend those tiny rents in the great fabric as I tell my part in it.'[30] By 'mending' through her own telling of the story, Lavinia refers to the reformative structure of the novel.

The guiding voice of the vision is not that of an oracle, but that of a poet, Vergil, who tells (but does not in any way dictate) Lavinia about her life: 'It was the poet who spoke. It was all the words of the poet, the words of the maker, the foreteller, the truth teller: nothing more, nothing less. But was I myself any more, or less, than that?'[31] The sense of the supernatural/divine in the novel lies in the poet, not in the gods governing the wars and male heroes as in the *Aeneid*. And while the heroine's character is presented differently in the novel than it was in the *Aeneid*, the most striking aspect of the novel is not her character but her conversations with her 'maker', Vergil. Lavinia's acceptance of her destiny is what helps her become creatively involved with it, freeing her in the resulting story. Her assent is testimony to her creative engagement in active imagination, which leads to her internalization and articulation of experience – textually. With this acquiescence, Lavinia takes a very important step: 'As the first step in engaging the transcendent function, the ego turns to the unconscious with an open and receptive attitude.'[32]

The creative power of active imagination also appears when Vergil uses the term 'invent' as he refers to Camilla, a warrior princess, in one of his poems: 'I suppose I did invent her. But I liked her.' He tells Lavinia, who asks him astonishingly, 'Invent her?', to which he answers: 'I am a poet, Lavinia.'[33] The answer pleases Lavinia and suddenly gives her the epiphanic connection between poetry and prophesy: 'I liked the sound of the word, but he saw I did not know it. "A vates," he said. I knew that word of course: foreteller, soothsayer.'[34] Vergil automatically replaces the oracle and is actually referred to as an oracle by the people of Lavinium later in the novel: 'An oracle has spoken. A promise has been given. If you defy the voice that guides us, if you break the treaty I made, you do wrong.'[35]

On the fantasy process, or active imagination, Jung mentions that 'We have to conceive of these processes not as immaterial phantoms we readily take fantasy-pictures to be, but as something corporeal, a "subtle body", semi-spiritual in nature.'[36] This was the portrayal of the poet in *Lavinia*: he was a vision, but one that is a mix between the ethereal and physical. Vergil was a summoning of worlds, a psychoid phenomenon – an unconscious content made conscious and 'real' in the empirical sense:[37]

> He was there, the shadow. He stood between me and the altar. His tall form was vague in the grey starlight. . . . The nod of a head is such a small thing, it can mean so little, yet it is the gesture of assent that allows, that makes to be. The nod is the gesture of power, the yes. The numen, the presence of the sacred, is called by its name.[38]

So he was a 'shadow,' and like the dark Albunea night, symbolized unconscious content. But he had a physical form, along with so much authority and power assigned to its materialized movements. Vergil becomes the noumenal made 'present,' which is a sacred power that is able to guide and create Lavinia's destiny. She asks him: ' "Wait – Only tell me – your poem, my poem, did you finish it?" He seemed to nod, but I could hardly see him, a tall shadow in shadows.'[39] So there was an answer there, within Lavinia, and there was a destiny and presence still in the making because she cannot see the answer clearly in the image, but it had to be freed from within her own self in order to project in front of her.

The poet himself, simultaneously being Lavinia's projected inner image and the mouthpiece of Le Guin, expresses this desire for redemption and freedom. The *Aeneid* did not give the whole picture of Lavinia, who was buried within verse, 'unfinished' and 'incomplete.' Through her practice of active imagination during her nights at Albunea, however, the poet asks her to return: ' "Oh my dear," he said, still very softly. "My unfinished, my incomplete, my unfulfilled. Child I never had. Come back once more." "I will." '[40] Her story must expand and continue within new lines, out of the patriarchic form of the epic, which, as mentioned earlier, is mainly concerned with tales of male heroes in battle. The space allowed in the novel is not a matter of format, of breaking from the tradition based on the hunter's craft, and turning to the carrier-bag culture, the culture that is more of a 'recipient', away from the 'botulism' of the epic-hero culture, as noted by Virginia Woolf. Moreover, Le Guin states that this break from the spear-culture gives freedom to characters as 'people':

> it's clear that the Hero does not look well in this bag. He needs a stage or a pedestal or a pinnacle. You put him in a bag and he looks like a rabbit, like a potato. That is why I like novels: instead of heroes they have people in them.[41]

Textuality and Existence

Lavinia learns to summon the dying poet (although he appears to her as a guest from the future, in a past that existed before he was even born). She becomes in contact with her inner guide, which later creates the wisdom that will free her from the clutches of Ascanius and the history of battles in verse, in which she barely had an existence. With time, this creates an awareness of her own textuality. She is guided by her 'poet' and inner 'storyteller' to continue her written life:

> After a long time, when the constellations had changed, I spoke to the poet, not aloud but in my mind. 'Dear poet, all you told me came to be. You guided me truly, up to Aeneas' death. Since then I've let others lead me. But I go astray. I can't trust Ascanius: he doesn't know his own enmity to Silvius. I wish you were here to guide me now. I wish you could sing to me.'[42]

Lavinia reflects on the two makers of her reality, which juxtapose her sexual and textual awakening:

> My question is which of them did I more truly love? And I cannot answer it. One was my husband, the beautiful man whose flesh my flesh enclosed to make my son in me, the author of my womanhood, my pride, my glory; the other was a shadow, a whisper in shadows, a virgin's dream or vision, yet the author of all my being. How can I choose? I lost them both so soon. I knew them only a little better than they knew me. And I remember, always, that I am contingent.[43]

The makers left her, but Lavinia remained, existing and conscious enough to realize her own being:

> in giving up my girl self and taking on the obligations of womanhood I found myself freer than I had ever been. If I owed duty to my husband, it was very easy to pay. And as understanding grew between us and we came to trust each other, there were no restraints on me at all but those of religion and my duty to my people. I had grown up with those, they were part of me, not external, not enslaving; rather, in enlarging the scope of my soul and mind, they liberated me from the narrowness of the single self.[44]

Here the textuality is juxtaposed with sexuality, as she is aware of her new level of transformation from girl to woman. And so it happens, like a poem with words and images, Lavinia continues to create her own being:

> Words and images drifted through my mind. The words were, Speak me! Then they turned and seemed to reverse themselves as they drifted away: I say your being. I saw Aeneas' shield very clearly for an instant, the turn of the she-wolf's head to her bright flank. I felt myself lying on a vault like a turtle's shell of earth and stone that arched over a great dark hollow.[45]

So Lavinia ultimately becomes her own creator. Her practice of active imagination in Albunea was the first step towards individuation, as her engagement with the poet is the initial step showing her integration of unconscious material with consciousness. When she had the poet with her, she had asked him to guide her (but not tell her the result of her destiny): 'A chill of fear had come into me. Too much was coming to me, too soon. I wanted the poet to tell me what was coming, and I didn't want it'.[46] She was ready for the journey and accepting of the forthcoming loss, pain, and violence as aspects of the world she is in; she did not strive, in any way, to avoid these harsh realities, but she knows how to bravely – and freely – act within them. She does not flee the patriarchic kingdom of her stepson Ascanius in the beginning but instead continues to live within it but with the authority and strength of piety of her voice: it was the voice of a princess (King Latinus's daughter), a queen (wife of Aeneas, and later mother of King Silvius), and a gifted visionary. What makes her stand out is that she neither flees nor gives in to silence but with the power of her visions strengthens her voice and overcomes the boundaries in her life. She dives in, rather than out. She found freedom during her own self-imposed exile; she chose her own destiny – and her conversations with the poet helped her discover that. She finally realizes this hidden freedom within: 'It was I who had the dream and heard the voice.'[47]

The Freedom in Quantum Space

Within this unique and autochthonous dimension of possibilities offered by Le Guin's novel is a non-conventional form of fiction resembling the laws of quantum mechanics, bringing life and liberation to Lavinia through the novel's alternative forms of reality. As Rowland points out, 'quantum experiments showed that the observer is always implicated in what is observed,'[48] and there is no separation. By giving Lavinia a voice through the novel, and by giving Vergil a voice through Lavinia, the novel steps into different levels and dimensions of reality where the observer and the observed work together as one force (e.g. Vergil working with Lavinia to continue to story and Le Guin working with the voices of both to write the novel). This creation of space counters the problem of 'the positing of *one* level of reality as foundational to all others.'[49]

Quantum mechanics states that the roots of matter lie in non-matter, which perhaps can be applied to the realm of storytelling and novel writing. This causal relationship, then, between matter and non-matter, resembles Jung's theories on the relationship between psyche and matter, rendering the psyche an important, highly advanced matter-forming technology:

> The discovery of a realm of non-material forms, which exist in the physical reality as the basis of the visible world, makes it possible to accept the view that the archetypes are truly existing, real forms, which can appear in our mind out of a cosmic realm, in which they are stored. Thus, we can confirm here on the basis of the quantum phenomena Jung's view that 'it is not only possible but fairly probable, even, that psyche and matter are two different aspects of one and the same thing.'[50]

It is the revelation of the psychoid, the manifestation of this relationship between psyche and matter, which gave 'space' for Lavinia's voice. It is through the quantum method of the author's active imagination, imposed on her protagonist as well, that a conversation with Vergil changed the level – and perception of – freedom that Lavinia had. Reading *Lavinia* from this perspective allows us to look more closely at the role of active imagination in writing the novel, which in itself is also about (and the result of) the active imagination of the heroine. The appearance of the invisible and numinous figure of Vergil is the most important factor in granting Lavinia the space and freedom she never had in the *Aeneid*:

> Analytical Psychology, embodied in the archetype structure, leads us to the view that there is a part of the world that we can't see, a realm of reality that doesn't consist of material things but of non-material forms. These forms are real even though they are invisible, because they have the potential to appear in our mind and act in it.[51]

And it is through these 'potentials' that Lavinia's mind, voice, and life are expanded.

Le Guin here is a writer, rather than author – the difference in that there is a sense of observance, of witnessing what is happening rather than 'informing' the readers by writing *about* it. Le Guin herself remarks that 'This story is in no way an attempt to change or complete the story of Aeneas. It is a meditative interpretation suggested by a minor character in his story – the unfolding of a hint.'[52] In this way, the structure of the novel is quite similar to quantum mechanics, where also, as Rowland observes, 'Quantum physics discovered that some reality cannot be evaluated objectively or by absolute separation between the observer and the observed because the way phenomena are measured changes the results radically.'[53]

Another quantum concept appears through the visions of Albunea and her meetings with Vergil. Lavinia's story unfolds within the temporality of parallel worlds and epochs: 'I had had a dream about a man who was dying somewhere else, in some other time. Nothing to do with me. And for that I had come back here, with my silly basket of food.'[54] Vergil tells Lavinia, his summoner, that she lives in his past, 'Centuries, centuries!'[55] before he was born. She had called him to life, which in turn created her own life: 'I think I know why I came to you, Lavinia. I have wondered – Of all the people of my poem, why were you the one who called my spirit?'[56] Lavinia's summoning of the poet, albeit unconsciously, is a calling for freedom, through textual space.

Lavinia realizes truth in dreams, in the visionary:

> the things my poet had said to me came and went in my mind, sometimes seeming as real as they did when he spoke them, but more often fading away like the shreds of a dream that vanish as you try to remember them. It was a true dream, but you cannot live your life in a dream even if it be true.[57]

However, this truth in text must escape the realm of 'dreams' and must be realized as a 'reality.' It is active imagination, echoing with Le Guin's claim about truth in fantasy: 'fantasy is true, of course. It isn't factual, but it is true.'[58]

Lavinia shows the performative, life-giving aspect of writing rather than the boundaries of authorship that come with a text. The poet is not an oracle, does not offer any finite-ness to Lavinia's life, or even her destiny, although he guides her through many of her life's major details. Vergil's intention is shown to have a limit; Lavinia's life is not *dictated* to her, but rather, it is *made* by her through her conversations with Vergil's verse rather than his 'prophecy', allowing the 'otherness' of her existence to come through. The death of the poet is very significant of this, especially towards the end of the novel when he does not to 'finish' the story and when Lavinia is left to continue her life without him: 'But what am I to do now? I have lost my guide, my Vergil. I must go on by myself through all that is left after the end, all the rest of the immense, pathless, unreadable world.'[59] Her existence never ceases, although it changes form, and that is not done according to anything 'dictated' by Vergil, but rather, it is the evolution of her own being. She questions: 'What is left after a death? Everything else. The sun a man saw rise goes down though he does not see it set. A woman sits down to the weaving another woman left in the loom.'[60]

Finally, Le Guin does the same as Vergil in performing the story rather than simply writing about it. Through active imagination, she creates the novel form of the text in which Lavinia is allowed to speak. By this, Le Guin is showing her readers that what it takes for redemption is to create a character and hear her. This is the liberation offered by active imagination in re-writing, which, in itself, offers life and autonomy to this 'otherness'. Lavinia is multi-dimensional, A vision (Le Guin's) within a vision (Lavinia's) within a vision (Vergil's). It is a parallelizing of realities, a juxtaposition of eras and forms of existence. This quantum style is in itself a redemption of the eros-aspect of storytelling, asserting Le Guin's carrier bag theory. There is freedom in the novel's text, which, like Lavinia, has a life of its own: 'Well, my poem will look after itself, no doubt, if I let it.'[61]

Notes

1 Susan Rowland, *C.G. Jung in the Humanities* (New Orleans: Spring Journal, 2012), Amazon Kindle e-book
2 Ursula Le Guin, *Lavinia* (New York: Houghton Mifflin Harcourt, 2009), p. 5.
3 Ibid., p. 89.
4 Ibid., p. 4.
5 *Lavinia*, p. 3.
6 Marc Slavin, *Metaphor and Imaginal Psychology: A Hermetic Reflection* (London: Routledge, 2018).
7 Ursula Le Guin, "The Carrier-Bag Theory of Fiction", in *Dancing at the Edge of the World* (New York: Grove Press, 1989), p. 166.
8 Ibid., p. 169
9 Ibid.
10 *Lavinia*, p. 145.

11 *Lavinia*, p. 273
12 Susan Rowland, *Jungian Literary Criticism* (London: Routledge, 2018), p. 38
13 *Lavinia*, p. 34.
14 Rowland, 2018, p. 38.
15 *Lavinia*, p. 36
16 Ibid.
17 *Lavinia*, p. 37.
18 Ibid., p. 39.
19 *Active Imagination*, p. 107.
20 *Lavinia*, p. 212.
21 Ibid., p. 41.
22 Ibid.
23 Carl Jung, *Mysterium Coniunctionis, The Collected Works of C.G. Jung, Volume 14*, ed. and trans. by Gerhard Adler and Richard Francis Carrington Hull (Princeton, NJ: Princeton University Press, 1970), p. 107.
24 *Lavinia*, p. 44.
25 Robert A. Johnson, *Inner Work: Using Dreams and Active Imagination for Personal Growth* (New York: Harper Collins e-Book, 1989), p. 9.
26 *Lavinia*, p. 79.
27 Ibid., p. 19.
28 Ibid., p. 58.
29 Carl Jung, *The Symbolic Life: Miscellaneous Writings, The Collected Works of C.G. Jung, Volume 18*, ed. and trans. by Gerhard Adler and Richard Francis Carrington Hull (Princeton, NJ: Princeton University Press, 1977), p. 171.
30 *Lavinia*, p. 144.
31 Ibid., p. 257.
32 Jefferey Raff, *Jung and the Alchemical Imagination* (Lake Worth: Nicolas-Hays Inc., 2000), loc. 525.
33 Ibid., p. 43.
34 Ibid.
35 Ibid., p. 124.
36 Carl Jung, *Psychology and Alchemy, The Collected Works of C.G. Jung, Volume 12*, ed. and trans. by Gerhard Adler and Richard Francis Carrington Hull (Princeton, NJ: Princeton University Press, 1968), p. 177.
37 As noted by Jefferey Raff in *Jung and the Alchemical Imagination*: 'Active imagination connects individuals with inner figures which, while very powerful, are clearly imaginal and derived from the psyche. These figures feel as if they were coming from within oneself. Typically one experiences them with eyes closed, and attention directed inward. These are the psychic figures that personify the forces of the unconscious. However, every so often, one may experience a figure that feels completely different. This figure feels as if it were coming from outside oneself, as if it existed in the external world, in the room in which one finds oneself, for example. One's eyes are open, and the felt sense is that one perceives a figure that does not come from within. The attention of the ego is focused outward, not inward. These are the experiences I refer to using the term "psychoid"' (location 665).
38 *Lavinia*, p. 86.
39 Ibid., p. 90.
40 Ibid, p. 68.
41 Le Guin, 1989, p. 169.
42 *Lavinia*, p. 253.
43 Ibid., p. 68.
44 *Lavinia*, p. 184.

45 Ibid., p. 253.
46 *Lavinia*, p. 67.
47 *Lavinia*, p. 254
48 Susan Rowland, *C.G. Jung in the Humanities*, New Orleans: Spring, 2012. Amazon Kindle, Location 2172
49 Susan Rowland, "Against Anthropocene: Transdisciplinarity and Dionysus in Jungian Ecocriticism", in *Feminist News from Somewhere* (London: Routledge, 2017), p. 11.
50 C.G. Jung, *The Structure and Dynamics of the Psyche* (Princeton, NJ: Princeton University Press, 1960; Collected Works, Volume 8, para 418); Diogo Valadas Ponte and Lothar Schafer, "Carl Gustav Jung, Quantum Physics and the Spiritual Mind: A Mystical Vision of the Twenty-First Century", *Behavioral Sciences,* Vol. 3, 2013, p. 604.
51 Ibid., p. 603.
52 *Lavinia*, p. 273.
53 "Against Anthropocene: Transdisciplinarity and Dionysus in Jungian Ecocriticism", p. 9.
54 *Lavinia*, p. 50.
55 Ibid., p. 40.
56 Ibid., p. 63.
57 Ibid., p. 94.
58 Ursula Le Guin, "Why Are Americans Afraid of Dragons", in *The Language of the Night: Essays on Fantasy and Science Fiction* (New York: Putnam, 1979), p. 44.
59 *Lavinia*, p. 173.
60 Ibid.
61 Ibid., p. 67.

References

Johnson, Robert A., *Inner Work: Using Dreams and Active Imagination for Personal Growth* (New York: Harper Collins e-Book, 1989)

Jung, C.G., *The Structure and Dynamics of the Psyche, The Collected Works of C.G. Jung, Volume 8* (Princeton, NJ: Princeton University Press, 1960)

Jung, Carl, *Psychology and Alchemy, The Collected Works of C.G. Jung, Volume 12*, ed. and trans. by Gerhard Adler and Richard Francis Carrington Hull (Princeton, NJ: Princeton University Press, 1968)

Jung, Carl, *Mysterium Coniunctionis, The Collected Works of C.G. Jung, Volume 14*, ed. and trans. by Gerhard Adler and Richard Francis Carrington Hull (Princeton: Princeton University Press, 1970)

Jung, Carl, *The Symbolic Life: Miscellaneous Writings, The Collected Works of C.G. Jung, Volume 18*, ed. and trans. by Gerhard Adler and Richard Francis Carrington Hull (Princeton, NJ: Princeton University Press, 1977)

Le Guin, Ursula, *Lavinia* (New York: Houghton Mifflin Harcourt, 2009)

Le Guin, Ursula, 'Why Are Americans Afraid of Dragons', in *The Language of the Night: Essays on Fantasy and Science Fiction* (New York: Putnam, 1979)

Le Guin, Ursula, 'The Carrier-Bag Theory of Fiction' in *Dancing at the Edge of the World* (New York: Grove Press, 1989)

Ponte, Diogo Valadas and Lothar Schafer (2013) 'Carl Gustav Jung, Quantum Physics and the Spiritual Mind: A Mystical Vision of the Twenty-First Century', *Behavioral Sciences* Vol. 3, p. 604

Raff, Jefferey, *Jung and the Alchemical Imagination* (Lake Worth: Nicolas-Hays Inc., 2000)

Rowland, Susan, *C.G. Jung in the Humanities* (New Orleans: Spring Journal, 2012), Amazon Kindle e-book

Rowland, Susan, 'Against Anthropocene: Transdisciplinarity and Dionysus in Jungian Ecocriticism' in *Feminist News From Somewhere*, ed. Frances Grey and Leslie Gardner (London: Routledge, 2017)

Rowland, Susan, *Jungian Literary Criticism* (London: Routledge, 2018)

Slavin, Marc, *Metaphor and Imaginal Psychology: A Hermetic Reflection* (London: Routledge, 2018)

Chapter 7

Mysterium Dissociationis

The Masculine in Crisis Towards New Forms of Thought and Relationship

Roberto Grande

Foreword

When Stefano Carpani gave me the idea of a reflection on current events and the possible future of the masculine,[1] I felt that my *Opus*,[2] to be authentic, needed the voice of several disciplines (history, sociology, politics, economics, psychology) and a suitable container for their comparison.

This is because the vision of the masculine that interests me cannot be only intellectual; it must be functional to the human race and to the environment that contains it: this is the container, the *vas hermeticum*[3] within which to mold a possible new 'masculine principle'.

Obviously, I do not intend to find the Aqua Regia, the essence that the alchemists themselves never found; however, I want to reflect on the fact that the discourse on the masculine can no longer be done arbitrarily by a single science or even by the male gender alone.

Today as I write this, the COVID-19 epidemic has irrevocably upset the existence of human beings, dramatically furrowed by a before- and after-virus. And who knows if there will be a post-virus, for humanity: the cornerstones of the psychological and social life of individuals, not only male, were already turned with the advent of extreme climatic phenomena, well before the manifestation of the pandemic in 2020. To this day, we only see the smoking vestiges of the past, democratically left around the world by the virus and by environmental pollution.

I do not intend to dwell on the analysis of these events, widely debated and whose criticality is evident, regardless of the debate on the causes, still of uncertain nature. For now, the only *post* we have is the socio-economic one, the postmodern society; if we have a future, it will be because we will build our psyche and our societies differently than in the past.

For this reason, the masculine principle needs an urgent consultation: more disciplines and more individuals must place themselves at his bedside and each one help the patient, for his part, by dialoguing with the others. The masculine must not be left to the males only.

Today the identity crisis of the masculine must be read in the light of the feminine battle, which is opposed to the male one-sidedness, and the battle to save the Earth, *Mother* Earth.

DOI: 10.4324/9781003168829-8

To be clear, I have no preconceived thoughts about the gender struggle, as I did not have about the class struggle. Women are at war with the patriarchal system, which for too long (and with obvious consequences to all) has monopolized culture, politics, society and the psyche. Just think of the masculine misrule of the environment and of his children (future generations) made the object of a predatory exploitation, characteristic of the herd, of the male horde.

The most useful orientation for reading the situation of the masculine seemed to me the one proposed by Jung in *Mysterium Coniunctionis*, and from it I took the title of my work, since the current tendency is towards dissociation, not towards conjunction, coincidentia oppositorum.[4]

I want to reflect on the current Mysterium Dissociationis: because the detachment between the natural environment and humanity grows, just as the lack of meaning in the way of life grows within the individual; the consequences are harmful for the individual (isolation in drugs, in obsessive rituals, in apparently inexplicable symptoms such as panic attacks, somatizations) and for the Earth.

My point of view will be subjective rather than masculine. On the other hand, subjectivity is ineluctable; not even time can be considered objective anymore, because it relates to the observer who measures it (Hawking 2010, 249).

Subjectivity it is not a privilege but a necessity of existence:

> In the last resort it is neither 'the eighty-million-strong-nation'[5] nor the State that feels peace and happiness, but the individual. . . . He has only the mystery of his living soul to set against the overwhelming might and brutality of collective convictions. It is the age-old drama of opposites, no matter what they are called, which he is fought out in every human life.
>
> (Jung 1963, § 196, 198, 199)

Masculine, Feminine

What does it mean to talk about the masculine? As Jung indicates, I will go through images: therefore, the discourse of the masculine gives me the sensation of standing on one leg, of being unbalanced; it always draws to another missing one. Masculine is impossible to define, as light cannot be defined without shadow:

> Males and Females are two types of individuals who are differentiated within one species for the purposes of reproduction; they can be defined only correlatively.
>
> (de Beauvoir 2012, 35)

It is like looking with one eye: it lacks depth and perspective, and the speech flattens out into one dimension. We need binocular vision; masculine and feminine are the two eyes that complement each other for the sake of sight and the individual.

We can define feminine and masculine as categories: biological (sex: female, male), social and psychological.

Sex, in biology, is the character that allows in living organisms a gamic reproduction, to distinguish individuals belonging to the same species in different gen-
era. The sex comes from the Latin etymology *sexe*, to separate, to distinguish.

Gender in sociology is the belonging to one or the other sex not based on differences of a biological or physical nature but on components of a social, cultural,
historical and behavioral nature.[6]

As psychological categories, masculine/feminine are considered by Jung
between the opposite polarities of the psyche:

> The factors which come together in the coniunctio are conceived as oppo-
> sites, either confronting one another in enmity or attracting one another
> in love. To begin with they form a dualism; for instance the opposites are
> *humidum* (moist)/*siccum* (dry), *frigidum* (cold)/*calidum* (warm), *superiora*
> (upper, higher)/*inferiora* (lower), *spiritus-anima* (spirit-soul)/*corpus* (body),
> *coelum* (heaven)/*terra* (earth), *ignis* (fire)/*aqua* (water), bright/dark, *agens*
> (active)/*patiens* (passive), *volatile* (volatile, gaseous)/*fixum* (solid), *pre-
> tiosum* (precious, costly; also *carum*) dear)/*vile* (cheap, common), *bonum*
> (good)/*malum* (evil), *manifestum* (open)/*occultum* (occult; also *celatum*) hid-
> den), *oriens* (East)/occidens (West), *vivum* (living)/*mortuum* (dead, inert),
> *masculus* (masculine)/*foemina* (feminine), Sol/Luna.
>
> (Jung 1963, § 1)

In *Mysterium Coniunctionis*, his last work, completed after the age of 80, he
summarizes his ideas regarding the conflicting nature of the psyche. The psychic
polarities are subject to the opposing forces of dissociation (δια-βάλλω, in Greek,
to separate, hence devil) and union (σύμ-βάλλω, to bring together, hence symbol).

> As is indicated by the very name which he chose for it – the "spagyric" art
> (from σπαειν, 'rend, tear, stretch out', αγειρειν, 'bring or collect together')
> – or by the oft-repeated saying "solve et coagula" (dissolve and coagulate),
> the alchemist saw the essence of his art in separation and analysis on the one
> hand and synthesis and consolidation on the other. . . . The obvious analogy,
> in the psychic sphere, to this problem of opposites is the dissociation of the
> personality brought about by the conflict of incompatible tendencies, result-
> ing as a rule from an inharmonious disposition. The repression of one of the
> opposites leads only to a prolongation and extension of the conflict, in other
> words, to a neurosis.
>
> (Jung 1963, Foreword XIV–XV)

His statements on natural processes as energy phenomena seems written today by
a physicist from the CNR in Geneva:

> But, young as the psychology of unconscious processes may be, it has nev-
> ertheless succeeded in establishing certain facts which are gradually gaining
> general acceptance. One of these is the polaristic structure of the psyche,

which it shares with all natural processes. Natural processes are phenomena of energy.

(Jung 1963, Foreword XVI)

Regarding the duality and the sparks that arise from the tension between masculine and feminine, (so much so that Jung speaks of *age-old drama of opposites*), Simone de Beauvoir also trusts in their pacification, although, more than coniunctio, she speaks of the division of the world.

To this day, the French philosopher's questions remain unanswered and refer to the Mysterium:

> how did this whole story begin? It is understandable that the duality of the sexes, like all duality, be expressed in conflict. It is understandable that if one of the two succeeded in imposing its superiority, it had to establish itself as absolute. It remains to be explained how it was that man won at the outset. It seems possible that women might have carried off the victory, or that the battle might never be resolved. Why is it that this world has always belonged to men and that only today things are beginning to change? Is this change a good thing? Will it bring about an equal sharing of the world between men and women or not?
>
> (de Beauvoir 2012, 25)

Now we want to reflect on the mysterious nature of masculine and feminine and on the complexity of their confrontation.

Mysterium

First of all, why does Jung define *mysterium* as the process of joining opposites (Coniunctio)?

> But the real reason was the imperative need to participate in *a* or perhaps *the* secret without which life loses its supreme meaning. The secret is not really worth keeping, but the fact that it is still obstinately kept reveals an equally persistent psychic motive for keeping secrets, and that is the real secret, the real mystery. . . . The essential thing is the hiding, an expressive gesture which symbolizes something unconscious and 'not to be named' lying behind it. . . . It points, in a word, to the presence of an unconscious content, which exacts from consciousness a tribute of constant regard and attention.
>
> (Jung 1963, § 312)

Surrounding with mystery means giving importance to the unknowable. We define as arcane, occult, mysterious, even, what is a reason for fascination or attraction, for the secrecy or mystery in which it is wrapped:

> I can do no more than demonstrate the existence of this image and its phenomenology. What the union of opposites really 'means' transcends

human imagination. . . . we are dealing with an eternal image, an archetype, from which man can turn away his mind for a time but never
permanently.

(Jung 1963, § 200, 201)

Mysterium is therefore a constitutive, fundamental image of the psyche; it is precious and must be protected. Dissociation is the starting condition:

Just as all energy proceeds from opposition, so the psyche too possesses its
inner polarity, this being the indispensable pre-requisite for its aliveness, as
Heraclitus realized long ago.

(Jung 1989, 346)

The aversion to the Other is an archetypal disposition; it is the force of the repulsion of the polarities, of the consciousness that does not want to recognize the
shadow. It is the root of homophobia, of gender discrimination, of incoherence of
human beings.

It is also the basis of the scapegoat mechanism (Girard 1992, 201–234): if the
animal is driven by instinct, man desires something because someone else has
it, becoming his equal and rival. The mimetic (imitative) rivalry is socially dangerous and must be resolved in a projection, in the sacrificed goat, that is, made
sacred. The fear of the same (for example, the residual fear of twins in archaic
cultures) generates deep, archaic fears.

And what a radical contrast, even before the masculine/feminine, if not that of
matter/antimatter:

In addition, corresponding to each of these subatomic particles there exists
an antiparticle. Antiparticles have the same mass as their sibling particles
but are opposite in their charge and other attributes. . . . There could be
whole antiworlds and antipeople made out of antiparticles. However, when
an antiparticle and particle meet, they annihilate each other. So, if you meet
your antiself, don't shake hands – you would both vanish in a great flash of
light!

(Hawking 2010, 169)

If taken into themselves, again, femininity and masculinity risk being empty
boxes:

True, the theory of the eternal feminine still has its followers. . . . Is femininity secreted by the ovaries? Is it enshrined in a Platonic heaven?. . . . concep-
tualism has lost ground: biological and social sciences no longer believe there
are immutably determined entities that define given characteristics like those
of the woman, the Jew or the black; science considers characteristics as secondary reactions to a situation. If there is no such thing today as femininity,
it is because there never was.

(de Beauvoir 2012, 19)

In any case, it is clear that the feminine and masculine archetypal components of the psyche are not empty abstractions: they are images, fantasies that structure 'complexes with an emotional tone' that are constitutive of the psyche. They can be devastating, or otherwise saving:

> The archetype is a force. It has an autonomy, and it can suddenly seize you. It is like a seizure. Falling in love at first sight is something like that. . . . And afterwards you may discover that it was a hell of a mistake. . . . He says: "For God's sake, doctor, help me to get rid of that woman!" He can't, though, he's like a clay in her fingers. That is the archetype, the archetype of the anima. . . . It's the same with the girls. When a man sings very high, a girl thinks he must have a very wonderful spiritual character because he can sing the high C, and she is badly disappointed when she marries that particular number. Well, that's the archetype of the animus.
>
> (Jung 1991, 110)

Just as one cannot make a list of archetypes, one cannot make a list of the characteristics of masculinity or femininity. The archetypal images that masculine and feminine draw on and that can come to life in the individual are many:

> There are dozens, if not hundreds, of feminine and masculine archetypes. . . . But not all archetypes are dominant at a particular period in the life of an individual, moreover every historical epoch has its dominant masculine and feminine archetypes. . . . This misunderstanding has led, for example, to the assumption in Jungian psychology that masculinity is identical with Logos and femininity with Eros, and that the essence of femininity is more personal, more related to one's fellow human, more passive, more masochistic; while the essence of masculinity is abstract, more intellectual, more aggressive, sadistic, active, etc. This naïve assertion could have been made only because the masculine and feminine archetypes that were dominant at that time and in that culture were understood as the only valid ones.

> The passage from one archetype to another, or the awakening of new, heretofore neglected archetypes is always fraught with difficulty. . . . During puberty, the archetype of the child recedes into the background, and the archetype of the adult emerges. Around the age of fifty, the latter one slowly begins to be suppressed by the senex archetype. When one archetype becomes detached from another, we find in the life of the individual the so-called transition depressions
>
> (Guggenbühl-Craig 2015, 584 et seq, K)

Concerning Jung's conception of the presence of Anima and Animus archetypes in relation to gender, and their primacy over other archetypes, I share Beebe's vision:

> his [of Jung —ed.] original formulation was sexist and rigid . . . we don't always know what archetype a partner in a sexual relationship will end

up personifying, and it is naïve to imagine that will always be anima or animus.

(Beebe 2020, 60, 72)

The Voice of History

On the historical level, by way of example of the comparison between the male and female principle, I will mention the events of the Cathars and the birth of gender history.[7]

Simone Weil speaks of Occitan civilization in 1942 in Marseille, in the middle of the war, writing about the *Chanson de la croisade albigeoise* composed in the Middle Ages and in the language of Oc, which describes "the need for purity of the Occitan country", "the last heartbeats 'Of a rich and tolerant civilization, wiped out by the sword and by burning at the stake'":

> What fruits has a civilization so rich in different elements brought? And what could it have brought? We ignore it; the tree was cut down.
>
> (Weil S. 1996, 21 personal translation)

It was a crossroads for European history that took the path of strength. Bulls, bullfights and referendums, in their own way, also talk about this.

In the "Occitan homeland", writes Weil, there was tolerance, openness to all spiritual currents. From the thirteenth century, Europe withdrew itself from with the absolute states and never left the territory of its continent except to destroy it. They are the germs of what we now call our civilization, based not on tolerance but on strength.

Tolerance, the protection of life, kindness are feminine qualities. An entire civilization has turned to male principles, to "violence, lady of this world" (Grande C. 2002).

As for gender history, it was born in the seventies, on the push of the feminist movement, and dealt with the history of feminism. Gender history is a sub-field of history and gender studies, which looks at the past from the perspective of gender. The "gender" point of view also concerns art, literature, medicine. Gender medicine deals with the influence of gender differences on health and disease (Glezerman 2017). The gender vision has not only enriched the disciplines in question; it has revolutionized them (Rose 2010).

The Psychology of the Developmental Age: Shaping the Male

The rethinking of the masculine principle must start from the psychology of the developmental age, from the early developmental stages of the child who builds the adult.[8]

That the Nomos,[9] the original order, is given by the father is not totally true. An authentic social feeling, the experience of harmony with oneself and with the world, are experienced very early on and are taught to children by those who, regardless of gender, exercise primary care.

Neumann said that the ordering law of the individual and society, alongside Eros and Logos, is derived from the masculine principle in the mother:

> Religion, morality and social feeling are still one and have their positive root in the primal relationship. . . . Phylogenetically, the order and morality of the Great Mother are conditioned by the child's experience of the order of its own body and of the cosmic rhythm of day and night and of the seasons. . . . To the infant the animus aspect of the mother, standing for order, for the *nomos*-principle, partakes at first of the Terrible Mother. . . . Later on, the child acquires a positive along with the negative experience of this masculine aspect of the Great Mother, which now, currently or successively, confers both pleasure and pain or discomfort.
>
> (Neumann 2002, 90, 103)

It is to be assumed that for many haters, racists and homophobes, the change of diaper, and with it the subsequent hygiene of the psyche, must not have worked very well. I add that Neumann's conception of an Animus exclusive of the woman (as I wrote previously) has had its time, as has the reference to the mother as the child's only caregiver.

Early experiences and development, whether good or bad, are not primarily related to gender differences:

> It has long been established that homosexual orientation is in no way related to any pathology, and there is no basis on which to assume that a parent's sexual orientation would increase the odds or induce a homosexual orientation in the child. Studies on the educational outcomes of children raised by homosexual parents, compared with those raised by heterosexual parents, do not suggest a different degree of instability in the parent-child relationship or with respect to developmental disorders in children.
>
> (American Academy of Child and Adolescent Psychiatry, in Lingiardi 2012, 151)

The quality of the relationship with a child also depends on the awareness and psychic balance of the parent: the desires and symptoms of a child could be the desires and symptoms of parents:

> the things which have the most powerful effect upon children do not come from the conscious state of the parents but from their unconscious background.
>
> (Jung 1977a, § 84)

If until now we have spoken of a *good enough mother*[10] (Winnicott 2005), it will be good to accept the discussion that the maternal function can be performed by other figures and that perhaps the worst trouble lies not with the caregiver's gender but with his involvement in the current *Zeitgeist*,[11] the commodification of individuals:

> What is around these adolescent children: a world of haste, of money, of consumption, of words that are bad or never said, of stifled emotions, of fear. Of distracted parents who, for a 'malfunctioning' child, only ask for a quick repair.
> Of an apparently adult world, which must be asked to grow up for its children, together with them, so that it becomes a better world than this one.
>
> (Grande 2009, dust jacket)

The characteristics of post-modern society, and the description of the liquid society (Bauman 2000), have a clear echo in childhood development. Concepts such as fluidity, indeterminate states, transience/transitional, instability, fragmentation are certainly not unknown to scholars of developmental psychology:

> according to Stern, the subjective life of the infant may consist of many distinct and vivid experiences. . . . But these single moments eventually begin to organise themselves into successfully larger, more comprehensive structures. The infant experiences what Stern[12] calls "an emergent self". . . . From the Jungian point of view, one could say that this is the primal form or what in later life is called the emerging of contents from the unconscious.
>
> (Jacoby 1999, 49, 50)

As happens in childhood development, in fact, the post-modern individual must learn to organize emotions and thoughts, and this can only be done through individual experience.

Post-modern society has regressed to fragmented, isolated, provisional and simplified experiences. Social media creators chase collective patterns of experience. From an original and dramatically naïve idea of increasing people's well-being and sociability, they have obtained the opposite effect, because the self-esteem generated by the hypertrophy of the Ego (due to collective judgment) does not hold up for long. The craving[13] of getting one more *like* produces anxiety; one fewer *like* generates depression and isolation. *The Social Dilemma*[14] focuses on how big social media companies manipulate users by using algorithms that encourage addiction to their platforms.

Postmodern man, disoriented and fragmented, needs a container (the *mandala*, the *vas hermeticum*, that circumscribe a limit) and an orientation (the meaning of life, individuation).

As a newborn seeks containment, *holding*,[15] so the surface of a *liquid* young reflects the collective. But a digital platform is not a container; it is entertainment.

A young woman, my client, complains that her partner left her: "Because he doesn't want to be with someone he met *online*."

The only *holding* we have today are the economic ones, the *Holding Companies*.

Another topic concerns the need for the mother to be able to leave the internalized patriarchy, which prevents her and her children from evolving. With respect to the daughter, an aggressive, socially competitive and overly performance-encouraging maternal model can be dysfunctional:

> The questions that emerged for me were to do with how we had internalized patriarchy and capitalism and how our psyches were not a thing apart from that but were constituted by it. That is why I turned to psychoanalytic ways of thinking. Feminism could show the collective mind, psychoanalysis could show through a deeper study, the individual mind which of course is also a collective mind. . . . I've had the experience with some young women, that they have ticked all the boxes, but they don't exist. I've got the boyfriend, I've got the body, I've got the job, but I don't – it's not even that I'm not happy. . . . It's not to blame their mothers, but it was the historical moment in which they were raised, which tended to project onto those girls and foster ambition.
>
> (Orbach 2020, 201, 205)

An indulgent and collusive maternal attitude with the patriarchal vision risks keeping the child's eros immature, and the son may want to replicate his mother in every woman. In other words, the possibility that the male respects the feminine by renouncing the symbiosis with the Great Mediterranean Goddesses-Complacent Mothers requires that women themselves demand it from children and partners. The male who does not evolve is a *Puer Aeternus*:

> The stage of the maternal uroboros[16] is characterised by the child's relation to its mother, who yields nourishment. . . . This stage of development is ruled by the image of the Mother Goddess with the Divine Child. . . . Even for the youthful god, the Great Mother is fate. How much more, then, for the child, whose nature it is to be an appendage of her body.
>
> (Neumann 2014, 43)

For the development of the male child, a father is also needed, good enough. The search for the father is an ancient and archetypal theme: Telemachus, Hamlet are the literary sons of the research (Zoja 2000, 287), Joker the post-modern version.[17]

In fact, more and more mothers have assumed the paternal function, but things get difficult with adolescents who organize themselves in gangs or, on the contrary, by social withdrawal (Zoja 2000, 301). The social withdrawal of many young males is often caused by the absence of the father and the rejection of what he represents today: the primacy of the neoliberal economy and the law of competition (Saito 2013).

Although the archetypal image of the father (*imago*)[18] is active in the individual, for better or for worse, even in the absence of the real father, nevertheless the son needs him in the presence: not with the word, which is not an example, but with acts. The male of the horde willingly renounces his role as father, tragically delegated to the leader in dictatorships; the father, on the other hand, does not give up, and returns, as Ulysses did.

Today we need *minimalist utopias* (Zoja 2013), not fathers of the Church, of the Fatherland or of Humanity.

Here are some examples of gorgeous inconsistencies; I am grateful to Fate that I had them as fathers of my utopia and not as personal fathers:

> Ernesto Guevara de la Serna, known as Che, possessed culture, charisma, high values for which he was ready to sacrifice his life . . . this 'absolute altruist' was essentially self-centered: the images he had in his soul, the life of myths that he carried inside, they counted more to him than the lives of real people. . . . Che had, as far as is known, six or seven children . . . according to Sebreli,[19] Che hardly saw them. . . . Che was really convinced that the future collective moral re-education would have made the presence of parents secondary.
>
> (Zoja 2013, 18–34, personal translation)

Carpani: "what is the masculine, what is the father, what is the *new* father?

> Beebe: "Jung doesn't really get into that subject very much. . . . In my own meeting with Jung's son, Franz Jung, he said, 'My father was someone to get to know on holiday or weekends, but actually he was in his study all the time. Emma Jung raised us, and when we needed advice, my father couldn't give it to me'. . . . A "father" is someone who fosters, parents, protects. . . . Jung was far more heroic than fatherly. . . . Jung was as good a grandfather as he was terrible as a father.
>
> (Beebe 2020, 50–54)

Yet, it is Jung himself who reveals the Shadow:

> a highly intelligent young man who had worked out a detailed analysis of his own neurosis . . . asked me to read the manuscript and to tell him why he was still not cured, although he ought to have been, according to his scientific judgement. . . . I therefore asked him who actually paid for these holidays, and it there-upon came out that a poor schoolteacher who loved him almost starved herself to indulge this younger man in his visits to pleasure-resorts. His want of conscience was the cause of his neurosis, and this also explains why all his scientific insight availed him nothing. His fundamental error lay in his moral attitude. He found my way of looking at it shockingly unscientific, for morals have nothing to do with science.
>
> (Jung 1972a, § 685)

What laws lead the gradient between what you say, what you are and what you do? In the inconsistency, we can see a confirmation of the archetypal tendency towards the expression of 'Dissociatio'. Dreams, actions are often an unconscious compensation to the speaking Ego, compensation that Che and Jung embodied; two human beings, exemplars of Opposites.

Were they aware of their *Felix Culpa*?[20]

> One can miss not only one's happiness but also one's final guilt, without which a man will never reach his wholeness.
>
> (Jung 1977b, § 36)

There is one hard thing that the male can do to renew himself: to become honestly aware of the Shadow's existence.

Psychiatry and Sociology

If the vision of social problems is the prerogative of sociology, while the understanding of an individual mental illness is the domain of psychiatry, the two disciplines go dissociated, and exclusively symptomatic psychiatry, which does not seek causes, collides with the substantially collective character, *mass individualism* of the second modernity (Beck 2001, 45).

But a new point of view tries to hold them together:

> The neo-Jungians find, in the following features of psychosocial studies, their purpose: . . . Psychosocial studies object to the idea of thinking separately about psychological and social processes and then examining the way they intersect with each other.
>
> (Carpani 2020b, 13)

Unfortunately, we are still far from that goal. The psychiatrists' bible, DSM 5 (Diagnostic and Statistical Manual of Mental Disorders 2013), takes into consideration an individual's symptoms; psychiatry treats individuals, of course, but often the treatments prescribed to the individual (drugs, psychotherapy) fail if the mental disorders are reduced to individual symptoms to be eradicated.

How can a person affected with unstable personality be cured if he is deeply influenced by a society sick with impermanence? Let's follow the definition of a post-modern liquid society:

> A most salient aspect of the vanishing act performed by old securities is the new fragility of human bonds. The brittleness and transience of bonds may be an unavoidable price for individuals' right to pursue their individual goals, and yet it cannot but be, simultaneously, a most formidable obstacle to pursue them *effectively* – and to the courage needed to pursue them. This is also a paradox – one rooted deeply in the nature of life under liquid modernity.
>
> (Bauman 2000, 170)

The manic search for oneself, related to troubles concerning 'a sense of inner direction and dependable, orienting values' (McWilliams 2011, 36), present in the narcissistic personality disorder, has the sociological equivalent in the phenomenon of the *individualization* (Beck 2001).

Panic attacks, generalized anxiety, social phobias, compulsions, present in a fragile and ambivalent personality structure, are reflected in the *anomie*, in the absence of limits of the liquid society.

Dependent or infantile personalities are favored by the lack of economic autonomy, not only by psychological factors. It is the same need that women have (especially in the role of mothers) to be economically independent in order to be psychologically independent as well.

Thus, disconnected from the impact of social unease (economic fluctuations and frailties, rapid life cycles, temporary working life), the individual phenomenology of mood disorders (bipolar oscillation with very rapid cycles, for example) is inexplicable and incurable, and social phobia disorders, never related to solipsistic isolation, are devoid of sociological sense. The fight against the provisional nature of the postmodern man requires energy, non-provisional libido:

> Our actions remain non-committal and this enables us to move forward quickly in favour of other possibilities. Jaspers calls this neurotic provisionality.
>
> (Daniel 2020, 142)

In short, it is evident that many of the dissociative symptoms (depersonalization, derealization) that my young patients suffer from are also due to the fact that:

> The individual . . . must master and practice the art of 'liquid life' with its attendant disorientation and absence of itinerary and direction.
>
> (Bauman 2005, 4)

On the other hand, sociology cannot interpret social phenomena and behaviors by excluding the individual's unconscious psyche, that is, without exploring the individuation concept (Carpani 2020a, 223). Individualization is generated by exasperated individualism, employed in neuromarketing strategies, which glimpse the dogma "I am if I consume" (Bauman 2007).

In doing so, the support that Social Service bestows on the fragmented *homo optionis* risks becoming wasted (Beck 2001, 5).

The authentic, profound quest for individuation, necessarily far from prepackaged objects of collective approval, is quite another thing from the *mass character*.

Rooting yourself in a collective emotional identity, drawing on the symbolic, mythological heritage expressed by humanity over the millennia, is not achieved by being a *follower* of an *influencer*. *Feeling* first of all means experiencing within oneself, certainly not buying a consuming emotion at the web supermarket. This is the root of creative fantasy (Carpani 2020a, 235).

In terms of developmental psychology (Stern 1985, 97):

> As a result of many episodes, which are recorded in memory, initial represen-
> tations and expectations will emerge; what Stern named with the abbreviation
> "RIGs," whose initials indicate *representations of interactions that have been
> generalised.*
>
> (Jacoby 1999, 55)

We are training our children in commodification, in the economic exploitation of
feelings.

Which therefore are no longer such; they are emptied of meaning if persons are
"desubjectivized" (Agamben 2006, 30). We cannot feel an emotion in the place of
others; we can only help them express it:

> psychoanalysis . . . is the absolute metaphor for what midwifery is.
>
> (Carpani 2020b, 7)

Mysterium Dissociationis

If the Coniunctio is Mysterium, Mysterium is also the opposite principle of repulsion, Dissociation. Referring to woman and man:

> In order to understand marriage it is also important to realize not only that
> masculine and feminine can behave hostile to one another, but that they do not
> even have to complement one another. . . . Marriage can be really understood
> only when we free ourselves from the "harmony complex." . . . Marriage is
> not comfortable and harmonious. Rather, it is a place of individuation where
> a person rubs up against oneself and against the other, bumps up against the
> other in love and in rejection, and in this fashion learns to know oneself, the
> world, good and evil, the high and the low ground.
>
> (Guggenbühl-Craig 2015, 741 K)

In the uroboric alternation, in the individual and in history, of attraction and
repulsion of opposites, today between male and female, the clash prevails; this is
because a change is taking place:

> For millennia, men have had more archetypal possibilities than women.
> The archetype of Ares, the simple, brutal warrior and soldier, . . . and so has
> that of Ulysses, the clever warrior and husband; and the archetype of the
> priest, the man of God. The archetype of the medicine man, the doctor; that
> of Hephaestus, the clever technician; that of Hermes the clever trader and
> thief; . . . The man of today is still bound to his role as provider, and this limits
> his possibilities.
>
> (Guggenbühl-Craig 2015, 648 K)

We are in a time of haters who kill; we are in the schizo-paranoid, angry Klein-ian position of the denial of the other, of dissociation (Klein 1952). To stay with Melania Klein, a healthy depressive phase has yet to come: the phase of introspec-tion, of the *reculer pour mieux sauter*, to use a phrase that Jung loved, about the regression that precedes change.

Religions, beliefs grow old; when humanity loses interest in 'current' arche-types, they have lost 'their shattering numinous quality' (von Franz 2000, 24–44, cit. in Daniel 2020, 35–36).

So, if in the year 2000, Guggenbühl-Craig wrote:

> The situation today is that women are somewhat lost at sea: . . . Such a transi-tion brings with it an archetypal emptiness.
>
> (2015, 679 K)

Today the rebellion is underway, and humanity in crisis needs a renewal of the archetypal images of the masculine and the feminine. The summer of the patriar-chy was torrid, and it is not over: we are still on the side of the female enslaved and exploited, in the sign of the archaic strength of the masculine that cancels the strength of the feminine.

Temperatures are out of control; opus requires the cooling of the masculine principle, the sizzling *solutio* of boiling patriarchy. The results are uncertain, but it is hoped that the human being survives. Alongside Ananke, the Necessity to which every Olympic is subjected:[21]

> only absolute necessity can effectively inhibit a natural instinct. When there is no need and no inexorable necessity, the 'sublimation' is merely a self-deception, a new and somewhat more subtle form of repression.
>
> (Jung 1972b, § 704)

If in 2020 the woman has new awareness, she too comes to terms with the need for renewal of her archetypal models. Here are a few:

> First there is the maternal archetype. . . . The archetype of Hera, wife of the heavenly father Zeus, symbol of the cruel wife who is jealous of everything that diverts her husband's attention from herself. . . . Another archetype is the *hetaera*, the uninhibited companion of men in sexual pleasure, in wit, and in learnedness. . . . Aphrodite, the goddess of pure sexual pleasure, the archetype of the lover. . . . Athene represents . . . the wise, energetic woman, self-sufficient, nonsexual, nevertheless helpful to men. . . . the archetype of the amazon, the female warrior. She needs men only for procreation. . . . This is the archetype of the independent career woman who renounces men. . . . Another feminine archetype is that of Artemis. Her disposition toward men is hostile also. She does not want to be seen or known by them. Men who

stalk her must die. If Artemis has a relation to anyone, it is to her brother Apollo.

(Guggenbühl-Craig 2015, 595 et seq. K)

When the archetype loses strength, it becomes an empty container, and the individual who embodies it feels, as Guggenbuhl said, an archetypal feeling of emptiness, risking becoming a caricature, such as in the so-called *Barbie & Ken syndrome*.[22] Today beauty is even more enslaving for women than for men, because it is an ancient collective heritage, a cultural obligation; however, we are fast approaching gender equality, as the cosmetics market and plastic surgery require all genders to do their part for the triumph of another expression of the *mass character:* The *Beauty Terror*, obsession and moral obligation of beauty (Orbach 2009, cit. in Daniel 2020, 107).

Perhaps the feminine today performs an *enantiodromia*,[23] because it experiences what has been removed from the feminine, to become prerogative of the masculine: aggressiveness, power, autonomy, sexuality. What I regret, since freedom and relationship are the highest of my values, is the masculine complex in woman, that is to say the use of the logic of aggression, the grammar of war, the arid lexical discriminations of rationalism devoid of Eros (*Complex of power*, Valcarenghi 2003, 138). It is not a question of defining as masculine or feminine aggression, thought, feelings and qualities of the psyche; it is rather about recognizing different ways of manifesting instinct, thought, feeling (Valcarenghi 2003, 10).

The *Weibermacht*[24] still and only reflects the absolute power of the masculine principle, which allows itself a mocking carnival overturning (Smith S.L. 1995). The primacy of the feminine that I would like is described in the alchemical images:

> This more exalted attitude raises the status of the anima from that of a temptress to a psychopomp. The transformation of the kingly substance from a lion into a king has its counterpart in the transformation of the feminine element from a serpent into a queen.

(Jung 1963, § 540)

In any case, between snakes and lions, the lion seems most disoriented, today.

In my analytic activity, a panic anxiety often emerges in young males because of the difficulty of choosing a partner (he who does not find the right woman or does not know how to choose).

The male falters because he has to face the demolition of his status: he can no longer rely on his Ego, nor on his virile member, having lost the exclusivity on rationality and aggression and having (finally) come out of the stereotypical role of inseminator. Moreover, it is needed to 'master and practice the art of liquid life'.

When he does not attack, he falls into self-aggression or/and depression of social withdrawal (Grande 2015, 18).[25]

He would need an Archimedean point, as Jung liked to say, but he still does not know what it is: the male still does not know the Law of feeling, in order to be able to choose. Having no self-relatedness, left alone to act, his Ego fails:

> Self-realisation becomes ego-realization, self-confidence becomes ego-confidence, and self-optimization is actually ego-optimization . . . ego is trapped in an autonomous complex that could be referred to as a God complex.
> (Daniel 2020, 59)

To overcome the current barbarism of relationships, what a hopeful Jung wrote can be used:

> Increasing psychological insight hinders the projection of the shadow, and this gain in knowledge logically leads to the problem of the union of opposites. One realises, first of all, that one cannot project one's shadow on to others.
> If the projected conflict is to be healed, it must return into the psyche of the individual, where it had its unconscious beginnings. He must celebrate a Last Supper with himself, and eat his own flesh and drink his own blood; which means that he must to recognise and accept the other in himself. But if he persists in his one-sidedness, the two lions will tear each other to pieces. In this perhaps the meaning of Christ's teaching, that each must bear his own cross? For if you have to endure yourself, how will you be able to rend others also?
> (Jung 1963, § 203, 512)

So, the real new attitude must be sought in the acceptance of the opposite that is in us. Humans do not derive greater freedom in canceling or mimicking the qualities of the other.

Freedom cannot be defined by a single point of view, by corporate or gender membership. Rights become privileges if they are the prerogative of a single category: sexual, economic, social, ideological as it is.

Therefore, if women conquer new responsibilities, there is no doubt that the male must take on a specific task: the ability to relate.

Without becoming a caricature of the woman, the man will have to cultivate non-narcissistic beauty, gentle firmness, the grace of obedience; he will have to tolerate the frustration of desire, he will have to accept defeat not as a negative value. He will be the author of *coagulatio*, that is, he will have the generative responsibility of assuming the feminine principle:

> Any specific form, manifestation, or structure that solidifies our life energies into particular, concrete expression is of the nature of woman. . . . Jung has

defined the feminine principle as the principle of relatedness. Thus, we can say, *relationship coagulates*.

(Edinger 1985, 96–97)

However, rebuilding the masculine and his freedom will not be an easy task, and the male cannot be left alone to do so. Basically, as Susan Orbach says, about true feminism:

pertains to how we construct psychologies of femininity and masculinity; it's a critique of those gendered binaries.

(2020, 202)

Reflecting on my personal female Pantheon, I feel alien to the Barbie archetype, and I defend myself as much as I can from Circe and the Sirens; I flee from Cruella de Mon (modern actualization of Hecate, Lilith), and I avoid Artemis and the Amazons (who are already fleeing me); I sympathize with Athena (favorable to the masculine), I need Beatrice (Sophia, the woman considered a link between man and God). Soon, also, the archetype of Amazon will be obsolete:

observations have proved that asexual multiplication can occur indefinitely without any noticeable degeneration. . . .

All that can be affirmed with certainty is that these two means of reproduction coexist in nature, that they both perpetuate species, and that the heterogeneity of both gametes and gonad-producing organisms seems to be accidental. The differentiation of individuals into males and females thus occurs as an irreducible and contingent fact. . . .

perhaps man's co-operation in procreation would one day become useless: that seems to be many women's desire.

(de Beauvoir 2012, 36, 37, 39)

It is therefore a change that will not lead to a lack of biological functionality will renew the human being? I do not know; the woman may not be more alone than she already is, since the dawn of time.

Unlike O. Wilde, who used to say: "I always pass on good advice. It is the only thing to do with it. It is never of any use to oneself", I conclude without lectures.

My reflection, as it had begun, ends with an image, which arises from Biology:

Male and female gametes merge together in the egg; together they cancel each other out in their totality.

(de Beauvoir 2012, 42)

I do not hope that woman and man cancel each other out but that they participate in the human 'mitsein' transformed by each other. We do not know if matriarchy really existed (Gimboutas 1989); maybe we have historical traces of a creative and generating masculine, too:

> sculpting Neolithic female statuettes required a pregnancy fantasy, albeit in a male mind.
> The thought of that era was dominated by a generative image.
>
> (Zoja 2000, 72)

If a new masculine will rise, capable of generating Eros, there is still some hope for all humanity.

Notes

1 I use female and male to refer to the sex of humans and animals, and *feminine/masculine* when I refer to the qualities that we consider typical of women or men https://dictionary.cambridge.org/it/grammatica/grammatica-britannico/masculine-or-feminine-male-or-female

2 The central image of alchemy. . . . Sacred work, a search for the supreme and ultimate value (Edinger 1985, 4).

3 Vas Hermeticum: the alchemical retort in which the alchemist cooked the prima materia into the Lapis.

4 In alchemy, coincidentia oppositorum is a synonym for coniunctio/conjunction.

5 Hitler's formula repeatedly cited by Jung even after the catastrophe.

6 www.treccani.it/vocabolario/gender/

7 I thank my brother, Carlo Grande, writer (reflections on S. Weil and the Cathars), and my son, Carlo Grande, future historian (concept of gender history), for their personal communications.

8 "The Child Is Father of the Man" (Wordsworth 2004, 515), in *My Heart Leaps Up*, also known as *The Rainbow*.

9 Nomos (Greek: Νόμος) was the spirit of laws, statutes and ordinances. Nomos' wife is Eusebia (mercy), and their daughter is Dike (justice).

10 The phrase "the good enough mother" was coined by the British pediatrician and psychoanalyst D. W. Winnicott.

11 *Zeitgeist* is a concept from eighteenth- to nineteenth-century German philosophy, meaning 'spirit of the age' (Jung, 1957 § 545).

12 Stern D. (1985) Self not in the Jungian way (see Jacoby 1999, 47).

13 Craving: "an intense desire or urge for the drug" (DSM-5 2013, 483).

14 Documentary 2020, Netflix, with interviews with figures like Justin Rosenstein (inventor of the Facebook "like" button).

15 *Holding* (literally "support") is a term introduced by D. Winnicott to define the mother's ability to act as a container for the child's anxieties, *holding company* is a company created to buy and own the shares of other companies, which it then controls.

16 Uroboros is the circular snake, the primal dragon of the beginning that bites its own tail, the self-begetting. It is the archetype of the All-One (Neumann 2014, 10).

17 The movie *Joker* (2019) is based on the DC Comics character of the same name (Batman's antagonist), inspired by Victor Hugo's novel, *The Man Who Laughs* (1869), the story of an abandoned orphaned child.

18 *Imago* "is a term introduced by Jung . . . many images (e.g., of parents) do not arise out of actual personal Experiences of parents of a particular character, but are based on unconscious fantasies or derived from the activities of the archetype" (Samuels 1986, 73).

19 Sebreli J. J., *Comediantes y mártires. Ensayo contra los mitos.* Editorial Debate Barcelona-Buenos Aires 2008, p. 76.
20 The Catholic Church comes to define Adam's guilt as "blessed", because it brought Jesus the Redeemer to men: "O felix culpa, quae talem ac tantum meruit habere Redemptorem" (Blessed sin, who deserved such and such great Redeemer). The phrase derives from a homily of St. Augustine.
21 "Not even a God can stand up to Necessity" (Platone 2013, 2515 e 2623, Laws, 741a, 818b, quoted in Hillman 1991, 89).
22 https://en.wikipedia.org/wiki/Jessica_Alves and https://en.wikipedia.org/wiki/Valeria_ Lukyanova
23 Enantiodromia (from the ancient Greek ἐναντιοδρομία, composed of *enantios*, opposite and *dromos*, race) literally means race in the opposite. With this concept, in the philosophy of Heraclitus is indicated the conception according to which everything that exists passes into its opposite: 'What is opposed is convenient, and from the things that differ harmony is generated more beautiful, and all things are born according to competition and contention' (Heraclitus, Fragment VIII, 343, (2006/2012)).
24 The 'power of women' (*Weibermacht* in German) is a medieval and Renaissance artistic and literary topos, showing heroic or wise men dominated by women.
25 For a study of self-harm and social withdrawal (hikikomori) in young people (males and females), see Grande R. (2015), Diploma Thesis at Jung Inst, 2015.

References

Agamben, G. (2006). *Che cos'è un Dispositivo?* Milano: Nottetempo srl
Bauman, Z. (2000). *Liquid Modernity.* Cambridge: Polity Press
Bauman, Z. (2005). *Liquid Life.* Cambridge: Polity Press
Bauman, Z. (2007). *Consuming Life.* Cambridge: Polity Press
Beauvoir, S. de (2012). *Il secondo sesso.* Milano: Il Saggiatore
Beck, U., Beck-Gernsheim, E. (2001). *Individualization: Institutionalized Individualism and Its Social and Political Consequences.* London: SAGE Publications Ltd
Beebe, J. (2020). C.G. Jung, Anima/Animus, Homosexuality, and Integrity, in Carpani, S. (ed.) *Breakfast at Küsnacht: Conversations on C.G. Jung and Beyond.* Asheville: Chiron Publications. Ed. Kindle
Carpani, S. (2020a). The Consequences of Freedom, in Brodersen, E. (ed.) (2020). *Jungian Perspectives on Indeterminate States: Betwixt and Between Borders.* London: Routledge
Carpani, S. (2020b). *Breakfast At Küsnacht: Conversations on C.G. Jung and Beyond.* Asheville: Chiron Publications. Edizione del Kindle
Daniel, R. (2020). *The Self. Quest for Meaning in a Changing World.* Einsiedeln: Daimon Verlag
DSM-5 (2013). *The Diagnostic and Statistical Manual of Mental Disorders, 5th Edition.* Washington, DC: American Psychiatric Publishing
Edinger, F.E. (1985). *Anatomy of the Psyche.* Chicago and La Salle, IL: Open Court.
Gimboutas, M. (1989). *The Language of the Goddess: Unearthing the Hidden Symbols of Western Civilization.* New York: Harper & Row
Girard, R. (1992). *La violenza e il sacro.* Milano: Adelphi
Glezerman, M. (2017). *Gender Medicine: The Groundbreaking New Science of Gender- and Sex-Related Diagnosis and Treatment.* New York: Harry N Abrams Inc
Grande, C. (2002). *La Via dei Lupi. Storia di una ribellione nel Medioevo romantico e crudele.* Milano: Ponte alle Grazie

Grande, R. (2009). *Il Bambino di Cioccolato*. Milano: Ponte alle Grazie

Grande, R. (2015). *Getting Hurt in Adolescence: From Blood to Ice. A Jungian Study on Clinical, Collective and Symbolic Aspects of Self-injury and Hikikomori*. Diploma Thesis – C.G. Jung Institute, Zürich SS 2015

Guggenbühl-Craig, A. (2015). *Marriage Is Dead – Long Live Marriage!* Washington, DC: Spring Publications, Ed. Kindle.

Hawking, S.W. (2010). *A Briefer History of Time*. London: Transworld Digital – Kindle Ed.

Hillman, J. (1991). *La vana fuga dagli Dei – Ananke e Atena*. Milano: Adelphi ed.

Jacoby, M. (1999). *Jungian Psychotherapy & Contemporary Infant Research – Basic Patterns of Emotional Exchange*. London: Routledge

Jung, C.G. (1957). *Collected Works*, vol. 10, *The Undiscovered Self (Present and Future)* Civilization in Transition. Bollingen Series XX. Princeton, NJ: Princeton University Press

Jung, C.G. (1963). *Collected Works*, vol. 14, *Mysterium Coniunctionis. An Enquiry into the Separation and Synthesis of Psychic Opposites in Alchemy (2nd edn.1974)*. Bollingen Series XX. Princeton, NJ: Princeton University Press.

Jung, C.G. (1972a). *Basic Postulates of Analytical Psychology*, in *Collected Works*, vol. 8, *The Structure and Dynamics of the Psyche. (2nd printing 1972)*. Bollingen Series XX. Princeton, NJ: Princeton University Press

Jung, C.G. (1972b). *Analytical Psychology and Weltanschauung*, in *Collected Works*, vol. 8, *The Structure and Dynamics of the Psyche. (2nd printing 1972)*. Bollingen Series XX. Princeton, NJ: Princeton University Press

Jung, C.G. (1977a). *Collected Works*, vol. 17, *The Development of Personality*. Introduction to *Wickes' Analyse der Kinderseele*. Bollingen Series XX. Princeton, NJ: Princeton University Press

Jung, C.G. (1977b). *Introduction to the Religious and Psychological Problems of Alchemy*, in *Collected Works*, vol. 12, *Psychology and Alchemy*. Bollingen Series XX. Princeton, NJ: Princeton University Press

Jung, C.G. (1989). *Memories, Dreams, Reflections*. A. Jaffe (ed.). New York: Vintage Books Editions.

Jung, C.G. (1991). *The Houston Films* in *Aspects of the Masculine*. John Beebe Editor. Princeton, NJ: Princeton University Press

Klein, M. (1952). *Developments in Psycho-Analysis. Notes on Some Schizoid Mechanism* Londra: Hogarth Press

Lingiardi, V. (2012). *Citizen Gay. Affetti e diritti*. Milano: Il Saggiatore Tascabili

McWilliams, N. (2011). *Psychoanalytic Diagnosis*. New York: The Guilford Press

Neumann, E. (2002). *The Child. Structure and Dynamics of the Nascent Personality*. London: Karnak ldt.

Neumann, E. (2014). *The Origin and History of Consciousness*. Bollingen Series XLII. Princeton, NJ: Princeton University Press.

Orbach, S. (2009). *Bodies*. London: Profile Books

Orbach, S. (2020). *How Are Women Today? Feminism, Love, and Revolution*, in Carpani, S. *Breakfast at Küsnacht: Conversations on C.G. Jung and Beyond*. Asheville: Chiron Publications. Ed. Kindle.

Platone (2013). *Leggi*, in Tutte le Opere. Newton Compton ed.

Rose Sonya, O. (2010). *What Is Gender History?* Cambridge: Polity Press

Saito, Tamaki (2013). *Hikikomori: Adolescence Without End*. University of Minnesota Press

Samuels, A. (1986). *A Critical Dictionary of Jungian Analysis*. London: Routledge

Smith, S.L. (1995). *The Power of Women: A Topos in Medieval Art and Literature*. University of Pennsylvania Press

Stern, D. (1985). *The Interpersonal World of the Infant – A View from Psychoanalysis and Developmental Psychology*. London: Karnak

Valcarenghi, M. (2003). *L'aggressività femminile*. Milano: Bruno Mondadori ed.

von Franz, M.-L. (2000). *The Cat. A Tale of Feminine Redemption*. Toronto: Inner City Books

Weil, S. (1996). *I Catari e la civiltà mediterranea*. Bologna: ed. Marietti.

Winnicott, D.W. (2005). *Playing and Reality*. London: Routledge

Wordsworth, W. (2004). *Poems* – Poemhunter.com – The World's Poetry Archive.

Zoja, L. (2000). *Il gesto di Ettore. Preistoria, storia, attualità e scomparsa del padre*. Torino: Bollati Boringhieri

Zoja, L. (2013). *Utopie Minimaliste. Un mondo più desiderabile anche senza Eroi*. Milano: Chiarelettere ed.

Chapter 8

False Start

A neo-Jungian Critique of Self-Help

Niccolò Fiorentino Polipo

In this chapter, I will address the question of why self-help is to be considered an unsatisfactory answer to the spiritual needs of modern individuals, from a neo-Jungian perspective. I will do so by reviewing Jung's theory of psychodynamics and reformulating it as a theoretical framework to foretell which ethical systems can be expected to lead to lasting individual or collective change and which cannot. Building on this framework, I will put forth the concept of False Start as a 'diagnosis' for the problem with self-help, from a neo-Jungian perspective.

What is self-help?

The term 'self-help' immediately makes us think of those books we are all familiar with whose purpose is to give instructions for personal or spiritual development (Starker, 2002). However, self-help is far more than a publishing industry. First, it is *not just literature*, because self-help books exist alongside self-help seminars, online programs, retreats, and so on. Second, self-help is *not just business* but, on a closer look, a whole attitude that modern individuals hold regarding the way in which happiness is to be pursued. There is a *fil rouge*, psychologically speaking, between the inspirational quote posted by an Instagram model below her selfie ("be your best self"), the motivational messages sliding on the screens of a local gym ("be stronger than your excuses"), and an auditorium packed with young men paying their guru to tell them how to get rid of their pornography addiction. This *fil rouge* is self-help as a "cultural complex", in the sense of an "emotionally charged group of ideas" revolving around a center of meaning (Singer & Kimbles, 2004, p. 69). As a cultural complex, self-help underlies also the popular idea in mainstream psychology that one should foster positive emotions or traits (e.g., resilience) and let go of the 'toxic' ones. In its broadest sense, then, self-help coincides with the general fixation with 'wellness' that is characteristic of most relatively affluent societies (Cederström & Spicer, 2015; Nehring, Alvarado, Hendriks, & Kerrigan, 2016).

In consideration of the multiplicity of meanings that the term self-help can have, I feel compelled to facilitate the discussion by clarifying how I will be using the term. In the context of this chapter, I will use 'self-help' mainly as a qualificator of propositions guiding life projects and, by transitive property, of life

DOI: 10.4324/9781003168829-9

projects themselves. In particular, I define a self-help project as any individual or collective attempt to catalyze self-change guided by a proposition of the type: '*let us strive for P and leave ¬P behind*', where P is a positive state (e.g., self-esteem, adventurousness, or abstinence) that one would like to see emancipated from its opposite (self-doubt, boredom, or dependence, respectively). Under this definition, the classic new year's resolution would qualify as a self-help project to the extent that it is guided by a proposition of the type 'let us strive for fitness', for instance, 'and leave all this laziness behind'. Typically, a self-help project is complemented by specific techniques to actualize its programmatic proposition. This is what we buy when we buy a self-help book: the experience of being let in on a method that, it is promised, will help us attain a certain ethico-psychological *desideratum* (e.g., getting back control over life, realizing one's potential, being happy) and leave all that was blocking it behind.

A neo-Jungian critique of self-help

The most striking feature about self-help projects is that, on average, they *do not seem to work*. It is not that these projects do not start; rather, they do not last. This is proverbially true about new year's resolutions. But the same holds for life projects generated by self-help books and programs. It might be argued that the ultimate proof for the ineffectiveness of these products is their mere multiplication. If any single self-help author were capable of making their readers happy ever after, they would run all others out of business. Instead, the mere fact that these products keep coming in, and that they are bought mostly by repeat customers (Salerno, 2005), is a powerful indicator for their seeming inability to transform people.

But if we accept the general premise that self-help projects on average do not seem to work, then we are left with the task of finding out why. It is not sufficient to criticize self-help projects because they *do not* work: what is needed is a theoretically informed explanation for why they *cannot* possibly work. I propose that Jungian psychology provides that. In contrast to the folk psychology explanation that self-help projects would fail because people are generally weak-willed, analytical psychology can inform a theorization for why something like a self-help project would be intrinsically doomed to fail, no matter how much willpower is put into it. To show this, I will first review Jung's theory psychodynamics and reformulate it into a theoretical framework to classify ethical systems on the basis of their likelihood of leading to lasting individual or collective change. Then, I will build on this framework to introduce the concept of False Start as a 'diagnosis' for the reason self-help should be considered an unsatisfactory answer to the spiritual needs of modern individuals, from a neo-Jungian perspective.

Jung's theory of libido

It is widely known that Jung, unlike Freud, did not conceive of libido in sexual terms but, more generally, as "the force of desire and aspiration" and ultimately as "psychic energy in the widest sense" (CW 5, par. 98).[1] However, the conse-quences of this paradigm shift are not as frequently appreciated.

Jung's theory of libido rests on two assumptions. The first is that conscious-ness depends on its energetic source for all of its endeavors. The second is that it does not fully dispose of this source as it pleases: libido stands only "in part at the disposal of the ego" (*ivi*). Both of these assumptions can be better understood in analogy with physical energy: not only does a machine need to be supplied with energy to perform any work, but the outflow of energy is subject to con-straints by the need of favorable gradients. In other words, libido, just like water, needs a slope to flow (CW 5, par. 337). These two basic coordinates of Jung's theory of libido already present us with a specific problem: the possibility of a *misalignment of consciousness with respect to its energy source*. If consciousness depends on libido, yet this energetic source ultimately lies out of its reach (in the unconscious), then what happens if consciousness finds itself unable to provide the gradient required for libido to outflow and be channeled into its projects? This misalignment can take two forms:

1. *Subtraction of libido* – If consciousness fails to secure its energetic supply by satisfying the psychodynamic requirements necessary for the outflow of libido, then in reaching towards a certain goal, it may suddenly experience an unpleasant loss of momentum. This corresponds to a subjective experi-ence that for the primitive is a "hard and concrete fact: his life ceases to flow, things lose their glamour, plants, animals, and men no longer prosper"; "modern man, in the same situation experiences" a sense of being "stuck" or "a depression" (CW 5, par. 250).

2. *Autonomization of libido* – If consciousness fails to convey energy into its projects, then the untamed libidinal flux, after reaching a certain threshold, could run uncontrolled, much like a dam breaks under an excessive pressure of water. This "absolute and inexorable, unjust and superhuman" element (CW 5, par. 89) is the natural aspect of libido, as natural are tsunamis or volcanic eruptions. This corresponds to the subjective experience of being at the mercy of a superior force that is determining the subject *malgré soi*. The impression of extraneousness given by the relative autonomy of the libidinal course typically leads to its projection as an external and invisible influence, either of a malignant or an indifferent but implacable nature (e.g., fate; CW 5, par. 644).

It is important to understand that if libido, like hydropower, is "morally neu-tral" (CW 5, par. 182), the energetic misalignment of consciousness represents an eminently practical and therefore also *moral* problem. In fact, as long as con-sciousness depends on libido for its endeavors, then among these there will be the morally relevant ones. Since moral action, like all action, requires motivation as its psychic correlate, then the energetic misalignment, in both of its variants, constitutes a problem of diminished "moral agency" (Polipo, 2020, p. 249): in the former case, because a reflux of libido might hit a person's righteous actions; in the latter, because a person might be coerced into doing the 'evil they do not want' (Romans 7:19). Ultimately, although libido in itself is neither good nor evil, individuals need it to do good and to avoid evil. Energetic alignment is key because "there is no morality without freedom" (CW 6, par. 357).

Thus, from a Jungian perspective, we might say that the predicament of the moral agent is at least two-fold. The moral agent needs, first of all, a direction to go in because, as Seneca famously put it, "there is no favorable wind for the sailor who does not know where to go" (*Ep.*, Book VIII, LXXI, 3). However, knowing where to go – in the sense of having a conscious project and the will to pursue it – is not sufficient. The sailor might know where they want to go, but be becalmed (*subtraction*) or have the wind blowing in the opposite direction (*autonomization*). To continue with the metaphor,[2] what the sailor needs, besides a compass, is an instrument similar to the ox-hide bag that Aeolus gave to Ulysses (*Od.*, X, 19–27), which allows to gain control of the forces of nature by capturing all the winds but the one that is favorable to the sailor's course.[3]

Jung's theory of symbol

This instrument, which consciousness uses to gain the collaboration of the unconscious and thus liberate libido into a state of conscious availability, is the symbol. Jung compares it to a *transformer* that is used to convert libido "from a 'lower' to a 'higher' form" (CW 5, par. 344). Beyond metaphors, a symbol is merely an expression with a fundamentally *indicative* nature: a representation hinting at something beyond itself (Pieri, 1998). However, Jung further defines it negatively by differentiating it from another indicative expression: the sign (CW 6, par. 814). While a sign is an abbreviated expression of a *known* thing, a proper symbol for Jung is the best currently available expression of something partially *unknown* (CW 5, par. 180). There is one side to the symbol that can be grasped by reason but another that remains inaccessible. As a suitable representation to provide that 'gradient' which libido needs to outflow, the symbol must be a representation that brings together not only known and unknown, but all of the opposites in the psyche: *a unified representation of the totality of the psyche in all of its incommensurable aspects*.

"The symbol is neither abstract nor concrete, neither rational nor irrational, neither real nor unreal" but "always both" (CW 12, par. 400). As a coincidence of opposites, a symbol is never a simple reality, such as only-'beautiful' or only-'good' one. It "unites antithetical elements within its nature" (CW 6, par. 211) and "has the quality of being related to all psychic functions": not only thinking or feeling, but intuition and sensation as well (CW 6, par. 187). In order to be effective in channeling the libidinal course, a symbol must be "unassailable": "an unsurpassed container of meaning . . . sufficiently remote from comprehension to resist all attempts of the critical intellect to break it down" (CW 6, par. 401). It must express "the inexpressible" (CW 6, par. 816), and as long as it maintains this quality and is not 'solved' by reason, then it is said to be a *living symbol*: but as soon as it loses this quality, it loses its life-promoting value as well and assumes merely a "historical" significance (CW 6, par. 819).

The crucial question, then, becomes: how is a symbol formed? On this, Jung is adamant: "such an expression cannot be contrived by reason, it can only be created through living" (CW 6, par. 169). If a symbol must be a synthesis of conscious and unconscious, and more generally of all psychic opposites, then it is logical that consciousness cannot create one for itself: not only because when consciousness creates something for itself, it is only able to "put into it" what it already knows (CW 6, par. 817), but also because consciousness works according to the principle of non-contradiction, by which it is either P or ¬*P*, and "*tertium non datur*" (CW 11, par. 738). That is why a symbol, as a *coniuctio oppositorum*, is not a rabbit that consciousness can take out of its hat but something that always *has to emerge from the unconscious*. From a Jungian perspective, then, consciousness is twice subjected to the unconscious: because from there comes the *problem* that consciousness faces (the energetic misalignment) but also its *solution* (the symbol).

The relativization of the role of consciousness in solving its own energetic predicament has an important ethical consequence: that, from a Jungian perspective, one places an unrealistic faith in willpower if one believes that it can generate any change in the absence of a living symbol. Consciousness is not like Baron Munchausen, who can get out of the stasis by pulling its own hair. "Psychic development cannot be accomplished by intention and will alone; it needs the attraction of the symbol" (CW 8, par. 47). The "voluntaristic decision" for Jung is an "ineffectual" solution to the "ethical problem" because "it requires in addition the auxiliary energies" of the symbol (Jung & Neumann, 2015, p. 368). One needs "two mutually complementary methods": "moral decision *plus* ritual action, based on the symbol"; otherwise, "one cannot command the drive without repressing it" (*ivi*). In light of Jung's psychodynamics, any spasmodic conscious effort that is not accompanied by a living symbol is *volens nolens* doomed to be short lived.

Even more specifically, Jung suggests that there is a proportional relationship between the ability of an ethical system to maintain itself close enough to the interrelation of opposites in the psyche and its motivating force: the more an ethical system moves away from that source, the less effective it becomes (CW 6, par. 415). This reflects in Jung's critique of Schiller's aestheticism as an ethical system that would not be "fitted" to solve the ethical problem because it simply poses a value ("beauty" or "pleasure") while rejecting all that opposes it ("anything evil, ugly, and difficult"; CW 6, par. 194). Schiller's aestheticism for Jung exemplifies, more generally, all those ethical systems that are too "differentiated" (CW 6, par. 415) on a rational level and which, in contrast to living symbols, take the natural interrelation of opposites in the vital process and attempt to emancipate the 'good' from the 'evil' all too clearly. In doing do, these ethical systems lose that mixture of pure and impure, "clear and muddy" sources from which "life itself flows" (*ivi*). For that, they pay a penalty: they lose "all moral force" (CW 6, par. 194), and "precisely because the muddy elements are excluded" (CW 6, par. 415). Unlike differentiated ethics, living symbols maintain themselves in greater proximity to the contradictory nature of the vital process, and that explains not only their great activating power but also their longevity: keeping close to the whole, in fact, is a way of avoiding the "unconscious disturbance of the conscious" (CW 6, par. 212).

A theoretical framework for the classification of ethical systems

Building on Jung's theory of psychodynamics, I will now outline a theoretical framework for the classification of systems of ideas aimed at orienting personal and spiritual development on the basis of their likelihood of giving rise to lasting individual or collective change. This framework will work as a bridge between Jungian psychodynamics and the question of why self-help should be regarded as unsatisfactory, from a neo-Jungian perspective.

The framework starts with a general assumption. The assumption is that there are some natural laws governing human life that one needs to become acquainted with and abide by as much as possible, if one wants to lead a good, happy, or, in the more teleological versions of this view, fulfilled life. Conversely, the same laws that would be conductive to such moral goods, if followed, can make an individual's life miserable if ignored or gone against. This assumption rests on a form of ethical realism by which this set of laws would exist 'out there', regardless of anyone's belief in their existence, just as the laws of physics are written in the book of nature. Although not universally shared, this assumption is predominant in traditional systems of ethics and is coessential to the very notion of wisdom. We find this assumption at the basis of most natural law ethical theories, from the pagan Aristotle, to the Christian Thomas Aquinas, to the non-Western Laozi (e.g., Shen, 2013). We find it in Jung when he stresses that morality is not the invention of "some vaunting Moses on Sinai, but something inherent in the laws of life" and that the "natural flow of libido" requires "obedience to the fundamental laws of human nature" in order to attain "life's *optimum*" (CW 6, par. 356). Finally, we find it underlying most self-help literature, which assumes precisely that there are some 'rules' in life which one should follow in order to be 'happy'.

For brevity, I will from now on hypostatize this assumption by referring to the ensemble of natural laws governing human life as the 'Truth (as Whole)' or simply as the 'Truth/Whole'. The Truth/Whole is traditionally assumed to have two key characteristics: *it is eternal* and therefore transcends most changes in history or culture, and *it is complex* and therefore transcends human comprehension. In particular, the Truth/Whole is complex not only for its vastness, but also because it fails to comply with the principle of non-contradiction recalled previously. Rather, the Truth/Whole contains contradictions or, as the poet would say, "multitudes" (Whitman, 1855). In metaphysical terms, we might say that "the true is the whole" (Hegel, 1807, p. 13) in the sense that it is what embraces the single dialectical movements that oppose each other. This reflects in Jung's idea that if something is (psychologically) true, then the opposite must be true as well. A traditional way to visualize this co-presence of opposites in the Truth/Whole is to picture it as having a circular or spherical form. This visual expedient has a long history: such a shape is typically attributed to all 'objects' invested with a transcendent quality, from Parmenides' Eternal Being to mandalas or even UFOs (CW 10, par. 622).

Moving downwards from the Truth/Whole, the framework envisages two levels. The first level (L1) is composed of all those ethical systems that attempt to express the set of laws underlying human life but necessarily do so imperfectly, due to the complex nature of the Truth/Whole. This reflects, for instance, in the idea expressed in the first chapter of the *Tao Te Ching* that 'the name that can be named is not the eternal Name' (Sabbadini, 2013). L1 is a level of *representation*: we find here 'maps' of the Truth/Whole, as opposed to the Truth/Whole itself. This is the place where living symbols belong, as representations of the psyche in all of its incommensurable aspects. To understand the representative nature of a living symbol, I propose to compare it to Achilles' shield (*Il.*, XVIII, 478–608). A living symbol is one that manages to accomplish the same that Hephaestus achieved in forging the hero's shield: carving out with divine craft *a microcosm in which the macrocosm reflects* (Taplin, 1980).[4] A symbol must be able to condense the *whole of life* within the boundaries of a given frame, like a tapestry. Here applies another traditional idea: that if the Truth/Whole is circular because it contains contradictions, then the more *well-rounded* an instance of thinking is, the more it will participate of the same properties of the Truth/Whole. In other words, an L1 ethical system is all the more long lasting the more it resembles the rotundity of the Truth/Whole by containing contradictions within itself (e.g., see 'circular thinking' in Gnosticism; CW 14, par. 123).

As noted, a crucial feature of the living symbol is that it cannot come from consciousness but has to emerge from the unconscious. This 'alien' origin (i.e., the fact that it comes from an intentionality that lies beyond consciousness) is a precondition for its ability to maintain itself close enough to the Truth/Whole and therefore to last. An example is the Christian symbol. The cross is a map of the Truth/Whole: a minimalistic representation that is able to signify at the same time the 'whole of life' as a coincidence of sacrifice and reward, death and eternal life. Two properties cannot be denied to the Christian symbol: (a) its great activating power[5] and (b) its longevity, having imposed itself for thousands of years as "a major source of the interpretation of life" (Browning & Cooper, 2004, p. xiii). The important lesson to be taken about symbol formation here is that the longevity of Jesus' words is put in direct relationship with their non-human (i.e., not only-conscious) origin when, for instance, the fact that people have found themselves coming back to those words with renovated meanings is adduced as proof of their divine nature[6]. 'They could not have been the words of a man', it is argued, 'for having had such a life-giving and long-lasting quality, they must be the Words of God'. This idea, together with other religious ideas such as that 'all that man does perishes, but all that God does lasts' (Ecc. 3:14), make perfect sense in light of Jung's theory of symbol formation. They express the psychological truth that, as long as consciousness creates a symbol for itself, this will prove unfitting as soon as consciousness is faced with the unknown. But if consciousness instead receives a symbol *from elsewhere*, that is, from a place lying beyond its borders (the unconscious or the Self as the *imago Dei*, CW 5, par. 612), then this expression will have a better chance to last, because it will rest not on the feeble and ever-changing foundations of consciousness but on the large 'shoulders' of the unconscious.[7]

Although L1 ethical systems are long lasting, they are not eternal. The Christian symbol itself entered a crisis, just as the Olympic gods did in their time: as consciousness evolves, living symbols eventually 'die', while the Truth/Whole survives them. Symbols are maps, not the territory. This is why Jung could praise the Roman Catholic church for its symbolic richness and consider it one of the last institutions where modern individuals could live a "meaningful life" (CW 18, par. 631) while at the same time declaring: "I know it is the truth, but it is the truth in a form in which I cannot accept it any more" (par. 632).[8] All representations of the Truth/Whole, since they are not the Truth/Whole itself, are subject to history: they expire, leaving a trail behind them, like a spiritual cemetery. The same is true for individual symbols emerging from the unconscious of creative personalities: they exercise the crucial function of bringing the individual *forward*, but as individuation progresses, they are surpassed and left behind like empty shells.

Descending further down in the framework, we find the second level (L2) of ethical systems. These are systems that are entirely made by 'mortals' or "consciousness-based" (Colacicchi, 2020, p. 2). We could think of them as a further 'emanation' from the Truth/Whole, in the neo-Platonic sense of a pouring forth that corresponds also to a loss of Being (Plotinus, *Enn.* II, 3.2). If L1 systems are already a 'betrayal' of the Truth/Whole, then L2 systems are "thrice removed" from the Truth/Whole (Plato, *Rep*, X, 598b), because they are not only representations of the Truth/Whole but representations that are tainted by the one-sidedness of consciousness. Since consciousness is only able to grasp one aspect of the Truth/Whole at a time, leaving its opposite out, L2 systems do not maintain themselves in proximity to the copresence of opposites in the Truth/Whole, but rather 'take the best and leave the rest': they distill the clear and leave the muddy out (CW 6, par. 415); in biblical terms, they separate the wheat from the chaff ahead of time (Mt 13:24–30). We may place at L2 ethical systems such as Schiller's aestheticism, the 'degraded' version of Christianity criticized by Neumann under the name of 'old ethic' (1949), and, most importantly, self-help propositions with their characteristic program to attain P to the exclusion of $\neg P$.[9] Just as living symbols derive their activating force and their longevity from keeping close to the Truth/Whole, so differentiated ethics, by getting further away from it, would be bound not only to lose "moral force" (CW 6, par. 194) but also to produce characteristically short-lived forms of individual or collective self-change. But to 'diagnosticate' more precisely what would cause a self-help project, as the product of an L2 ethical system, to be short lived, I will introduce the concept of False Start.

False Start as a diagnosis for the problem with self-help

I argue that the problem with self-help projects, from a neo-Jungian perspective, can be identified in the fact that they systematically trigger a dynamic that I propose to refer to as a 'False Start'. A False Start is a psychodynamic pattern occurring in two phases.

1. In the first phase, consciousness orients itself towards a 'pseudo-symbolic proposition'. With this term, I indicate a representation with a prescriptive tension that, at the same time, falls short of satisfying the prerequisites to constitute a living symbol. In particular, a pseudo-symbolic proposition is a representation of the one-sidedly positive form given previously: '*let us strive for P and leave ¬P behind*'. Orientation of consciousness towards a pseudo-symbolic proposition allows a momentary liberation of libido that sets the psyche in motion.[10] Yet, at the same time, it lays the ground for an "inflation" as the psychic event "by which any part of the psyche identifies itself with the whole psychic life" preluding to a "transformation with a catastrophic character" (Pieri, 1998, p. 215).
2. In the second phase, as a function of the compensation principle, the "puffed-up" conscious attitude (CW 7, par. 110) is taken down precisely at the hand of whatever negative the pseudo-symbolic proposition was trying to liberate consciousness from. This is the phenomenon of enantiodromia as the "emergence of the unconscious opposite in the course of time" that "always occurs when an extreme, one-sided tendency dominates conscious life", with the result that it "first inhibits the conscious performance and subsequently breaks through the conscious control" (CW 6, par. 709). It is a return of that same loss of moral agency that one wanted to avoid: "inflation may provide a sense of temporary joy, but it undermines moral freedom" (Colacicchi, 2020, p. 17).

This two-step pattern might remind the reader, more generally, of the physiological alternation between centrifugal and centripetal movements in psychological development (CW 6, par. 428). However, what is distinctive about a False Start is the *rapidity* with which consciousness goes from 1 to 2 and ends up flat on its back. Why would something like speed be important? Because there are two ways to block the dialectical development of personality. One is to shut it down, as in certain 'mindfulness' versions of self-help (Carpani, 2020; see also Purser, 2019). Yet an equally effective way is to speed it up to excess. The acceleration of the history of consciousness, ironically, coincides with its end (see Vidali, 2020, pp. 225–230, 238–243). Timing is as important to psychic development as it is to music: a theme in a musical piece needs to be given time to develop in other to give rise to a counter-movement that can culminate into a meaningful resolution. This is true at other levels of analysis. A State with too many governmental falls and re-formations, for instance, is one without history precisely because of an excess of historical events.[11] False Starts are a series of stop-and-go movements that risk 'jamming' the engine of the psyche.

The rapidity of a False Start is also what surprises the subject as well as any third spectator. The whole pattern looks as if consciousness 'stumbled', not without a comical effect. In reaching towards a certain goal, the subject sees its project slip through its fingers: a short movement forward, followed by a sonorous plop. The fall is so unexpected that, as in the case of the autonomization of libido, one would be tempted to invoke the action of an invisible sprite 'tripping' consciousness. But a False Start is the action of no contingent intruder: it is *inflation* itself that causes a return of the negative that makes the conscious project fall apart shortly thereafter. A False Start is precisely this time-bound surge forward causing a resurgence of whatever 'vice' wanted to be canceled from the face of the Earth.

To illustrate in what sense the second phase of a False Start does not occur randomly but as a precise *sequitur* from its premise, let us take this passage from Dostoevsky (1864):

> I have a friend . . . Oh, gentlemen! He's a friend of yours too and in fact to whom is he not a friend? When he undertakes to do something this gentleman will immediately expound to you, lucidly and grandiloquently, exactly how he should proceed, according to the laws of truth and logic . . . and then, exactly a quarter of an hour later . . . prompted by some inner impulse which is stronger than all his interests, he'll take a completely different tack, that is to say, he'll blatantly go against what he was just saying.
>
> (p. 20)

Everybody can recognize here one of their friends: the one who says s/he is going to start a diet and orders junk food only minutes later, or the one who uninstalls a dating app in the morning and reinstalls it during the night. But Dostoevskij adds a revealing sentence: "*I'm warning you that my friend is a collective person, so it's rather difficult to pin the blame on him individually*" (ivi, my italics). In other words, a False Start is not the defect of a few individuals, perhaps the hypocrites or the weak-willed ones. Rather, it is a dynamic embedded into the fabric of the human soul: a psychodynamic law and, I would argue, even a metaphysical necessity.[12]

How easy is it to quit smoking?

How many smokers have said in their lifetime, 'this is the last one', and that turned out to be a False Start? The author of the most famous self-help book against tabagism thinks that 'it's easy to quit smoking, if you know how to do it' (Carr, 1985). After reading through the drawbacks of being a smoker, one arrives at the chapter "The advantages of being a smoker", where the author has jokingly left a blank page. This blank page, I propose, is the perfect illustration of the concealment of the negative made by pseudo-symbolic propositions in their eagerness to present a one-sidedly positive picture of self-change. No 'symptomatic' behavior, in fact, is without secondary gains. In the case of smoking, these gains could be killing time, fitting in, being able to ask a lighter of the person one fancies at a bar, and so on. *Of course* it is easy to quit smoking, if one is presented with the only-positive side of things (in this case, ironically, the negative-only side of smoking). And what may happen is that the subject will get motivated enough to give up smoking – after all, they have *nothing* to lose. But will those secondary gains not pay them a visit, perhaps on a night out? The subject, then, could even be naively scandalized at *how easy*[13] it was to fall under their invisible spell, and will be entitled to complain like Polyphemus: 'Nobody (Οὖτις) has failed me!' What will have failed them is what did not appear on the blank page. We see, then, how such over-simplifications do not bring "a greater sense of humanity and universal happiness" but "a particular form of cruelty and dishonesty" (Drewermann, 1982, p. 63). The reader will blame themselves rather than the book. But what if the teacher, not the pupil, is the one in error? What if there is nothing 'spiritually' easy about stopping smoking? Unless one means it as in the joke attributed to Twain: then it is the easiest thing in the world, when one has done it a *thousand times* – that is, a thousand False Starts.

False Start as a defective aircraft

In a sense, all of our life projects – be they a romantic relationship, a career prospect, or an attempt at self-improvement – are things that we throw forth (lat. *pro-jacere*) and hope to see 'fly': that is, take off, sustain their trajectory, and land somewhere safely. From this perspective, we might get some insight into the reason behind the characteristically short-lived trajectory of self-help projects by examining the *complex balance of dynamic forces* that makes actual flying possible.[14]

How does an aircraft work?[15] The basic aerodynamic forces are four: Weight (W), Lift (L), Thrust (T), and Drag (D). Starting from the situation where the plane is still firmly on the ground, W is the main force at play as the one that is keeping the object down ($\downarrow$). In order to get the plane to fly, W needs to be overcome by generating L as a force going in the opposite direction ($\uparrow$). This is achieved by applying T, a force pushing the object forward ($\rightarrow$). Here is where the shape of the object starts to matter: if the plane were a cube, then T would be able to move it but not to lift it. Instead, a plane is shaped as it is so that, as speed increases, the air moving below the aircraft will determine a difference in pressure which provides L. Finally, what is D for? D is the force that goes in the opposite direction of motion ($\leftarrow$) and is essential to balance T. D becomes essential during landing, for instance, when the plane needs to decelerate to avoid crashing. We learn from these rudiments of the theory of flight that there are three general factors that one should consider whenever *projecting* a plane. As any child who has participated in a paper airplane contest already knows, it is a matter of (a) throwing the object with sufficient force (*propulsion*), (b) giving the launch the right inclination (*attitude*), and (c) folding the paper in the right way (*shape*).

Let us try to translate now from the aero-dynamics of aircrafts to the psycho-dynamics of life projects. We noted that the peculiarity of self-help projects is that they *do take off*, only they seem to crash shortly thereafter. Assuming a lack of unfavorable atmospheric agents, is it possible to predicate this characteristic trajectory on a single problem in the balance of dynamic forces that should sustain their flight? If we compared *propulsion* to willpower, then surely it could not be that: people put plenty of willpower into their projects of self-change, and these crash nonetheless. Could it be the *attitude*, then? This second element is more difficult to interpret, but if we were to compare it, for instance, to the life contingencies surrounding the launch of a life project, then it could not be that either, because people from all kinds of starting positions still characteristically report their self-help projects going down. We are left with the hypothesis that the reason self-help projects would be bound to be short-lived has to be predicated chiefly on their *shape*. But we know what the *eidos* of a pseudo-symbolic proposition guiding a self-help project is: '*Let us strive for the positive and leave the negative behind*'. We notice in this shape an *asymmetry*. Unlike the balanced form of a living symbol, a pseudo-symbolic proposition is 'tilted' in one direction – on the side of whatever positive is being prescribed.

How can this asymmetry be interpreted in keeping with our analogy? We could interpret it literally and note that an asymmetry in the wings of a plane hinders the possibility of a straight flight, with possibly disastrous consequences. Yet, another way to interpret it is to postulate that the shape of a self-help project is asymmetrical in the sense that it is designed so as to gain as much T as possible while neglecting the importance of balancing it with proportional D. It is as if these projects were 'pointy' enough to cut through life in the short term but had no in-built systems to decelerate, which would explain why they rarely land anywhere safe. D, in general, is the resistance exercised by a fluid against a moving object and, as such, is the force that has to be overcome in order to fly. However, there is another type of D (the so-called 'Form Drag') which is built *into the shape* of an aircraft. Pilots purposefully rely on this force, for instance, when they use speed brakes to slow down an aircraft. Self-help projects would appear to lack the spiritual equivalent of this safety system, and that might explain their ruinous trajectory.[16]

To illustrate what this lack of Form Drag looks like, let us take the movie *Yes Man* (Reed, 2008). Carl's life is in shambles. After a divorce, he has become depressed and says 'no' to all life opportunities. A friend convinces Carl to attend a self-help seminar where a guru makes him promise that, from now on, he will live according to a single rule: whatever the occasion, he will have to say 'yes' to life. The rule, in effect, gets Carl's life back into motion: he enjoys a period of existential 'fireworks', between continuous adventures and a new romance. However, soon the negative that had been excluded from life in order to gain momentum starts to creep back in: the rule turns against him, romance goes bad, a friend gets fired because of him. Eventually, Carl ends his 'shooting-star' parabola on a hospital bed. In this example, the D that would be lacking is the acknowledgement of all the times when Carl should have balanced the 'yeses' with the 'nos' in life.[17] The lesson seems to be that, if a self-help project does not 'brake' itself, it will be stopped *from without* (by life as the Truth/Whole). The self-help subject, like Kant's dove, perceives as a burden what is actually a pre-condition of a steady and sustained flight. Psychic movement requires both meaning and all-that-resists-meaning, as that which provides *grounding*.

If our hypothesis was correct, then self-help authors would be selling defective airplanes: these would be thrown in the air only to watch them go in nosedive, just like the early prototypes by the Wright Brothers. The strength of a Jungian perspective, in this case, is that it can be used to tell *in advance* whether a spiritual endeavor will last, just by looking at the shape of the proposition that guides it. Judging by the one-sidedness of the pseudo-symbolic proposition guiding a self-help project, one could make the *a priori* judgment that a certain life project will not go very far; and that judgment will be resting on the same irreproachability of *physis* which dictates that chickens cannot fly very high, no matter whether they believe themselves to be eagles.[18]

False Start as an artificial boost of libido

According to Jung's theory of psychodynamics, differentiated ethics should have no "moral force" (CW 6, para. 194), and the motivational culture paradoxically should have no motivating power at all. However, this is the where I believe that the classic theory might need updating. Observation, in fact, suggests that self-help projects are able to summon, if not a steady flow of libido, then at least an artificial boost of it. This is reflected in the enthusiasm, even the frenzy, with which they are embraced. But what is the mechanism through which a pseudo-symbolic proposition is able to give rise, if not to an actual Start, then at least to a False one?

I propose to think about this mechanism in analogy with what happens in most behavioral addictions (e.g., pornography addiction, binge watching, compulsive shopping). A behavioral addiction is a condition that arises in interaction with a product that is able to arouse a specific form of excitement in the human mind. The mechanism through which an addictive product is able to release such an artificial boost of libido can be described loosely as one of pressing an 'archetypal button' in the psyche, in the sense of taking advantage of a trans-individual tendency to exhibit a "*pattern of behavior*" in response to *stimula* that satisfy certain characteristics (CW 8, par. 841). Porn, for instance, is able to have the effect that it has, especially on young males, because it presses an archetypal button in their psyche, which is their response to certain *stimula* that are consequently exaggerated in an artificial way. There are entire categories of professionals who rely on such buttons in order to give rise to desired action tendencies. Screenwriters, for instance, purposefully strive to create an effect of suspense around the end of an episode in order for the viewer to click on the next episode (Lehne & Koelsch,

2015). Similarly, marketing experts purposefully strive to increase the perceived value of everyday objects by wrapping them in archetypal fantasies in order for the customer to make the purchase (Dichter, 1960). It can be hypothesized that pseudo-symbolic representations are able to summon their 'feel-good' injection of meaning and purpose in a similar way by pressing a yet-unspecified archetypal button in the psyche and giving rise to an associated 'call to action'.

It would be erroneous, then, to consider a living symbol the only ethical device that can arouse libido. A pseudo-symbolic representation can release as much libido as a living symbol. Rather, the problem seems to lie in the fact that most addictive products, including pseudo-symbolic propositions, are able to release their boost of libido only through an *artificial* manipulation of the archetype which, as such, triggers compensation from the Truth/Whole. The general principle is that "excessive happiness must always be paid for very dearly, psychologically speaking" (CW 3, par. 257). That is why gratification through porn tends to translate into post-coital *tristesse*, why one experiences that peculiar sense of emptiness after binge watching an entire TV series, or why the victim of a particularly persuasive salesperson is likely to be hit by buyer's remorse soon after the purchase. Following "excessive happiness", a regression towards the mean is observed: but not merely in the sense of a return to reality; rather, as an actual enantiodromia or conversion into the opposite. Besides behavioral addictions, we see this clinical phenomenon in the characteristic 'come-down' experienced by MDMA users or in the depression following a manic episode in certain types of bipolar patients. It is not just that the elevating effect is *not meant to last*: it is that it directly attracts vengeance from the Truth/Whole.[19]

We are back to the general principle underlying the theoretical framework outlined above, which has both a psychodynamic and a metaphysical background, that anything that is not round will be surpassed by life; anything that starts already partial will be taken down by its own partiality. When it comes to channeling libido into conscious projects, the more well-rounded a symbolic representation is, the more lasting will be the change that it can lead to. Conversely, the single gravest fault that a symbolic proposition can have is one-sidedness, as that 'injustice' (*adikia*) which Anaximander thought had to be paid for in the course of time in order to bring back justice (*dike*)[20]. Pseudo-symbolic propositions are too 'falsifiable' in the sense of being liable to be made false by the Truth/Whole.[21] They are not protected against enantiodromia because the only way to do that would be to keep close to the whole. Like most addictive products, self-help projects *give you now what they take from you later*.[22] They give the individual the impression of a movement forward, but the mechanism through which they achieve that occurs at the expenses of the possibility of any *subsequent* movement. The way in which they are made to work in the short term hinders their possibility of working long term. Modern individuals become addicted to False Starts because they fail to see the link between the way in which self-help projects are able to gain momentum and the reason why they end prematurely, leading to a cycle of repetitions.

False Start as a defense against legitimate suffering

If it is true that self-help projects give you now what they take from you later, then how are people persuaded to trade something as precious as individuation for something as caducous as a False Start? The answer, I believe, lies in a peculiar form of spiritual *desperation* that is characteristic of modern individuals and which causes them to be drawn to anything that will promise to fill their underlying 'sense of emptiness' (Carpani, 2020). Jung provides a touching description of this sensation: "That thing in you which should live is alone; nobody touches it, nobody knows it, you yourself don't know it; but it keeps on stirring, it disturbs you, it makes you restless, and it gives you no peace" (CW 18, par. 632). One wonders how anyone could be blamed for desiring a False Start when naked life, as the one exemplarily embraced by Sonja at the end of *Uncle Vanya* (Chekhov, 1898), is just too much to bear. As the poet says, we all need to be constantly "drunk" to distract ourselves from the horrible burden of time (Baudelaire, 1869). We all need our 'fix' of libido. But the problem is that, in order to flee immobility, modern individuals end up embracing an "experimental life" that is "condemned to activity" (Beck & Beck-Gernsheim, 2002, pp. 26, 24) – which is merely its dialectical reversal.[23] The restlessness of False Starts resembles the one found in the so-called masked depression. Frantically planning one's self-improvement is a defense against reckoning with oneself as the heaviest burden or, as Jung would put it, it is a substitute for "legitimate suffering" (CW 11, par. 129).

The counterintuitive logic is that the suffering that one tries to leave behind by falling into the arms of a False Start is like that legendary lady of Samarra with whom we all have an appointment, wherever we have run to escape her (O'Hara, 1934). To use another image, among the children who are learning to swim, it is the one who for a moment has enough 'faith' to let go of the poolside that water will keep afloat; instead, the child who rigidly clings to his armbands, when the moment comes, will sink like a stone. We could mimic the logic of the biblical beatitudes and say, then, that it is the one who is willing to go without libido that will receive it in abundance. This is why Jungians insist on the lesson that salvation is where risk is and that, conversely, "whoever wants to save their life will lose it" (Mt 16:25). The self-help subject, constantly escaping suffering, is thereby nailed to it. Self-help promises a pain-free development: only-conscious, only-pleasant, only-upwards. It aims at maximizing one's wellbeing and minimizing one's sufferance. But whatever can be outrun today will make its reappearance tomorrow, if it is part of life: we might as well walk with it.

Conclusions

In this chapter, I analyzed self-help projects as individual or collective attempts to catalyze self-change that are guided by the formal proposition 'let us strive for P and leave ¬P behind'. I started from the general observation that self-help projects on average do not seem to work and proposed that Jungian psychology could provide a theoretically informed explanation for their ineffectiveness. To show that, I first reviewed Jung's theory of libido and symbol formation and drew some ethical implications. One is that the predicament of the moral agent requires finding, besides a direction to go in, a way to obtain the collaboration of the unconscious. The second is that knowledge and willpower are insufficient to bring the subject out of its predicament in the absence of a living symbol, which has to emerge from the unconscious. Then, I reformulated Jung's theory of psychodynamics into a theoretical framework for the classification of ethical systems on the basis of their likelihood of giving rise to lasting self-change. The framework rests on the assumption, predominant in traditional ethical systems, that life's *optimum* can only be attained by conforming to the natural laws governing human life. I hypostatized this set of natural laws as a transcendent Truth/Whole and structured the rest of the framework as a series of neo-platonic emanations in two levels. L1 contains representations of the Truth/Whole that maintain themselves in sufficient proximity to its contradictory nature; these systems are activating and long-lasting, although not eternal. L2 represents a further degradation from the Truth/Whole and encompasses ethical systems that are differentiated on a conscious level; these systems are supposed to have inferior moral force and to generate short-lived life projects.

To diagnose more precisely what would cause life projects generated by L2 ethical systems to be short lived, I introduced the concept of False Start. I claimed that the pseudo-symbolic proposition guiding self-help projects systematically triggers an accelerated psychodynamic pattern by which consciousness first orients itself towards a one-sidedly positive representation, allowing a momentary liberation of libido; yet, due to the compensation principle, the inflated position of consciousness is taken down by whatever negative the pseudo-symbolic proposition was trying to emancipate consciousness from. Then, in a neo-Jungian (i.e., integrative) spirit, I analyzed the dynamic of False Starts by drawing parallels with a variety of other fields. To understand the characteristically short-lived trajectory of self-help projects, I established an analogy with aerodynamics and concluded that self-help projects seem to have an *eidos* that is designed to gain as much thrust as possible while lacking any in-built system to provide drag. To understand the mechanism through which a pseudo-symbolic proposition is able to liberate an artificial boost of libido, I established an analogy with the way in which most addictive products work and concluded that the mechanism that a self-help project uses to gain momentum is what triggers compensation from the Truth/Whole. Finally, to understand why modern individuals might be eager to receive now (a False Start) what is taken from them later (individuation), I discussed False Starts as a defense against legitimate suffering.

The concept of False Start could bridge the gap between the psychological and the sociocultural level of analysis by providing a psychodynamic rationale to what, in characterizing modern individuals, sociologists have described as a "constantly starting again from the beginning" (Beck & Beck-Gernsheim, 2002, p. 6) or a "succession of new beginnings" (Bauman, 2005, p. 2). Self-help is one of the many declinations of the *'homo optionis'* condition analyzed in this book. Modern individuals would like to engineer every aspect of their life: from their haircut, to the sex of their newborns, to the symbol guiding their life projects. False Starts are a problem characteristically faced by modern individuals living in the 21st century: they are a consequence of freedom and an obstacle to individuation. In a time when people think they can do and be whatever they want, Jung's psychodynamics can be used as a theoretical framework to re-think the natural constraints imposed on omnipotent self-plasmation, but also the pre-conditions for rooting oneself in the current of the unconscious. By showing how the failure of self-help projects might not be *contingent* (i.e., owing to the weak-willed subject) but *necessary* (i.e., owing to the shape of the ethical system), analytical psychology helps uncover also the ethical sadism of self-help that follows from the straightjacket of moral intellectualism. As Spinoza noted as early as in 1677, "[m]ost of those who have written" on human conduct "give the impression that they are discussing things that are outside of nature rather than natural things that follow the common laws of nature"; they seem to believe "that human beings disrupt rather than follow the order of nature and that they have absolute power over their actions", so that when human beings happen to fail, they attribute this not to the "power of nature but to some sort of fault in human nature", which accordingly they "deplore, despise and ridicule", and the one who "shows superior eloquence or ingenuity in denouncing" that supposed fault is looked upon as a seer (p. 93). This is what happens with self-help authors today. If a minimum of knowledge and willpower are sufficient to solve the ethical problem, and the rules of the game have been clearly laid out once and for all, there is not much room for discussion: if one is still unhappy, they only have themselves to blame. And what is the prescribed remedy for that? More self-help. From this perspective, self-help is really a self-eating monster, an *ouroboros*. Desperate for orientation, people devour one book after another; and since bulimia is misunderstood as good appetite, new books are printed identical to the ones on the shelves. This is an unprecedented scenario typical of our time, a new Dantesque circle that we could label the 'meaning seekers': not having dared to seek it in depth, where it is found, they shall be condemned to chase it eternally on the surface.

At this point, the reader might be left wondering: *if not self-help, then what?* One would be very tempted to answer: Jungian psychology.[24] However, recommending Jungian psychology as an 'antidote' to self-help, and proposing to go for the former as pertaining to 'depth' and to abandon the latter as pertaining to 'surface', would be to fall back on the logic of self-help: *'let us strive for P instead of ¬P'*. What I think we should wish for analytical psychology, instead, is to find a creative synthesis from the tension that exists *in its own house* between 'esotericism' and self-help, as reflected by episodes such as Jung *contra* Neumann (Jung & Neumann, 2015), Giegerich (1998) *contra* Hillman, or Samuels (2018) *contra* Peterson. Even at this metalevel, embracing both sides (each of which has good arguments as well as limitations) would appear to be preferable than choosing one over the other (see also du Toit & du Toit, 2019). In other words, the validity of the principle that one should strive to hold the opposites is confirmed by the fact that *one should and one should not*, in fact, strive to hold the opposites.

Notes

1 Passages from the Collected Works of C. G. Jung are cited from the *Complete Digital Edition* published by Princeton University Press in 2014, edited and translated by G. Adler and R. F. C. Hull.
2 Wind is a classic libido-symbol (e.g., CW 5, par. 151).
3 Jungian psychology is defined as a method to change the attitude of consciousness in order to establish a collaborative relationship with the unconscious (CW 18, par. 1388; CW 6, par. 204).
4 It is no accident that Achilles' shield was the *poiesis* of a god, not a mortal (see subsequently).
5 Consider martyrdom in its name, as described, for instance, in Cantarella (2013).
6 Interestingly, this is also one of the criteria to define a 'classic' in literature (Calvino, 1991).
7 The 'unsurpassed' nature of the living symbol, as a catalyst of psychic life, resembles the one of the living body, as a catalyst of biological life (CW 8, par. 80–81). 'Mortals' apparently struggle to recreate both through only-conscious means. This reflects in the characteristically short-lived life projects of scientists in animal cloning. An ingredient seems to be missing, which causes the whole enterprise to fall apart: in religious terms, the 'breath of life' (Gen. 2:7).
8 The crisis of the Christian symbol brought the upsurge of Eastern (New Age) spirituality in the West (CW 9.1, par. 11).
9 In light of this framework, self-help books and programs can be seen as satisfying the universal need to address the ethical question, and their popularity should inform us foremost of the demand that is out there for ethical guidance (modern individuals "compulsively . . . search for the right way to live"; Beck & Beck-Gernsheim, 1995, p. 2). However, our framework also suggests that qualitative differences exist between the sources of orientation, so we need to critically appraise the spiritual resources "for modern living" (Browning & Cooper, 2004, p. 3). Self-help may be tapping into the same old need for meaning, but is its bread any good in satisfying the collective hunger?
10 See the correction to the classic Jungian theory proposed later in "False Start as an artificial boost of libido".
11 Politics, as a field where the "attractive power of a collective image" can easily bring about "a high degree of inflation" (CW 7, par. 233), is an important area of application of the concept of False Start. In particular, the pattern of False Start can be discerned in the period leading up to the elections, when it is common for a politician to paint a one-sidedly positive picture of collective change in order to gain momentum and activate citizens in the short term. But any 'fresh start', as a start that fails to acknowledge the resistance against which it is working, is likely to be a False Start. This is confirmed by the fact that often precisely whatever aspect of the complexity of reality has been disregarded at time 1 (election campaign) is what causes the political project to fall apart at time 2 (the moment of political action).
12 The compensation principle governing the dynamic of False Start has ontological and cosmological connotates that go beyond the vicissitudes of 'mental states' in somebody's head. Jung took it from the metaphysician Heraclitus (CW 7, par. 111). We

may think about it as a law that has to be taken into account whenever designing a life project, just as the law of gravity has to be taken into account whenever designing a building. The compensation principle does not care about the contents it is being applied to, any more than the law of gravity cares about whether it is working on a bridge or a pencil. In mythological terms, it is Ἀνάγκη (Necessity), higher in rank than gods because gods, too, are subject to it.

13 "How could I be unfaithful to my dear Doña Julia. . . . How could I sleep with another woman. . . . How could I forsake the purity of love. . . . Actually, I was surprised at *how easily* the past can be overcome" (*Don Juan De Marco*; Leven, 1995).

14 Even self-help authors have embraced the idea that understanding why self-change projects fail would be the only way to learn how to make them work one day (Norcross, 2012).

15 I am indebted to my uncle Giuseppe Fiorentino, aerospace engineer, for explaining this to me in simple language.

16 The analogy has obvious limitations. Most importantly, the life project generated by a living symbol, as a well-rounded (as opposed to 'pointy') object, should theoretically be unable to fly, just as the cube in the example. Furthermore, a plane, in order to be aero-dynamic, does not need to 'resemble' air in any intelligible sense, just as a submarine, in order to be hydro-dynamic, does not need to resemble water. Yet, apparently, a symbolic proposition, in order to be psycho-dynamic, needs to resemble the 'rotundity' of the fluid it traverses: namely, the Truth/Whole or life as the medium through which all of our life projects are launched. These attempts to establish connections between the psychic and physical level may appear naïve, but they are just analogies; they do not need to be exact (see CW 11, par. 279).

17 Another example in popular culture is Michael Scott's trip to Mexico in s7e7 of the TV series *The Office* (2005–2013).

18 Reference is made to the title of a popular self-help book by De Mello (1990).

19 The so-called 'planned obsolescence', typically invoked for smartphones or washing machines, applies to existential or spiritual projects as well.

20 This notion is ridiculed by Žižek (2001) as a "New Age cliché according to which the sin of modern Western civilization . . . is man's hubris . . . this notion that underlies all returns to 'ancient wisdom' . . . disturbing of cosmic balance, the privileging of one aspect of the cosmic antagonism in favor of its opposite" (p. 74). However, from a Jungian perspective, an idea with such a long tradition cannot be but psychologically true.

21 Self-help products are 'unfalsifiable' in another sense: that, when the reader of a self-help book does not get the end result (e.g., happiness), they are told that they have not properly applied a certain step in the method. The author, as if to justify himself, "has architected a dogma about all the tragic forms of failure of goodwill" (Drewermann, 1982, p. 64).

22 Also fizzy drinks are sold as a 'cure for thirst', but what they give is a momentary sense of refreshment followed by an even greater thirst, triggered by a spike of sugar. This paradox effect is true at a biological but also at a philosophical level: all capitalistic objects are the "embodiment of the supra-sensible aura of the ineffable spiritual surplus" that entails "an artificial promise of a substance which never materialized" (Žižek, 2001, p. 20). Coke has "the paradoxical property that the more you drink the thirstier you get" (p. 19).

23 A term inspired by Jungian psychology that is tainted by such pseudo-activity is 'Shadow work', which has become popular on the web, although Jung did not use it. It gives the idea that the integration of the Shadow is something that one does (on oneself), while for Jung "evil is never assented to . . . it is suffered." (Jung & Neumann, 2015, p. 367).

24 There are indeed key differences between a self-help and a Jungian approach to personal/spiritual development. To name a few: if self-help provides a method, Jung (2009) thought that one should seek their own method; if self-help over-simplifies things, Jung programmatically named his psychology 'complex' (CW 10, par. 887); if self-help wants to bring undisturbed happiness, Jung thought that life needs its problems (CW 16, par. 185).

References

Baudelaire, C. (1869). Get drunk. In *Paris spleen*. Middleton: Wesleyan University Press, 2009.

Bauman, Z. (2005). *Liquid life*. Cambridge: Polity.

Beck, U., & Beck-Gernsheim, E. (1995). *The normal chaos of love*. Cambridge: Polity.

Beck, U., & Beck-Gernsheim, E. (2002). *Individualization: Institutionalized individualism and its social and political Consequences*. London: Sage.

Browning, D. S., & Cooper, T. D. (2004). *Religious thought and the modern psychologies*. Minneapolis: Fortress.

Calvino, I. (1991). *Perché leggere i classici*. Milano: Mondadori.

Cantarella, E. (2013). *La passione di Perpetua e Felicita*. Milano: Bur.

Carpani, S. (2020). The consequences of freedom. In E. Brodersen, & P. Amezaga (Eds.), *Jungian perspectives on indeterminate states: Betwixt and between borders*. London: Routledge.

Carr, A. (1985). *The easy way to stop smoking*. London: Arcturus.

Cederström, C., & Spicer, A. (2015). *The wellness syndrome*. London: John Wiley & Sons.

Chekhov, A. (1898). Uncle Vanya. In *Plays*. London: Penguin, 2002.

Colacicchi, G. (2020). *Psychology as ethics: Reading Jung with Kant, Nietzsche and Aristotle*. London and New York: Routledge.

De Mello, A. (1990). *Messaggio per un'aquila che si crede un pollo*. Casale Monferrato: Piemme.

Dichter, E. (1960) *The strategy of desire*. Garden City, NY: Doubleday.

Dostoevsky, F. (1864). *Notes from the underground and the double*. London and New York: Penguin Books, 2009.

Drewermann, E. (1982). *Psicanalisi e teologia morale*. Brescia: Queriniana, 1993.

du Toit, D. H., & du Toit, S. (2019). Giving positive psychology interventions depth: A Jungian approach. In L. E. Van Zyl & S. Rothmann (Eds.), *Theoretical approaches to multi-cultural positive psychological interventions* (pp. 391–412). Cham: Springer.

Giegerich, W. (1998). *The soul's logical life: Towards a rigorous notion of psychology*. Frankfurt am Main: Peter Lang.

Hegel, G. W. F. (1807). *The phenomenology of spirit*. T. Pinkard (trans.). Cambridge and New York: Cambridge University Press, 2017.

Jung, C. G. (2009). *The red book: Liber novus*. S. Shamdasani (ed.). M. Kyburz, J. Peck, and S. Shamdasan (trans.). New York and London: W. W. Norton.

Jung, C. G., & Neumann, E. (2015). *Analytical psychology in exile: The correspondence of C. G. Jung and Erich Neumann*. M. Liebscher (ed. and intr.). H. McCartney (trans.). Princeton: Princeton University Press.

Lehne, M., & Koelsch, S. (2015). Toward a general psychological model of tension and suspense. *Frontiers in Psychology*, *6*, 79.

Leven, J. (1995). *Don Juan De Marco*. San Francisco, CA: New Line Cinema & American Zoetrope.

Nehring, D., Alvarado, E., Hendriks, E. C., & Kerrigan, D. (2016). *Transnational popular psychology and the global self-help industry: The politics of contemporary social change*. Basingstoke: Palgrave Macmillan.

Neumann, E. (1949*). Depth psychology and a new ethic*. Boston & London: Shambla, 1990.

Norcross, J. C. (2012). *Changeology: 5 steps to realizing your goals and resolutions*. New York: Simon and Schuster.

O'Hara, J. (1934). *Appointment in Samarra*. New York: Harcourt, Brace, and co.

Pieri, P. (1998). *Dizionario junghiano*. Torino: Bollati Boringhieri.

Polipo, N. F. (2020). Vulnerability and incorruptibility: An aretaic model of the transcendent function. In E. Brodersen, & P. Amezaga (Eds.), *Jungian perspectives on indeterminate states: Betwixt and between borders*. London: Routledge.

Purser, R. (2019). *McMindfulness: How mindfulness became the new capitalist spirituality*. London: Repeater.

Reed, P. (2008). *Yes Man*. Los Angeles, CA: Warner Bros.

Sabbadini, A. (Ed.). (2013). *Tao Te Ching: Una guida all'interpretazione del libro fondamentale del taoismo*. Milano: Feltrinelli.

Salerno, S. (2005). *SHAM: How the self-help movement made America helpless*. New York: Crown.

Samuels, A. (2018). Jordan Peterson and Jung. Video posted on 2nd April 2018 in "Andrew's Rants". Available at www.andrewsamuels.com/jordan-peterson-and-jung/

Shen, V. (2013). From gift to law: Thomas's natural law and Laozi's heavenly Dao. *International Philosophical Quarterly*, *53*(3), 251–270.

Singer, T., & Kimbles, S. L. (Eds.). (2004). *The cultural complex: Contemporary Jungian perspectives on psyche and society*. New York, NY: Brunner-Routledge.

Spinoza, B. (1677). *Ethics: Proved in geometrical order*. M. Kisner (Ed.) & M. Silverthorne (Trans.). Cambridge Texts in the History of Philosophy. Cambridge: Cambridge University Press, 2018.

Starker, S. (2002). *Oracle at the supermarket: The American preoccupation with self-help books*. New Brunswick and Oxford: Transaction.

Taplin, O. (1980). The shield of Achilles within the Iliad. *Greece & Rome*, *27*(1), 1–21.

Vidali, C. (2020). *Fine senza compimento: La fine della storia in Alexandre Kojève tra accelerazione e tradizione*. Milano: Mimesis.

Whitman, W. (1855). Song of myself (Section 51). In *Leaves of grass*. Philadelphia: David McKay, 1883.

Žižek, S. (2001). *The fragile absolute, or, why is the Christian legacy worth fighting for?* London and New York: Verso.

Chapter 9

Natality, Individuation and Generative Social Action

From *Amor Mundi* to Social Generativity

Chiara Giaccardi and Mauro Magatti

Premise

Hannah Arendt's call for a specific attitude towards the world, which she called *amor mundi*, can be seen as a precursor to the idea of 'social generativity', a theoretical paradigm that intends to respond to many of the global challenges and pathologies of the contemporary world, especially in the post-COVID era.

Starting from her critique of the desertification of our common world, due to the transformation of the whole society into a 'laboring-consuming' society, some crucial ideas in Arendt's work (especially *natality* and *plurality*) open the way to a generative idea of freedom. In particular, the possibility of free acting, springing from *amor mundi*, linking past and future and combining individual initiative and mutual cooperation, can be seen as a forerunner of the relational, dynamic construct of 'social generativity'.

In fact, generativity is an anthropological *character* that is comparable, in depth and breadth, to consumption and therefore is essential to balance the excesses of consumerism.[1] Generativity is also able to open the road to a different, broader idea of freedom and self-realization which is not alternative (in a dualistic perspective) but rather complementary (in a polar tension) to consumption.

The initial hypothesis was that 'generating' – as an act of 'ex-corporation', that is, 'putting out', 'giving life to' or 'initiating' – can be considered as elemental as consuming from an anthropological point of view. Generating is neither something that has to be learned nor a moral duty or imperative; it is, rather, innate to human beings able to initiate, to bring to bear, to begin something new. In that way, individual action is able to contribute positively to the environment, as a (relational) response to the context rather than a form of self assertion.

This hypothesis is rooted in the psychology of the second half of the 20th century. Carl Gustav Jung, for instance, qualified the process of individuation (that is, of 'becoming an individual'), saying that "The self is relatedness. . . . The self appears in your deeds and deeds always mean relationship".[2]

Jung did not use the term 'generativity', but his vision anticipated the work of Erik Erikson (1950), who first introduced the term, suggesting that in the path

DOI: 10.4324/9781003168829-10

towards adulthood, the subject inevitably faces the dilemma between 'stagnation' (or self-absorption) and 'generativity', or displacement towards others.

And yet, this attitude has been overlooked, since the consumeristic culture has been effective in equating *individuation* – the long-term, relational and always open process of personal development – with *individualization*, a social condition that seeks to maximize individual autonomy and liberty.

This collapse is problematic, as it elides the complexities of elements at play and most of all the intrinsically relational character of individuation. It also fosters one-sided interpretations of the relations between individuals and between them and their environment that turn either in domination or alienation.

On a similar line, although with different terms, Hartmut Rosa (2019, p. 163) underlines the failure of modernity

> in the confusion of a *mute*, results-oriented concept of self-efficacy geared towards domination and control with the experience of a *resonant*, influential, process- and response-oriented form of self-efficacy that not only takes into account but is even constitutively reliant on which remains even *inaccessible*, which cannot be mastered, which resists.

Arendt was very convincing, and let's say prophetic, in showing that without affection, there can only be labor but not action. In other words, we can only fabricate but not generate. Without affection, action can become violent, and any power unbalance can easily turn into domination. *Amor mundi* is the force of self-transcendence, of ex-centricity that sustains freedom as the capacity to bring something new into the world, beyond any determinism, thanks to, with and for others.

Social generativity is not an abstract, utopian model but something already there, rooted in social reality,[3] as well as in different traditions of social thought.

In our view, it is a positive way to reimagine a collective future beyond capitalist consumer society, especially after the COVID crisis, at the same time bringing a contribution to social theory.

Diagnosis and critique

Development as indefinite quantitative increase, information overload, homogenization and de-differentiation as a paradoxical result of individualization . . . these are just some of the elements that contribute to the increase of entropy, the one we can observe in the era of advanced capitalism and its crisis. A model of individualized hyperconsumption that (never like today) cannot be revived, because it has exhausted the resources on which it was based; it has created disorder, paralyzed change, increased social inequality.

Today we face a paradox: the cult of the individual leads to normalization, to the leveling of differences (reduced to superficial variations in the supermarket of identities): as Stiegler (2013) has pointed out, "mass individualism does not allow individuation of mass, and thus *individualization,* in the sense that consumerist individualism understands it, is a *deindividuation*". Which is in fact the true meaning of entropy when applied to the interpretation of the social world: increase in disorder and fragmentation, loss of variety and differentiation (Stiegler, 2018).

The market is unable to contribute to a world order while rather increasing inequality, exploitation, fragmentation, chaos. Populism and repulsive attitudes are growing. No one is happy with the situation, but it seems impossible to change it, and resignation, cynicism, anger tend to prevail. Despite criticism, the consumerist capitalist model continues to dominate the imaginary of freedom and economic growth, without seemingly viable alternatives, even after the third global crisis of COVID (after the Twin Towers attack in 2001 and the consequent escalation of terrorism and fundamentalism and the financial crisis of 2008).

In this situation, the weakest sections of the population are paying the highest price.

A new idea of development, qualitative and multidimensional, is urgent today.

Even on the pages of the *Harvard Business Review,* Ref_356_FILE-150325198009Porter and Kramer (2011) were speaking about the creation of "shared value" as a way to overcome the individualistic anthropology of contemporary capitalism.

The basic idea – even in a vision internal to capitalism – is that the production of economic value is linked to the relationship between subjects and between them and their environment, to the convergence towards common goods rather than to the divergence in the pursuit of one's own individual interests.

Also, on the part of the social milieu, there is an emerging social demand for 'contextual' self-realization through the various links (relational, institutional, environmental. . .) inherent to our concrete life. In sum, a relational idea of human being, very different from that of *Homo oeconomicus,* as well as a conception of value much broader than mere economic revenue, is today much needed.

Perhaps it's time to imagine a way which is neither that of the economic imperative 'we must consume more and more' nor that of the moral imperative 'we need to consume much less'. The negative idea of restriction cannot be motivating, while recognizing the positive relationship between individuation, bond and social change can become crucial. Arendt's critique of the "laboring society" is still very precious for understanding what is at stake and opening new directions of thought and action for today.

First of all, when labor becomes dominated by instrumental and technical aspects, we enter a regime of production that turns us into the servants of our machines (Arendt, 1958, pp. 147 and 151). In addition, we cease to see labor as the toll we have to pay so that we can devote time to "those other higher and more meaningful activities for the sake of which this freedom would deserve to be won" (Arendt, 1958, p. 5), namely 'thinking' and 'action'. Labor then becomes the colonizing model that we extend to the whole realm of human activities.

Today the economic crisis, made even worse by the effects of pandemics, reveals a paradox: we are a society of laborers *without labor*. Yet, we live in a society in which fabrication seems the only legitimate and desirable way of action.

According to Arendt, the only activity left in a world colonized by labor is consumption, which literally 'annihilates' the world: a world colonized by labor is a 'worldless world'.

If we do not abandon the task of thinking "what we are doing", we will see that the consumer society is just another name for the laboring society. Even our choice as consumers, the 'burden' of choosing among products, is driven by algorithms that process our data and know what we want even better than we do.

In contrast to this technical, functional knowledge, 'thinking' is first of all contemplation; it originates in our sense of wonder toward the world that is precisely the starting point of thought. It is for this reason that in Arendt, as in Heidegger, *denken is danken*, thinking is thanking (Arendt, 1978, p. 150). Losing wonder (gratitude) means losing thought and hence the possibility to form our original and critical point of view, to take our place into the world, to express our uniqueness and preserve plurality, that is, contrasting entropy.

A change of paradigm is needed at this stage. A shift from abstraction to concreteness, if we intend to promote a social critique that is more effective than a lamentation or even a denunciation. The notion of 'resistance' needs also to be reconsidered, as the system is smart in turning any attempt of opposition in fuel for its own growth, which leaves no room for social critique. 'Consumer citizenship' and 'prosumerism' are a good example of that logic of pro-active consumption that turns into voluntary submission to the consumerist capitalist logics. 'We are like a hot dog putting ketchup on itself', as ironically, but also sadly, Rob Horning (R. Horning, 2016) puts it in the columns of *The New Inquiry*, stressing the fact that alienation is far from overcome in the consumer society.

Our idea is that no critique is possible within this framework.

Within the production/consumption model, even the proactive movement of 'contribution' ends in reinforcing the system to the detriment of people (especially the weakest). Participation through consumption fosters proletarianization, in Stiegler's words: a process of *disapprenticeship* that makes people more and more dependent on consumption.[4] And political "populism" is but one of the consequences of "industrial populism", which has produced a "new form of proletarianization", where we have lost not only our know-how but our very capacity to live a meaningful life.

Today, we are certainly contributors to a system (the data economy), but this contribution is impoverishing and disabling, which leads to the opposite of market declarations, namely to de-individuation and conformism.

According to Stiegler, in the present situation and before it is too late, it is absolutely essential to rethink the question of 'collective' (as organic solidarity). "If we do not succeed in reconstructing collective social horizons . . . we will fuel processes of extremely violent destruction. . . . Our bet is to produce a negentropic disruption, able to create noodiversity".[5]

The challenge, then, is to build an economy of contribution which, on the contrary, increases us,

> not in the way of the enhancement of transhumanism, which would serve only an economic, techno-scientific elite; I am talking about an increase in our intelligence, our ability to work with others, our desire for collaboration, with our neighbors or other partners, with peers, near and far.[6]

At this stage, not an opposition to the system (that in the end plays its game) but a new, different paradigm is mostly required.

The paradigm of social generativity is the framework within which contribution can be enabling for everyone, even the most disadvantaged.

A negentropic paradigm that preserves noodiversity or, in Arendt's words, plurality.

In fact, Arendt perfectly grasped, although in different language, the entropic and leveling outcome of a laboring society, with its economy of neglect and carelessness.

And she pointed to a different direction: one where freedom is rooted in natality.

Natality and generativity: individuation beyond individualism

> Our problem isn't that we're individualists. It's that our individualism is static rather than dynamic.
>
> (Fernando Pessoa)

Among the conditions of human existence that Arendt describes, those most crucial for the dynamics of action and consequently most relevant to the paradigm of generativity are 'natality' and 'plurality'. These interdependent concepts open up the possibility of a 'generative freedom', which can lead us out of the radical individualism and worldlessness of consumer society.

With the term 'natality', Arendt denotes a profound dimension of human experience that influences her entire philosophical and political analysis. Natality is the simple fact that each human life begins with birth, that is, a new beginning, out of any determinism. This is the human condition in which freedom – the capacity for beginning – is rooted. Freedom is the miracle that human birth discloses, as the capacity to bring the unpredictable and unexpectable into the world.[7] We have been brought into the world by others, as a radical 'newness', and thanks to that fact, can we give birth to something new.

This, however, is not only a matter of *knowing* where we are from but also of *experiencing* a sense of gratitude for the fact of our own natality.

In Arendt's words, then, freedom is the capacity to bring something new into the world, that is, to 'generate' what wasn't already there. And – very importantly – to do that in condition of non-sovereignty, a crucial recognition that helps us to escape the fallacious dualism activity/passivity, according to which if we do not dominate, we are dominated. Limits are inherent to any situation and constitute the concrete condition in which we can exert freedom.

We can generate because we have been generated. Even in thought or political action, we do not generate from scratch but "on the shoulders of giants", thanks to, with and for others. We can really act only to the extent that we are able to receive and then to give. The relation to alterity[8] is essential both for coming into the world and for bringing into the world.

Being able to give is also the very feature of the stage of maturity for Erickson. It is not matter of generosity (being 'good') but of generativity (being fully alive in responding to the bonds with others and with the environment).

While natality has to do with initiative, 'plurality' is related to interdependence (or, better, 'inter-independence', in Ramon Pannikar's words). Arendt understands plurality as "the basic condition of both action and speech"; it "has the twofold character of equality and distinction".[9] Equality, as she means it, is different from the abstract notion of symmetry, rather indicating "the paradoxical plurality of unique beings".[10]

Plurality is another way to say that "men, not Man, live on the earth and inhabit the world".[11]

Like natality and plurality, generativity is intrinsically relational but not in the mode of interpersonal relationships (as 'built' by individual, already individuated subjects). Rather, is a dynamic process, thanks to which individuation can take place.

Here the work of Gilbert Simondon[12] is vital, as individuation is always relational: "a relation does not spring up between two terms that are already separate individuals, rather, it is an aspect of the internal resonance of a system of individuation".[13]

Relation is the very condition of our being here, as well as of our becoming.

The paradigm of social generativity

With the idea of social generativity, we are suggesting a new paradigm that is rooted both in living practices and in the history of thought of different disciplines, one that is able to acknowledge as well as support social action as positive, creative and effective without falling into the self-referential, individualistic and abstract perspective of the 'sovereign self'.

In fact, and in other words, social generativity is a way of becoming individual through a nonindividualistic process, thanks to a dynamic that recognizes and strengthens relations (not reducible to interpersonal exchanges).

Generative social action (GSA) is a way of starting processes that go beyond the individual, as they are made possible by a 'preindividual charge', in Simondon's terms (traditions, deeds, archetypes, collective memories, heritage . . .) and by the transindividual (which is larger than inter-individuality). Simondon defined it as "the systematic unity of interior (psychic) individuation, and exterior (collective) individuation".[14]

That is to say: the unity of individuals is more than identity. As Barthélémy says in commenting on Simondon, such a perspective allows one to overcome both "the mistake of psychologism – which only sees the interindividual – as well as of sociologism – which merely sees the intrasocial". Both of them, in fact, "have forgotten this reality of the subject which is 'vaster than the individual'[15] and which alone enables one to explain the birth of a real collective" and to create a domain of the transindividual, which is different from the community. It is rather the horizon of collective meaning thanks to which new processes of individuation can take place.

GSA, as a nonindividualistic mode of individuation, is a process of becoming oneself that lasts a lifetime. In fact, life is for Simondon a "perpetual individuation".[16]

We can recognize social generativity when:

* an entrepreneurial initiative in the personal, economic, social, political or cultural field can bring something new to the world or is able to renew or regenerate something that already exists
* in doing so, it is able to offer an original, recognizable and sustainable contribution to the social context and also
* effectively promote the capacitation of others through direct empowerment or indirect improvement of contextual conditions, which in turn regenerate the initiator, providing further transindividual conditions for individuation.

We recognize GSA afterwards by the presence of three movements, all of them essential to the whole process (without the last, in particular, the whole process collapses and reverses into its opposite): namely giving birth, taking care and letting go.

Giving birth

When a generic aspiration becomes a concrete realization, this is the moment of creation and enterprise that turns the generative momentum into a social fact.

As Arendt has suggested, the experience of putting into the world is essential to freedom: as human beings, we are "born to begin", to bring our original contribution to the world. But this is never a mere individualistic accomplishment: we can give birth because we have been brought into the world; we can give because we have received.

In fact, for Arendt, "nobody is the author or producer of his own life story",[17] as action is never possible in isolation.

Acting is less a matter of self expression than of gratitude, the experience of our original 'being in debt', our 'indebtedness'.

A quantum leap occurs at this stage, a phase-shift that turns apparent incompatibilities and seemingly disparate levels in a 'metastable' resolution that opens new paths for individuation.

Someone who puts something into the world is a center of transductive activity, a mediator of non-deterministic processes of reconfiguration, thanks to which the initiator is regenerated in turn.

Bringing in the world also implies a massive emotional investment. Without *amor mundi*, generative processes can not take place. Affection is an element of concreteness, involvement and engagement, in the face of the abstraction of scientific detachment and the depersonalization of technical procedures. It is also the condition of care.

Taking care

There is an interdependence between initiating and taking care, also indicated by Arendt with the ancient Greek terms *archein* (to begin) and *prattein* (to fulfill).

If we love what we have generated, we are also motivated to maintain it and make it last, a movement that is one of "care".

In a generative logic, taking care is not a one-way action, an isolated act of generosity: rather it is a movement of reciprocity, an enduring process entering which all the subjects involved are transformed within a dynamic of co-individuation. It also provides a positive context of mutual recognition, that is, of realization and appreciation of the uniqueness of the other.

Reciprocity does not mean equivalence (which is but an abstraction): in interhuman relations, there is always a differential in power, skills, charisma, status, personal capacities. While it can be played for domination, as normally happens, in GSA, it is played for the improvement of the context and the capability of others (including further generations).

Taking care, in fact, is a practice (there is a concrete, even carnal, aspect) that deeply engages subjects in all their dimensions because they can express and also cultivate their own singularity, originality and gifts while contributing to something that goes beyond them. Both in initiating and taking care, de-coincidence is the condition as well as the effect of the individual becoming more than one ego. It is the paradoxical structure of generative individuation: the 'inner desire' of self-satisfaction is realized through self-transcendence.

Letting go

The last step in the generative process is very difficult to accomplish yet essential. Without 'letting go', the whole generative process fails: in fact, there is generativity only when the initiative does not end in a closed, self-referential form of mutual dependence.

The problem arises when care and affection turn into possession (for the sake of the 'good' rather than for the sake of love) that suffocates what has been brought into the world.

Generative social action accepts risk as a peculiar articulation of life and death, one that is for the sake of life. When the fear of loss is overcome rather than becoming paralyzing, people can establish a specific social bond based neither on domination nor obligation but rather on empowerment and capability. In that way, their own realization contributes to the realization of others: to their freedom – beyond any logic of control or influence. Letting go is the ultimate proof that social generativity is not just a rhetorical or ideological discourse. It certainly implies a loss, a death in a sense: yet dispossession as a way of stepping back to make room to others is the very condition by which those who came into the world can freely give their own contribution and do so in a way that was neither planned nor imagined and then contributes to the dynamism and variety of social life. This qualifying dynamic of GSA helps to establish a successful transition in intergenerational relations as well.

Social generativity is a force of individuation that preserves plurality and contrasts entropy.

In fact, by stimulating individual desires and creativity, as well as a circulation of experiences, GSA brings a "surplus" of value, which is capable of counteracting indifference, fragmentation and carelessness, among the worst consequences of a consumer society.

GSA fosters a concrete, relational, processual, transindividual regime of individuation, where subjects individuate themselves while drawing from – and giving shape to – the world around them as a starting point for further dynamics of individuation, in other words, a relational dynamics where relations are not only interpersonal but intertemporal and transindividual.

There is not a generative subject that commits generative actions by relating to others; rather, there is a generative logic, a logic of being as becoming, entering which people are constituted as generative subjects in relation to their *milieu*. Finding new 'metastable'[18] forms of life (beyond any dualism between stability/instability) is a way to overcome abstraction, to give shape to the environment while shaping themselves, to set new processes in motion that are able to strengthen the outcome of GSA and its capability to inform the social world by opening new possibilities for further individuations. That is relational social change.

In other words, GSA is a way of becoming individual through a nonindividualistic process thanks to a dynamic that recognizes and strengthens relations (again, not reduced to interpersonal exchanges).

In overcoming the I/you gap and competition (Girard's mimetic rivalry),[19] temporal fragmentation and the subject/context dichotomy, GSA 'informs', that is, gives reality a different shape through its peculiar way of individuation, one that is at the same time a source of inspiration for further individuations in the same or even different directions.

That is why generating is always an adventure, the experience of "a subject other than the ego taking hold", in Simmel's words.[20]

Thanks to the three previous steps, we can say that 'generative individuation' produces at least three relational, negentropic effects for social change:

i) a *specific relation between self and other(s) (transitivity)* operating as a transductive force among differentials of competence that do not end in domination but in capacitation. In fact, GSA brings about a specific pattern of individuation that we call *authorization:* that is, enabling others as a way to accomplish one's own individuation. The circulation of freedom as capacity to begin is the ultimate goal of authorization, the main feature of a 'generative authority'.

ii) *a temporal effect (transtemporality)*: GSA is able to give continuity to past, present and future in the same dynamic of becoming: individuation as producing durability. On the line of Hannah Arendt, accepting the responsibility to care for our posterity is an act of freedom. It is *amor mundi* that protects freedom from the risks of arbitrariness and encourages it to take responsibility for posterity.

(iii) *a contextual effect (transindividuality)* as individuation gives shape both to the subject and its environment. Within this process, unfruitful dichotomies are recomposed, and the conditions and inspiration for new processes of individuation are set in place: we call it *exemplarity*. Exemplarity generates a knowledge that overcomes many unfruitful dualisms, like subject/object, theory/practice or model/reality, rather providing a concrete source of inspiration for further individuations. GSA can play an exemplary role, that is, encouraging the initiative from others, opening a possible space for contribution.

GSA is neither a model nor a recipe. It is not even matter of 'best practices' that can be replicated thanks to formalized procedures. It is rather an inspiring experience that encourages others to trust their own capacities to bring something worthy to the common world: contribution as a way of self-realization.

Beyond abstraction and dualism: new directions for generative social practices and theories

Concreteness is the crucial feature of the paradigm of social generativity, a way to positively contrast both abstraction and dualism, two aspects that must be questioned, as they have produced great amounts of practical and symbolic violence.

Abstraction means to drag away, to detach from the complexity of the concrete that always entangles a number of different and even contradictory dimensions. When applied to human beings, it is a way of de-humanizing by reducing them to members of categories, which makes inhuman practices (like marginalization, expulsion, domination, even suppression) easiest and morally viable, as Arendt and Bauman have shown.[21]

Within this framework, universalism has been equated with abstraction, which is indeed an arbitrary reduction. In fact, there can be a 'concrete universalism', one that does not cancel singularity.

Inasmuch as it entails an arbitrary separation of what is connected, abstraction fosters dualism: in fact, it leads to detaching what is linked (force and form, particular and universal, individual and collective, psychological and social, stability and change) and then to opposing the two poles, and finally to putting them in a hierarchical relation, where the aim is to cancel one of the two poles for the supremacy of the other.

The opposite of abstraction (as radical separation and opposition) is fusion (as indistinction, dedifferentiation, assimilation), and in fact, modernity oscillates between extreme abstraction and occasional rituals of fusion via excess (drugs, sex, extreme experiences) that are functional to bear the frustration of abstraction – without changing the overall framework.

Concreteness is instead the way to inhabit the tension between separation and fusion, detachment and total absorption, in the situation as it is by recognizing that the two poles cannot stay the one without the other, as they rather imply each other.

The challenge is precisely to find a way, which is always temporary, to keep both dimensions alive: not a synthesis (that, again, cancels the difference) but a metastable, creative, generative equilibrium always open to change.

Abstraction is also the condition for domination, while concreteness is the condition for generation: two opposite ways to relate to reality.

Concreteness means to give priority to the process of individuation over the product of individuality.

As a matter of fact, in concrete life, being is always dynamic. Being is becoming.

In Simondon's words, the consequence of the ontogenetic postulate ('the conservation of being through becoming'),[22] central to a philosophy of individuation, is that individuals consist of relations, as the individuality of the individual increases through the demultiplication of the relations that constitute the individual; as a consequence, relation has the status of being (it is relation that constitutes its terms, rather than the opposite: it is what Simondon calls 'realism of relations') instead of being the operation of an individual subject.

Focusing on the process means recovering time (abstraction, in fact, is atemporal) and most of all the transindividual character of individuation. Both Jung and Simondon, although with different arguments, agree on the fact that individuation is based on something that precedes us and takes place within a world of visible and invisible relations that transcend us.

The same is true for GSA, which is not the product of a willing subject (although it requires initiative and responsibility) but a dynamic entering which subjects are constituted as the terms of a relation that is not only interpersonal but transindividual.

GSA can be seen as a concrete, relational, processual, transindividual regime of individuation, where subjects individuate themselves while drawing from – and giving shape to – the world around them as a starting point for further dynamics of individuation.

Individuation is thus a 'field' in which subject and object are no longer opposed. There is no dualism, including the one between being and becoming, or subject/object of knowledge.

Becoming is a dimension of being corresponding to a capacity of being to fall out of phase with itself,[23] that is, to resolve itself by dephasing itself (de-coincidence). Dis-identity is the condition of becoming for change, and for GSA as well.

Concrete being is being that is more than a unity.[24] Unity, which is characteristic of the individuated being, and identity, which permits the use of the law of the excluded middle, can apply to individuals but not to individuation.

Being has not a stable unity but a transductive unity: which is to say that it can overflow out of itself; it 'exceeds' itself.

For Simondon, transduction is a notion that is both metaphysical and logical. It applies to ontogenesis and is ontogenesis itself.[25]

Within this framework, contribution is the participation, for the individual, in the fact of being an element in a greater individuation, where the psychic (personal) and the collective are reciprocal to one another.

For all those reasons, assonance and affinities among very different thinkers who in their different languages point to the same dynamic, we believe that social generativity can be considered a negentropic paradigm able to put life back in the desert of a consumeristic-individualistic society.

In Arendt's words:

> Only those who can endure the passion of living under desert conditions can be trusted to summon up in themselves the courage that lies at the root of action, of becoming an active being. Only then we . . . are able to transform [the desert] into a human world.[26]

Notes

1 Leading to what B. Stiegler (2013) calls an "addictogenic society".
2 C.G. Jung (1939). "The Relations between the Ego and the Unconscious". In *Two Essays on Analytical Psychology*. CW 7. *Conscious, Unconscious and Individuation*. CW 9i (1969, p. 73)
3 As the basis of the paradigm, long-running research that since 2012 has allowed the collection of more than 100 case studies now published online in the Archivio della generatività (www.generativita.it).
4 B. Stiegler, *What Makes Life Worth Living,* Polity Press, Cambridge, 2013, p. 53.
5 The term 'noodiversity' is opposed to 'generalized proletarianization' and responds to "the need for a diversity of forms and singularities, not only on the biological terrain, but on that of knowledge, know-how and know-how to live". B. Stiegler, *La disruption rends fou*, culturemobile.net. our translation.
6 Ibid.
7 H. Arendt, 1969c [1961], pp. 169–171.
8 From the Latin *alter*, that is, 'one of two', the other that is constitutive, versus *aliud*, the radically other, the alien.
9 H. Arendt, 1958, p. 175.
10 Ibid., p. 176.
11 H. Arendt, 1958, p. 7; see also p. 234.
12 See especially G. Simondon *L'individuation psychique et collective: A la lumière des notions de Forme, Information, Potentiel et Métastabilité*, Aubier, Paris, 1989. Now in *L'individuation à la lumière des notions: De forme et d'information,* Millon, Grenoble, 2017.

13 G. Simondon, "The Genesis of the Individual," in J. Crary and S. Kwinter (eds.), *Incorporations*, Zone Books, New York, 1992, p. 306.
14 G. Simondon, *L'individuation à la lumière des notions: De forme et d'information*, p. 29: "le collectif intervient comme résolution de la problématique individuelle, ce que signifie que la base de la réalité collective est déjà partiellement contenue dans l'individu, sous la forme de la réalité préindividuelle".
15 G. Simondon, *Du mode d'existence des objets techniques*, Aubier, Paris, 1958, p. 248.
16 G. Simondon, *L'individuation à la lumière des notions: De forme et d'information*, p. 27.
17 H. Arendt, *The Human Condition*, The University of Chicago Press, Chicago, 1958, p. 184.
18 See Simondon in Crary, pp. 301–302.
19 R. Girard, *Violence and the Sacred*, Johns Hopkins University Press, Baltimore, 1977.
20 G. Simmel, "Das Abenteuer," *Phiosophische Kultur. Gesammelte Essays* ([1911] 2nd ed.; Alfred Kroner, Leipzig, 1919. Now in English in J. Cosgrave (ed.), *The Sociology of Risk and Gambling Reader*, Routledge, London, 2006, pp. 215–224.
21 H. Arendt, *The Origin of Totalitarianism*, Schocken Books, New York 1976 [1951]; Z. Bauman, *Modernity and the Holocaust*, Cornell University Press, New York, 1989.
22 G. Simondon, *L'individuation à la lumière des notions: De forme et d'information*, p. 25.
23 G. Simondon, Ibid.: "il est possible aussi de supposer que le devenir est une dimension de l'être, correspond à une capacité que l'être a de se déphaser par rapport à lui-même, de se résoudre en se déphasant".
24 G. Simondon, "The Genesis of the Individual," in J. Crary and S. Kwinter (eds.), *Incorporations*, Zone Books, New York, 1992.297–319. p. 301.
25 Ibid., p. 314.
26 H. Arendt, *The Promise of Politics*, Schocken Books, New York, 2005, p. 202.

References

Arendt, H. (1958). *The Human Condition*. Chicago: The University of Chicago Press
Arendt, H. (1976 [1951]). *The Origin of Totalitarianism*. New York: Schocken Books,
Arendt, H. (1978). *The Life of the Mind*. New York: Harcourt Brace Jovanovich
Arendt, H. (2005). *The Promise of Politics*. New York: Schocken Books.
Bauman, Z. (1989). *Modernity and the Holocaust*. New York: Cornell University Press.
Crary, J., and Kwinter, S. (1992). *Incorporations*. New York: Zone Books.
Erikson, E. (1950). *Childhood and Society*. New York: Norton & Company.
Girard, R. (1977). *Violence and the Sacred*. Baltimore: Johns Hopkins University Press
Horning, R. (2016). "Mass Authentic," in *The New Inquiry*, December 20, 2016. https://thenewinquiry.com/blog/mass-authentic/
Jung, C. G. (1939). "The Relations between the Ego and the Unconscious," in *Two Essays on Analytical Psychology*, CW vol. 7. London: Routledge, 2007.
Jung, C. G. (1969). *Conscious, Unconscious and Individuation*. CW vol. 9. Princeton, NJ: Princeton University Press, p. 73.
Porter, M. E., and Kramer, M. R. (2011). "Creating Shared Value," in *Harvard Business Review*, Vol. 89, No. 1, pp. 2–17.
Rosa, H. (2019). *Resonance. A Sociology of Our Relationship to the World*. Cambridge: Polity Press.
Simmel, G. (1911). "Das Abenteuer," in *Phiosophische Kultur. Gesammelte Essays*. Leipzig: Alfred Kroner. Now in English in (2006) *The Sociology of Risk and Gambling Reader*, J. Cosgrave (ed.). London: Routledge.

Simondon, G. (1958). *Du mode d'existence des objets techniques*. Paris: Aubier.

Simondon, G. (1989). *L'individuation psychique et collective: A la lumière des notions de Forme, Information, Potentiel et Métastabilité*. Paris: Aubier. Now in Simondon, G. (2017). *L'individuation à la lumière des notions De forme et d'information*, Grenoble: Millon.

Simondon, G. (1992). "The Genesis of the Individual," in J. Crary and S. Kwinter (eds.), *Incorporations*. New York: Zone Books, 297–319. p. 301.

Stiegler, B. (2013). *What Makes Life Worth Living*. Cambridge: Polity Press.

Stiegler, B. (2018). *The Neganthropocene*. London: Open Humanities Press.

Stiegler, B. *La disruption rends fou*. culturemobile.net.

Chapter 10

'Roots in a Pot'

The Identity Conundrum in Global Nomads

Elias Winterton

Introduction

This chapter aims to develop the seeds of a reflection which started in 2018 during the IAAP/IAJS conference in Frankfurt upon the topic of *Indeterminate States: Transcultural, Transracial, Transgender* within an inter-disciplinary Jungian and post-Jungian psychoanalytical framework (Broadersen & Amezaga, 2021). The papers presented in this forum indicated a change of direction in the Jungian community towards the exploration of psychosocial dimensions and confronting contemporary issues related to race, sex, gender, identity, migrations, human rights, multi-culturalism and global politics.

This collective thinking stemmed from the original works of Singer and Kimbles (2004), Kimbles (2014), Rasche and Singer (2016) on cultural complexes, cultural diversity and cultural trauma after environmental disasters, political violence and exile. In a fast-changing world and emergent new territories, it is pivotal to aspire to redesign a psychological cartography of multiple indeterminate states (Iberni, 2021). A local identity encompasses the experience of being rooted in one territory, speaking the same language throughout one's life and connecting with a stable relational matrix and offers predictability, safety and a sense of belonging. Moving across physical, geographical, virtual and psychic borders activates ambivalent feelings and requires the capacity to hold the process of 'not knowing' with creative hope. From a clinical perspective, it is crucial to introduce innovative conceptions of the unconscious and intersubjective dynamics to understand 'multiple indeterminate states'.

Jungian and post-Jungian psychology offer an ideal point of observation and interpretation of liminal and hybrid manifestations of life. Jung posed the transcendent function at the core of his analytical psychology, describing it as a process of synthesis between opposite polarities and mediation of conflicting conscious and unconscious tensions. The symbol appears as a third apex apt to rebalancing the ego and its capacity to function (Jung, 1923: 825–826). Broadersen and Amezaga (2021) clarify that the term *indeterminate* refers to a different type of rational thinking process, which Jung defined as introverted symbolic thinking (Jung, 1911–1912: 4–54, 1921: 533). This type of indirect symbolic thinking

DOI: 10.4324/9781003168829-11

operates in a different manner in contrast to the *directed*, logical, hierarchical, abstracted thinking (logos) used for empirical scientific observation. Through introverted thinking, it is possible to encompass different thinking processes, transforming emotional states and affective responses of the inter-subjective field into symbols and mental representations.

This chapter attempts to apply to the clinical realm the original theoretical framework traced by Carpani (2021) and his endeavour to enrich the field of ana-lytical and depth psychology by integrating the idea of a 'social unconscious'. Moving from Ulrich Beck's individualization theory and Zygmunt Bauman's con-cept of liquidity (Bauman, 2001, 2005, 2006), he suggests revising the Jungian individuation considering the contemporary second modern epoch and liquid soci-eties. He also proposes to introduce the sociological concept of anomie to explore 'indeterminate states' (betwixt and between). For this purpose, the first part of this chapter will focus on recent studies on global nomads and third culture kids and adults, with specific attention to generational differences in relation to societal and cultural transformations. The second part of the chapter discusses the clinical material referring to the case of Muriel using a bio-ethnographic perspective (Lu, 2020) and shining light on multiple liminal states and forms of hybridity (social, cultural, racial and gender). The clinical case serves as a mirror to reflect on the process of development and individuation of an increasing number of individuals, families and communities living in a globalized and interconnected world.

Tales of global nomads and digital natives

Globalization has been the topic of studies for sociologists, political analysts and scholars for over two decades, since Zygmunt Bauman (1998) elucidated the ambivalent and ambiguous features of this complex phenomenon with its irrevers-ible human consequences. He described the nomadic lifestyle enabled by faster and cheaper global mobility, allowing people to move across countries, relocat-ing, settling and moving again to another destination (Bauman, 1998, p. 75). Besides geographical and physical border crossing, Bauman envisaged *digital nomadism* as a different way to connect and travel around the world through tel-evision, media and the Internet. In his writings, Bauman expresses rather directly concerns over the intensifying mental pain due to the uncertain and unstable conditions of the human life. More recently, psychologists have started to focus attention on understanding the complexity of personal identities for individuals who have crossed borders (for different reasons, immigrants, refugees or cross-nationally married) for a long or short term (e.g. for work or study); people who live in border areas; or people raised in multicultural or dissonant environments, including child migrants, children of migrants and mixed race/ethnic/national children (Cottrell, 2000). This case study refers more precisely to the category of so-called third culture kids (TCKs), a term originally coined by two sociologists, Ruth and John Useem (Useem et al., 1963; Useem, 1973; Useem & Downie, 1976; Useem & Cottrell, 1996; Cranston, 2017). They wanted to study how US

Americans who lived and worked in India during post-colonialism and after World War II would interact with their Indian colleagues (and vice versa), also observing power dynamics among the two groups. The term originally defined predominantly American children who lived their childhood years outside their country of citizenship because of a parent's employment in a representational role abroad. During the last three decades, anthropological, psychological and developmental researchers aimed to bring to light the emotional and psychological realities that come with the TCK journey (Pollock & Van Reken, 2009; Pollock et al., 2017). Currently, the term 'third culture kids' describes "children of expatriates, missionaries, military personnel, and others who live outside their passport country – due to a parent's choice of work or advanced training" (Pollock et al., 2017, p. 27). TCKs are considered a subcategory of the much wider group of cross-cultural kids (CCKs),[1] individuals experiencing a cross-cultural childhood for different reasons, for example, refugees, immigrants, international adopters, or born in cross-cultural marriages (Pollock & Van Reken, 2009). TCKs share unique experiences and personality traits. First of all, they have developed a global mindset, as they have experienced some conscious cultural dislocation and challenges to cultural verities and generally have a broader world view and more complex sense of self than those who are culturally and geographically centred. Of note, many TCKs do not think of themselves as an identifiable socio-cultural "type" (Cottrell, 2000). In this chapter, the term "global nomads" is used interchangeably with TCKs, which was originally coined by Norma McCuaig (2011) to refer to TCKs who grew into adulthood and preferred not to be referred to as 'kids'. The word 'nomad' also belongs to the mainstream of psychological gender studies and philosophy of difference.

Until 2000, most research on TCKs focused on psychological trauma, reverse culture shock, alienation, rootlessness, marginality, non-adjustment, homelessness and lack of identity, primarily at the time of (re)entry to the home country and in the teen and early adult years. These studies included TCKs, who, becoming adults, could articulate narratives relating both the pain and the gain of such multifaceted identities (e.g. Hoersting, R., & Jenkins, 2011; Nette & Hayden, 2007). In the first study, the differences of TCKs' childhood experiences in third cultures were analysed, taking into consideration several variables: 1) age at which they lived overseas and returned to their passport country, where impact appears to increase with age; 2) parent's sponsor (e.g. diplomatic service, military, missionary, corporate kids); 3) mobility;[2] 4) length of time overseas (in the same sample, the length of time ranged from 1 to 18 years abroad); 5) limited experience of life as a member of a "home" culture; and 6) experience of the host culture as a culture they connect with (in terms of local practices, values, language etc.) without belonging and experience of the home culture or of the country of parents' citizenship as the 'other' (especially after repatriation). TCKs experience a physical and internal dislocation (Papadopoulos, 2021), feeling either in one place and in another at the same time and neither in one place or another. Pollock et al. (2017) clarify that "the TCK builds relationships to all of the cultures, while not having full ownership in any" (p. 27) and explain that TCKs' "sense of belonging is in relationship to others of the same background" (p. 29); hence, TCKs identify with this shared experience, termed third culture. Furthermore, TCKs feel that mainstream labels and categories aiming to encapsulate them as adults into one group are uncomfortable, as these descriptions are inconsistent with their self-definition and too restrictive to describe the complexity of their subjective experience. Consequently, adult TCKs often report a lack of deep connection with national communities but rather prefer connecting with others who share analogous pasts. Adult TCKs recognize as a common identity to relate to similar others the pluralistic sense of identity derived from having a third culture childhood, creating an instant sense of community. The third culture is a shining example of the liquidity of the psychosocial experience of a sharply increasing number of individuals across the world. It is an abstract, interstitial ethos created from the shared experiences of persons from a variety of cultures but living the same mobile international lifestyle. Paradoxically, in TCKs, the differences are the fundamental element of their identities that create a sense of belonging. In this sense, TCKs' hybrid identities can transcend boundaries of geographical places or nationalities, allowing TCKs to find their roots to interstitial places and cultures in a "both/and way, rather than having to choose either/ or" (Pollock et al., 2017, p. 68).

In the last decade, with globalization and continuous developments of technology and digitalization, the number of people living cross-culturally due to their mobility has rapidly increased. Consequently, more attention has been dedicated to investigating the impact of these psychosocial conditions on the emotional, relational and identity development of children living mobile cross-national lives and their personality development as adults. Tan et al. (2021) published the results of a systemic review of the literature on the state of art of empirical research on third culture kids. The study included 31 (out of initial 399) peer-reviewed research publications in international journals. Three main domains were addressed in several investigations: 1) emotional development, 2) social and relational development and 3) identity development. The meta-analysis shows that the body of research focusing on the emotional development of TCKs includes three themes: adjustment, mental wellbeing and grief and loss. Most of the studies related to adjustment have tackled the emotional challenges related to repatriation or the return to the country of citizenship of their parents, which represents a typical experience of TCKs not shared by other cross-cultural and mobile populations (Smith & Kearney, 2016). Adjusting and fitting into the passport country is often difficult because of the experience of estrangement with the dominant culture after living abroad. TCKs can struggle to build friendships and can report being bullied, especially when moving to college life (Walters & Auton-Cuff, 2009; Choi et al., 2013). Mental distress, depression, anxiety and low self-esteem are higher than in other populations and often related to cultural homelessness, lack of belonging and loneliness (Davis et al., 2010; Hervey, 2009; Rounsaville, 2014). This data is also reported in studies focusing on grief and loss, as TCKs often experience several separations and multiple goodbyes. Unresolved grief has been highlighted as a crucial issue due to alienated or hidden losses (Gilbert, 2008; Pollock et al., 2017).

Another key domain of inquiry concerns TCKs' capacity to develop relationships and maintain friendships, as well as their special intercultural sensitivity and competence and tolerance towards other cultures and religions. The relational development of global nomads is highly challenging due to their need to form-lose-reform meaningful emotional relationships and to maintain then at a distance in a virtual space (Lijadi & Van Schalkwyk, 2018). Compared to mono-cultural individuals, global nomads show significantly higher social sensitivity and ability to read social situations and reflect on others' feelings, cognitions and personalities (Lyttle et al., 2011), and they are more competent as intercultural communicators (Moore & Barker, 2012). A different comparative study by Greenholtz and Kim (2009) seems to reflect the paradox of the cultural hybridity of global nomads. TCKs compared to non-TCKs were shown to have a unique intercultural sensitivity and a worldview able to hold two polarities simultaneously, being both ethnocentric and ethno-relative, demonstrating skills in bridging and frameshifting.

With regard to the third topic, the process of identity construction among TCKs received special attention to explore their confusion in cultural identification, struggle with sense of belonging and home (Nette & Hayden, 2007) and identity negotiations. TCK respondents reported two major foundations for their sense of belonging at a young age: familiarity with physical aspects of their environment and meaningful relationships, being able to identify at the same time with two or more countries as their home countries. A fascinating aspect of the studies investigates how TCKs navigate through their life holding a single multicultural identity and/or multiple identities. Holding multiple identities and being able to shift depending on the circumstances to meet expectations and fit within a specific environment seems a common identity negotiation strategy, as described in the literature (Berry and Sam, 2016). In-depth qualitative studies describe the struggles and disruptions in the development of identity for global nomads and their intense mental pain and longing to share a specific culture or home, with negative impact on their mental and emotional wellbeing. Overall, an important research finding shows that TCKs feel most content when with others who share similar cross-cultural lifestyles or international mobile experiences (Greenholtz & Kim, 2009; Selmer & Lam, 2004; Selmer & Laurig, 2014; Smith & Kearney, 2016), showing that the internalization of multiple experiences and blended identities can be adaptive and function as a permanent mindset (Jensen, 2012).

Freedom and individuation among global and digital travellers

Besides the nomadic lifestyle as internationally mobile people, global nomads are also navigating the massive digitalization that occurred over the last decades, so that they are also digital travellers. Of note, generational differences are key to understanding the impact of technology and global connectivity on human habits, and the members of Gen Zero (Gen Z) – born from 1995 to 2010 – represent the first cohort of true digital natives (McKinsey, 2018). In a context of continuous exposure to the internet, to social networks and to mobile systems, this generation has developed "hypercognitive skills, the ability to collect and cross-reference many sources of information and to integrate virtual and offline experience" (ibidem). As a result, youth have become powerful influencers of the broader population across socioeconomic classes. The study investigated how the behaviours of Gen Z in three major Brazilian cities, as well as in other countries around the world, can affect other generations. The results of the survey showed that Gen Zers are "in search for truth, value individual expression and avoid labels". Compared to the previous generation, the Millennials, born in an era of economic prosperity that made them "more inclined to focus on themselves and to be less willing to accept diverse points of view", Gen Zers appear are more likely to "mobilize themselves for different causes and to relate to institutions". The research indicated that Gen Zers make decisions in a highly analytical and pragmatic way and deeply value dialogue to solve problems and to improve the world. In fact, their behaviour as consumers shows that they "conceive consumption as a matter of ethical concern and expression of individual identity". By virtue of technological advancement and digitalization, their influence is decidedly transformative for brands and businesses, pushing the market to rethink the values that they "promote and to rebalance scale and mass production against personalization".

The results of this recent survey seem to reply to the questions posed by Bauman at the beginning of the third millennium. More than any other group of people, these *global and digital travellers* share an existential horizon of "fragility, temporariness, vulnerability and inclination to constant change" (Bauman, 1998, 2000, p. 82) and by default remain underdefined and literally open to new lives against certainty.

Observing *global and digital travellers* through the lens of the concept of individualization and liquidity, it appears that for them, freedom is a source of generative power rather than leading to a state of anomie or *broken individualization*. Agreeing with Beck, who defined individualization as a "choice among possibilities" where all aspects of human life can be subject to autonomous decisions (2002, p. 5), the case of global and digital travellers clearly demonstrates that "any generalization that seeks to understand individualized society only in terms of the extremes of autonomy or anomie abbreviates and distorts the questions about the real meaning of individualization" (Beck, 2002, p. 6).

The key to understanding how the developmental outcomes of this specific group can be oriented towards generativity and authentic autonomy against anomie could be in Jung's concept of individuation, described as a process "of differentiation, having for its goal the development of the individual personality" (CW6, para: 757) and, in a clinical setting, "the process in which the patient becomes what he really is" (CW16, para 11). Jung thought that individuation was a process related to the "second half of life", at the beginning of the midlife transition corresponding to age 35 or 40 (1933, p. 100), and that the purpose of the first half of life "undoubtedly lies in the development of the individual, our entrenchment in the outer world, [and] the propagation of our kind and the care of our children" (1933, p. 109). Jung conceived the transition from childhood into an independent adulthood as an innate instinctual process, guided by healthy sexuality (1948/1960, par. 113) and enabled by a functional ego complex. The theory of individuation has been further explored and explained as a process of separation and the resolution of parental complex to become independent and autonomous, which can take place through a conscious engagement with collective consciousness, roles and norms (Kast, 2000, p. 308). In a liquid society, however, young individuals not only are missing the traditional rituals of passage born of an innate necessity to fundamentally transform the ego and support their access into adulthood (1968, p. 175) but also lack guidance and adequate culturally institutionalized systems to prepare them for life in a world that underwent widespread social changes (Arnett, 2000).

Stein (2006a, 2006b) revised the framework of the *principium individuationis*, describing individuation as a long-life dynamic process unfolding through different stages: containment/nurturance 0–12, adapting/adjusting 12–21, centring/integrating above 21. Individuation involves a continuous cycle of synthesis and analysis to integrate the unconscious into a self-aware personality (Stein, 2006a, 2006b). To understand the developmental pathway of TCKs, and global and digital nomads in an individualized/liquid society, the concept of individuation can both serve as a theoretical point of reference and allow the creation of a suitable clinical approach. Psychological individuation can fully enable TCKs to embrace their precarious life and identity with self-awareness and responsibility, a crucial aspect to avoid anomie (Beck and Beck-Gernsheim, 2002). The adapting/adjustment stage of individuation (Stein, 2006a, 2006b) can provide a solid basis to develop a clinical framework able to understand the perilous risks that incessant life changes and diversity present to the global and digital nomad. Building on the solid scientific findings that show how mental health problems and emotional distress are highly present among TCKs and global nomads (Tan et al., 2021), it is possible to find evidence of the importance of the role of individuation to integrate unconscious and dissociated levels of experience and to establish a strong ego (Jung, 1928/1954; Fordham, 1957). In a liquid and individualized society, they face multiple difficulties in becoming themselves: starting with research of wholeness and a coherent sense of self while facing painful compartmentalization's of their experiences, the impossibility of fully sharing their emotional experiences and a sense of marginalization and alienation, traumatic losses and forced separations, the quest for a sense of belonging and home and the negative effect of bullying and discrimination that might be triggered by their diversity. They climb a dangerous cliff that can weaken their ego; their physical separation from parental figures at the moment of entering college is highly correlated with the risk of a mental break down and often underrecognized (Smith & Kearney, 2016).

Another challenge is the integration of the virtual dimensions in the present moment and the illusion of omnipotence, of being able to stay interconnected with many places and people while not developing meaningful relationships, reciprocity, interdependence and intimacy.

A therapist working within the framework of the principium individuations adapted to the contemporary challenges of global and digital nomads can enhance the wellbeing not only of individuals but of an entire generation. Successful individuation can activate generativity, the capacity to maintain a dialogue between the ego and the self and to foster by virtue of digital interconnectivity the value of diversity and truth.

Clinical case

Treatment history

This case study illustrates the process of differentiation and individuation of a young patient through different stages of the analytical treatment and the attempt to integrate diverse aspects of the self, linked to distinct experiences of global mobility. Facing the liquidity of a nomadic life, patient Muriel has to learn to deal with the paradoxes and with a profound sense of loneliness and alienation, living in both a virtual and material reality pervaded by variations and endless possibilities. Working through the cycles of transference and countertransference, synthesis and analysis, the patient and the analyst co-create a safe container to elaborate and transform omnipotence, negative projections and dissociated traumatic experiences. The patient's experience that initially could not be told started to tessellate, reconciling the divergent opposites and creating the capacity to hold mindfully the conundrum of their identity. At the beginning of treatment, gender identity represented the major theme, as Muriel expressed the desire to be recognized and validated as a non-binary person. Therefore, gender-neutral and inclusive language is adopted (Merriam-Webster, 2019), and in the narrative of the clinical material, the pronoun used is the third-person plural 'they'. The therapeutic relationship developed a relational matrix able to sustain individuation embracing multiplicity of the self and to shape Muriel's persona.

Patient's background

Muriel was a 23-year-old student in political science. They are an energetic, ironic and sensitive young adult, with a remarkable artistic talent in photography and music. They enjoy friends and show a genuine curiosity for the surrounding and more distal world, human rights, civil rights, the environment and global politics. Their academic performance remains below their potential, and this kindles frustration and envy. Muriel was conceived and born in a South American country, with a mono-ethnic society, religious and traditional culture and authoritarian political system. They remember their life in the country until the age of 8.

During the first two years of their life, Muriel and their mother were living with their paternal grandparents, in a little town with a tight-knit community strictly observing traditional rules. The first memories refer to the birth of a sister when Muriel was 3 years old, which coincided with their father re-joining the family full time. Muriel was very close to their strong and masculine father and remember a sense of distance and detachment towards the mother, who was closer to the little sister. They felt jealous and hurt by the mother's neglect and lack of interest in their achievements and growth. Muriel experienced their mother as a "narcissist, womanly and instable" and speculated that her problem was that she was conditioned by the patriarchal society and submissive towards the traditional rules, limiting her capacity to develop as a human being. Muriel felt contempt and dislike towards the mother, repressing feelings of anger and sadness to maintain detachment.

At the age of 8, the family made its first move to Mexico due to their father's diplomatic career. These years were dark, and Muriel showed signs of depression, missing the caregiving grandparents and in particular suffering after the sudden the death of the grandmother. Muriel's condition was unrecognized and non-validated, as the family seemed unable to connect and elaborate the losses and negative emotions. When they were 12 years old, the family relocated to Australia, which Muriel remembers as a chunk of their life like a rollercoaster, getting to know the open and multicultural society, the enthusiasm for learning and education but also the terrifying experience of sexual abuse. When Muriel was 16 years old, they moved to New York without their family to start college studies with a scholarship. During these American years, two younger twin brothers were born. In this phase, Muriel developed a large capacity to enjoy exploration, discovery of new worlds and diverse people and started becoming aware of sexual and relational desires, sensuality, gender identity and sexual orientation. Moving to Europe, four years after, to live with their family again represented a powerful setback that made them regress to an earlier stage, re-ignited the old, heated feelings towards the mother and created a sense of disorientation for not being able to re-connect with their father. Their chief complaint at the beginning of the treatment was being confused and muddled with regard to aspects of their life, unaware of their authentic needs and desires, terrified of remaining stuck in this uncertainty and precariousness.

Immersed in the fog

For the first four months, Muriel found it difficult to use the therapeutic space of analysis. They remained silent and embarrassed, excusing themself for being unable to focus or to say the 'right thing'. The sense of discomfort during the sessions in the first four months was often captured by a somatic countertransference filled with stomach tension and blushing faces. When Muriel was invited to talk about themself, their reaction was to gasp in anxiety, as they were incapable of articulating any stories about themselves, finding it difficult to focus on a specific thought to describe a trait of personality and the relationships with meaningful others. They said that

> it's like being immersed in the fog, I cannot see my thoughts, ideas, preferences or desires. I cannot detect the shapes and the directions of the things I have inside. Sometimes I fear of looking at all those things. Other times I am afraid to discover being empty. But what terrifies me the most is being unable to understand who I am, and what I can become, and I need to find it out quickly.

Muriel was facing the possibility of having to leave Europe in the short term, as their resident status was bound to a visa provided by the national government to individuals and families with diplomatic status, expiring with the end of father's assignment. In addition, Muriel did not know if they wanted to continue their studies or to find a job, and this dilemma was opening a set of different questions around their actual skills, capacities, passions and preferences. Their most aching uncertainty was where they wanted to live, as they could not identify any place as home.

A series of dreams appeared during this initial part of the treatment, most of them presenting recurring sensorial elements, such as mud, humid ground and worms, grass, paths in rural landscapes, rainfalls and storms. The images of natural elements, like earth and water, evoked a sense of curiosity for hidden life forms and had a strong association with a mindscape of their home country. Muriel seemed surprised to connect to those memories that they considered an irrelevant part of their life experience.

Sinking in countertransference and shame

The therapeutic relationship between the therapist and Muriel was characterized by a series of intense unconscious interactions generating a sense of impasse in different moments, mostly due to the racial difference linked to their South American heritage. The social identity of Muriel was shaped around their physical diversity, the features of their body and, to their shame, very often connected to the experience of discrimination and humiliation that they had faced in many situations and different places. Despite having been born and grown up in a privileged environment and the possibility to attend schools for global elites, looking at their image reflected in the mirror had always made them feel a pervasive embarrassment and interiorized racial judgements. Muriel's transference was injected with shame, eliciting a deeply uncomfortable feeling in the therapist. On the other hand, the therapist was defensively avoiding openly mentioning the topic of racial diversity, fearing that Muriel could express anger towards the White therapist. The unconscious fear of the high risk of ruptures of the therapeutic relationship was keeping the analytical process blocked. Jung considered that to initiate a truly transformative process, mutual transference was a critical part of the work, and the two personalities of the patient and analyst had to mix as chemical substances (Jung, 1954, p. 71). In contemporary terms, Benjamin (2013, 2010) considers that the fact that both patient and therapist bring their unconscious to the process can allow them to engage in a process of rupture and repair for mutual recognition. In this case, the possibility of a collaborative break-through and the flowing into the relationship of ambivalent feelings and negative projections could start when positive elements of the racial identity could be associated with unknown memories and with the image of a loving relationship with their grandmother and her sudden death. The painful experience of loss and unresolved mourning, shared within the analytical setting, emotionally connected the therapist and patient and allowed the transformations of shame and overwhelming anxiety into sadness and reparation of precious element (grandmother) representing the roots of their biological, sexual, racial and social identity. Racial difference entered the therapeutic dialogue in a fruitful manner, and Muriel could unfold dissociated stories of micro-aggressions undermining their sense of self-love and self-acceptance. While progressively increasing a sense of self-awareness, Muriel's confusion and disorientation around the lack of a material and internal home (Papadopoulos, 2021), and their longing to have a specific cultural background began to integrate. Muriel could start to make sense and create a meaningful narrative of that hybrid, contradictory and at the same time globally standardized, mosaic blend of many different cultural experiences across several countries. They realized that what before appeared a vulnerability and weakness was a strange sort of gift, or super-power: the chameleonic capacity to identify with many different types of people, being naturally curious and eager to explore new dimensions. The distress related to discrimination and their defensiveness turned into a proactive attitude of care and promotion of inclusion in community settings. Their tendency to avoid social contacts diminished as Muriel engaged more freely with new situations and people.

Nor female or male: omnipotence, fluidity and the emergence of a third possibility

Muriel started the analysis feeling unable to define themselves but paradoxically clarified a key element referring to gender identity: being non-binary, gender-fluid, both male and female, not bounded to the limitations of sexual biology, nor rules, traditions and religious beliefs. By defining the non-binary nature of being a human, Muriel wanted to assert the right to become free and unbounded, to exercise the power of self-expression and creativity. Their identification with a global, cosmopolitan culture inspired by diversity, respect, tolerance and individual rights and freedom provided them a solid ground to orient themselves in the world.

In the surface of their rationalized narrative, being gender-fluid served to give cohesion to their persona and enabled Muriel to be an activist, to network with other individuals and organizations and to participate in political and cultural movements with important goals to improve human society. As the analytical relationship became more trustful and therapeutic goals clearly delineated towards individuation and the capacity to operate short and midterm life choices, Muriel started to question this definition of gender identity, to reflect on their difficulties with creating intimate relationships and to enjoy pleasure in sexual activities. The analytical focus shifted from their archetypal identification with the fascinating image of the androgenic Sygizia, to unpack the experiences of Animus and Anima referring to their parental figures and to an excruciating experience of sexual abuse during the pre-puberty period. Being identified with a male toxic predator provided a false sense of psychological safety from potential threats to self-integrity and at the same time protected from the fear of being like the mother, insensitive, unpredictable and neglectful. Femininity was referred to a positive vital element, the racial and cultural roots, the unique way of being in the world, and connected to meaningful others, representing the capacity to nurture, comfort, repair and love. Working through alienated parts of self, filling gaps of meaning left by invisible losses by mourning patiently, Muriel learned to integrate their polyphonic identities in a whole. Fostering self-love and acceptance, the therapist offered a safe space for Muriel to begin to connect with new potential partners in the effort to express authentically as vulnerable but worthy of being chosen and loved.

Roots in the pot: reconciling the opposites

Muriel was born as a 'digital native', being exposed to technology since early childhood and using multiple digital tools in educational settings. Moving across countries and cultures, digital media and innovative applications represented for Muriel the main way to stay connected, to maintain relationships at distance and to relate to the world as a global citizen, gathering information and interacting with the world on different topics and with diverse people. In this virtual dimension, compared to their attitude in the material world, Muriel can stretch their limits and appear more confident and mature, also because their virtual image is improved by using sophisticated filters on pictures and self-portraits. Living hybrid forms of experience and relationships is surely a huge advantage and offers endless opportunities for learning and growing. Nevertheless, virtual reality functioned for long years as a defensive barrier, giving Muriel an illusionary sense of control and balance, introducing self-serving distortions in relation to social and personal relationships, for example, those conveyed by Instagram's beautification of life. In analysis, Muriel explored their feelings of unease and perceptions of rejection or being spurned when facing real people and situations. Their active imagination provided a formidable instrument for exploring the internal reality of their body; mastering emotions and sensations; and defining external boundaries through massage, sensorial stimulation and physical contact. Muriel's dislocation in both the virtual and external world was influenced by both digital and global nomadism. Unquestionably, this restless movement was generating and maintaining in a mutual circle their unstable sense of belonging, fragile sense of self and hyper-inclusive hybrid identity, blurring boundaries and distinctions of different parts of themself. After two years of treatment, Muriel embraced the need to adapt to the limited possibilities and to financial and time constraints and decided to make a clear choice about their professional career. They decided to become a digital content manager. Transcending the opposite instances of their aspirations as human rights activist and artist, Muriel desired to use their skills and experiences to serve non-governmental organizations and brands to mainstream diversity and equity in the collective representation of all individuals, granting the maximum freedom of self-expression and individuation.

In one of their last sessions, Muriel brings a dream to analysis that offers an internal picture of their different level of individuation.

> "I am travelling in New York's underground, with all my family, and I am surprised because also my grandmother is there, I know she is dead but I am excited for being able to talk to her and hug her. I am careful to warn all my relatives that we need to step out at the next stop. They actually ignore or don't listen to me. I finally get out of the metro, and in a moment I realize that I left all behind me, my bag with money, cards and documents and my family including my grandmother. I am in panic in front of a new place feeling so vulnerable and disoriented. I try to breathe deeply and then I put my hands in my pockets, and I find new keys and identity cards. I am sad, alone in a place that I don't know, but there are posters with reassuring messages inspiring a better future for all the people. I follow the path and climb the stairs going to explore this new place and life."

Muriel showed surprise observing their resilience and capacity to regulate emotions facing the traumatic loss and separation in the dream. The closure of the doors behind them anticipates the end of the analytical process, which offers them a new possibility to learn losing and mourning pursuing reparation instead of falling into alienation and dissociation.

Conclusion

The case study of Muriel suggests the chance to develop and refine theoretical ideas that can inform and guide the analytical process and therapeutic work with global nomads and with third culture kids and young adults (Pollock & Van Reken, 2009; Damon, 2004; Purnell & Hoban, 2014; Peterson & Plamondon, 2009). The case proposes to reflect on the importance of extending the boundaries of analytical psychology with an innovative conceptual framework integrating the social dimension. Bauman and Beck eloquently described the effects of the globalization on the life of individuals and the massive impact on their (liquid) intimate relationships (Bauman, 2003, 2006), family conditions, working conditions, mobility and outlook on the future. Precariousness, uncertainty and vulnerability are the common experiential denominators for a large majority of individuals, who can enjoy many sorts of freedom but also suffer alienation and mental pain. The Jungian lens of analytical psychology can offer an original approach to activate the integrative process of individuation in young global nomads. Analysis can promote the creation of a more balanced worldly mindset apt to hold the ambiguity and liminality of their identity and relationships and can trigger the generative/reparative capacities of taking care of the community, society and environment.

Global nomads present specific challenges for the psychotherapeutic treatment, as their development of a sense of identity takes place in asynchronous spaces and times, being here and there, nowhere, anywhere: life between embodied and virtual reality (Lee et al., 2007; Lerner et al., 2014). Global nomads can resonate with the image that Dante offers of souls stuck in Purgatory: exiled, expats are aliens, who cannot feel at home but can transplant their roots as rhizomes and reopen a new space for growing another part of self somewhere else while continuing in parallel their previous lives and relationships, although in a virtual hyperconnected space.

In conclusion, a few venues of further research and clinical exploration are suggested to incorporate the psychosocial dimension in the analytical setting. The first line of inquiry could focus on the countertransference of the analyst working with internationally mobile individuals. The therapist's capacity to tolerate indeterminate states of mind is crucial for the patient's unfolding reflective function and the elaboration of negative emotions and mental pain inherent to the condition of precariousness and uncertainty. Unconscious biases and implicit assumptions about gender, race, the experience of migration and acculturation, trauma and power can unconsciously orient the analytical process in search of premature definitions. The emergence of the transcendent function through the holding of the analyst can facilitate the creation of an inclusive, plural and hybrid identity and of a strong Ego complex able to flexibly adapt a manifold persona. The second thread of research could focus on the effect of sociological and generational factors in therapy and their role in shaping emotional, relational and cognitive growth; self-identity; and personality of young adults, regardless of their mobility. Being exposed since early childhood to a hyperconnected and virtual environment can set the basis of a worldly attitude and offer the possibility of finding new ways of self-expression, as well as increasing the possibility of experiencing undefined, queer, hybrid identity; dislocation; and rootlessness. Analysis serves to protect the roots and enable them to grow everywhere flexibly and to adapt virtuously to visible and invisible traumas. A third field of clinical investigation could address alienated states of mind and dissociated negative emotions derived from discriminatory experiences (i.e. micro-aggressions, bullying or racist violence). The analytical setting elicits transference responses reproducing power relationships and conflicts that can remain undetected and undermine therapeutic alliance.

Analytical psychology has a large potential for clinical applications and to address the complexity of new emerging conditions generated by social changes and technological innovations. From a theoretical standpoint, a constant dialogue with other disciplines and human sciences is crucial to produce a clear and updated understanding of contemporary realities. On the clinical side, the Jungian ideas on transference and countertransference resonate with current developments in relational and intersubjective psychoanalysis, suggesting the opportunity to invest more efforts in researching the factors that contribute to determine successful therapeutic outcomes.

Notes

1 The CCK concept clarifies that individuals raised in more than one culture share: 1) the feeling of connection to more than one culture and often, because of that, not fully belonging to either and 2) a sense of commonality with others whose lives are also multicultural in ways similar to their own. Mobility patterns, time of permanence in other cultures, political status and acculturation strategies might widely differ.
2 A longitudinal study, including 603 adult TCKs (Useem & Cottrell, 1996), showed that the overseas experience of the sample ranged from a single overseas residence to 12 residences in six countries, averaging four different places of residence outside the United States by age 18. Many were additionally mobile in the United States, some living in 18 places by high school graduation.

References

Arnett, J. J. (2000, May). Emerging adulthood: A theory of development from the late teens through the twenties. *American Psychologist*, 55(5), 469–480.
Bauman, Z. (1998). *Globalization: The Human Consequences*. Cambridge: Polity Press.
Bauman, Z. (2000). *Liquid Modernity*. Cambridge: Polity Press.
Bauman, Z. (2001). *The Individualized Society*. Cambridge: Polity Press.
Bauman, Z. (2003). *Liquid Love*. Cambridge: Polity Press.
Bauman, Z. (2005). *Liquid Life*. Cambridge: Polity Press.
Bauman, Z. (2006). *Liquid Times: Living in an Age of Uncertainty*. Cambridge: Polity.
Beck, U., & Beck-Gernsheim, E. (2002). *Individualization: Institutionalized Individualism and its Social and Political Consequences*. London: Sage.
Benjamin, J. (2010). Where's the gap and what's the difference? The relational view of intersubjectivity, multiple selves and enactments. *Contemporary Psychoanalysis*, 46(1), 12–119.
Benjamin, J. (2013). *Shadow of the Other: Intersubjectivity and Gender in Psychoanalysis*. London: Routledge.
Berry, J., & Sam, D. (2016). Theoretical perspectives. In D. Sam & J. Berry (Eds.), *The Cambridge Handbook of Acculturation Psychology* (Cambridge handbooks in psychology) (pp. 11–29). Cambridge: Cambridge University Press. https://doi.org/10.1017/CBO9781316219218.003.
Broadersen, E., & Amezaga, P. (2021). *Jungian Perspectives on Indeterminate States. Betwixt and between Borders*. London: Routledge.
Carpani, S. (2021). The consequence of freedom: Moving beyond the intermediate states of broken individualization and liquidity. In E. Broadersen & P. Amezaga (Eds.), *Jungian Perspectives on Indeterminate States. Betwixt and between Borders*. London: Routledge.
Choi, K. M., Bernard, J. M., & Luke, M. (2013). Characteristics of friends of female college third culture kids. *Asia Pacific Journal of Counselling and Psychotherapy*, 4(2), 125–136. https://doi.org/10.1080/21507686.2013.779931.

Cottrell, A. B. (2000). *Global Mobility and Personal Identity*. Paper presented at Pacific Sociological Association Meetings, San Diego, CA.

Cranston, S. (2017). Self-help and the surfacing of identity: Producing the third culture kid. *Emotion, Space, and Society*, 24, 27–33. https://doi.org/10.1016/j.emospa.2017.07.006.

Damon, W. (2004). What is positive youth development? *The Annals of the American Academy of Political and Social Science*, 591(1), 13–24. https://doi.org/10.1177/0002716203260092.

Davis, P., Headley, K., Bazemore, T., Cervo, J., Sickinger, P., Windham, M., et al. (2010). Evaluating impact of transition seminars on missionary kids' depression, anxiety, stress, and well-being. *Journal of Psychology and Theology*, 38(3), 186–194. https://doi.org/10.1177/009164711003800303.

Fordham, M. (1957). *New development in analytical psychology*. London: Routledge, Tailor and Francis (2014).

Gilbert, K. (2008). Loss and grief between and among cultures: The experience of third culture kids. *Illness Crisis & Loss*, 16(2), 93–109. https://doi.org/10.2190/IL.16.2.a.

Greenholtz, J., & Kim, J. (2009). The cultural hybridity of Lena: A multi-method case study of a third culture kid. *International Journal of Intercultural Relations*, 33(5), 391–398. https://doi.org/10.1016/j.ijintrel.2009.05.004.

Hervey, E. (2009). Cultural transitions during childhood and adjustment to college. *Journal of Psychology and Christianity*, 28(1), 3–12.

Hoersting, R., & Jenkins, S. (2011). No place to call home: Cultural homelessness, self-esteem and cross-cultural identities. *International Journal of Intercultural Relations*, 35(1), 17–30. https://doi.org/10.1016/j.ijintrel.2010.11.005.

Iberni, E. (2021). Challenges to the individuation process of people on the move. Developing a sense of global citizenship. In E. Broadersen & P. Amezaga (Eds.) (2021), *Jungian Perspectives on Indeterminate States. Betwixt and between Borders*. London: Routledge.

Jensen, L. A. (2012). Bridging universal and cultural perspectives: A vision for developmental psychology in a global world. *Child Development Perspectives*, 6(1), 98–104. https://doi-org.fuller.idm.oclc.org/10.1111/j.1750-8606.2011.00213.x.

Jung, C. G. (1911–1912/1952). 'Two kind of thinking'. In *Collected works*, Vol. 5, *Symbols of Transformation* (2nd ed.). London: Routledge and Kegan Paul, 1995.

Jung, C. G. (1921). 'Indeterminism versus determinism'. In *Collected Works*, Vol. 6, *Psychological types*. London: Routledge and Kegan Paul, 1989.

Jung, C. G. (1923). 'Definitions'. In Collected Works, Vol.6, *Psychological Types* (2nd ed.). London: Routledge and Kegan Paul, 1989.

Jung, C. G. (1933). The stages of life (W. S. Dell & C. F. Baynes, Trans.). In C. G. Jung, *Modern Man in Search of a Soul* (pp. 19–114). New York, NY: Harcourt

Jung, C. G. (1954). Child development and education. In H. Read, M. Fordham, G. Adler, & W. McGuire (Eds.), *The Collected Works of C. G. Jung* (Trans., R. F. C. Hull, 2nd ed., Vol. 58, pp. 49–62). Princeton, NJ: Princeton University Press. (Original work published 1928)

Jung, C. G. Collected Works. Vol 7, Part 2, Individuation. New York: Pantheon (Bollingen Series, Vols 1–20), 1957–1979.

Jung, C. G. (1968). *Analytical Psychology: Its Theory and Practice*. The Tavistock lectures. New York, NY: Vintage Books. (Original lectures given in 1935).

Kast, V. (2000). Individuation. In G. Stumm& A. Pritz (Eds.), *Wörterbuch der Psychotherapie*. Vienna: Springer. https://doi.org/10.1007/978-3-211-99131-2_836

Kimbles, S. (2014). *Phantom Narratives: The Unseen Contributions of Culture to Psyche.* Lanham, Rowman & Littlefield.

Lee, Y., Bain, S., & McCallum, R. (2007). Improving creative problem-solving in a sample of third culture kids. *School Psychology International*, 28(4), 449–463. https://doi.org/10.1177/0143034307084135.

Lerner, R. M., Lerner, J. V., Bowers, E. P., & Geldhof, G. J. (2014). Positive youth development and relational-developmental-systems. In W. F. Overton, P. C. M. Molenaar, & R. M. Lerner (Eds.), *Handbook of Child Psychology and Developmental Science: Theory and Method* (Vol. 1, pp. 1–45). Wiley. https://doi.org/10.1002/9781118963418.childpsy116.

Lijadi, A., & Van Schalkwyk, G. (2018). "The international schools are not so international after all": The educational experiences of third culture kids. *International Journal of School & Educational Psychology*, 6(1), 50–61. https://doi.org/10.1080/21683603.2016.1261056.

Lu, K. (2020). Racial hybridity. *International Journal of Jungian Studies*, 12, 11–40.

Lyttle, A., Barker, G., & Cornwell, T. (2011). Adept through adaptation: Third culture individuals' interpersonal sensitivity. *International Journal of Intercultural Relations*, 35(5), 686–694. https://doi.org/10.1016/j.ijintrel.2011.02.015.

McCuaig, N. (2011). Raised in the margin of the mosaic: Global nomads balance worlds within. In G. Bell-Villada & N. Sichel (Eds.), *Writing out of Limbo: International Childhoods, Global Nomads and Third Culture Kids* (pp. 45–56). New Castle upon Tyne, UK: Cambridge Scholars Publishing.

McKinsey (2018). *True Generation*, available at: www.mckinsey.com/industries/consumer-packaged-goods/our-insights/true-gen-generation-z-and-its-implications-for-companies

Merriam-Webster (2019). *Online Dictionary: They*. Retrieved February 11, 2021, available at: https://www.merriam-webster.com/dictionary/they

Moore, A., & Barker, G. (2012). Confused or multicultural: Third culture individuals' cultural identity. *International Journal of Intercultural Relations*, 36(4), 553–562. https://doi.org/10.1016/j.ijintrel.2011.11.002.

Nette, J., & Hayden, M. (2007). Globally mobile children: The sense of belonging. *Educational Studies*, 33(4). https://doi.org/10.1080/03055690701423614, 435–435.

Papadopoulos, R. (2021). *Involuntary Dislocation Home, Trauma, Resilience, and Adversity-Activated Development*. London: Routledge.

Peterson, B., & Plamondon, L. (2009). Third culture kids and the consequences of international sojourns on authoritarianism, acculturative balance, and positive affect. *Journal of Research in Personality*, 43(5), 755–763. https://doi.org/10.1016/j.jrp.2009.04.014.

Pollock, D. C., & Van Reken, R. (2009). *Third Culture Kids: Growing Up among Worlds* (2nd ed.). Boston: Nicholas Brealey Publishing.

Pollock, D. C., Van Reken, R., & Pollock, M. V. (2017). *Third Culture Kids: Growing Up among Worlds* (3rd ed.). Boston: Nicholas Brealey Publishing.

Purnell, L., & Hoban, E. (2014). The lived experiences of third culture kids transitioning into university life in Australia. *International Journal of Intercultural Relations*, 41, 80–90. https://doi.org/10.1016/j.ijintrel.2014.05.002.

Rasche, G., & Singer, T. (Eds.). (2016). *Europe's Many Souls. Exploring Cultural Complexes and Identities*. New Orleans: Spring Journal Books.

Rounsaville, A. (2014). Situating transnational genre knowledge: A genre trajectory analysis of one student's personal and academic writing. *Written Communication*, 31(3). https://doi.org/10.1177/0741088314537599, 332–332.

Selmer, J., & Lam, H. (2004). "Third-culture kids": Future business expatriates? *Personnel Review*, 33(4), 430–445. https://doi.org/10.1108/00483480410539506.

Selmer, J., & Lauring, J. (2014). Self-initiated expatriates: An exploratory study of adjustment of adult third-culture kids vs. Adult mono-culture kids. *Cross Cultural Management an International Journal*, 21(4), 422–436. https://doi.org/10.1108/CCM-01-2013-0005.

Singer, T., & Kimbles, S. (2004). *The Cultural Complex. Contemporary Jungian Perspectives on Psyche and Society*. London: Routledge.

Smith, V., & Kearney, K. (2016). A qualitative exploration of the repatriation experiences of us third culture kids in college. *Journal of College Student Development*, 57(8), 958–972. https://doi.org/10.1353/csd.2016.0093.

Stein, M. (2006a). Individuation. In R. Papadopoulos & A. Samuels (Eds.), *Handbook of Analytical Psychology*. London: Routledge.

Stein, M. (2006b). *Principium individuationis*. Asheville: Chiron Publications.

Tan, E. C., Wang, K. T., & Cottrell, A. (2021). A systematic review of third culture kids empirical research. *International Journal of Intercultural Relations*, 82, 81–98. https://doi.org/10.1016/j.ijintrel.2021.03.002.

Useem, J., Useem, R., & Donoghue, J. (1963). Men in the middle of the third culture: The roles of American and non-western people in cross-cultural administration. *Human Organization*, 22(3), 169–179.

Useem, R. H. (1973). Third culture factors in educational change. In C. S. Brembeck & W. Hill (Eds.), *Cultural Challenges to Education*. Lexington, MA: D.C. Heath & Co.

Useem, R. H., & Cottrell, A. B. (1996). Adult third culture kids. In Carolyn D. Smith (Ed.), *Strangers at Home: Essays on the Effects of Living Overseas and Coming "Home" to a Strange Land* (pp. 22–35). Bayside, NY: Aletheia Publications.

Useem, R. H., & Downie, R. D. (1976, September–October). Third culture kids. *Today's Education*, 103–105.

Walters, K. A., & Auton-Cuff, F. P. (2009). A story to tell: The identity development of women growing up as third culture kids. *Mental Health, Religion & Culture*, 12(7), 755. https://doi.org/10.1080/13674670903029153.

Chapter 11

The Necessity of Guilt

A Freeing Movement of the Soul Towards Individuation

Elizabeth Leuenberger-Kajs

Guilt is her name. What have you done?! Look. What. You. Have. Done. She stands, guilty. She is Guilt herself, guilty as charged. She demands to be seen, and she is irresistible – horrible and beautiful at the same time, a seductress. You cannot say no to Guilt, try as you may to reject her. Once she has taken a foothold, you are captured. Like a siren, her incessant song gives no rest; merciless, she seeks recognition and can be quite persistent, a strong hand of the law or a nagging, inner voice. Adam and Eve accepted their guilt – what choice did they have? Verdict handed down, they took their punishment: banished from the Garden of Eden. But couldn't they have fought it, arguing their innocence, begging for mercy, blaming it on the serpent? On the other hand, should they really have wanted to stay in the garden? Remaining, forever, in that state of bliss otherwise known as ignorance? If the sin is to taste the forbidden fruit of the Tree of Knowledge, guilt may just be a price for freedom some are willing to pay.

C. G. Jung (1942/1948/1969c) spoke of a healing "psychic activity not caused or consciously willed by man himself," which leads towards wholeness and is felt to be daemonic or from some divine source (p. 162 [CW11, para. 242]). James Hillman (1996) described each individual as having an inner soul-companion, or "daimon," that guides them through life towards a unique destiny (p. 8). Edward Edinger (1995) stated:

> The devil is a personification of all those aspects of an individual's psychology which contradict one's conscious, ideal self-image and which therefore must be repressed. . . . The devil will be all that is unChristlike – sexuality, power, self-interest, and material desires as opposed to spiritual ones.
>
> (p. 115)

Thus, willingly or unwillingly, when destiny comes calling and demands an action, ingrained moral codes and old ideas of right and wrong aside, sometimes the gods, the daimon, the devil, trickster, or serpent – in whatever form that inner voice appears – whispers in your ear, "just do it." It becomes a necessity. The drive for individuation surges forth from within with a need for freedom, an inner calling to break the bonds that hold one back. Necessity calls to free oneself from

DOI: 10.4324/9781003168829-12

old limitations, binding restrictions, obligations. Hearts must be broken, laws disobeyed, unpopular decisions made, disappointments inflicted, while the perpetrator chooses guilt in their pursuit of destiny.

In mythology, the Greek goddess Ananke, or Necessity, is said to govern being (Hillman, 1974/2016, p. 37). Explaining Jung's archetypal approach to psychology and therapy, Hillman described it as a Greek mythic method, which seeks an internal explanation for what is going on in the psyche. Viewing the figures of myth as metaphors for the archetypes of human psychic patterns and behaviors, Hillman stated the behaviors of those figures, with all their cruelties, cheatings, revenges, and other morally and ethically questionable antics, are exhibitions of *necessary* patterns of human behavior, and thus their pathologizing mirrors ours (p. 34). He observed that necessity, as one of two Platonic first principles of being, "operates through deviations," and that "abnormal, scared, and crazy movement of the soul is not only necessary; it is Necessity itself" (pp. 46–47). Thus, he noted, "Necessity resides as an internal cause in the soul and perpetually produces irksome results" (p. 45–46), adding, "When you flee Necessity you suffer" (p. 52).

One of those irksome results, guilt, can be internally felt, as an emotion – "feeling guilty" – as well as an objective fact or state of being, as in to "be guilty" of something, and the two may or may not always go together. Jung (1945/1970a) pointed out the difference between the psychological use of the word "guilt" and the legal or moral sense of the word. In the psychological sense, he described it as "the irrational presence of a subjective feeling (or conviction) of guilt, or an objective imputation of, or imputed share in, guilt" (p. 195 [CW10, para. 403]). If we commit an act of transgression – be it a sin, when it is a transgression against our religious code of ethics, or a broken law or rule, if the transgression goes against society's laws or our own personal code or standards to which we have bound ourselves – then the fact, or state, of guilt is established. We *are* guilty, in the eyes of the Church, the law, or our prexisting moral code. If we steal, we are guilty of theft. Whether or not and to what extent we *feel* the suffering *emotion* of guilt, that plaguing, persistent, nagging inner siren-cry that so often accompanies the state, might be said to depend primarily on whether Guilt is accompanied by her twin sister, Shame. Like Adam and Eve, we must accept our guilt and the penalty that goes with it, but whether to accept the ongoing presence of Shame along with it may be optional.

To accept and come to terms with guilt is like an arranged marriage. Once the deed has been done and the vows have been exchanged, we have entered into a binding contract. We must live with it. We can try to rectify it, we can pay the penalty for it – but we must accept our fate and accept the union, the bride to whom we have been wed, for better or for worse; what is done is done. But with every marriage comes the question of in-laws. Is it then possible to marry Guilt, without her sister, Shame, moving in? There is always that universal problem in marriage, the balancing act of keeping in-laws at a comfortable distance. Guilt and Shame are close, like twins – almost inseparable, but not *necessarily*.

To differentiate the feeling of shame from guilt can be challenging. In Greek mythology, Tartaros is the name for the hellish place where the wicked are punished. Yet the gods of Greek myth were not concerned with morality or ethics. Here the Erinyes dwell, "where they punish the guilty, besides their pursuit of . . . offenders in this world. . . . They are a sort of embodied curse" (Rose, 1928/1958, p. 87). Those who suffered in Tartaros were not necessarily all terrible sinners or fundamentally evil but were often simply guilty of an action or crime that offended or insulted the gods (p. 80). In this place of suffering, Odysseus saw the likes of Tityos, bound with vultures tearing out his liver for raping Leto; Tantalos, who suffered everlasting hunger and thirst for testing the gods' omniscience and abusing the privileges he had been granted; Sisyphos, condemned to eternally roll a stone up a hill; or Ixion, who offended the gods in trying to seduce Hera, for which he was eternally bound to a revolving wheel (pp. 80–82). Such punishments handed down to those found guilty by the gods, in that they often brought not only physical but also psychic suffering, could be said to have been designed, as well, to inflict shame. In the early archaic "shame culture" of the Greeks, to bring punishment and shame upon the guilty party in the eyes of the public served to appease the angered god and occupy the avenging Erinyes in handing out the punishments. But guilt in the archaic sense by the Greeks themselves was viewed as a "pollution," an "automatic consequence of an action, [which] belongs to the world of external events, and operates with the same ruthless indifference to motive as a typhoid germ" (Dodds, 1951, p. 36). The shift towards a "guilt culture" with an internalized sense of guilt that weighed on the conscience of the guilty party, or sinner, was something that came about later, along with the Christian sense of morality, "in the haunting fear of falling into mortal sin" (p. 36), and became common much later, when the motive of an act became recognized as an important factor for consideration in the eyes of the law (p. 37).

According to Douglas Cairns (1993), the term *aidos*, appearing in Greek literature as a social and psychological entity representing a "considerable emotional and motivational force in literary representations of human agency" (p. viii), is frequently translated as "shame," though it is actually a concept with a much more complex essence, which includes aspects that could, based on context, be translated in other terms such as embarrassment as well. While the concepts of *aidos* and shame are not identical, Cairns noted, they both refer to emotions with overlapping phenomenology and associations (pp. 7–14). One key shared characteristic of shame and *aidos* is that they both involve an external judgment, or witnessing factor.

In differentiating feelings of shame from guilt, on the other hand, Cairns (1993) clarified that in a shame-culture, "Shame is caused by fear of external sanctions, specifically the disapproval of others," while in a guilt-culture, "guilt relies on the internal sanctions provided by the individual conscience, one's own disapproval of oneself" (p. 15). Yet the catalyst for shame can originate either within or without, with the judging audience in both the English shame and Greek *aidos* being often merely anticipated but in absence of actual criticism, or the judging element may be a self-judgment, criticism of one's self based on internalized standards (pp. 16–17). Similarly, guilt, as an emotion, Cairns noted, can be described as a "transgression of an internalized prohibition" (p. 20). Boundaries blur between the emotions of guilt and shame, and the two frequently overlap. "Neither is differentiated from the other by the fact that it may occur before a real audience, before a fantasy audience, or before oneself," stated Cairns (p. 27). Jungian analyst Lawrence Staples (2010) acknowledged the significant difference between shame and guilt on an intellectual level but noted that the two, at a "gut" level, are experienced as identical, with guilt being based on one's acceptance and acknowledgement of having done (or imagined doing) something which is, on some level, bad, while shame is an experience of devaluating humiliation (whether from outside or internal), leading to a sense of self as intrinsically bad (p. 15).

Thus, the tendency in Greek mythology is towards acceptance of guilt with a sense of detachment, and even integrity, rather than a self-deprecating moral struggle, viewing actions and consequent guilt as a fact or state of being, a "pollution" that results from divine intervention or infatuation planted by the gods known in Greek as *ate*. Agamemnon, for example, did not deny his guilt in stealing Achilles' mistress but blamed Zeus, the Fates, and Erinyes: "Not I . . . they it was who in the assembly put wild *ate* in my understanding . . . so what could I do? Deity will always have its way" (Dodds, 1951, p. 3). Yet, while explaining his actions as such, he did not attempt to evade responsibility. He simply accepted it as a matter of fact, without internalizing shame. He acknowledged acting of his own volition, stating, "I am willing to make my peace and give abundant compensation" (p. 3). For Homeric man, moral failures, such as Agamemnon's, were simply projected onto a divine agency. Behavior was swayed not by a moral force seeded in a fear of Godly disdain but rather in *aidos*, or respect for the opinion of the public. Only much later, as the sense of morality-based guilt and shame gradually grew, did *ate* and the Erinyes come to be associated with punishment, with Zeus as "an embodiment of cosmic justice" (p. 18).

When the marriage to Guilt is entered yet there is no room for Shame in the house, Ananke can sort things out with Shame. If shame, as a (either self- or externally sourced) deprecating, demoralizing emotion originates in receipt from without and/or perception of criticism from within, Shame does not necessarily have to move in with Guilt; she does not have to be invited or even embraced. She does not share the same close relationship to Necessity as does her twin. While Necessity may answer the daimon's call for an act (or even thought) of transgression, making the accompanying guilt also a necessity, self-criticism and shame are not. Cairns (1993) stated, "shame accompanies failure because it is concerned with goals and ideals" (p. 20). While Shame certainly belongs in some places, she does not have to always accompany Guilt. By acknowledging the role of Necessity in certain acts themselves, the act of transgression is credited a meaningful purpose, which may override, nullify, even redefine old goals and ideals. In turn, the sense of failure and self-torment of internalized shame or self-deprecating guilt can be relieved, even avoided.

In his central focus on the process of embracing the whole of one's full individual potential he termed *individuation* (Jung, 1939/1969b, p. 275 [CW 9i, para. 490]), Jung addressed the occasional necessity and teleological purpose of acts that invoke a sense of guilt. He observed that while it is not easy to become aware of and embrace or acknowledge one's guilt of shadow – even evil – aspect, to suppress them brings about no personal benefit, stating, "When we are conscious of our guilt we are in a more favourable position – we can at least hope to change and improve ourselves" (Jung, 1945/1970a, p. 215 [CW10, para. 440]). To repress those things that invoke guilt feeds the shadow, grows the darkness, and we remain unconscious. We are not free.

Jung (1944/1968b) described a "loss of soul" as a regressive state in which the personality splits off aspects of an integrated whole and projects them instead out into the world, for example, onto family members, blaming the mother or father for elements of discontent instead of owning responsibility, stating, "the individual loses his guilt and exchanges it for infantile innocence" (p. 115 [CW12 para. 152]). In line with this perspective, Hillman (1996) defined what he called the "parental fallacy," whereby he viewed parents as scapegoats upon whom the burden of responsibility and subsequent guilt for all the problems or failings in the life of a child is projected (pp. 63–91) rather than each individual assigning or accepting the role of fate and their own individual, personal responsibility for their lives. Like the Greeks, it is our natural inclination to seek a scapegoat, someone else, or the gods, on whom we might project blame in order to relieve responsibility and guilt. Jung (1944/1968b) added that to focus our attention on the guilt of others' sins against us is worthless, because it is outside our power to change it. To be a mature, free individual requires viewing others' transgressions and how they impact ourselves personally as our own condition, stating, "The man who is really adult will accept these sins as his own condition which has to be reckoned with. . . . The wise man learns only from his own guilt" (p. 117 [CW12, para.152]). At the end of the day, we must focus on reckoning the sins and transgressions in our own shadow and their atonement. As Jung (1944/1968a) also noted, "one can miss not only one's happiness but also one's final guilt, without which a man will never reach his wholeness" (p. 30 [CW12, para. 36]).

Additionally, by viewing struggles with inner conflicts of guilt as a debt exacted by Fate, Jung believed, our guilt may not only be reduced, but may even become a gain, a form of wealth, because, as he stated, it enables us to see our own worth. "Nobody can owe a debt to a mere nothing," he declared (Jung, 1955/1956/1970b, pp. 363–364 [CW14, para. 511]). Thus, to own one's guilt is to attain maturity in moral freedom and responsibility for a more complete, valuable sense of self.

While the overall ideas of individuation, in the case of personal or collective growth and movements towards self fulfillment and wholeness, may appear to be positive in nature, the act of individuation requires difficult or unpleasant actions that challenge us to step outside our ego's boundaries or go against the "norm." If to individuate means to go your own way and to find your truest, most complete sense of self, then it means acknowledging and incorporating your shadow, or those aspects which may have been suppressed, shunned, split off, or projected as undesirable. Based on Jung's ideas towards the often guilt-inducing, self-serving acts at times required in the pursuit of individuation, Staples (2010) differentiated from "bad guilt" what he referred to as the seemingly contradictory concept of "good guilt": the guilt that we experience by engaging in behaviors, thoughts, or feelings that are contradictory to our or society's accepted norms and guidelines for the sake of individuation. This may include seemingly selfish transgressions that result in contribution towards individual, personal growth, or it may mean self-sacrificing transgressions that break rules or old standards but are motivated by ultimately good intentions that potentially help others serving a wider, collective, societal good (p. 25).

In the myth of Prometheus, Hesiod (2013 Version) told the tale of how the Titan sought to trick Zeus, "the father of men and of gods" (507–543), siding with the mortals. In retaliation, Zeus withheld fire from mankind. Once more going against the gods, Prometheus then used his trickery, stealing "the far-seen gleam of unwearying fire in a hollow fennel stalk" (561–584) to give man. Zeus, upon seeing the fire's light among the men, in vengeance not only ordered the creation of Pandora to unleash evil onto mankind as the price of fire; he also punished Prometheus for his attempt to enlighten man by having him cruelly bound to a barren, rocky cliff, to suffer eternal torture while an eagle devoured his liver daily.

"For the gods keep hidden from men the means of life" (Hesiod, 42–53). To have fire is to have passion, creativity, drive, will, and determination. To "light a fire under" something is to initiate action. Fire brings warmth and life itself; there is cold darkness in death and the warmth of fire in life. Fire gives off sparks, the divine spark being the life-source of the soul. Fire gives light, it illuminates, and to illuminate is to "shed light," or bring to awareness, bringing consciousness and knowledge. To enlighten is to bring truth and liberation, transcendence, and pureness of being. Giving fire and light to mankind, Prometheus would grant them heightened freedom, giving access to all these things of their own power and reducing their subservience to the gods. While the flip side to this is, indeed, the danger of titanic hubris, or unchecked, unlimited pride, the idea of ultimate enlightenment would bring the power of absolute consciousness. However, without access to fire, or light, mankind would remain in complete darkness, a primal state of unconsciousness; without it, there would be no chance for depolarization. Access to light allows the possibility to move towards freedom from darkness, towards unity, centering. The fire's light is a necessity for wholeness, a necessity for individuation.

Jung (1928/1935/1966) addressed the phenomenon of heightened consciousness and its inherent side effect of an inflated state of personality (pp. 156–157, [CW7, para. 243]). He noted any new knowledge can lead to a puffed-up sense of "almighty self-conceit", thus referring to the story of Adam and Eve's guilt of eating from the tree of knowledge as representing a "taboo infringement," an overstepping of a "sacrosanct barrier," or otherwise phrased, "Promethean guilt"(p. 156 [CW7, n1]). Stealing the light of consciousness, eating the fruit of the tree of knowledge, is a transgression against the gods, because it brings mankind closer to them and threatens to reduce their power. It must be kept in check to prevent the hyperinflation of hubris. "Something that was the property of the unconscious powers is torn out of its natural context and subordinated to the whims of the conscious mind" (p. 156 [CW7, n1]). The price for this transgression, this transformation to a level of freed, elevated consciousness and step forward in individuation, is a form of suffering, a Promethean torment, a feeling of being isolated out on the craggy cliffs, never to return to the blissful garden of unconsciousness. Jung stated, "He has raised himself above the human level of his age . . . but in so doing has alienated himself from humanity. The pain of this loneliness is the vengeance of the gods" (p. 157 [CW7, n1). Isolation and loneliness is a price we occasionally must pay for Promethean guilt, a price we often pay for such freedom.

Prometheus was guilty in the eyes of the gods. As Hephaestus, who was sent to nail him to the rocks, in Aeschylus's *Prometheus Bound*, declared:

> I shall nail you in bonds of dissoluble bronze . . . far from men. Here you shall hear no voice of mortal; here you shall see no form of mortal. . . . Always the grievous burden of your torture will be there to wear you down.
>
> (Aeschylus, 1959, p. 311)

Prometheus was guilty of enlightening mankind and bore his punishment with acceptance. As David Grene (in Aeschylus, 1959) stated, his actions symbolize mankind's ongoing conflict between brute force and mind. He is a symbol of the rebel going against a tyrant, or the struggle of knowledge against force (p. 306). He is a mythic Robin Hood of titanic proportions. He stood by his act, stating:

> So must I bear . . . the destiny that fate has given me; for I know well against necessity, against its strength, no one can fight and win. . . . I hunted out the secret spring of fire . . . which when revealed became the teacher of each craft to men, a great resource. This is the sin committed for which I stand accountant, and I pay nailed in my chains under the open sky.
>
> (p. 315)

Thus, despite his suffering, despite pressure from the gods and comments from the collective (chorus), Prometheus willingly entered into marriage with Guilt. As the chorus stated, "I see your form wasting away on these cliffs in adamantine bonds of bitter shame," Prometheus retorted, "My enemies can laugh at what I suffer . . . there shall come a day for me when he [(Zeus)] shall need me" (Aeschylus, 1959, p. 317), and he stood by his sacrifice with conviction, adding, "To the unhappy breed of mankind he gave no heed . . . none stood save I: I dared. I gave to mortal man a precedence over myself in pity: I can win no pity" (p. 320). Prometheus accepted his marriage with Guilt. Yet, standing by the greater purpose of his actions and acknowledging them consciously, he did so with Integrity, leaving no space in the house for Shame to move in.

Prometheus's crime and punishment were not, however, for naught. Despite receiving punishment in his effort to enlighten mankind with the gift of knowledge through fire, Prometheus also granted them optimism, in the form of "blind hope" (Aeschylus, 1959, p. 320). For when Pandora's jar was opened, releasing countless evil plagues, diseases, and mischief upon earth, "only Hope remained there in an unbreakable home within under the rim of the great jar, and did not fly out at the door" (Hesiod, 90–105). Without hope, there is no will for life – hope is sustenance. Without hope, we wither in darkness. Thus, the hope retained in Pandora's jar is the retained spark of life, of light, a crack in the jar, a glimmer of freedom. Hope gives birth to imagination, and escaping from the jar, it is set free; with hope, we can imagine more and imagine our way forward. Hope is the torch, which shines the light into the darkness. Thus, through Hope's retention, Prometheus did, after all, outwit Zeus one more time. He accepted the guilt of an action that had to be undertaken as means to a worthwhile end: a guilt, which set free hope and enlightenment.

There are numerous examples in real life, as well as myth and legend, of rule breakers guilty of "good guilt," who, like Prometheus, go against societal expectations and collectively accepted behavior in order to incite change for the ultimate good. Well known are the acts of such public figures as Rosa Parks, who broke segregation laws and sparked a significant movement towards civil rights in America, or Socrates, who opted for the punishment of death in defense of his principles and teachings (p. 23). More recently, US Congressman John Lewis, a champion for the civil rights movement and causes such as action against gun violence, called for the people to seek ways of getting into "good trouble," to accept guilt for the type of trouble-making he referred to as *necessary* trouble.

Good guilt, however, does not only come in forms easily recognized as good deeds by brave and self-sacrificing guilty parties for the good of the collective or a less privileged minority. Good guilt may be difficult to comprehend, Necessity's role hard to ascertain, appearing on the surface as senseless, harsh acts of selfishness or betrayal. Hillman (1964/2013) wrote of betrayal as a painful act of transgression that brings an overwhelming sense of suffering to the betrayed and thus guilt upon the betrayer. However, as he demonstrated, in seeing through an act of betrayal, a purpose may be served and its necessity brought to light. With the example of a Jewish parable of a father who intentionally betrayed his young son's trust, allowing him to fall in order to teach him a lesson, the cruelty of the father's actions and the guilt it incurred could be said to be necessary side effects of the lesson the father sought to instill. Yet while the necessity of his actions could be viewed as a lesson about trust he was willing to sacrifice his good image in his son's eyes for, it could also be merely the Fates acting upon a calling of the higher Self or daimon for the sake of deeper self development in both parties (p. 201).

While the potential negative reactions by the betrayed, such as revenge, denial, cynicism, self-betrayal, and loss of trust, must be overcome by the betrayed, Hillman (1964/2013) noted, in the ultimate act of forgiveness and allowing atonement of the betrayer, the betrayed may grow to face their own betrayals, "less unconsciously, implying an integration of man's untrustworthy nature" (p. 205). The betrayer, facing and owning their guilt, while accepting forgiveness and atonement, develops integration of their own dark side, lest they "remain stuck in unconscious brutality," which would result not only in continued wrongdoing towards the other but also (especially important for individuation) wrongdoing to the self, as they may continue through life incapable of self-forgiveness (p. 204).

Plagued by un-integrated guilt, Hillman (1971/2016a) observed an unconscious burden may appear, for example, as dreams of an abandoned child, for which the dreamer feels a sense of acute worry and guilty responsibility (p. 84). The usual reaction, however, to these feelings of guilt leads to an ego-driven moral sense of need for action, to correct or clean up the situation, at the expense of a deepened state of understanding that could bring growth by relating to the emotions – such as helplessness, fright, or loss – that the abandoned child represents. Thus, taking the role of the "fixer" or parent, we distance ourselves from the childish needs where the potential for real growth lies, instead merely strengthening the ego's stance. Perhaps, if we follow Hillman's approach, to face Necessity and "collapse with the child's crying" (p. 85), allowing and accepting guilt rather than attempting to rid ourselves of it, we, like the archetypal child whose function is "that which alters," may discover growth; instead of correcting it, allowing it to transform and correct us (pp. 88–89).

Allowing the transformative process is not, typically, a happy course change made on sunny days sailing smooth waters. Sailing smoothly along, we tend to stick to the course, sit back and relax in the sun, letting ourselves passively drift along with the current, pulled by gentle breezes. For Ego to step aside from the helm and allow transformative course-change often requires a dreadful storm: rumbling, dark, ominous skies that wake us from the daydream, stormy gale-force winds, crashing waves that slam the boat against treacherous rocks, crushing the boat and leaving our dismembered bodies in pieces on the shore. Jung (1942/1954/1969d) looked at guilt's role in the transformative process, referring to dismemberment and torture not as punishment for guilt but rather as an initiatory necessity of a neophyte, or "the indispensable means of leading him towards his destiny" (p. 271, [CW11, para. 410]). Dismemberment is a recurrent theme found in myths, as a form of vengeful punishment by angry gods. Prometheus's dismemberment at the hands of an angered Zeus, of having his liver pecked out by the eagle, is just one example. Dionysus, who was intended by Zeus to have dominion over the world, was lured and dismembered by the Titans. His dismemberment is viewed as a metaphor for a state of madness, a psychic breakdown, a form of psychological dismemberment that can be viewed as initiatory. It is a movement towards disintegration of the old ways of psyche, to make room for psychic rebirth. Before a new house can be built, it is necessary to tear the old house down.

Psychological dismemberment in the form of moral punishment for some guilt or sin and subsequent reconstitution can lead to a rebirth into a higher state of being, a transformative process Jung (1942/1954/1969d) pointed out is a necessary part enacted in rites of shamanic initiation, for example (p. 271, [CW11, para. 410]). The Promethean torment of guilt is often seen as punishment enough. Whether internally or externally inflicted, guilt can feel like a psychological dismemberment, which eats away at our conscience day in and day out, until it is faced, come to terms with, and the reconstitution and rebirth begin. And this is the key – because the torments enacted on the guilty in the underworld of Tartaros by the Erinyes, like any underworld power, are connected with fertility. It is the seed planted below ground from which new life grows (Rose, 1958, p. 87).

If, as Hillman stated, attempts to run from Necessity lead to suffering, repressed guilt that hides in the shadow of psyche or is rejected and projected away lingers and brings about suffering in other forms. Attempts to avoid some form of dismemberment are futile. The symptoms that arise from repressed material may appear in form of physical illness or haunting dreams, for example. Jung (1916/1969a) addressed the symbolism of guilt in dreams, with an account of erotic guilt appearing in the dreams of a man who, unconsciously suffering from a bad conscience after an erotic encounter with a woman, dreamt of plucking the apple of Paradise. The dream indicated the dreamer's suppressed tendency to experience erotic encounters as self-condemnation and guilt. In this way, the dreamer's guilt served as a moral compass (pp. 242–244, [CW8, para. 460–466]), which, from its place buried in the personal unconscious, insisted on being acknowledged. Jung noted the universality of the apple motif as a typical, archetypal way of representing guilt that appears not only in the story of the Garden of Eden but is recurrent throughout myths and fairytales of all ages and cultures (p. 248 [CW8, para. 474–476]). As painful as it may be and as much as we might try to deny and suppress it, accepting and coming to terms with guilt, through a process of psychic death by dismemberment, rebirth, and reconstruction, can serve a teleological purpose, planting the seeds of new growth, leading to higher states of freedom of consciousness on the individuation journey.

Conclusion

Hillman said that if we flee Necessity and try to resist guilt, there will be a price to pay. That price is the lack of fire, remaining in darkness, a stagnation of the individuation journey. Was it necessary for Adam and Eve to taste the apple? In theory, they could have said no to the serpent, refusing the apple (but they were yet too unconscious for such freedom!) and simply abstained from original sin, remaining free from guilt, blissfully remaining in the Garden. Like Prometheus, however, they chose the fire and set off an individuation journey for mankind of titanic proportions. Jung (1944/1968a) stated that "wholeness is in fact a charisma which one can manufacture neither by art nor by cunning; one can only grow into it and endure whatever its advent may bring" (p. 30 [CW12, para. 36]). Addressing the purpose of evil, he argued that the purpose served in confronting shadow surpasses moral superiority that lends judgment, adding, "without sin there is no repentance and without repentance no redeeming grace, also that without original sin the redemption of the world could never come about" (p. 30, [CW12, para. 36]).

As we move forwards in Jung's concept of individuation, if the goal is to bring balance to the polarized opposites in our personality by making conscious and reintegrating split-off, repressed, and undeveloped or undesirable aspects, then such sins and transgressions, and working through the guilt they invoke, are occasional necessities for our consciousness to be brought to light and granting the freedom for integration to occur. Sometimes we have to let the devil out, to open Pandora's jar, setting free all possibilities, while preserving Hope as the light that cuts through the darkness, keeping us moving forward on the path of individuation.

References

Aeschylus. (1959 Version). Prometheus bound. In Grene, D. & Lattimore, R. (Eds.). Grene, D. (Trans.). *The complete Greek tragedies*. Chicago, IL: The University of Chicago Press.

Cairns, D. L. (1993). *Aidos: The psychology and ethics of honour and shame in ancient Greek literature*. Oxford: Oxford University Press.

Dodds, E. R. (1951). *The Greeks and the irrational*. Berkeley, CA: University of California Press.

Edinger, E. F. (1995). *Melville's Moby-Dick*. Toronto: Inner City Books.

Hesiod. (2013 Version). *The complete works of Hesiod*. Delphi Classics. [Kindle Edition]

Hillman, J. (1996). *The soul's code: In search of character and calling*. New York, NY: Grand Central Publishing.

Hillman, J. (2013). Betrayal. In G. Slater (Ed.) *Uniform edition of the writings of James Hillman, Vol. 3: Senex & Puer*. Putnam, CT: Spring Publications. [Original work published 1964]

Hillman, J. (2016a). Abandoning the child. In *Uniform edition of the writings of James Hillman, Vol. 6: Mythic figures*. Thompson, CT: Spring Publications. [Original work Published 1971]

Hillman, J. (2016b). Athene, Ananke, and the necessity of abnormal psychology. In *Uniform edition of the writings of James Hillman, Vol. 6: Mythic figures*. Thompson, CT: Spring Publications. [Original work published 1974]

Jung, C. G. (1966) The relations between the ego and the unconscious. In R. F. C. Hull (Trans.), *The collected works of C. G. Jung* (Vol.7, pp. 156–162). Princeton, NJ: Princeton University Press. [Original work published 1928/1935]

Jung, C. G. (1968a). Introduction to the religious and psychological problems of alchemy. In R. F. C. Hull (Trans.), *The collected works of C. G. Jung* (Vol. 12, pp. 1–38). Princeton, NJ: Princeton University Press. [Original work published 1944]

Jung, C. G. (1968b). Individual dream symbolism in relation to alchemy. In R. F. C. Hull (Trans.), *The collected works of C. G. Jung* (Vol. 12, pp. 39–224). Princeton, NJ: Princeton University Press. [Original work published 1944]

Jung, C. G. (1969a). General aspects of dream psychology. In R. F. C. Hull (Trans.), *The collected works of C. G. Jung* (Vol. 8, pp. 237–280). Princeton, NJ: Princeton University Press. [Original work published 1916]

Jung, C. G. (1969b). Conscious, unconscious and individuation. In R. F. C. Hull (Trans.), *The collected works of C. G. Jung* (Vol. 9i, pp. 237–280). Princeton, NJ: Princeton University Press. [Original work published 1939]

Jung, C. G. (1969c). A psychological approach to the dogma of the trinity. In R. F. C. Hull (Trans.), *The collected works of C. G. Jung* (Vol. 11, pp. 107–200). Princeton, NJ: Princeton University Press. [Original work published 1942/1948]

Jung, C. G. (1969d). Transformation symbolism in the mass. In R. F. C. Hull (Trans.), *The collected works of C. G. Jung* (Vol. 11, pp. 201–298). Princeton, NJ: Princeton University Press. [Original work published 1942/1954]

Jung, C. G. (1970a). After the catastrophe. In R. F. C. Hull (Trans.), *The collected works of C. G. Jung* (Vol. 10, pp. 194–217). Princeton, NJ: Princeton University Press. [Original work published 1945]

Jung, C. G. (1970b). Rex and Regina. In R. F. C. Hull (Trans.), *The collected works of C. G. Jung* (Vol. 14, pp. 258–381). Princeton, NJ: Princeton University Press. [Original work published 1955/1956]

Rose, H. J. (1958). *The handbook of Greek mythology*. London: Methuen & Co. Ltd. [Original work published 1928]

Staples, L. H. (2010). *Guilt with a twist: The Promethean way*. Carmel, CA: Fisher King Press. [iBooks Edition].

Chapter 12

Floating and Taking Root

Individuation in Contemporary Traumatic Conditions

Monica Luci

Although conceived before the outbreak of the COVID-19 pandemic, this chapter has been written during the pandemic, a time of great uncertainty and exceptional conditions coloring everything we do and affecting every aspect of private and public life.

This crisis arrived following about three decades of intense globalization (e.g., Tomlinson, 1999; Giddens, 2000; Held et al., 1999; Sen, 1999), which contributed, at least in part, to the pandemic's rapid spread, with the fervent rhythm of contacts and exchanges of people and goods favoring rapid contagion of the virus.

Globalization and its impacts on societies, cultures, and individuals have produced many relevant sociological reflections since the 90s. Some have focused on the consequences of globalization for subjectivity. As discussed by Stefano Carpani in the introduction of this book (pp. 1–14), the individualization thesis advanced by Beck (1992) and Giddens (1991) and Bauman's concept of *liquidity* provide a portrait of the arising characteristics of Western societies, as we know them nowadays as quite established.

Beck and Giddens claims that under globalization, individuals in Western societies are increasingly set free from both cultural constraints, such as religion, tradition, and conventional morality, and structural constraints, such as class, status, nation, gender, and the nuclear family. What was once inherited from tradition or assumed instead requires an individual to make a conscious decision, and, consequently, identity is no longer ascribed but achieved (Beck, 1992; Beck and Beck-Gernsheim, 1995: 43–60). Education has replaced traditional modes of thinking with more universalistic and reflexive ones; social and geographical mobility have dissolved formerly primary social bonds, demanding one interpret their destiny personally. Moreover, economic globalization processes have broadly enhanced the labor market's flexibility, producing massive unemployment, spectacular increases in fixed-term employment, and widespread economic insecurity. Notably, these phenomena are often interpreted by individuals as personal failure.

Bauman's work analyzes the consequences of new social and economic conditions that are marked by uncertainty and rapid change. Interweaving philosophical and sociological reflections, Bauman describes solidity and liquidity as the

DOI: 10.4324/9781003168829-13

distinctive features of modernity and postmodernity (2013). During liquid epochs, social forms and institutions no longer have enough time to solidify, precluding them from serving as frames of reference for human action or long-term life plans, prompting individuals to organize themselves in other ways, producing lives held together by strings of short-term projects and episodes. These fragmented lives require individuals to be flexible and adaptable, constantly ready and willing to change approaches, abandon commitments and loyalties without regret, and pursue opportunities as they appear. Constant changes and transformations turn identity into a continuous process (Bauman, 2007).

In times of COVID-19, the situation has become even more unstable and uncertain, further complicating being an individual: the previous balance between individual and collective dimensions has changed profoundly due to the altered style of living and the dangers of contagion; also our body, health, and physical existence are under a severe threat together with material possessions, given the expected economic crisis.

Psychologically, stable social and familial environments, along with feeling secure and at ease in one's body, enable the self to take root and develop harmoniously (Winnicott, 1971; Kohut, 1977; Bowlby, 1969; Damasio, 1999). The entire body of knowledge of psychoanalysis and social psychology suggest that the self is not created in isolation: we are not born with perceptions of ourselves but develop such a perception through interactions with others and their observation. In other words, given the self only has meaning within social contexts, the social realm substantially defines one's self-concept, self-identity and self-esteem.

Thus, it is worth questioning what happens when the self is seriously and continuously threatened by instability and how the self reacts to structural and constant uncertainty.

Self, identity, and individuation

The concept of identity is so complex and includes such a wide range of domains and self-definitions that its essence is elusive. Identity's status is apparently a transitional aspect of selfhood that exists between intimate, personal, and even innate inner dimensions and socially constructed outer dimensions of the self. Demonstrating the breadth of the topic, relevant studies have emphasized these issues from sociological perspectives (e.g., Callero, 2003; Owens et al., 2010), from social identity perspectives (e.g., Jenkins, 2004; Ellmers, Spears, and Doosje, 2002), and from a social psychology perspective (e.g., Swann and Bosson, 2010).

For example, Papadopoulos, relying on his decades of experience in working with refugees, observes the difficulty of coherently and distinctively defining identity by demonstrating the ways different studies considering the topic have struggled with its complexity and vastness (2021: 118–130). Essays on identity have argued that identity constitutes the most personal sense one has of oneself, a personal impression constantly interacting with the identity bestowed upon them, a social, collective, or ascribed identity (*personal vs. collective*). It is often emphasized that identity comprises elements of sameness and difference in different combinations with respect to other people and their definitions of self (*sameness vs. difference*). Meanwhile, identity also features dimensions of constancy and change over time: the passing of time and experiences impacts some aspects of identity but not others (*constancy vs. change*). Finally, identity comprises very concrete realities that are both individually and socially constructed. For example, sensory elements of our environment, especially those from infancy and childhood, form part of who we are and how we experience ourselves. Simultaneously, social construction theorists have recognized identity as socially constructed rather than naturally occurring (*essence vs. construct*). Upon careful consideration of these and other aspects connected to identity, Papadopoulos (2021) concludes, "Our identity is not an abstract and solipsistic concept but implies a lived and constant interaction between the totality of our being and the totality of our environment, the entire spectrum of the ecology that surrounds us" (131).

According to Rattansi and Phoenix (2005), identity should be considered multiple, fluid, decentered, and changing rather than singular, centered, and stable, a view that resonates with the perspectives of some psychoanalysts on self (Bromberg, 1998: 186, 256, 311; Mitchell, 1991: 127–139; Jung, 1921, para. 789; 1928, para. 274). Power relations also play a considerable role in identity, which can be influenced by parental expectations, religion, and cultural and social norms and values, along with unique and unprecedented social conditions and individual experiences that interfere with the structural characteristics of self and that trigger certain survival functioning modes.

Ultimately, identity is a domain of negotiation between who we are internally and externally in terms of needs, definitions, aspirations, requests, roles, and motivations. And the center of gravity of our identity may be more outside or more inside, more stable or more liquid and changing, but it is always the result of these tensions.

The Jungian concept of individuation somewhat relates to identity and its development. Jung (1921) writes,

> In general, it is the process by individual beings are formed and differentiated; in particular it is the development of the psychological individual as being distinct from the general collective psychology. Individuation, therefore, is the process of differentiation, having for its goal the development of individual personality.
>
> (par. 757)

For Jung, individuation has a somewhat "salvific" value for one's true sense of self. From the perspective of analytical psychology, "individuation refers to the process of becoming the person the one innately is *potentially* from the beginning of life" (Stein, 2006: 198). Stein identifies three stages of individuation by common features, hazards, and breakdowns: the containment/nurturance (i.e., maternal) stage, the adapting/adjusting (i.e., paternal) stage, and the centering/ integrating (i.e., individual) stage. For Stein, the two major crises of individuation "fall in the transitions between these stages, the first in adolescence and early adulthood and the second at mid-life" (2006: 199).

The containment/nurturance phase serves the psychological purpose of supporting and protecting a child's incipient ego, which analytical psychology conceives of as the center of consciousness – featuring certain executive functions and elements of innate anxiety about reality – and which gradually comes into being over the course of early childhood.

During the second stage of individuation, between early puberty and early adulthood (approximately around 12–21), a person is exposed to a world in which standards of performance are paramount, and consequences for behavior are explicit and forceful. In this "father world," unconditional love is no longer the norm; instead, strict and even harsh conditions are imposed upon the distribution of all rewards, including love and positive perception. Nonetheless, completing the passage from the containment stage to the adapting/adjusting stage is fraught with crisis and emotional turmoil.

Entering the third stage of centering and integrating means gradually abandoning previous collective definitions of identity and assuming a self-image that emerges from within. However, this does not mean leaving collective reality behind. There is a shift of emphasis towards reaching for dimensions of life that have been less connected to survival and more connected to meaning.

The psyche's underlying structure – referred to by Jung as the Self (capitalized to denote its transcendence and essential difference from the ego) – is newly involved, taking control of the dominant position formerly held by external authorities, by the voice of reality, by the "father," and by the social "persona." The ego begins to answer to inner demands and call for obedience from the psyche.

Two clinical cases

The rest of the chapter develops the argument that, not exclusively but especially in traumatic conditions, *floating* on the surface of the self or the world can constitute an effective survival strategy in times of predicament, connoting the self's reaction to traumatic conditions. I intend to illustrate this strategy's key processes but also demonstrate that it is possible to move from a survival mode to a more rooted existence.

Two very different clinical cases exemplifying contemporary identity issues are discussed as vehicles for consideration of the important aspects of the dynamics between internal and external *liquidity*. First, a severely traumatized refugee struggling with the inner difficulties produced by different kind of traumas and living in a culturally and socially alien world. Second, a lesbian woman processing her childhood family abuse and her present sexual identity issues. Both seem to struggle to define their identity, using the floating strategy first in response to trauma and then searching for a significant internal point to which they might anchor themselves for a more rooted sense of self.

A totally heroic ego: the case of Gidom

Gidom is a 26-year-old Gambian man who has just arrived in Italy. He is married to a young woman and has a 2-year-old son, both of whom remained in Gambia. We meet in the office of an organization that offers legal and psychosocial support to asylum seekers. Although Gidom's mother tongue is Mandingo, he also speaks fluent English, enabling easy communication. His physical appearance is that of a strong man, which is discordant with his present mental state. Gidom presents symptoms of an acute and very painful post-traumatic disorder, describing persistent insomnia, vivid flashbacks, frequent headaches, social avoidance, intense fear for men in uniform, difficulty concentrating, hyper-arousal, tachycardia, and sudden and unmotivated outbursts of anger. Additionally, he suffers from depressed moods that focus on intense feelings of sadness and despair and produce a limited appetite and difficulty concentrating. Furthermore, chronic conjunctivitis is quite visible in his permanently red eyes. He discusses missing his family very much and the fact of being worried for them because they are potentially under threat from the government.

Gidom outlines his story. He was formerly a policeman in his country, and he was assigned to the "border police" between Gambia and Senegal just before Gambia's presidential elections. During his service, he refused to distribute false electoral cards to non-Gambian citizens, an order that he had received from people he did not recognize as his superiors and that he understood as intended to alter the electoral results. For this reason, he was arrested, imprisoned, and tortured with electric shocks, sleep deprivation, beatings, threats to his family, mock executions, and other forms of violence while detained illegally in the cell of a police station. He was forced to sign a statement admitting that he opposed the current government to make his arrest "lawful." Following two months of imprisonment, during a period of turmoil due to the cancellation of electoral results, he succeeded in bribing a prison officer, allowing him to flee the prison and then, immediately after, the country.

Our first meeting made clear that Gidom was suffering from acute PTSD combined with a depressive syndrome, a typical consequence of having been subjected to torture. The brain stem's elemental self-system and the emotion-producing limbic system are substantially activated when people face death threats, which produce overwhelming feelings of fear and terror accompanied by intense physiological arousal (Frewen and Lanius, 2006). People who experience torture are often trapped in a "life or death" mindset, a state of paralyzing fear. The mind and body are constantly on alert, as if still in the presence of imminent danger. It is, thus, common to respond with panic to even minor noises and to be frustrated by minor irritations. Such subjects often demonstrate chronically disturbed sleep and difficulties regulating arousal, emotions, and relationships. These experiences can trigger desperate attempts to extinguish symptoms through freezing, dissociation, and self-harm behaviors (Solomon and Siegel, 2003; Schore, 2003; Van der Kolk, 2014).

At the time of our first meeting, Gidom is living in a reception center, waiting to learn when his asylum claim will be heard. A psychiatrist in a hospital has already given him some antidepressants, which make him feel somewhat better but far from recovered. As he tells his story, he weeps bitterly about a sense of betrayal and shame at being in such a "miserable" condition. While recounting his torture episodes, his flashbacks begin, and it is clear that he is not telling, but vividly reliving those moments, in which his torturers tied him to an electric chair and sprinkled him with water before attaching electrodes to his arms, legs, and penis before starting the electric shocks that generated an "earthquake" in his body and brain.

Gidom is incredulous of what happened to him and cannot accept it because it is in stark contrast to his self-image as a faithful man dedicated to his family and country. He is prey to a searing sense of disappointment and disillusionment that prompts depersonalization, derealization, depression, and a persistent sense of guilt accompanied by continuous self-recrimination.

Life story

Gidom's accounts of his life make clear that, before the traumatic events, he identified completely with his Mandinka ethnicity, his country, his government, his family, and his job as a policeman. Furthermore, he was proud of that identity. While still seemingly very determined and of strong will, at the time of therapy, he is suffering intensely.

Gidom is the third of five sons from a family of farmers that mainly grows peanuts. He describes it as a "poor but honest" family. Despite his love for them, and unlike his brothers, he refused to work in agriculture with his family. Busy with hard work and the material needs of a large family, Gidom's parents were essential in their caregiving, probably not providing enough to their children. His father, in particular, was rather absent during Gidom's childhood and adolescence; nonetheless, his figure represented a guide and a reference for values, principles, and rules to follow. Gidom compensated for his parents' shortcomings by adhering to traditional values, developing a very determined will and a strong ego that was identified with his "persona" to replace the actual presence of his father as a "real" person – however, in a culturally syntonic way. Gidom's mother was apparently a warmer and more present parent, more skillfully nurturing his trust in himself.

At 18 years old, Gidom moved to a nearby town, first joining the army and then the police force, where he made a career. At the age of 22, he married a woman his family had chosen. The following year, they had a son. He was happy with his family despite being occasionally stationed far away. He did not expect such an epilogue to his career and life: although he was aware of the president's concentration of power and heard that journalists were fleeing to Senegal, he considered the president "a father of the country."

The journey

The journey across West and North Africa was perilous for Gidom. After enduring hunger, thirst, and assaults by bandits in the Sahara Desert, Gidom stayed in a Libyan migrant detention center for four months, renewing his trauma. Every morning, detainees were beaten and tortured for no reason, the daily ration of violence designed to prepare them for whatever requests might later be made (e.g., ransom demands, unpaid job offers, sexual favors).

Gidom worked for five months doing construction works in exchange for the sea journey to Italian shores on a crowded and dangerous boat across the Mediterranean Sea. Abandoned by traffickers in the middle of the Mediterranean, the boat drifted without fuel for four days before being intercepted by a fishing ship, whose crew rescued the castaways and delivered them to an Italian navy frigate. A moving account of Gidom's journey, especially his attempts to take control of the boat to avoid shipwreck, produces a heartbreaking image of Gidom as someone desperately struggling for his life, for his family, for other migrants.

Present life

Gidom has the moral strength and courage to face difficulties and does not easily give up. He regularly attends language courses and is learning to speak Italian very quickly. He is determined to find a job ("to protect my family," he comments). Obtaining asylum, the maximum international protection, would boost him and provide encouragement.

He is in contact with his family and has learned that men connected to the government are looking for him in Gambia, having recently interrogated his family to obtain information, threatened his wife and the family by setting their house on fire. Gidom feels even more guilty than before, finding confirmation of his preoccupations about his responsibilities. The only helpful thing I can do is attempt to accelerate the family reunion procedure following asylum.

Gidom's condition worsens drastically, highlighting the fragility of his personality structure. Frustration and powerlessness fuel a powerful anger that reactivates the energy of trauma. In these circumstances, I begin to understand more clearly how his experience had threatened his inner psychological balance and probably sustained his PTSD. Beyond the appearance of strength and heroism, I speculate that Gidom has a very fragile ego and a dis-integrated self that was previously compensated for by his family, uniform, identifications with ethnicity, country, and religion (he is Muslim and quite religious).

I understood Gidom's appearance of force as excessive identification with his "persona," which had been shaped according to his physical appearance and the imago of a father figure responsible for his family and extremely diligent regarding the duties implied by this role, something that had been affectively absent during Gidom's childhood and adolescence. Here, although I refer to adolescence as understood in Western culture, I am aware that in Gidom's culture, this phase of life does not exist: at 13 years of age, Gidom experienced rites of passage (removal from family and circumcision) marking the transition from childhood to adulthood. He belongs to a very traditional society that prescribes definite roles to its members, culturally far from the liquidity of the Western society he will encounter later. However, Gidom did not follow the path his family traced for him. At the age of 18, Gidom sought his own path, enlisting in the police, a body of the state that provided him with another element of collective identification in a historical moment characterized by the Gambian president's nationalist movement. This strengthened and compacted Gidom's ego by anchoring it to a male image promoted by political propaganda. Then, young but of a suitable age for his culture, Gidom's family chose a wife for him, with whom he had a child and who provided him with another role and his ego with another collective dimension.

Gidom's torture was the first severe blow to Gidom's organization of self, shaking its foundations and undermining his bases, especially upon such a political 'betrayal' that forced him to leave 'home', both in a concrete and symbolic sense. Gidom's organization of self depended considerably upon his "collective props": his uniform, his family, his muscular body, and his "persona." These "props" represent his identity as a rigid pre-determined external container, an interface with the outside world established to protect a fragile and now fragmented self. The traumatic event that broke this defense prompted the adoption of a mode of survival of "floating" on the surface of the world by escaping from his country, undertaking a perilous journey from sub-Saharan Africa to North Africa, arriving in Italy, and seeking asylum. His ego is still dictating a clear agenda (asylum, language-learning, work, family reunification) – indicating a still-good adaptation functioning – but this is in stark contrast to the post-traumatic suffering that is very resistant to treatment, probably deriving from the breakdown of his previous inner organization that cannot rely anymore on its previous armor, his ego cemented by his culturally syntonic "persona."

Floating or diving: Veronica's dilemma

Veronica is Italian and is 26 years old when she arrives at my private practice. She has just won a scholarship for a Ph.D. in linguistics. She is slender and kind but very controlled. Although she cannot explain why she has decided to enter psychotherapy, she seems to suffer from a sense of emptiness provoked by her inability to maintain a stable relationship with any of the men she has been engaged to. The only lasting relationship was a long-distance one, with the two living in different cities. Her sexual life is dominated by dissociation: she drinks alcohol to let herself go, which leads her to detach from herself during intercourse, seeing herself from outside. She does not think she has ever experienced an orgasm.

Nonetheless, Veronica appears well adjusted. She has a successful academic career, often travels to fascinating locations for research purposes, has friends and hobbies. Nonetheless, a sense of emptiness and despair is pervasive, and she cannot build significant relationships. I wonder how such a well-adjusted and successful person can suffer so intensely in her intimate life.

After some time, I will understand that Veronica suffers from complex PTSD resulting from a childhood marked by her father's sexual abuse and totally inadequate maternal caregiving, along with the family's subsequent denial of what had happened. Her only supportive close relationship is apparently with her sister.

Following the first phase of therapy, which involves overcoming Veronica's resistances to telling the stories involving her father, a series of nightmares reveal the sexual abuses suffered during her childhood. Veronica feels very guilty, as if she were responsible for what happened. At one point, she explicitly declares, "knowing about that does not help me [and] on the contrary, it makes me feel worse." Veronica's mother is apparently an extremely fragile person who is insecure about herself but extremely rigid and prescriptive towards her daughter. Furthermore, her mother has covered up her husband's sexual misconduct for Veronica's whole life.

Over a lengthy period and many sessions, I sense that Veronica's "success" at work constituted the socially acceptable facade her mother has constructed through very subtle but indubitable manipulation. This manipulation included subjecting her to food restrictions and a harsh physical exercise regime during her childhood. Veronica has adhered to her mother's perfectionist demands; additionally, her mother continues to control her life. I learn that even the choice of the research doctorate represents her mother's desire for an academic career. I begin to understand Veronica's feelings of emptiness and high levels of dissociation, recognizing Veronica as an empty shell, behind which only intolerable pain opens up. At this point, and during the COVID-19 pandemic, Veronica develops an autoimmune disease that forces her to return to live with her parents for a few months, unable to manage the daily tasks of an independent life. Veronica's illness appears a somatic fight against an internal enemy which compels her to recognize who her parents are and how they have manufactured the dynamics of her reality. Following a series of epiphanies occur, a series of dreams begins, "marine" dreams featuring sharks of different sizes and levels of threat. Sometimes Veronica is frightened of these sharks, and sometimes she is not, convinced that if she knows how to behave, they will not attack. When asked about sharks, she suggests that they are very beautiful animals that are full of strength; although they are aggressive, she is fascinated by them. In her dreams, Veronica makes a series of dives, and all the dangers of seas emerge: giant octopuses, prison-like coral reefs, abysses, and so on.

At this point, I understand something fundamental about Veronica's therapy. She has adapted to her situation – the manipulation and trauma – by floating on the surface of relationships and reality, fully adhering to her mother's prescriptions as a survival strategy. Her frequent journeys represent a fugue from her inner world, attempts to find relief by plunging herself into "other realities." This has produced an adult woman who does not know who she is, what she desires, what she hopes for herself, or what she feels: a totally rootless being. This generates enormous amount of denied anger which is represented by the sharks in her dreams that she cannot recognize as dangerous.

However, as an adult, this strategy of floating has revealed the voids of meaning and subjectivity previously masked. Veronica is now even more frightened, not only by her illness but by the incipient awareness that she has never owned her own self and does not know where to begin the process. She does not know who she really is; she feels herself 'floating' on the surface of a void.

This begins a phase of therapy involving a struggle to discover her authentic emotions and thoughts, which begins with her relationships. Veronica does not feel safe with men and begins to feel attracted to women, identifying herself as lesbian. Although more satisfied from emotional and relational perspectives, her body still does not respond sexually, and she feels awkward and not completely at ease. A series of short-term relationships follow. Only one seems significant; however, in this relationship, Veronica feels like a vulnerable, abandoned child, despairing for weeks when she is abandoned. She starts attending a feminist collective and resumes dancing, something she used to practice in childhood but that she now cultivates as a hobby and which makes her feel more authentically herself. Her new homosexual identity aligns with her self, connoting a space for experimentation in which she recomposes the various fragments of herself to constitute a slightly more coherent and authentic picture.

After some months of significant improvements, the isolation and interruption of these activities provoked by the pandemic disrupt this moment of grace, plunging Veronica back into total desperation. Not too long before the conclusion of her doctoral studies, Veronica begins to believe she has made a huge mistake in her thesis' data collection process. Despite being in the middle of a disaster, she is calmer than I have ever seen her, almost relieved. This is the crisis of an entire system on which her life was constructed.

A few sessions later, Veronica recalls an idea she had as a teenager, a pale but seemingly authentic fantasy of herself. She imagined she would someday be a journalist, "an investigative journalist." This leads the therapy to take a completely new turn, prompted by active research. Dreams often concern recognizing real jewels from costume jewelry or children's toys, objects found on the water's edge or on the beach. Veronica's self-reflective abilities have definitely improved, with her awareness of her own dynamics and her sense of distrust in relationships and in the future apparently creating space for safety and the possibility of finding her true self.

Individuation, the ego and the hero's birth

In analytical psychology, the hero represents individual excellence and symbolizes the vicissitudes of a person's unconscious self and its dynamics with the ego complex in the differentiation of an individuality. It is an archetypal motif based on overcoming obstacles and achieving certain goals. The hero's birth, his initial condition, is one of fragility (the abandoned and exposed child):

> Abandonment, exposure, danger, etc. are all elaborations of the child's insignificant beginnings and of his mysterious and miraculous birth. This statement describes a certain psychic experience of a creative nature, whose object is the emergence of a new and as yet unknown content.
>
> (Jung, 1940: par. 285)

The lack of protection literally characterizes Gidom's condition for his being a victim of torture by the Gambian regime and for being forced, like other asylum seekers, to flee across national borders and confronting natural or human dangers during often long and perilous travels. However, this is not only a concrete condition of exposure but also an intra-psychic condition in which the self is deprived of containment and protection. For Veronica, the dangerous beginning is the failure of her doctoral study, the breaking of the mask of efficiency and adaptation. Jung writes: "The motifs of 'insignificance', exposure, abandonment, danger, etc. try to show how precarious is the psychic possibility of wholeness" (1940: par. 282).

For Jung, the ego complex is merely one complex among many; however, it is the dominant complex, featuring the image of the hero at its core, which represents the archetypal tendency to mastership (Gidom as the captain of the boat and Veronica as a diver confronting sharks and other underwater perils). For Jung, the ego is the complex at the center of consciousness, a unifying and integrating function that promotes a stable identity perspective, a sense of "being an ego."

Nonetheless, in certain circumstances, such as following a severe trauma like torture or familial sexual abuse, multiple split selves, despite lacking the ego's thrust towards stability, can potentially establish as predominant states of mind. In such threatening situations, the pressure of uncontained emotions can provoke consciousness to splinter and the psyche to resort to dissociation to reduce damage to the core self. *Autonomous complexes* that one can observe in action in PTSD (Gidom) and in complex PTSD (Veronica) derive from this dissociation, which affects the self at different depths, with splintered parts of the psyche capable of thought, feeling, desire, and intention. These parts are held together affectively by, for example, memories, in an unconscious grouping that is dissociated from other mental functions. These emotional groupings constitute a normal phenomenon that contributes to psychopathology when they cannot or refuse to bear legitimate suffering (Jung, 1921, 1934). In the Jungian model, the dissociation caused by trauma may, under certain circumstances, promote PTSD; in its extreme form, a dissociative identity disorder can result. According to Van der Kolk, McFarlane, and Weisaeth (1996: X), PTSD severely disrupts an individual's capacity to perceive, represent, integrate, and act on internal and external stimuli because of disruptions in the neural systems associated with attention, working memory, and the processing of affective stimuli. Therefore, trauma leads to abnormal coding of sensory and affective elements; when these are later recovered in memory as visual, olfactory, affective, auditory, and kinesthetic experiences, they remain dissociated from any coherent semantic component (Van der Kolk, 2014).

Initially, Gidom's ego cannot accept his suffering because suffering does not correspond to his self-image, which is constituted by traditional male ideals of strength, justice, self-control, and respect for religious and cultural values. However, his ego is incontrovertibly small and fragile now that is uprooted from its environment that had cemented it and after that trauma has dealt a serious blow to his sense of core self fragmenting his psyche. For Jung, "states of identity" and *participation mystique* describe a state of primitive lack of psychic distinction between subject and object or between two subjects, a primordial unconscious state existing between one's self and an other, between one's self and a group, between one's self and the environment. Given Gidom's ego needs to adhere to an external authority to function, betrayal by the collective through his unlawful arrest and torture severely undermined his ego-based "sense of self." In his sessions, Gidom often talks about his feeling constantly activated, on alert, irritable, and hostage to his post-traumatic symptoms, and he is experiencing compulsive thinking about saving his family. I long considered this understandable and justified because of his family's political persecution. However, the repetitive and unreasonable quality of his thinking provoked me a series of "reveries" on topic of the hero as a way out of fixity that helped us to understand the deep meaning of developments in therapy.

Similarly, at the beginning of her therapy, Veronica cannot consciously recognize that her suffering is connected to her exposure to abusive caregivers. Thus, her disconnection from her body and her feelings constitutes a necessary strategy for tolerating unbearable suffering. Growing up in such a threatening environment prevented her ego from creating roots in either herself or her environment, leading it to adhere to surfaces and float on them to survive her experiences, her post-traumatic bodily memories, her perceptions, and her memories of sexual abuse. Even her university subject and her doctoral research suggest this floating strategy, involving floating among words and geographical locations. Her dives beneath the ocean in her dreams represented encounters with dangerous and aggressive animals that would tear her to pieces if she could not sustain herself through a quest for truth.

The hero's journey

Returning to the mythological perspective, the hero's goal is to find, for example, the treasure, the princess, the ring, the golden egg, or the elixir of life, i.e., a mature self. These metaphors for one's true feelings and unique potential form part of the process of individuation, in which the heroic task is to assimilate unconscious contents instead of being overwhelmed by them. The potential result is the release of energy that has been bound by unconscious complexes:

> In myths the hero is the one who conquers the dragon, not the one who is devoured by it. And yet both have to deal with the same dragon. Also, he is no hero who never met the dragon, or who, if he once saw it, declared afterwards that he saw nothing.
>
> (Jung, 1955: par. 756)

Often, this hero is represented in the context of a journey. In myths and legends, heroes frequently travel by ship, fight sea monsters, are swallowed, and struggle against being bitten or crushed to death; a famous example is Jonah, who, after arriving inside the belly of the whale, seeks the vital organ and cuts it off, liberating him. This illustrates how the birth and development of consciousness constitutes heroic adventure and perhaps the most extraordinary example of such. However, the ego must first enter into a dialogue with the self to establish the individual.

Erich Neumann has extensively documented this myth as the prototype of the mature self struggling to break free from the dominance of unconscious forces. This process depends on awakening the ego and is experienced as the progressive activation of one's own self-consciousness. The ego locates itself through differentiation from the maternal matter (Neumann, 1949), which can be understood as the original unconscious state, the starting point, the Great Mother, the symbol of psychic fusion, and the co-presence of all indistinct psychic parties. Within this preconscious totality, there develops an impulse to eject a partial aspect of it, namely the consciousness.

According to this mythologem, establishing broader forms of awareness depends upon breaking with the past. In Gidom's experience, arrest and torture constitute such a breaking point: the transition from one dimension to another through destroying what is old and imposing what is new: fragility and vulnerability as existential conditions.

For Veronica, this breaking point was failing her Ph.D., which put into crisis the entire system upon which her life had been based. In a diving dream during this phase, Veronica saw a light deriving from a crack in the depths of the abyss. The rocks were covered with plant and animal life forms; in every ravine, she could see life forms pertaining to the deep sea. She became disoriented because she no longer knew which was up and which way was down; nonetheless, she was at once fascinated and afraid of the light. In this moment of bewilderment, a sea turtle – a helper figure – arrived to guide her back to the surface of the sea before diving back down again. Although relieved, Veronica knew she would return to that place.

The psychological development in question in the myth of the hero is that of *individuation*, which concerns how this human being and this (internal and external) world are simultaneously constituted and their interconnections. The meetings of Gidom and Veronica with the external world were opportunities to save themselves from their own personal traumas, a survival strategy that allowed them to navigate the difficulties of an impossible true identity. For Jung, individuation means to become what you always were *in potentia*, to fulfill your unique promise, and to accomplish your nature, producing an individual in the real sense of the word, a whole self that can no longer be hijacked by splintered aspects or complexes (Jung, 1935: para 11). This also represents the broad aim of psychotherapy.

Accordingly, Gidom's story represents a journey through experiences that enabled him to abandon an idealized self built from a received cultural model that comprised masculine strength and plain adhesion to nationalistic collective values and a prescribed self-image in favor of a strengthened true self. This identity does not abandon its original values and attachments but is more substantially founded on significant affective experiences. Meanwhile, Veronica's story represents a long journey of discovery of her self, revealing deep unexplored dimensions that teem with life with all its threats and opportunities.

Jung understood psychotherapy as the dialectic relation between two individuals. When therapist and patient sit in front of each other, this recreates the mirror function that is fundamental to any development. While critical to every therapeutic process, this emphatic function becomes absolutely fundamental to non-verbal exchanges, implying the use of the imagination from not only the patient but also the analyst. Both imagination and modes of empathetic intervention relate to what is known as right-brain activity, a subject of neuroscience research, especially studies considering the role of the right hemisphere in socio-affective development (Schore, 2003 , 2009, 2011).

The emergence of a broader and more flexible and articulated personal identity may be facilitated through work that occurs "at the border between ego and complexes," building "bridges" between autonomous complexes, the ego complex, and external/social reality. Such "psychological complexes" are experienced as motivating forces with highly arousing affective core and image components (Jung, 1934). When these complexes overtake ordinary consciousness, they seek another person's participation in the form of invitation, offer, or demand.

I realize while sitting with these two patients that I am always pressured to do something for them, undertake some action to save them, investing considerable energy in my therapeutic role. I realize that I am totally identified with the "heroic savior" archetype. In contrast, I sometimes feel totally powerless and insignificant, prey to some inner persecutor, literally a victim. Notably, I experience myself as the savior when my patients are vulnerable. Meanwhile, when they are more active and seem more in control of their life, I experience counter-transferential phantasies of being their victim.

I understand such a dynamic of transference-countertransference as partially due to the power differential between us and transference-countertransference dynamics. In order to get out of this apparently unavoidable dynamic, I invite Gidom to attend a meeting of a group of torture survivors whom I am working with to develop methods for increasing personal empowerment. I am following my intuition that a group setting could be a productive context for Gidom to work through his trauma and contend with the theme of power, and for both of us not feeling threatened. We also continue individual therapy to reflect on what is going on in his life and what eventually happens in the group. Gidom accepts and makes powerful contributions to the group's work. Over 12 meetings, he approaches various issues, including trust and safety, connectedness, empathy, identity, recognition, hope, and empowerment. In this context, he discovers his true leadership skills, which differ from those he imagined he had, more connected to attachment needs, courage, openness towards others, and openness to recognizing one's own vulnerabilities and strengths. Additionally, his identifications are reframed within the group context as concerning African identity versus the white Western world with more self-aware consciousness of contributing to a variety of post-colonial African identities.

Gidom's experience in this group is so significant that he develops a desire to work in the field of migration services. After three years, his dream comes true, and he finds a job in a reception center.

About Veronica, I invite her to choose a physical activity that might work for her as an activity involving her body in our process of reflecting on herself. She chooses to practice modern dance in a dance school managed by a feminist circle. This offers her the occasion to experience more freely and safely her body and a totally new identity. Additionally, Veronica invests energy in significantly improving her relationships through new encounters. In her homosexual relationships, Veronica can explore her feelings and bodily reactions in relative safety. Her work in therapy involves exploring her authentic feelings towards people and her personal interests and preferences. This was precipitated by the slow reconstruction of pieces of her authentic subjectivity and creating distance from her previous psychic attitudes, and, above all, from the psychic fog that impeded her certainty that she was abused in reality and not in phantasy.

When this reconstructive work reaches critical mass, Veronica's natural drive towards individuation manifests itself through the desire to find a new and authentic professional identity after having established her new sexual identity. Now, she wants to become an investigative journalist.

For both Gidom and Veronica, the turning points in their therapy were occasions offering the possibility of reconnection, in different and more differentiated ways, with elements of identification with which, earlier, they were only superficially connected: for Gidom, a new way to connect to his gender role (being a man, a husband and a father) and cultural identity; for Veronica, to her sexual and professional identity.

Individuation as taking root

According to Jung's work, individuation can be observed at two levels. First, at a *subjective* (internal or intra-psychic) level: individuation concerning psychic elements, functions, and structures which differentiate themselves to allow the ego and consciousness to engage in the difficult confrontation with the unconscious components of personality (Jung, 1947). Second, at an *objective* or intersubjective (relational or inter-psychic) level: the differentiation of the individual through a state of identity with another and the subsequent integration or interaction either or both between these individuals and between the individual and the group. At both levels, individuation concerns differentiation and integration between the ego and the self and between the ego and the world:

> Individuation means becoming an "in-dividual," and, in so far as "individuality" embraces our innermost, last, and incomparable uniqueness, it also implies becoming one's own self. We could therefore translate individuation as "coming to selfhood" or "self-realization."
>
> (Jung, 1928: par. 266)

This implies the reintegration of traumatic complexes through a reconnection between the complex of ego and the entire self. However, a significant pair of risks are apparently those linked to an inflation of the hero archetype: on the one hand, the conviction of being someone special; on the other hand, the feeling of inferiority that promotes the heroic martyr through negative inflation. At the beginning of therapy, both Gidom and Veronica alternately lived both risks. Despite their opposite characters, the forms are identical because the conscious megalomania – the inflation of the ego – corresponds to an unconscious compensatory inferiority, while the conscious inferiority corresponds to an unconscious megalomania. Gidom and Veronica oscillate between superiority and inferiority, these swings being attempts to integrate the complex of ego and autonomous complexes in a wider sense of self. Confronting inflation risks, the ego, a part of the self, has to be functional and contribute to overall mental balance. The ego is more likely to participate in the overall psychic balance if it can consider itself a part of the self and therefore be aware of its own one-sidedness and its existence in relation to all of the other psychic parts, which have dignity and opportunity – cognitive and affective – equal to that of the ego. The ego must also be able to simultaneously differentiate itself from and identify with different psychic instances.

At the intersubjective level, Gidom's ego, which previously identified rigidly with his ethnicity, profession, and family role, has become able to differentiate itself from and integrate with the particular psychic constellation known as the "Persona." Forced to acknowledge the failures of past identifications, Gidom increasingly develops trust in the meaning of what happens to him, his attitude becoming more and more self-listening.

Jung speaks of the Persona as a "mask," which indicates a mode of relationship between the individual and the world. The mask is an external façade disguising an internal façade; the connection between the two fundamentally demonstrates how ego's adhesion to the world is relative to the ego's adhesion to the self. The latter does not occur directly but through an internal mediator, the Anima, the relation function, which is considered to exist in a complementary relationship with the Persona. Development of Gidom's Anima constituted one of the foremost demands of our therapeutic work. A similar process occurred in Veronica's therapy. Her unconscious led her to fail her Ph.D., which pushed into crisis her false self and her identification with the Persona her mother had constructed for her, allowing her to liberate her energies to dive into her traumatic complexes and recognize the dangers as such (the light that enlightens the depth of the sea).

At one point, a social assistant proposed that Gidom attend a professional course to become a private security guard. Gidom responded that the role no longer suited him, that he did not feel able to do it because he felt profoundly changed. When asked about his motivation in working in the field of migration, he replied: "I want to help others like me and also understand their experience. In the group I learned that everyone has a different experience and also that our experiences are interconnected." In this group, the members coming from African countries commented on how African group identities have been profoundly altered by the arbitrary divisions of borders of the colonial period and how their own education, now purely Western, ignores local traditions. To these participants, it was very clear the impact that the colonial period had on their societies. A cogent political analysis emerged from this group, and my impression was that that helped to establish definite new African 'post-colonial' sense of identity among group members. Gidom's identity, less monolithic, is still significantly bound to its cultural origins but in a new, more flexible, and personalized way.

In Veronica's case, through dance and therapeutic explorations of several aspects of herself, including her homosexuality, she was able to discover her true emotions, feelings, perceptions, and thoughts, ultimately developing a sense of freedom. She could attend a course of professional journalism and start a career in that field, motivated to pursue such a career by a potential to discover the "truth" behind the appearances of things. In her own wording, "only the truth makes people free." Her relational life becomes richer when she meets a young woman, a painter, and they fall in love and have the opportunity to discover their respective interests, personal characteristics, and shared pleasures.

Conclusion

From his sociological perspective of liquidity, Bauman (2003) considers refugee-dom and homosexuality both an expression of our time: refugees in the refugee camps as an expression of *extraterritoriality* (not truly belonging to the place), with its effect on their identities (pp. 141–148), and homosexuality as an expression of the *homo sexualis*, a product of our cultural *scientia sexualis*, in which "what does matter it is up to *homo sexualis* to determine (discover or invent)" (pp. 54–55), with the consequence of a life fraught with anxiety.

However, he has in mind refugees in the camps, not refugees in an asylum country recognized as refugees, that is, with a determined status and the opportunity to work through their trauma and rework their identity. Although Bauman's analysis is brilliantly suitable to describe our reality from a sociological critical perspective, liquidity is not necessarily an individual destiny. It can be the starting point of an individual's development line that injects peculiar challenges to the contemporary psyche of refugees throughout the process.

Similarly for *homo sexualis*, according to Bauman, the under-definition, incompleteness, and non-finality of their sexual identity are at the same time a poison and its antidote guiding towards never-ending anxiety.

However, as seen with Veronica, this itinerary can also be an opportunity to discover one's true self and a path towards self-fulfillment. Floating can be a temporary strategy of survival, and instead diving into one's autonomous complexes can also mean to discover an unexpected homosexual identity to be lived authentically and as self-exploration.

The Jungian idea of *individuation* is helpful for thinking that there exists a way out of the toxic and disintegrating effects of social liquidity on human identities. There is an ultimate possibility towards a personal synthesis, an emergence from an unconscious state of identity or *participation mystique* (Jung, 1921: par. 781) with one's group or the environment; this is possible by taking root in some part of one's own authentic Self, in a natural endowment of the individual psyche. Through differentiation from collective processes and entities, it becomes possible to develop a unique and authentic existence, to reach one's true self-containing and nurturing identity, one's mature and developed self, that might significantly connect to the social reality and one's own essence. In this sense, psychotherapy can provide a constant container, a vas, in which social fragmentation or liquidity can be held to promote self-containment, personal integration and the development of a true self.

References

Bauman, Z. (2003). *Liquid Love. On the Frailty of Human Bonds*. Cambridge: Polity Press.
Bauman, Z. (2007). *Liquid Times: Living in an Age of Uncertainty*. Cambridge: Polity Press.
Bauman, Z. (2013). *Liquid Modernity*. Cambridge: Polity Press.
Beck, U. (1992). *Risk Society: Towards a New Modernity*. London: Sage.
Beck, U., and Beck-Gernsheim, E. (1995). *The Normal Chaos of Love*. Cambridge: Polity.
Bowlby, J. (1969). *Attachment and Loss*. Vol. 1, *Attachment*. London Hogarth Press and the Institute of Psycho-Analysis.
Bromberg, P. M. (1998). *Standing in the Spaces: Essays on Clinical Process, Trauma, and Dissociation*. Hillsdale, NY: The Analytic Press.

Callero, P. (2003). The sociology of the self. *Annual Review of Sociology*, 29: 115–133.

Damasio, A. R. (1999). *The Feeling of What Happens: Body and Emotion in the Making of Consciousness*. New York: Harcourt Brace.

Ellmers, N., Spears, R., and Doosje, B. (2002). Self and social identity. *Annual Review of Psychology*, 53: 161–186.

Frewen, P. A., and Lanius, R. A. (2006). Toward a psychobiology of posttraumatic self-dysregulation: Reexperiencing, hyperarousal, dissociation, and emotional numbing. *Annals of the New York Academy of Sciences*, (July), 1071: 110–124. doi: 10.1196/annals.1364.010.

Giddens, A. (1991). *Modernity and Self-Identity. Self and Society in the Late Modern Age*. Stanford, CA: Stanford University Press.

Giddens, A. (2000). *Runaway World: How Globalization is Reshaping Our Lives*. London: Brunner-Routledge.

Held, D., McGrew, A., Goldblatt, D., and Perraton, J. (1999). *Global Transformations: Politics, Economics and Culture*. Stanford, CA: Stanford University Press.

Jenkins, R. (2004). *Social Identity*. London: Routledge.

Jung, C. G. (1921). Definitions. In *CW*, vol 6.

Jung, C. G. (1928). The Function of the Unconscious. In *CW*, vol. 7.

Jung, C. G. (1934). A review of the complex theory. In *CW*, vol. 8.

Jung, C. G. (1935). Principles of practical psychotherapy. In *CW*, vol. 16.

Jung, C. G. (1940). The psychology of the child archetype. In *CW*, vol. 9i.

Jung, C. G. (1947). On the nature of the psyche. In *CW*, vol. 8.

Jung, C. G. (1955). Mysterium coniunctionis. In *CW*, vol. 14.

Kohut, H. (1977). *The Restoration of the Self*. New York: International Universities Press.

Mitchell, S. A. (1991). Contemporary perspectives on self: Toward an integration. *Psychoanalytic Dialogues*, 1: 121–128.

Neumann, E. (1949). *The Origins and History of Consciousness*. With a Foreword by C. G. Jung. Translated from the German by R. F. C. Hull. London: Routledge and Kegan Paul, 1954.

Owens, T. J., Robinson, D. T., and Smith-Lovin, L. (2010). Three faces of identity. *Annual Review of Sociology*, 36: 477–499.

Papadopoulos, R. (2021). *Involuntary Dislocation. Home, Trauma, Resilience, and Adversity-Activated Development*. London & New York: Routledge.

Rattansi, A., and Phoenix, A. (2005). Rethinking youth identities: Modernist and postmodernist frameworks. *Identity: An International Journal of Theory and Research*, 5(2): 97–123.

Schore, A. N. (2003). *Affect Regulation and the Repair of the Self*. New York: W.W. Norton & Company.

Schore, A. N. (2009). Right brain affect regulation: An essential mechanism of development, trauma, dissociation, and psychotherapy. In D. Fosha, D. Siegel, and M. Solomon (Eds.), *The Healing Power of Emotion: Affective Neuroscience, Development, and Clinical Practice* (pp. 112–144). New York: Norton.

Schore, A. N. (2011). The right brain implicit self lies at the core of psychoanalysis. *Psychoanalytic Dialogues*, 21(1): 75–100. doi: 10.1080/10481885.2011.545329

Sen, A. (1999). *Development as Freedom*. New York: Alfred Knopf.

Solomon, M. F., and Siegel, D. J. (2003). *Healing Trauma: Attachment, Mind, Body and Brain*. New York: W.W. Norton & Company.

Stein, M. (2006). Individuation. In R. K. Papadopoulos (Ed.), *The Handbook of Jungian Psychology. Theory, Practice and Applications*. London & New York: Routledge, pp. 196–214.

Swann, W. B., and Bosson, J. (2010). Self and identity. In S. T. Fiske, D. T. Gilbert, and G. Lindzey (Eds.), *Handbook of Social Psychology*. Hoboken, NJ: Wiley, pp. 589–628.

Tomlinson, J. (1999). *Globalization and Culture*. Chicago: University of Chicago Press.

Van der Kolk, B. (2014). *The Body Keeps the Score: Brain, Mind, and Body in the Healing of Trauma*. New York, NY: Penguin.

Van der Kolk, B., McFarlane, A. C., Weisaeth, L., Aarts, P. G., and Solomon, Z. H. (1996). *Traumatic Stress. The Effect of Overwhelming Experience on Mind, Body and Society*. New York: Guildford Press.

Winnicott, D. W. (1971). *Playing and Reality*. Harmondsworth: Penguin, 1985.

Chapter 13

Paranoia, Politics and the Tyranny of the Identical

Is there Civilization in the Transitions we are Crossing?

Marcus Quintaes

If every analyst should place himself in the subjective horizon of his time, how can we face the new images of psychological distress of our time? If there is transition in civilizations, we should recognize what is more idiosyncratic in these cultural, social, psychological and political formations in order to avoid the temptation of finding an absolute element that could erase and minimize the differences in each historical moment.

In this regard, I would like, first of all, to take a kind of retrospective look and postulate a theoretical hypothesis about considering that each historical-cultural moment produces, almost symptomatically, a given clinical structure that will last and gain a prominent place in this context. In this respect, if we consider the end of the 19th century and beginning of the 20th century, one of the many names of a civilization in transition, we could think that hysteria was the prevailing clinical structure that presented the highest protagonism in that cultural moment in a time marked by so many transformations and changes.

This idea considers the assumption that each cultural moment produces or has its own and particular way of producing what James Hillman (1993) called *infirmitas*, its wound. Such perspective considers that certain socio-cultural contexts have a very peculiar way of expressing their psychological distress. And, in this sense, what we want to bring in here is the idea that, in this turn of the 19th century and early 20th century, hysteria (Quinet, 2006) was the prevailing mode of psychological distress. History brought to light the elements that were in the shadow of a given collective social construction of the time. This shadow concerns sexuality, pleasure and the female body but the word of the woman as well, a woman who had become a kind of modern Cassandra. Hysteria appears as the prevailing clinical structure with its multitude of symptoms, presenting its somatic conversion with its infinite plasticity of pains that wander in women's bodies.

Advancing our theoretical hypothesis, we will consider that, by the end of the 20th century – the mid 80s – until the early 21st century – the early 2000s – there are a new subjective ordering and new symbolic coordinates, and now hysteria no longer appears as the fundamental or main category of psychological distress. Such psychological distress we will call depression. What we see in the late 20th century is what many historians call an epidemic of depressive affections.

DOI: 10.4324/9781003168829-14

Depression becomes this clinical manifestation that affects the whole collective conscience of a given time. It can be considered both something from the order of mental suffering, a disorder – as the DSM (Whitaker, 2010) will interpret – but also a social symptom, one symptom of psychological distress but social distress as well. Depression arises as a symptom of a mode of social arrangement of a culture.

Depression can be the effect of a type of social and economic construction in force in this period of time. We can think of a relation of the capital and the psychic life, of ways of structuring of subjectivities produced by productive and economic neoliberal models that cause psychological distress. Considering that, as neoliberal models promote the exaltation of a subject that is entrepreneur of himself, a performing subject, a subject that makes of himself his own organization to be managed, those that do not respond to this rule or somehow are not adapted to these principles prove to be a part out of gear. In this regard, we can think that the person under depression is the part out of gear of the capital system or a capital ruled by a given neoliberal modality.

The depressed subject presents a new fantasy about man and the force of a new myth about the psyche. Where, until the 1960s, there was the fantasy of a psychic man with an instance called unconscious, this psychological subject, divided, marked by conflicts, is replaced by another configuration, and the neuronal man, the biological man, the organic man appear.

We are here, inside what we could call a new mythology or a new archetypal fantasy that coordinates and rules these new symbolic coordinates. This new archetypal fantasy is the mythology of the brain man, from the unconscious to the brain. In other words, biological psychiatry comes to propose a kind of biologization of the psychic, that is, a physicalism of what was formerly considered mental.

The subject identity is no longer in the conflict he experiences, in his biography or in his personal history, in his subjective dramas, in symptomatic manifestations of his unconscious. The subject identity is now embedded in synapses, neurotransmitters and dopamines. In this regard, depression becomes this place where the subject is exiled, divorced, separated from his subjectivity.

However, we have advanced, and what I would like to present is that, somehow, on February 26, 2021, we are witnessing another dramatic historical moment – and I'm not referring to the pandemic. Paranoia is back. We are living in paranoid times. We are, almost all of us, entangled within the relentless paranoid logics that bring inevitable consequences both in the construction of social bonds with the culture and in the new constructions of contemporary subjectivity. The resurgence and election in several countries of extreme right parties and politicians with populist, xenophobic, racist, misogynist, intolerant discourses, with extreme conservative attitudes, makes us formulate the following question: is politics paranoid? How can we keep and preserve democratic spaces both in psychic life and political life in face of the insurgence of paranoid affections characterized by the tyranny of the identical and exclusion of difference? Even when, in the last editions of the DSM (Whitaker, 2010), paranoia as clinical identity was dismembered and divided into several symptomatologies, into several disorders, it is important to think that the classical paranoia is back.

In fact, it has always existed. However, it seems to me that here exactly the differential jump is revealed: paranoia no longer inhabits only hospitals, psychiatric clinics or even offices. Paranoia is in the polis. Paranoia is in the media. Paranoia contaminated us with its logics. Somehow, we are all running into paranoid practices, dynamics, logics and interpretations of the existence.

Speaking of paranoia implies an attempt to recover some part of its history or what it means. If we ponder carefully, in the second half of the 19th century, paranoia means, by etymology, "the one who thinks beside" (Quinet, 2006) In Germany, this concept gains a more precise description with a psychiatrist called Kahlbaum (cited in Quinet, 2006) in 1863, when he refers to paranoia as a clinical structure associated with the category of systematized delusions. And here there is an important detail: systematized delusions without intellectual weakening. The intellectual capacity of the paranoid is preserved. It is not disturbed. That is, the paranoid subject is a subject with his thinking functions intact, preserved and active, and that will explain why the paranoid delusion is so well systematized, so strictly coherent. From there the difficulty is to dissolve it, question it or even metaphorize it.

Paranoia is basically characterized by its irrefutable belief. That is, paranoid has no doubt: he doesn't hesitate, and he doesn't vacillate. The delusional construction that sustains the paranoid subject is constituted by a delusional certainty, an irrefutable belief. It's not by chance that some psychiatrists call paranoia a "rationalizing" madness, a madness that thinks. Freud (Quinet, 2006) will call it "the intellectual psychosis" (cited in Quinet, 2006). What does it mean? It basically means that we would have to consider paranoia as follows (this is Kraepelin's concept): the delusion is an ideational form – it is an idea – that leads to an unbreakable conviction, to a conviction that is not subject to doubts or even changeable by confrontation with reality. Confronting the paranoid with reality, attempting to correct the delusion, attempting to indicate to the paranoid that what he interprets is mistaken, is absolutely innocuous and sterile and has no purpose. His conviction is unbreakable. It is unshakeable. Saying that implies saying the following: the paranoid subject, sustained by its unbreakable conviction, becomes an interpreter. Every paranoid is an interpreter. That is, he is an interpreter that sees indications, signs, hints, proposals, intentions in everything – and all that against him. If the delusion of observation and the persecutory delusion characterize paranoia, we can think that, precisely for this fantasy – which in paranoia is not a fantasy but is taken as one dimension of reality – this subject will be always interpreting everything that happens as something turned to him, against him.

For the paranoid, there is no chance; everything is premeditated. There is a meaning in everything, and only the paranoid sees it. There is a meaning that only the paranoid can construe, because he holds the key of interpretation. The key of interpretations is: I am observed, watched, controlled; they talk about me. So, what is it that we want to say? We want to say that, ultimately, every paranoid is a narcissistic par excellence. Everything always refers to him. It is inside-out narcissism. The paranoid is a self-referential subject, and therefore he eliminates chance. It is this narcissistic character of the paranoid subject that will explain the megalomaniac character of his delusions.

While this subject is essentially narcissistic, what could we consider a development of an archetypal dynamics of paranoia? We can think that, in this way, the paranoid is a subject that does not trust. He watches. He is always alert. The paranoid is an eternal vigilante. Therefore, every paranoid considers himself unique. That is, one that considers and believes he is unique is always paranoid. For believing that he is unique, the paranoid is the one that believes that he holds the truth, reason, knowledge about the other. Of course, believing that one is unique brings the shadow, as Jung puts it very clearly. Where there is an excessively consolidated position, this consolidated position will constellate its opposite in the shadow. And the shadow that here appears is always the suspicion of being betrayed. Every paranoid considers that he will always be betrayed, that there is a plot to defeat him. Every paranoid always suspects something of someone. Because, for him, all the others want to render him destitute, remove him from the place he holds. And what place is that? The place of the One, the One of truth, the One of knowledge, the One of wisdom. So, the paranoid does not trust. He distrusts. He is always doubting those that surround him, an absolutely common and routine phenomenon in institutions. A phenomenon that, we can say, is easily constellated in collective groupings.

Every paranoia is, according to Luigi Zoja in his fabulous book *Paranoia* (2013), a collective contagion. Paranoia is not only an individual drama; it contaminates groups, nations and cultures. We can think that the paranoid subject that becomes a mass leader will always consider himself a target of plots, conspiracies and coups to overthrow him. And we don't need to go very far to see this dynamic clearly working in the field of politics: political subjects that feel themselves threatened all the time because someone will remove them from their position. The plot fantasy, the betrayal fantasy, a typical paranoia symptom.

Why is paranoia so present? Or, why it is so seducing? And this is a basic characteristic of paranoia. Paranoia is a speech that seduces. Why is it a speech that seduces? Because the paranoid discourse presents certainty, truth and warranty. That is, the paranoid seduces due to the conviction of his interpretations. He seduces with the conviction of interpretations and delusional conclusions he draws. Think about religious phenomena; think about churches and the figure of a pastor or a politician. Both in religion and politics, the pastor and the politician – some, not all – prove to be paranoid leaders dictating to their flocks, their believers, their electors the primers of the good life. In religion: what is it to be a man, a woman, a father and so on. In politics: what is it to be a patriot, a subject aligned with the commitments and traditions of the Brazilian family, the places of women, children and minorities. The paranoid seduces for his certainty. And this certainty is precisely the element missing inside the neurotic structure. It is not by chance that paranoids carry, herd, regiment crowds around them – by the persuasive power of their conviction. This adhesion is almost instantaneous, because the paranoid interpretation seduces, convinces, persuades. The paranoid, then, is the one that possessed the meaning. It is the empire of meaning. Paranoia is the pathology of interpretation. In paranoia we find this endless exercise of assigning meanings to everything that happens. These meanings, as previously mentioned, will always refer to the paranoid subject.

James Hillman, in his book *Paranoia* (1993), identifies two interesting aspects present in paranoia. The first is to consider that paranoia is a disorder of meaning. If paranoia is the empire of meaning, the pathology of interpretation, and is the excessive attribution of meanings, Hillman will say that paranoia is a disorder of meaning. And, if meaning is an attribution, condition or characteristic of the Self archetype, Hillman will say that paranoia is a disorder of the Self, a pathology of the Self, a very specific and particular form of Self operation. This is a first interpretation, but Hillman goes further and presents a second interpretation: paranoia is the failure of metaphorization; that is, there is a lack of the functional particle referred to by Jung as the "as if". This functional particle will enable us to establish a fictional, poetic, symbolic, imaginative, metaphorical relation with images. Based on this metaphorical game is the creation of a polysemy of meanings, a plurality of meanings. If this fictional particle is not present in paranoia, if the "as if" fails, we can think that paranoia is the prevalence of literalism. It is the prevalence of literalism and the failure of the metaphorical.

In paranoia, the freezing of images does not let the transforming game of soul-making be operated. Prevented from sliding in the open weave caused by the metaphor effects on and with image, to the paranoid, the primary activity of a clinic grounded on archetypal psychology is refused: what Hillman calls 'Seeing-through' (1995), an act that frees every and any psychic event from being reduced or captured by its literal meaning. So, the activity of the imaginative heart fails in its attempt to set free the images of its imprisonment in an univocal meaning to enter the fictional world of imagination. Without the action of the image fiction, the paranoid is prevented from opening himself to the multiple meanings present in images that appear to him, and the whole polysemic field is compromised and reduced to its value as sign: finite, univocal, invariable, consolidated. The imaginative heart of a paranoid is a heart infarcted with frozen images transformed into signs of pain and persecution.

Paranoia is so considered a disorder of the self and a failure in metaphorizing, the impossibility of soul making, precarization of the fictional and prevalence of literalism. But there is a third aspect: paranoia as the tyranny of unification, the curse of the One. That is, the paranoid subject can't open himself to plurality. While not being able to be open to what is different from him, the paranoid establishes a kind of relation with the world that is binary and excluding: me or the other, never me and the other. There is no condition of alterity, a condition of permission of existence of difference. This rivalry logic – either me or you – rules and fully dominates paranoid logic, for example, in politics or a given political group. This "either me or the other" means that either the other is converted into me, becomes identical to me, adopts my truth, is persuaded by my convincing power, or this other should be destroyed. In other words, we are here, once again, in the tyranny of the One – one single truth, one point of view, one reason, one possibility of existence, one modality for production of knowledge – whatever.

What we can say, then, is that paranoia is the aversion to multiplicity, because this multiplicity is fully reduced to the One of the identical. If paranoia is, as I said before, and as sustained by Hillman, the failure of metaphor and prevalence of literalism, then we can think that paranoia walks hand in hand with fundamentalism. In other words, fundamentalism is one of the forms of paranoia. The notion of belief is a tributary of the paranoid discourse, and the fundamentalist discourse is also the "rivalry" discourse, of the cancellation of alterity, difference. In this regard, everything that is difference to the paranoid, for this subject encapsulated in himself, he pushes to the margin.

Isn't it precisely the dynamics that we are seeing in Brazil and in several other countries? A kind of upsurge of populist, right-wing extremist discourses? Exactly: a paranoid logic now with a format of political device, political activity and doubtful political ethics where these extreme right leaders – Trump, Bolsonaro and others, identified with the idea of a single truth, monotheist in their hearts and minds, state to be contrary to everything that does not fit in the logic of meaning of paranoid identities and push all these differences to the margin. That will explain why paranoia in politics or paranoia as political activity is xenophobe, homophobic, racist, misogynist. Because it can't find a place where this difference, a difference that incorporates multiplicity – a multiplicity of psychic styles – can have voice.

The paranoid discourse is the discourse of the One, the tyranny of the One, the curse of the One. And this curse of the One erases everything that appears as element of difference, differentiation, contrast, ambiguity, ambivalence. We live in a very dangerous moment, politically, because, with the upsurge of these political practices and ultranationalist discourses, we find a paranoid mode of functioning, in full force and politically legitimated. We know that for the paranoid to exist, he needs to choose an opponent: he needs an enemy. Here, we have a paranoid practice and a paranoid strategy; that is, it is necessary to create an opponent. An opponent? What for? Because this opponent wants to destroy me – the betrayal plot is constellated. The paranoid does not trust; he watches. And this opponent justifies my hate speech, my aggressiveness and my actions to stop him. The paranoid individual needs the other, whom he will transform into the opponent so the paranoid speech can act typically, that is, aggressively, violently. Paranoia is violent. Paranoid logic is the logic of violence.

That's what we are experiencing in Brazil. The point is how we, Jungians, can be articulated and what to do in face of this phenomenon. Maybe the matter is that, for analytical psychology, a practice fully tributary of the right to multiplicity, plurality, as a founding condition of psychism – the Jungian unconscious is a plural, multiple, diverse unconscious – it is an ethical task to somehow raise flags, without shame, in favor of the multiple, in face of the homogenous speeches that try to silence us or try to transform both the social and cultural reality and the psychic reality in a devastated land where only one meaning prevails – the meaning of the religious-political leader.

In this regard, the Jungian clinical practice is a practice of dissension, of what attempts to make difference against this homogenous speech that is not captured by the paranoid logic and so assumes an ethical and psychic commitment to emphasize the freedom that is embedded in the multiplicity as a condition of the psychic living, as a condition of the civilizing life, civilized life. I believe that this is the point; that's what is it all about. Somehow, there is a big challenge in front of us, from which we, Jungians, should not retreat, in our clinics, in our private spaces of offices – or on the screens of computers and cell phones, as the pandemic obliged us to – but we should not retreat on the streets either, in the polis, in order for us to be loyal heirs of a lesson learnt with the teachings of Jung – of an unconscious that is plural, multiple, diversified, the praise of the difference, a kind of co-existence of differences, a tension between opposites. It seems to me that these Jungian qualities can serve us as absolutely interesting and useful tools and markers to face this terrible disaster called the politics of paranoia.

References

Adams, Michael Vannoy, *The Fantasy Principle: Psychoanalyses of the Imagination*, New York: Routledge, 2004.

Calligaris, Contardo, *Introdução a uma clínica diferencial das psicoses*, Porto Alegre: Artes Médicas, 1989.

Corbin, Henry, *Mundus Imaginalis, or The Imaginary and the Imaginal*, in *Working with Images: The Theorical Base of Archetypal Psychology*, Sells, Benjamin (Ed.), Woodstock, CT: Spring Publications, 2000.

Freud, Sigmund, *Notas psicanalíticas sobre um relato autobiográfico de um caso de paranoia – Caso Schreber*, Vol. XII, Rio de Janeiro: Imago Editora, 1969.

Hillman, James, *Paranoia*, Petrópolis: Vozes, 1993.

Hillman, James, *The Thought of the Heart and the Soul of the World*, Woodstock, CT: Spring Publications, 1995.

Jung, C.G., *Psicogênese das doenças mentais*, Petrópolis: Vozes, 1986.

Jung, C.G., *Nietzsche's Zarathustra: Notes of the Seminar Given in 1934–1939*, Princeton, NJ: Princeton University Press, 1988.

Jung, C.G. and McGuire, William, *Freud/Jung: Correspondência completa*, Rio de Janeiro: Imago Editora, 1974.

Nasio, Juan David, *Os Grandes casos de Psicose*, Rio de Janeiro: Zahar Editor, 2001.

Quinet, Antonio, *Psicose e laço social*, Rio de Janeiro: Zahar Editor, 2006.

Samuels, Andrew, *Psychopathology: Contemporary Jungian Perspectives*, London: The Guilford Press, 1991.

Solomin, Hester, *Contemporary Jungian Clinical Practice*, London: Karnac, 2003.

Whitaker, Robert, *Anatomy of an Epidemic: Magic, Bullets, Psychiatric Drugs and the Astonishing Rise of Mental Illness in America*, New York: Broadway Paperback, 2010

Zoja, Luigi, *Paranoia – La locura que hace la historia*, Buenos Aires: Fondo de cultura econômica, 2013.

Chapter 14

The Applicability of Analytical Psychology in China

How a Western Psychological Lens Might be Adapted in the East

Huan Wang

The application of psychoanalysis in China

As the founder of the China American Psychoanalytic Alliance (CAPA), Dr Snyder, states, 'from the beginning of the twentieth century until the present, a "pure" form of psychoanalysis was never introduced or received in China. There were all always cultural interpretations and adaptions that added Chinese characteristics to the mix' (Kirsner & Snyder, 2009, p. 46). This is true in the sense that there has been a long history of assimilating the thoughts imported from other cultures in China, and Chinese people have never been obsessive about the concept of 'purity'. I will expand on this later when discussing the use of analytical psychology in China. Zhang, who explored psychoanalysis in China in the early years, concedes that, 'the Chinese who promoted Freud's ideas turned those ideas to their own purposes' (1992, p. 10). Saporta, who offers teaching and supervision in CAPA, also supports this view, claiming that 'the Chinese have always taken what they need from the West and discarded the rest' (2014, p. 110). Thus, we can infer that, first, from the first day that psychoanalysis arrived in China, the Chinese began to apply it, and second, they have not copied psychoanalysis directly and entirely from the West but have selected what they need in relation to their own concerns, sometimes even reinterpreting and modifying it. Therefore, we can say that the Chinese use a 'hybrid' form of psychoanalysis.

However, this has caused a number of concerns. Schlosser suggested that psychoanalysis in China 'cannot be expected to be taken over-like a counterfeit-1:1' (2009, p. 223); in the same article, however, she also asks, 'Is Chinese psychoanalysis a fake copy?' (ibid., p. 220), like a fake copy of an LV purse or a Burberry coat, which are commonly seen on the streets of China. In addition, many Western teachers from Chinese and Western training programmes have observed (Haag, 2014; Fishkin & Fishkin, 2014; Schlosser, 2009; Snyder, 2014) that their Chinese students and supervisees are difficult to work with in therapeutic settings, that they struggle to maintain neutral and abstinent attitudes and that they have a tendency to challenge these rules with their patients during their training period. One International Psychoanalytical Association (IPA) candidate in China, Li Yawen (2014), confessed that there are some ethical problems among Chinese therapists,

DOI: 10.4324/9781003168829-15

but as Schlosser has argued, after appropriate training, Chinese students will become more deeply involved with the psychoanalytic experience. Based on my own observations, when Chinese students fully understand the rationale behind the settings, they show great willingness to keep them rather than breaking or contesting them. They challenge these settings and encounter ethical problems due to a lack of training and commitment to being analysed. However, these phenomena are declining among young Chinese therapists who have more training opportunities.

Another difficulty that is frequently encountered when trying to apply psychoanalysis in China is the attempt to combine or integrate it with Confucianism, Taoism and Buddhism, which are the basic elements of Chinese culture. Such localisation began when Chinese doctors first applied psychoanalysis and Confucian ideas to treat their patients in the 1930s. Nowadays, Chinese therapists who claim to be psychoanalytically oriented argue that there are many similarities between psychoanalysis and Chinese medicine (Li, 2014) and between psychoanalysis and Buddhism (Xu, 2012). Such ideas are welcomed in China, and Chinese people are very proud of their long historical heritage and tend to believe that all ideas and beliefs from other cultures, particularly the 'good' ones, can find a counterpart in their own culture.

The attempt to combine or integrate Chinese beliefs has been termed the 'localisation' of psychoanalysis in China. The first Chinese member of IPA, Lin Tao, argued that Taoism and Confucianism facilitated his understanding of psychoanalysis and that, as psychoanalysis develops in China, efforts should be made to integrate these Chinese cultural elements (Lin, 2014, pp. 81–84). He claims that Chinese cultural elements like *Zhong Yong* in Confucianism help him to gain a deeper understanding of the neutral attitude required in psychoanalysis, while 'the actual experience of living' in Tao helps him 'not be trapped in psychoanalysis concepts' but to explore real feelings and 'the real world' (Lin, 2014, pp. 86–88, 2015). A local self-educated therapist, Xu Jun, compares the death instinct with *anitya*[1] and inter-subjectivity with *hetupratyaya*[2] and draws parallels between relations in psychoanalysis and in Buddhism. He has found similarities between psychoanalysis and Buddhism and then applied the Buddhist system in psychoanalytical settings (Xu, 2012, pp. 60–84).

However, during my interview with Lin, he also cautiously emphasised his belief that 'we shouldn't break the boundaries between' Chinese culture and psychoanalysis. Nevertheless, even when Lin tried to illustrate how to do so, it became apparent that there is no clear and operable way to maintain these boundaries. Wang Xiao, who finished his training as a psychoanalytic therapist at the Tavistock Centre, and who has lived in London since 2008 to undertake his training, says that it is not possible to combine such different, even conflicting, elements in Chinese culture and psychoanalysis. This is seen as a 'weird' and characteristically Chinese tendency (Wang, 2015). Li and Xu both attended training programmes in China; most of Lin's IPA training was held in Beijing, while Wang was the first person from the Chinese mainland to be trained in a Western country from the very beginning of his training. It is likely that the more a Chinese person knows about psychoanalysis, the more negative an attitude he/she will have towards combining or integrating Chinese cultural elements with it. The current tendency towards integration may be due to the fact that Chinese therapists do not have sufficient understanding of psychoanalysis and are therefore inclined to rush into the idea of 'localisation'. I will also discuss this tendency in relation to the realm of analytical psychology.

The application of psychoanalysis is unstoppable in China, and this has given rise to a number of debates, which are explored in the following.

The debate about the differences between applying psychoanalysis in Chinese and Western settings

The strongest point of contention regarding the applicability of psychoanalysis in China is whether therapists should apply psychoanalysis in a different way in Chinese settings, given that psychoanalysis is deeply rooted in Western culture. In general, there are two opposing views.

The first view is that there are huge differences between Chinese people and Westerners. Schlosser (2009), Haag (2014) and Hansen and Pang (2014) have discussed the 'self' in China and the relationship between 'family interests', social requirements and 'individual concerns', and all have reached the same conclusion, namely that there are no clear boundaries between Chinese people or, in other words, that, in China, 'self-boundaries are permeable' (Haag, 2014, p. 46). Individualism is seen as negative in Chinese society, and so collectivism takes precedence. This gives rise to the concern that it is difficult to maintain boundaries between the analyst and analysand and to observe psychoanalytical rules and practices. Based on their professional experience in CAPA, Fishkin and Fishkin (2014) expressed the same concern. These discussions are very important in demonstrating the difficulties involved in applying psychoanalysis in clinical practice in China. However, this does not mean that they are impossible to overcome. As pointed out previously, all the instances of invasion that they observed occurred during the training process, indicating that immature therapists or those who have not been properly trained have a tendency to make these types of mistakes. This problem can be solved by further training and analysis of trainees by a training analyst.

The second view is that 'there is no actual difference between the Chinese mind and the western mind' (Varvin, 2014). In other words, working with patients in a Chinese context is similar to working with patients in a Western context. Some of the experiences of Western lecturers who offer supervisions and analysis support this assertion (Scharf, 2014, p. 143; Gerlach, 2014; Wang & Zachrisson, 2014). Comparing her work in China with that in the United States, Snyder pointed out that 'what is clear is that it is not a difference between East and West, but more like between rural and urban, primitive (in the psychoanalytic sense) and sophisticated, and non-middle class versus middle class' (2014, pp. 126–127). She further suggests that if the patients or therapists over-emphasise the cultural differences, this could be interpreted as 'a resistance' or a 'defensive manoeuvre[s]'. This is quite understandable. In the past 30 years, China has undergone a drastic social shift. Globalisation, also known as Westernisation or Americanisation, has had a profound effect on Chinese people. When young Chinese people grow up exposed to the same commercialism as Western youth, their psyches might come to share common elements with their Western counterparts. Both in a conscious and unconscious sense, they no longer totally identify with their Chinese ancestors. In addition, the basic family structure in modern China is founded on the marriage between a man and woman who raise children together; this also offers a similar experience of family and personal development to that of Westerners. In this sense, there is no real significant difference between the Chinese and Western minds.

However, a more realistic view on the issue of differences, I think, would be that there are some differences between the Chinese and Western psyches but that it is unnecessary to exaggerate these. As Varvine and Rosenbaum state, there are no myths about Narcissus or Oedipus in ancient Chinese narratives. However, even if the contexts appear different at a superficial level, it is possible to find some resonance in their Chinese counterparts, because 'the struggle of the human mind in dealing with transitional processes from the primarily non-verbal pre-Oedipal aspects and Oedipal language-bound experiences' (2014, p. 158) are common elements in the mental processes of human beings. However, the appearance of these conflicts and the approaches to solving them vary between contexts.

Therefore, in contemporary China, the otherness coexists with the similarities. If we ignore the otherness, we risk overlooking the uniqueness of the Chinese psyche and misunderstanding our patients, but if we ignore the similarities, this could make us too cautious to apply psychoanalysis effectively in China. Therefore, it is necessary to create a dialogue between Chinese and Western minds and to develop more mutual understanding (Saporta, 2014; Snyder, 2014; Varvin, 2014, Xu, Qiu, Chen, & Xiao, 2014; Lin, 2014, 2015; Zhong, 2014; Wang, 2015; Jia, 2016). Zhong Jie, one of the IPA candidates in China, described his dilemma when applying psychoanalysis to treating his patients (2014). He admitted that he encounters some difficulties when attempting to work with his patients in psychoanalytical settings. However, like many other therapists who are interested in psychoanalysis, he and his Chinese and Western colleagues will continue to apply it in the Chinese context and will eventually find the right way to do so.

'The psychology of the heart' – the modification of analytical psychology in China

As Chinese psychoanalysts have done from the very beginning, the leader of the Chinese team in the analytical psychology realm and the first member of the

International Association of Analytical Psychology (IAAP) from mainland China, Shen Heyong, has tried to apply and develop analytical psychology based on his Chinese roots. His first interest in analytical psychology was from his reading of *The Secret of the Golden Flower*. He enthusiastically wrote:

> I didn't find the secret of the golden flower, but I did find a secret of Jungian psychology, its inner connection with Chinese culture. It seemed as if I got a key to the door of Jungian Psychology.
>
> (Shen, 2009, p. 7)

Shen believes that Chinese culture is the key to understanding Jungian psychology because of the interconnection between them, and this belief is the foundation of all his work in China. Further, when he tried to introduce analytical psychology into Chinese settings, he modified what he had learnt from Western Jungians and developed his localised ideas based on both analytical psychology and Chinese culture, which he first named 'psyheart' but later modified to 'the Psychology of the Heart'.

In a presentation at Fudan University, Shen emphasised that there are three steps in his analytical work (2007a). In my interview with him, I asked him what changes should be made when we apply analytical psychology in Chinese settings, and he responded along the lines of his previous work (2015b). The modification he made is as follows.

Translating terms in analytical psychology into the Chinese language is the first step. Translation itself is a cultural exchange. When Chinese people translated Buddhist sutras into Chinese, they had already modified them. Initiation is a two-way thing. The West has its influence on China, and China also influences the West. For example, when Gao Juefu translated Freud's works into Chinese in the 1920s, the words he selected already showed his modification and reworking of psychoanalysis, which made it understandable and applicable to Chinese people. When Shen and his team introduced Jung's work to the Chinese, the same thing happened. I will expand on this point in the following.

Second, Chinese culture has a long history of assimilating other cultures. There is a Chinese archetype, 'Shen nong', which symbolises 'taming and nourishment' (2007a). This is the cultural archetype whereby the Chinese both tamed and nourished Buddhism, which came to China via India (Brook, 1993; Barrett, 2005). Jungian psychology would thus undergo the same process when introduced to China.

Third, timing is crucial for transformation. Here, 'transformation' means integrating Western psychology into Chinese culture. What is fantastic about the *I Ching* is its timing. It offers an effective way to bridge the conscious and unconscious minds. It is 'Jung's Archimedean point' (Jung, 1931, p. 141). When Shen and his team translated Jung's *Collected Works*, he examined all the images relating to the *I Ching* in these books and found that Jung had used them entirely appropriately. He found this an incredible feat for a Westerner who had no knowledge of the Chinese language. Thus, if we have sufficient patience and allow time for analytical psychology to flourish, Chinese analysts will find an appropriate way to understand and work with Jung's ideas (Shen, 2015b, 1:26–22:10).

Shen continuously emphasises that Chinese analysts should study analytical psychology based on their understanding of Chinese culture, as the latter was crucial to the formulation of the former. As he mentioned in our interview, archetypes on assimilation are common in Chinese culture. These modifications also show that Shen believes the Chinese to have advantages in terms of assimilating and applying analytical psychology and that the Chinese language itself is a wonderful tool for understanding it. After all, it might be easier for a Chinese person to understand the *I Ching*, since it was written in Chinese. Furthermore, the philosophy and logic of the *I Ching* are more understandable for the Chinese psyche, as it is immersed in their cultural unconsciousness.

Based on this trend of assimilation, another core aspect of Shen's modifications is integration. When he trained in Zurich and San Francisco, the first person from mainland China to do so, he received opportunities to work with famous analysts. Moreover, while Samuels pointed out that there are three schools of analytical psychology (Samuels, 1985, pp. 11–21), Shen said that there is also a fourth one – the San Francisco school (2015b).[3] Analysts from all four schools have visited China and offered their lectures and training there. Shen also worked with Gao Juefu, an important translator of Freud's works in the Chinese edition, and studied psychoanalysis from Gao before entering the Jungian frame. Therefore, the Chinese therapists in his team are very open to different schools of analytical psychology and psychoanalysis. This has fuelled Shen's belief that a coalition of analytical psychology will happen in China. His strong ambition to develop an integrative psychology has encouraged him to use his own method of applying analytical psychology in Chinese culture.

Contributions of the Chinese team to analytical psychology

The Chinese team led by Shen have made three main contributions to analytical psychology. The first contribution is to epistemology. For Shen, Chinese characters are 'readable archetypes' (2009), and he regards Chinese language as an 'archetypal formation of character' (1996). In Chinese language, a simple character can express multiple meanings. When he translates terms from analytical psychology into Chinese, he tries to interpret them by combining multiple meanings of Chinese characters, and he relates these characters to Chinese classics and old narratives. In other words, he amplifies them and eventually gives these terms meanings that are more comprehensive than their original meanings in Western languages. He also introduces Chinese terms into analytical psychology to describe complicated situations.

Shen translates *individuation* as *ZiXing*:

Xing (heart-minded) combined with *Zi* (nature) brings the idea of "heart" and "life" together; it gives a word picture of the original psychological image of what we are which we carried from the very beginning of our life and gave it psychological meaning.

(2009, p. 6)

From his words, we can see that 'heart' is a very important term for him. In many of his translations, he tries to insert the meaning of heart into the psychological and therapeutic terms he uses. He associates the multiple meanings of 'heart' in Chinese, and for him, 'heart' means a) the core centre of the human body, which is beyond the brain; b) thinking, emotion, consciousness, attitude, character and will; and c) the core of the Tao[4] (1996, 2007a). These meanings of 'heart' are totally based on the Chinese language and rooted in Chinese philosophy, covering several important elements in psychology. Eventually, Shen named his localised analytical psychology 'the heart of psychology' and named his respective programmes 'psyheart' and 'Gardens of the Heart-Soul'.

In another article, Shen translated the word 'containing' into '*bao chi*'. In Chinese, the two characters have multiple meanings. '*Bao*' can be expanded to mean 'cherishing', 'protection', 'care', 'maintaining', 'giving birth to' and 'hatching', while '*chi*' can be related to 'holding and control', 'proper limit' and 'companion'. Thus, the meaning of *bao chi* goes beyond the meaning of 'containing'. It comprises an analytical attitude and a basic technique that is used to confront symptoms and the shadows and complexes behind symptoms and to deal with transference and counter-transference (2015a). Again, his translation is not merely a transposition between languages; it reworks the terms and develops new meanings and applicable methods. In the same way, he translated 'thinking' and 'integrity' (1996), 'happiness' (2007a) and 'love' (Cai & Shen, 2010), reinterpreting these words from Jungian psychological perspectives.

He has also introduced the Chinese term 'gan ying' into the area of analytical psychology, and this term is the foundation of his psychology of the Heart:

Since both of the Chinese characters, gan (influence) and ying (response), are 'heart' characters (i.e., Chinese characters that have heart as the main structure), we could translate this dynamic into English as 'touching by heart and response from heart.' This kind of interaction can be compared with the Western notion stimulus and response. Naturally, because these languages reflect two different systems of psychology, they represent different levels of psyche, even if the dynamic is archetypally, finally, the same (Shen, Gao, & Cope, 2006, p. 71).

Gan ying is a typical Chinese term, and Shen uses it to emphasise the importance of his 'heart' and to describe a different level of the psyche that cannot be found in Western languages. At the technique level, gan ying could appear in hypnosis, free association and active imagination, and, in terms of intervention, it covers transference, projection, empathy and 'resonance'[5] (Shen, 2007b).

Again, this is another case of using a Chinese word to integrate many aspects in psychotherapy. These Chinese characters and words represent a combination of reflections, actions and situations.

Because of Shen's work, the Chinese language could be seen as reworking the terms of analytical psychology, and this could represent a unique Chinese contribution to the field. However, there is also a danger of over-interpretation. If every word in the Chinese language has various meanings, which can cover everything, they might ultimately come to mean nothing. Too many abstract, unidentified meanings in the language will make the proposed terms vague. Thus, the integrative trend in translating terms may lead to greater confusion rather than clarity. This issue became very salient in Shen's speech at the Fey lecture in Huston in 2018, in which he attempted to introduce 'the Psychology of the Heart' to Western audiences. To a certain degree, his presentation was successful: he organised his thoughts on 'the Psychology of the Heart' in a systematic way, established his understanding of psychology based on Chinese culture and brought to the Western audience vivid pictures of the images of relevant Chinese characters and the typical Chinese way of thinking. He amplified the core concept 'the Heart' and discussed the meaning of the derived characters and relevant images in depth, but throughout, he failed to provide a clear definition of 'the heart'. Hence, his speech was very rich but vague, perhaps leaving the audience with the feeling that while they seemed to have understood the meanings behind the words, it was very difficult to elucidate what exactly they had learned. Hence, Shen's speech might bring an incomplete understanding or misunderstanding of Chinese culture and his ideas and made it difficult for him to engage in a profound dialogue with his Western audience.

The second contribution is in the realm of practice. Based on Shen and his team's clinical practice and on their understanding of Chinese philosophy, he uses three phrases to describe analytical work. The first phrase is 'settling the unsettled', the second is 'settling the settled' and the third is 'settling with destiny' (Shen, 2004, pp. 43–50). In my understanding, the first phrase involves understanding the patients and dealing with their symptoms, problems and transference. The second phrase relates to development, with the aim of educating analysands to be better versions of themselves. The third phrase involves individuation, the core and aim of analysis. In *Problems of Modern Therapy* (*CW 16*), Jung developed four stages of analysis, which are 'confession' (CW16, para 123), 'elucidation' (CW16, para 136), 'education' (CW16, para 150) and 'transformation' (CW16, para 160). Comparing Shen's phrases with Jung's stages, 'settling the unsettled' is roughly equivalent to 'confession' and 'elucidation', while 'settling the settled' is roughly equivalent to 'education'. However, the third phrase, 'settling with destiny', is a typical attitude of Taoism. It is not about 'changing' or 'becoming' (Samuels, 1985, p. 178) who you are, nor is it about adapting actively. It is more like remaining who you are and accepting your fate peacefully. Thus, it is another direction of 'individuation'. This extends the notion of 'individuation', but in clinical practice, this has remained a very obscure idea and hence difficult to instruct trainers in.

The third of Shen's contributions is academic in nature. In China, students use sand play both in their clinical practice and academic studies. Shen's current students study dreams from children, adolescents, old people, prisoners and pregnant mothers as well as conducting cross-cultural research. China is a large country with 56 ethnic groups; thus, there are many materials and resources available for cross-cultural studies. In recent years, papers have been published on the difference between Tibetan and Han dreamers in an attempt to address the cultural influence on their respective dream images (Yin, Shen, He, Wei, & Cao, 2013; Li, Yin, & Shen, 2015; Yin, & Shen, 2015). Most of these studies concentrate on the images from various groups. Researchers are collecting and studying on materials from dreams, sand trays and images, which they think are all very close to the unconscious. However, as Jia (2016) points out, in the realm of psychoanalysis, there continues to be a lack of high-quality papers (p. 380), with research facing the same problems. Although the numbers of theses and papers in analytical psychology has been rapidly increasing year by year, and the passion for such research has remained at a high level, the number of international researchers referencing such work is rather low.

Even with its obvious shortcomings, however, all of this work suggests that the application of psychoanalysis and analytical psychology is unstoppable in China.

Discussion

When psychoanalysis came to China, while Western therapists showed much concern about whether it could be successfully applied to Chinese patients, their Chinese colleagues took a more positive approach. Ng (1985) claimed that psychoanalysis could be better understood by Chinese people and, through his empirical studies, showed that non-directive and exploratory therapies are effective with Chinese patients. This view is shared by Lin (2014, 2015). Comparing his work with Western patients in London to his work with Chinese patients in Shanghai, Wang (2015) came to the conclusion that there are no significant differences between the two groups in psychoanalytic therapy. Chinese therapists likely believe that psychoanalysis can definitely be successfully applied in China, and the only problem that concerns them is how to 'localise' it, that is, to integrate it effectively with Chinese cultural elements. In the world of analytical psychology, there is little discussion about its applicability in China. Because Jungian psychology contains some Chinese elements and quotes Chinese terms and since some studies have been conducted on these aspects, both Western analysts and their Chinese colleagues tacitly agree that it can be effectively applied to the Chinese psyche.

In fact, many studies have been conducted on therapeutic work in cross-cultural and cross-racial settings, in other words, on working with patients from non-Western cultures in Western countries, including looking at Western therapists working with non-Western patients or therapists and patients who both come from non-Western cultures (Roland, 1996a, 1996b; Akhtar, 1995; Layton, 2006;

Yi, 1995). None of these studies are completely negative about the applicability of psychoanalysis to non-Western patients. Instead, some researchers state that emphasising racial or cultural differences might act as a tool for transference (Holmes, 1992), that it demonstrates non-Western therapists' sense of inferiority as a minority group and white therapists' sense of superiority as the majority group (Yi, 1998) and that it creates a distance between the therapist and patient and provokes racially based prejudices (Evans, 1985; Bradshaw, 1978). As mentioned previously, when Western analysts work in China with Chinese patients and students, the arguments focus on whether they should apply psychoanalysis differently with Chinese patients;[6] however, the premise of its applicability is undeniable.

In analytical psychology, in the final chapter of *From Traditional to Innovation: Jungian Analysts Working in Different Cultural Settings*, Crowther and Wiener concluded, after reading about their colleagues' work with analysands and trainees in intercultural settings, particularly in countries without a culture of analytical psychology, that despite the challenges and disagreement on certain issues, such work is valuable and benefits both sides – both the deliverers and receivers. Finally, 'working in different cultural settings permits practice to make a greater impact on theory' (2015, pp. 209–293). It validates the applicability of analytical psychology in China. Further, in the same book, Beebe shares his experience of applying Chinese philosophy to understanding the dreams and images of his analysts and himself. Furthermore, from his experience of working with patients in China, he not only confirms that analytical psychology is applicable there but also foresees that engaging with Chinese Jungians will enrich and enliven Western Jungians and help 'Chinese therapists become freer to use their own self-experience in their work as counsellors and healers' (2015, p. 269). The groundwork laid by Shen and the achievement of his team are endorsements of its applicability in China, and its use in that context is unstoppable.

The dilemma of 'colonialism'

When we talk about 'difference', we are confronted with a complex issue. All therapists working with patients from non-Western backgrounds in Western settings must discuss the differences, regardless of whether they come from Western or non-Western cultures. Cushman criticises the idea of ignoring the cultural difference as a form of 'psychological imperialism' (1996, p. 479). However, overemphasising differences or encouraging Western psychotherapists to follow an 'emphatic-introspective approach' (Yi, 1995, p. 380) in order to adapt to their Asian patients seems to place Westerners and non-Westerners in unequal positions. It makes the Western culture appear more mature, sophisticated and stronger, or, in other words, it represents Western superiority. Haag compared American 'guilt culture' with Eastern (including China and Japan) 'shame culture', claiming that ' "guilt" . . . was seen on a more developed, namely Oedipal level deriving from an internalized moral standard or superego' (2014, p. 47). She also asserted that Chinese people lack curiosity and find it difficult to be abstinent in therapeutic settings. This kind of Western superiority is very common among Western analysts and, though they may not recognise it consciously, is often concealed under the guise of sympathy, encouragement and careful adaption to Chinese people.

Even Jung could not avoid succumbing to Western superiority when he talked about the difference between the Eastern and Western psyches. As Clark (1994, 1995) and Blower (2015) point out with reference to Jung's description of the one-sidedness of the East and West, he automatically placed the West on the 'high developed intellectual' side (Blower, 2015, p. 281) with the natural inference that the Eastern psyche is, conversely, undeveloped and unintellectual. However, I think this assessment is unfair and can be disproved given sufficient knowledge of Chinese history.

Herein lies a dilemma. If a Western analyst ignores the cultural difference, he might be accused of 'psychological imperialism', or there is a danger that he will use his values, which are based on 'Euro-American culture', to diagnose his non-Western patients and consequently reach the wrong conclusions in terms of the psychopathology. However, if a Westerner tries to adapt his approach to take account of the patient's background, this would suggest that the patient is not intelligent or developed enough to 'fit' the original tenets of Western psychology. Therefore, the treatment would still be Western ethnocentric.

Because of this dilemma, further exploration is required of how to 'adjust' Western-rooted psychotherapy in China to make it more adaptive without putting the two parties in an unequal position explicitly or implicitly. Some Chinese therapists have shown their interest in and concern with this topic. For example, the Chinese psychoanalyst Jia Xiaoming wrote a paper, 'Psychoanalytic Training in China: Cultural Colonialism or Acculturation' (2016), in which she warned Chinese therapists to be careful about absorbing Western teachings without thinking. She suggested that training psychoanalysis in China should be based on dialogue, not on monologue, and encouraged Chinese therapists to be more creative based on integrating their own cultural rooting, such as relying more on self-experience (a special term for Chinese psychotherapists' own therapy or analysis) with local psychoanalysts, even if these analysts are not qualified by international standards, and reducing the frequency of analysis. This is the first paper to discuss this issue in a direct way, and it reflects a common concern and further thoughts of the first generation of psychoanalysts in China after having learned, applied and taught psychoanalysis in China for many years. At the second Asia Pacific Conference of the International Psychoanalytical Association in Tokyo, Wang Xiao, one of the younger generation of Chinese psychoanalysts, gave a presentation that showed a different attitude. In his speech, he emphasized that, in China, psychoanalysis is at the beginning stage of development and has quietly challenged traditional Chinese values, with many misunderstandings and assumptions. Therefore, at this stage, as beginners, Chinese psychotherapists should, like little babies, rely on their Western teachers, who offer a 'holding environment' to teach and correct them so that they may learn more original psychoanalysis rather than a modified or adapted edition thereof (2018). This speech caused a hot debate amongst his Chinese and Western colleagues, with the main argument revolving around how much Chinese therapists should absorb from Western masters in the realm of depth psychology and how much independence they should retain.

In my opinion, Shen's work in China might offer a solution to this disagreement. As a Chinese man brought up in Shandong province (the hometown of Confucius), he is equipped with in-depth knowledge of Chinese culture. As the first person from mainland China to complete full training in both Jungian psychology and sand play therapy and to qualify as an IAAP member and International Society for Sandplay Therapy member, Shen completed his training in Zurich and San Francisco and as such gained rich experience and knowledge of analytical psychology in the Western setting. Furthermore, having undertaken clinical groundwork with Chinese people from all over the country, he and his team have a comprehensive understanding of the contemporary Chinese psyche. In the past few years, they have built a bridge designed to facilitate a dialogue between East and West. He offers a more egalitarian perspective, which can help Westerners understand the Eastern psyche, and, more importantly, he makes Western psychological ideas and concepts accessible, coherent and applicable to Chinese people.

Furthermore, Shen also offers the possibility of a new, integrative school of Jungian psychology. Samuels revised his classification of the schools of analytical psychology, so that the four new schools 'could be presented as a simple spectrum: fundamentalist-classical-developmental-psychoanalytic' (2011, p. 10). In some ways, the new classification is based on the different attitudes that exist towards psychoanalysis, from rejecting it completely to warmly embracing it. In China, people do not make the same distinctions between psychoanalysis and analytical psychology as do Westerners. They are interested in both and focus on the similarities between them, tending to regard them as different levels of interpreting human nature. As such, they do not see the two psychologies as in any way contradictory. Shen is a great believer in hypnosis and Winnicott, and he always emphasises the importance of Chinese cultural elements in the human psyche. Therefore, in his claim that there is also a 'San Francisco' school of analytical psychology, there could be a hint that he intends to develop his own 'Chinese school' which would not necessarily integrate all of the schools within analytical psychology but would offer a more integrative perspective with which to understand and work with the human psyche.

Nowadays, Taoism and Buddhism are no longer unfamiliar and exotic to Westerners and, in fact, have an influence on the Western psyche (Plankers, 2013). There have already been discussions about how ideas and methods from Buddhism can be applied within psychoanalytic therapy in Western countries (Epstein, 1988, 1990, 1995, 2013). In studies of analytical psychology, many Western analysts and scholars use Chinese cultural elements, particularly the *I Ching*, to enrich their understanding of Jungian ideas and phenomena in relation to the human psyche, like synchronicity and individuation (Coward, 1996; Cambray, 2005; Stein, 2005; Zabriskie, 2005; Beebe, 2008). In recent years, Chinese Jungians have also contributed to offering new ways of understanding dreams, the unconscious and

feminine aspects in human beings (Shen, 2011; Ma, 2011). However, in this reciprocal process, challenges and problems could not be ignored, for Chinese teams in
particular, and these require more examination and further discussion.

Problems and challenges of applying depth psychology in China for Chinese teams

The first problem of applying depth psychology in China is the tendency to ide-
alise Western masters, such as Freud, Jung, Winnicott and so on, due to the long
history of authoritarianism there. Jia (2016) points out that Chinese people have
put Freud in a very high and authoritative position, taken his writings as the truth
and treated IPA members as his preachers (p. 379). Amongst Jungians in China,
the situation is almost identical. They have remained stuck to Jung's classic works
and treat his words as gospel, ignoring the fact that Jung and his theory were
rooted in Jung's own time and culture. Some of Jung's thinking and writing is
limited and outdated in today's world, particularly his perspective from a superior
white male stance, which may have been normal during his time in Zurich but
could be seen as racist and sexist in a broader context today. Among post-Jungians
today, these issues are debated and Jung's thinking and works are criticised; however, dissenting voices have rarely been heard in China, and instead, the Chinese
team prefers to treat Jung as a wise man who was highly influenced by Chinese
culture and who adeptly adapted the Chinese lens to understand the deepest layer
of the human psyche (this tendency is very obvious, for example, in Shen's book
Jung and Chinese Culture). Hence, even with the emphasis on being integrative,
the delivery and development of Jungian psychology have remained monocultural
until now.

Second, when discussing 'integrating' or 'localizing' depth psychology in
China, in both the realms of psychoanalysis and Jungian psychology, Chinese
teams all focus on interpreting such Western-rooted ideas and notions by their
understandings from Chinese culture. In other words, they assume an a priori
sameness and similarity between them and never mention the differences. Particularly in quoting Jung, the Chinese team highlights places where Jung mentioned Chinese elements to prove how important Chinese culture was to Jung
but neglects the context or tone of these words; rarely mentions that Jung also
used many terms, perhaps even more, from Indian and African culture; and never
challenges Jung's understanding of Chinese culture. On the other hand, at most
international conferences that I have attended, Chinese speakers use special Chinese terms that are unfamiliar to audiences from other cultures and combine these
terms with those from Western psychology to interpret their case or establish their
understanding of the psyche. However, they rarely make any real comparison
between the two groups of terms, which would mean evaluating both the similarities and differences, not to mention discussing the possibility of a mismatch and
inadequate relevance. Although this approach might enrich the perspectives of
depth psychology, sticking to the one-sided approach might make the presentation

into a monologue, giving the audience a 'crash course' on Chinese culture but hindering further communication.

Due to these two main problems, the current fever of depth psychology in China might imply the possibility of narcissistic idealization. On the surface, people seem to be very open, curious and flexible, and to admire their Western masters and teachers very much, but underneath, people only value one voice, that of their counterparts in other worlds, while ignoring or discarding voices which are less harmonious with their own. This attitude brings three challenges for the further development of depth psychology. First, different Chinese teams, without idealization and tolerance of differences, are quite sensitive to competition and do not know how to prompt authentic and deep cooperation. Second, in Russia, during the process of delivery of analytical psychology, it was noticed that there had always been 'a disjunction between [the] sophisticated understanding of theory' and the method of practice with patients (Crowther & Wiener, 2015, p. 278). In China, because of the rush to integrate Chinese elements, this phenomenon could be even worse. The ideas and notions from Buddhism, Taoism and Confucianism are very obscure, ambiguous and even controversial. Hence, the attempt to combine these elements with clinical practice would be less friendly for new therapists. During the process, without clear definition and specific instruction, many therapists simply copy their teacher's words rigorously without full understanding, and this brings confusion and frustration to both themselves and their patients. Third, the real dialogue between East and West has not been fully engaged by either side. The current main approach for Chinese therapists to express themselves in international communication brings obstacles to mutual understanding, because specific Chinese terms are overly quoted without deep examination and adequate comparison. As a result, Western audiences require time to follow the meaning, and it is difficult to challenge or criticise the ideas, as well as difficult to reference. Therefore, although such presentations bring fresh and extended materials to the field, the delivery of such voices from Chinese therapists has been very limited, and they have not been heard by a broader audience.

The core of these three challenges is how to promote dialogue between Chinese teams, between therapists and patients and between East and West. People who have devoted themselves to the delivery and development of depth psychology in other cultures are aware of the importance of dialogue and emphasise that the foundation of such dialogue is putting the two parties in equal positions; having mutual curiosity, recognition and respect; and developing a negotiated relationship (ibid, p. 277; Beebe, 2015, p. 267; Jia, 2016). The next question is how to promote such dialogue. Cushman points out that the only way 'to understand others and live with others in peace and with respect' is to have a 'genuine conversation' based on 'conceptualiz[ing] the dialogic meeting and mutual cultural exploration' (1996, p. 489). Hence, for Chinese teams, this means, in the first place, initiating real curiosity about other cultures by putting aside their cultural pride for a while, carefully listening to what their Western masters and colleagues are trying to express, noticing and understanding the difference between the various cultures, not being in a rush to recognise the similarities or integrate what they have just learnt with what they already know and, most importantly, providing space for disagreement. The key to 'authentic dialogue' is accepting the fact that the dialogue could fail and the two parties may never reach agreement.

Further, beyond their own internal problems, all Chinese teams also encounter other challenges which are quite unique for China and for this era. The first is the prevalence of online training programmes and therapy. Cyber work is still new in the realm of depth psychology, and further research should be conducted on its applicability and validation. In China, as a large country with a large population and a huge gap between different regions, for many people, their only option is to obtain services over the internet. The positive side is that this makes depth psychology more approachable for more people who are interested in this area in a cheaper and more convenient way; the negative side is that such online work has immediately gained popularity in China without scrutiny. No one can guarantee the long-term results of such work. Further, heavy reliance on cyber work also carries a high risk of breaking confidentiality and their work being exposed under monitoring and intervention from the government. The second aspect is that because of the prevalence of online work, accompanied by the increased market and lower cost, capital is also demonstrating an interest in depth psychology in China. Many online platforms for training and therapy oriented in depth psychology have received support from investment companies. However, work in this area requires patience and a slow pace for the growth of the psyche, and a focus on immediate profit, which is the only aim of such companies, is totally contrary to this aim and likely to damage the area. However, resisting the enchantment of hot money has ever been a challenge for humanity.

Nevertheless, even with the problems and challenges discussed previously, from all the work that the Chinese team has already done, we can conclude that applying psychoanalysis and Jungian psychology in China is reciprocal. This process will reshape the ideas and techniques used in both psychoanalysis and Jungian psychology and make resources for understanding the human psyche more abundant and comprehensive. Furthermore, as Varvin suggests, 'this process may change not only our scientific perspectives and viewpoints but also [our] view of ourselves' (2014, p. 116). This will in turn affect the Western psyche. After all, according to the concept of the 'collective unconscious', we all share the same vast psychological space.

Conclusion

It is apparent that China has been through a great shift in recent years. This has presented many new issues, while the old problems have emerged into consciousness. 'Individualisation' has arisen in the younger generations, and we have gradually had to face our traumatic history, maintain a distance from our long traditions and learn to mourn the separation and loss during the process. In this context, psychoanalysis can be very helpful. Furthermore, materialism and an eagerness for achievement and money cast heavy shadows among Chinese people today. The Jungian idea of 'individuation' might be a good remedy for this condition.

In my eyes, the modifications that have been made to psychoanalysis and analytical psychology in China are not too few but too many. Most Chinese therapists are still only on the first step and need to learn more, undertake more training and develop a better understanding of the real meanings of Western ideas. Thus, modification and integration are the next step. This will happen spontaneously, however, and there is no need to force the process.

As Cushman suggests, 'analyst and patients might be better served by confronting what a dialogue with others reveals about one's own culture frame' (1996, p. 487). This could also be put into practice by applying Western psychological approaches in Chinese settings. Both the West and the East would be affected by so doing and would benefit from the process.

I would like to end this chapter with a story. In 2013, I went to Laoshan with Shen and a group of analysts from the Institute of Jungian Studies in Zurich. These analysts were sitting around a circular stone table. Paul Brutsche[7] began to imitate Jung's way of speaking. Shen asked him whether Jung would come back to this world and build another tower like his building in Bollingen near Kusnacht – but in China. Just as Brutsche was saying, 'YES, I will. . .', a sudden gust of wind whipped up around the group. Jungians would probably call this 'synchronicity'.

Notes

1 A term in Buddhism meaning nothing can last forever, and everything is in the process from birth to death.
2 A term in Buddhism meaning interdependent origination.
3 Samuels classified Jungian analytical psychology into three different schools – the 'Classical School', the 'Development School' and the 'Archetypal School' (1985a, p. 15). However, he later revised his classification, as I will present later.
4 A term in Taoism and one of the central concepts of Chinese philosophy, symbolising the principle of the world.
5 Ammann, 2004, pp. 245–246.
6 The three main themes are the interpretation of creativity, the Oedipus complex and the interpretation of dreams; Scharff (2014) wrote an article called 'Five Things Western Therapists Need to Know for Working with Chinese Therapists and Patients'. Apparently, in his opinion, Chinese people should be treated specially and carefully.
7 A Jungian analyst from Basel, Jung's hometown, who played Jung in the play *The Red Book*.

References

Akhtar, S. (1995). 'A third individuation: Immigration, identity, and the psychoanalytic process'. *Journal of the American Psychoanalytic Association*, 43: 1051–1084
Barrett, T. (2005). 'History', in D. S. Lopez Jr (ed.), *Critical terms for the study of Buddhism* (pp. 139–157). Chicago: The University of Chicago Press.
Beebe, J. (2008). 'Individuation in the light of Chinese philosophy'. *Psychological Perspectives*, 61: 70–86

Beebe, J. (2015). 'Returning to China', in C. Crowther & J. Wiener (eds.), *From tradition to innovation: Jungian analyst in different cultural settings* (pp. 255–271). Cham: Spring Journal Books.

Blowers, G. (2015). 'Jung and Chinese culture', in M. E. Mattson (ed.), *Jung in the academy and beyond.* Cham: Spring Journal, Inc. (April, 2015)

Bradshaw, W. (1978). 'Training psychiatrists for working with blacks in basic residency programs'. *American Journal of Psychiatry*, 135: 1520–1524

Brook, T. (1993). *Praying for power: Buddhism and formation of gentry society in late-Ming China.* Cambridge, MA: Harvard University Asia Center.

Cai, C. & Shen, H. (2010). ' "Garden of the Heart-Soul" in the Earthquake Area of China'. *Jung Journal: Cultural and Psyche*, 4:2: 5–15.

Cambray, J. (2005). 'The place of the 17th century in Jung's encounter with China'. *Journal of Analytical Psychology*, 50: 195–207

Clark, J. (1994/2005). *Jung and Eastern thought: A dialogue with the orient.* London: Routledge, 2005.

Clark, J. (1995). 'Introduction', in J. J. Clarks (ed.), *Jung on the East* (pp. 1–32). London: Routledge, 1995

Coward, H. (1996). 'Taoism and Jung: Synchronicity and the self'. *Philosophy East and West*, 46:4 (October): 477–495.

Crowther, C. & Wiener, J. (2015). 'From tradition to innovation: What have we learned', in C. Crowther & J. Wiener (eds.), *From tradition to innovation: Jungian analyst in different cultural settings* (pp. 273–295). Cham: Spring Journal Books.

Cushman, P. (1996). 'More surprises, less certainty: Commentary on Roland's paper'. *Psychoanalytic Dialogues*, 6: 477–488.

Epstein, M. (1988). 'Attention in analysis'. *Psychoanalysis and Contemporary Thought*, 11: 171–189

Epstein, M. (1990). 'Beyond the oceanic feeling: Psychoanalytic study of Buddhist meditation'. *The International Journal of Psychoanalysis*, 17: 159–165

Epstein, M. (1995). 'Thoughts without a thinker'. *Psychoanalytic Review*, 82: 391–406

Epstein, M. (2013). 'The devil we know'. *Psychoanalytic Perspectives*, 10:2, 285–290

Evans, D. (1985). 'Psychotherapy and black patients: Problems of training, trainees, and trainers'. *Psychotherapy: Theory, Research and Practice*, 22: 457–460

Fishkin, R. E. & Fishkin, L. P. (2014). 'Introducing psychoanalytic therapy into China: The CAPA experience', in D. E. Scharff & S. Varvin (eds.), *Psychoanalysis in China* (pp. 244–255). London: Karnac Books Ltd.

Gerlach, A. (2014). 'German psychoanalysts in China and the start of group therapy work', in D. E. Scharff & S. Varvin (eds.), *Psychoanalysis in China (pp. 256–265).* London: Karnac Books Ltd.

Haag, A. (2014). 'Psychoanalytically oriented psychotherapy and the Chinese self', in D. E. Scharff & S. Varvin (eds.), *Psychoanalysis in China* (pp. 44–56). London: Karnac Books Ltd.

Hansen, M. H. & Pang, C. (2014). 'Idealising individual choice: Work, love, and family in the eyes of young, rural Chinese', in D. E. Scharff & S. Varvin (eds.), *Psychoanalysis in China* (pp. 24–43). London: Karnac Books Ltd.

Holmes, D. E. (1992). 'Race and transference in psychoanalysis and psychotherapy'. *The International Journal of Psychoanalysis*, 73: 1–11.

Jia, X. (2016). 'Psychoanalytic training in China: Cultural colonialism or acculturation'. *Journal of Neuroscience and Mental Health*, 16:4: 377–382.

Jung, C. G. (1931). *The secret of the golden flower*, 2d ed. New York: Harcourt Brace & Company, 1962.

Kirsner, D. & Snyder, E. (2009). 'Psychoanalysis in China', in S. Akhtar (ed.), *Freud and far East: Psychoanalytic perspectives on the people and culture of China, Japan, and Korea* (pp. 43–60). Lanham, Boulder, New York, Toronto, Plymouth, UK: Jason Aronson.

Layton, L. (2006). 'Racial identities, racial enactments and normative unconscious process'. *Psychoanalytic Quarterly*, 75: 237–269.

Li, Q., Yin, F. & Shen, H. (2015). 'Death dreams from a manifest perspective: A cross cultural comparison between Tibetan and Han Chinese dreamers'. *Dreaming*, 25:1 (March): 32–43.

Li, Y. (2014). 'Research on the development of Chinese psychoanalysts and psychotherapists', 'The encounter of psychoanalysis and Chinese cultural', in D. E. Scharff, & S. Varvin (eds.), *Psychoanalysis in China* (pp. 266–272). London: Karnac Books Ltd.

Lin, T. (2014). 'The encounter of psychoanalysis and Chinese cultural', in D. E. Scharff & S. Varvin (eds.), *Psychoanalysis in China* (pp. 81–89). London: Karnac Books Ltd.

Lin, T. (2015). Interview with Huan Wang. 13/03/2015. London

Ma, S. (2011). *Footbinding: A Jungian engagement with Chinese culture and psychology*. London: Routledge.

Ng, M. L. (1985). 'Psychoanalysis for the Chinese – applicable or not applicable?'. *International Review of Psycho-Analysis*, 12: 449–460.

Plankers, T. (2013). 'When Freud headed for the East: Aspects of a Chinese translation of his works'. *The International Journal of Psychoanalysis*, 94: 993–1017

Roland, A. (1996a). 'The influence of culture on the self and self-object relationships: An Asian-North American comparison'. *Psychoanalytic Dialogues*, 6: 461–475

Roland, A. (1996b). 'Culture, comparativity, and psychoanalysis: Reply to commentary'. *Psychoanalytic Dialogues*, 6: 489–495.

Samuels, A. (1985). *Jung and the post-Jungians*. New York: Routledge, 2005

Samuels, A. (2011). 'Introduction', in P. Young-Eisendrath (ed.), *The Cambridge companion to Jung (Cambridge companions)*. Cambridge, MA: Cambridge University Press; 2 edition (26 October 2011)

Saporta, J. (2014). 'Psychoanalysis meets in China: Transformative dialogue or monologue of the western voice?', in D. E. Scharff & S. Varvin (eds.), *Psychoanalysis in China* (pp. 102–115). London: Karnac Books Ltd.

Scharff, D. E. (2014). 'Five things western therapists need to know for working with Chinese therapists and patients', in D. E. Scharff & S. Varvin (eds.), *Psychoanalysis in China* (pp. 143–153). London: Karnac Books Ltd.

Schlosser, A-M. (2009). 'Oedipus in China: Can we export psychoanalysis?'. *International Forum of Psychoanalysis,* 12/2009; 18(4): 219–224

Shen, H. (1996). *Heart and psychology: The meaning of Chinese culture*. Fulbright Scholar Presentation in the University of Nebraska, U.S.A.

Shen, H. (2004). *Analytical psychology: Understanding and experiencing*. Beijing: SDX Joint Publishing Company.

Shen, H. (2007a). 'Analytical psychology and Chinese cultural'. The Academic week on Analytical Psychology and Chinese cultural, Fudan University, China.

Shen, H. (2007b). 'Psychology of heart: The happiness and the cultural psyche in China'. Eranos Round Table session, Switzerland.

Shen, H. (2009). 'C.G. Jung and China: A continued dialogue'. *Jung Journal: Cultural & Psyche*, 3:2: 5–14.

Shen, H. (2011). *The dreams of Xixin island*. Guangzhou: Guangdong Technology Publishing House.

Shen, H. (2015a). 'Bao Chi'. *Analytical Psychology*, 01: 96–98.

Shen, H. (2015b). Interview with Huan Wang. 09/04/2015. South China Normal University, Guangzhou, China.

Shen, H. (2018). *The psychology of the heart*. Huston: Fay Lecture,

Shen, H., Gao, L. & Cope, T. A. (2006). 'The I Ching's psychology of heart and Jungian analysis'. *Psychological Perspectives: A Quarterly Journal of Jungian Thought*, 49:1: 61–78.

Snyder, E. (2014). 'The shibboleth of cross-culture issues in psychoanalytic treatment', in D. E. Scharff & S. Varvin (eds.), *Psychoanalysis in China* (pp. 121–129). London: Karnac Books Ltd.

Stein, M. (2005). 'Some reflections on the influence of Chinese thought on Jung and his psychological theory'. *Journal of Analytical Psychology*, 50: 209–222.

Varvin, S. (2014). 'Discussion on Chapter seven', in D. E. Scharff & S. Varvin (eds.), *Psychoanalysis in China* (pp. 116–120). London: Karnac Books Ltd.

Varvin, S. & Rosenbaum, B. (2014). 'West-East differences in habits and ways of thinking: The influence on understanding and teaching psychoanalytic therapy', in D. E. Scharff & S. Varvin (eds.), *Psychoanalysis in China* (pp. 155–169). London: Karnac Books Ltd.

Wang, X. (2015). Interview with Huan Wang. 11/03/2015. Tavistock, London

Wang, X. (2018). 'Shall we depend on the Western Professionals to Learn, Psychoanalysis', in The Second Asia Pacific Conference of the International Psychoanalytical Association, Tokyo

Wang, Z. & Zachrisson, A. (2014). 'Transference and countertransference in a Chinese setting: Reflections on a psychotherapeutic process', in D. E. Scharff & S. Varvin (eds.), *Psychoanalysis in China* (pp. 202–213). London: Karnac Books Ltd.

Xu, J. (2012). *The encounter of Freud and Buddha: A dialogue between psychotherapist and Buddhism*. Shanghai: Thread-Binding Books Publishing House

Xu, Y., Qiu, J., Chen, J. & Xiao, Z. (2014). 'The development of psychoanalytic psychotherapy at Shanghai Mental Health Center', in D. E. Scharff & S. Varvin (eds.), *Psychoanalysis in China* (pp. 234–243). London: Karnac Books Ltd.

Yi, K. Y. (1995). 'Psychoanalytic psychotherapy with Asian clients: Transference and therapeutic consideration'. *Psychotherapy*, 32: 308–316.

Yi, K. Y. (1998). 'Transference and race'. *Psychoanalytic Psychology*, 15: 245–261.

Yin, F. & Shen, H. (2015). 'Death dreams from an implicit perspective: A core cultural comparison between Tibetan and Han Chinese dreamers'. *Dreaming*, 25:2 (June).

Yin, F., Shen, H., He, Y., Wei, Y. & Cao, W. (2013). 'Typical dreams of "being chased": A cross culture comparison between Tibetan and Han Chinese dreamers'. *Dreaming*, 23:1 (March): 64–77.

Zabriskie, B. (2005). 'Synchronicity and the I Chin: Jung, Pauli, and the Chinese woman'. *Journal of Analytical Psychology*, 50: 223–235.

Zhang, J. (1992). *Psychoanalysis in China: Literary transformations 1919–1949*. Ithaca, NY: Cornell University East Asia Program.

Zhong, J. (2014). 'Working with Chinese patients: Are there conflicts between Chinese culture and psychoanalysis?', in D. E. Scharff & S. Varvin (eds.), *Psychoanalysis in China* (pp. 184–191). London: Karnac Books Ltd.

Index

Note: Page numbers followed by "n" indicate a note on the corresponding page.

For Product Safety Concerns and Information please contact our EU
representative GPSR@taylorandfrancis.com
Taylor & Francis Verlag GmbH, Kaufingerstraße 24, 80331 München, Germany

www.ingramcontent.com/pod-product-compliance
Lightning Source LLC
Chambersburg PA
CBHW050347270326
41926CB00016B/3632

9 780367 768959